THE TEAM THAT DARED TO DO

THE TEAM THAT DARED DO

TO DO

TOTTENHAM
1994/95

BY GERRY FRANCIS
AND CHRIS SLEGG

First published by Pitch Publishing, 2017

Pitch Publishing
A2 Yeoman Gate
Yeoman Way
Worthing
Sussex
BN13 3QZ

www.pitchpublishing.co.uk
info@pitchpublishing.co.uk

A CIP catalogue record is available for this book
from the British Library.

ISBN 978-1-78531-309-7

Typesetting and origination by Pitch Publishing

Printed in the UK by TJ International, Cornwall

Contents

Foreword

by Jürgen Klinsmann

WHAT I remember most about the 1994/95 season with Tottenham is the amazing energy that surrounded the club. It wasn't just a team spirit. It was a club spirit. It was a spirit that was created by Alan Sugar and his fight against the FA, and which filtered out to everyone, no matter what position they were working in, whether front office, back office, on the training ground, or in the stands.

White Hart Lane is a stadium which harnesses that energy too. I still feel it when I drive up to the stadium today, on the occasions when I am able to come and visit. The Tottenham fans are a really knowledgeable and sophisticated crowd. They know when the team needs them, they can sense the momentum of a game. I couldn't stop running during that season, because the crowd was always there right behind me. If the game had stopped and the crowd had still been there after the final whistle, I would have still been running.

The memories I have of that season will stay with me forever. I was privileged to win the World Cup, Euro 96, the Bundesliga with Bayern Munich and the UEFA Cup with both Bayern and Inter. I was fortunate to play for some great managers and with some great players. I include the Tottenham players and both Ossie Ardiles and Gerry Francis among that number. I learnt things at Tottenham that served me well in the rest of my career as a player and then also as a manager too.

The Liverpool goal in the FA Cup quarter-final is the goal I remember the most. It was a great team goal, because it was a lovely flick by Teddy that set me up. At the end of the game, when we were walking towards the Tottenham fans at Anfield to say thank you, and the Liverpool players had already left the pitch, we realised the home fans had stayed on to clap us too. That was an incredible experience. It summed up the English spirit, that the Liverpool supporters were prepared to honour us as winners of a great game. That was a really special moment in a season which was full of them. I hope you enjoy reliving many of those moments in this book.

Introduction

by Chris Slegg

I T'S close to 6.30pm on Sunday 14 May 2017. The White Hart Lane pitch looks like it has never looked before. Barely a patch of green is visible. It's white and it's blue, and it's a heaving mass of movement, a heaving mess of emotion. Around 15,000 Tottenham fans have reclaimed it in a fond farewell to the place that's been home for almost 118 years. Some are on their knees kissing the turf, some are taking selfies, some are walking round trance-like, struggling to take it all in. Moments ago referee Jonathan Moss blew the final, final whistle ever to be sounded at White Hart Lane, sparking a joyous pitch invasion. Tottenham have beaten Manchester United 2-1, but to some the result barely mattered. This day was all about the occasion. From tomorrow morning, when the demolition wrecking balls move in, this stadium will be no more.

The PA pleads with the fans to return to their seats so that the formal farewell ceremony can get under way, and many respectfully begin to do so. As the pitch thins out of bodies a gap opens up in the corner between the Paxton Road end and the West Stand. It gives three or four fans who are still on the pitch enough room to undertake an action they've clearly been desperate to carry out. In almost exactly the same spot where their hero did so after scoring on his home debut against Everton almost 23 years ago, they each re-enact Jürgen Klinsmann's dive celebration, hurling themselves to the turf.

Tottenham aren't just saying goodbye to White Hart Lane today, they're doing so as North London's top club, for the first time since that Klinsmann season of 1994/95. They've been sure of that for a fortnight now. A 2-0 win here against Arsenal on 30 April ensured their rivals could no longer catch them and put an end to St Totteringham's Day, the day on which Gunners fans had celebrated finishing above Spurs for each of the last 21 seasons.

When the formal farewell ceremony is eventually able to get under way, seven members of that 1994/95 squad are among the 48 Tottenham playing legends from the 1960s onwards invited on to the pitch to take the acclaim of the fans. Klinsmann himself has been unable to make it, but Darren Anderton, Justin Edinburgh, Micky Hazard, David Howells, Gary Mabbutt, Teddy Sheringham, and Erik Thorstvedt are here. Admittedly they aren't being honoured for 1994/95 *per se*, but the fact that squad contained so many players held in high enough esteem to warrant an invite today helps explain why it was such a special year. They were players who gave their all, players who generated not just a special team spirit in the dressing room but a bond with the fans which perhaps hasn't been felt so strongly at White Hart Lane again until now, in 2016/17.

After the legends have taken their places on the pitch, current manager Mauricio Pochettino and his players do likewise. Make no mistake, as a team, Pochettino's is unquestionably better than Tottenham's 1994/95 incarnation, but the last Tottenham side to finish above Arsenal certainly shares many qualities with the modern-day heroes of White Hart Lane: a gift for the spectacular; playing the game for the love of it; and an acceptance that the club motto 'To Dare Is To Do' is an apt mantra by which to approach every match.

For supporters of the vast majority of football clubs, the vast majority of seasons end without a trophy. That's true even for a club as big as Tottenham Hotspur. That was true in 1994/95, and in 2016/17, just as it has been in all but two of the last 26 seasons. A fan's love of his or her club though remains undimmed. The love doesn't come from silverware, it comes from the sharing of memories, the sharing of unforgettable moments, the sharing of heightened emotions, be they good or bad. To be a Tottenham fan in 1994/95 was to experience every single one of those heightened emotions football is capable of stirring in the space of ten short months.

It seems that wasn't just true from a fan's perspective, but from the manager's too. Gerry Francis has had a long and distinguished career spanning 50 years. Most recently, while working as assistant manager to Tony Pulis at the Hawthorns, he has helped steer West Bromwich Albion to respectable mid-table finishes in 2015/16 and 2016/17. Even at the time that he took over as Tottenham manager in November 1994, aged 42, he had already achieved so much. As a player he captained England at the age of 23 and was skipper of the QPR team that so narrowly missed out on the league title to Liverpool in 1976. As a manager he guided Bristol Rovers to the Third Division title and to Wembley for the first time in their history, then he returned to Loftus Road to lead Rangers to fifth place in the inaugural Premier League season of 1992/93, seeing them finish as London's top club.

For all of that though, it was 1994/95 – a season when he repeated that feat of finishing as the capital's top dogs with Tottenham – that has left the greatest impression on him. So great in fact that, when I first met him to interview him about his memories, he mentioned he had committed many of his experiences to paper during his days at White Hart Lane, and so we set about incorporating those diary entries into this book.

As a result, this story comes together in three parts. Part One covers the months before Francis took over, the FA's punishment of Spurs with a six-point deduction and FA Cup ban, the height of Klinsmania, the thrilling, yet ultimately failed, attempt of manager Ossie Ardiles to make a success of the 'Famous Five' forward line and the Argentinian's eventual sacking by chairman Alan Sugar. We flash back to the matches as they took place and also hear the present-day views of the players who were at the heart of it all.

Part Two begins with Francis taking over from Ardiles, having been forced out of QPR. It includes Francis's writings as he set about moulding Tottenham into a team capable of some magnificent performances. His introduction of intense running sessions – which the players labelled 'Terror Tuesdays' – video analysis, and a greater emphasis on defence, created a side in which the forwards were still able to express themselves but could now do so under the cover of a new-found stability.

Spurs hadn't kept a clean sheet all season prior to the arrival of Francis, but with no money to spend, and the same players at his disposal, they went on to equal the club record of six consecutive shutouts – a record that still hasn't been broken at the time of publishing. Having got the balance right, his team played some fantastic football, beating early-season title contenders Newcastle 4-2, disposing of North London rivals Arsenal 1-0 and seeing off eventual champions Blackburn Rovers 3-1. They also embarked on a dramatic FA Cup run, as they came close to winning the trophy they had started the season banned from. An exit from the competition loomed as they trailed Southampton 2-0 at half-time in a fifth-round replay. Then Francis sent on substitute Ronny Rosenthal who hit a glorious hat-trick to turn the match on its head with Spurs going on to win 6-2 after extra time.

Next up was a daunting visit to Anfield to take on Liverpool. In a match of the highest quality, Spurs went behind but hit back with a brilliant Teddy Sheringham goal and a coolly-taken winner from Jürgen Klinsmann with just one minute remaining. Sadly the road to Wembley was blocked by Everton who bundled out an injury-ravaged Spurs side at the semi-final stage.

In Part Three we talk to Francis today, and get his thoughts on the aftermath of that FA Cup defeat and the difficulties posed by three key players – Klinsmann, Gica Popescu and Nicky Barmby – deciding to leave in the summer of 1995. We look at what happened next, and assess how Tottenham's action-packed 1994/95 campaign helped shape the modern-day Premier League.

In writing this book I tried to make contact with as many players and staff as possible who were at the club in 1994/95. I was unable to make contact with everyone, and not everyone replied to my messages – some may not have got them. Understandably, not everyone I did manage to contact had the time or inclination to talk to me. I am truly grateful though to everyone who was willing to share their memories with me either face to face or on the telephone. Interviews with everyone I was able to speak to are included in the book.

Talking to me over the phone from his home in California, Jürgen Klinsmann spoke of the 'unbelievable energy' that enveloped the club, saying that he had never before, or since, experienced anything like it. Teddy Sheringham told me that, for all he achieved at Manchester United, Tottenham's 1994/95 FA Cup sixth-round win against Liverpool was one of the standout memories of his illustrious career.

Over tea at The Grove Hotel in Hertfordshire, 1999 League Cup winner Darren Anderton agreed that 1994/95 was the season he enjoyed the most. David Howells – an FA Cup winner in 1991 – invited me to Charterhouse School, where he now works as director of football, and spoke of the amazing team spirit that embraced the club in 1994/95. Despite the acrimony caused by the manner of his departure from Spurs, Sol Campbell told me his memories of the Klinsmann season will always be treasured, perhaps even more so than winning the League Cup with Tottenham in 1999.

Dean Austin has recently been coaching in the Premier League with Watford, Stuart Nethercott is a PE teacher in Braintree and former captain Gary Mabbutt is a club ambassador at Spurs. All of them were happy to share with me the stories of their highs and lows throughout an action-packed campaign.

Kit man Roy Reyland served Tottenham for 29 years before leaving for rugby union Premiership side Saracens. I met with him at Sarries' training ground in St Albans where he offered great insight into life in the dressing room. Nick Hewer – Alan Sugar's head of PR at Spurs, and now famous for his appearances on *The Apprentice* – did likewise when it came to painting a picture of what went on in the boardroom. BBC commentator Jonathan Pearce, who was then employed by the Capital Gold radio station, and lifelong fan Daniel Wynne also relayed their experiences of watching Tottenham take part in a series of unforgettable games.

Add to all of this the contemporaneous writings of Francis and his further recollections in our many meetings, and we are left with a wonderfully comprehensive account of life behind the scenes at a club that was the talk of English football in 1994/95. Everyone I was privileged enough to speak to recalled that season as fondly as I do. Football is about far, far more than winning trophies. Tottenham's Team That Dared To Do certainly proved that.

Author's Note

THE Premier League is the organisation that has run the top division in England since 1992/93. The competition under its auspices was called the Premier League in 1992/93, the Premiership from 1993 until 2008, and then the Premier League again, as it is today. As a result, both names are used in this book.

In 1994/95 the tiers below the Premiership were Divisions One, Two and Three. Today they are known as the Championship, League One and League Two. The top non-league division was called the GM Vauxhall Conference, today it is the Vanarama National League. The Emirates FA Cup was the FA Cup, with no title sponsor, the League Cup (which will be known as the Carabao Cup from 2017/18) was the Coca-Cola League Cup, the Champions League was, as it still is, the Champions League, the Europa League was the UEFA Cup, and there also existed a European Cup-Winners' Cup, for domestic cup winners, which was dispensed with in 1999. The Community Shield was the Charity Shield and an assistant referee was called a linesman.

Also, a word on how this book was put together. As a 16-year-old in August 1994, I can still remember when my younger brother came running up to me on the beach during a family holiday in Greece with a copy of an English newspaper and the back page headline that Jürgen Klinsmann had signed for Spurs. This wasn't speculation, this was a done deal. A true superstar of the game, a former World Cup winner, a man who had hit five goals at that summer's tournament in the USA, had arrived at our club – a club which appeared, until now, destined for relegation having been hit with a six-point deduction by the FA.

I have been able to call on a great many research sources. First among them are my own match reports. I attended nearly every home game and many of the away matches in 1994/95. As a boy who aspired to a career in sports journalism, I would write my own reports as soon as I returned home. When I was unable to get to games I would write them while watching on TV or listening on Capital Gold where commentator Jonathan Pearce would transport his audience to the stadium by painting such a vivid picture of proceedings. I am truly grateful to him for his time talking to me about his memories of 1994/95.

I also kept a great many of the newspaper cuttings from the 1994/95 season as well as match programmes from all the games I attended. I bought the club's official VHS review of the season. Alas, I no longer have a VHS player, but fortunately I was able to track down a DVD, and of course many of the highlights are available on YouTube.

When interviewing David Howells he mentioned that he has never watched a replay of any part of the Everton v Tottenham FA Cup semi-final. It is likewise something I had avoided doing, until now. Thank you to the BBC Sport library for their efforts in tracking down the game and allowing me to view it. After all these years, I was surprised to discover that Stuart Nethercott didn't hit the post with the chance that could have made it 2-2 seconds before Everton went 3-1 up – Neville Southall actually saved his shot. Strangely, everyone I interviewed also remembered Nethercott hitting the post, even Nethercott himself!

Books which have provided me with considerable assistance include Bob Goodwin's brilliant *Tottenham Hotspur: The Complete Record* and, every sports journalist's essential companion, the *Rothmans Football Yearbook* (which is today known as the *Sky Sports Football Yearbook*).

Acknowledgements

Chris Slegg
I would like to thank my former BBC colleague Lance Hardy whose wonderful book *Stokoe, Sunderland and 73* inspired me to write about the season that meant most to me. Friends, and hugely talented authors, Sarah Crossan and Ed Davey also provided me with no end of helpful advice and guidance as did good friend Michele Young. Thanks also to mum and dad, and my wife Sonja for all their time and support, and to my little boy Archie.

Gerry Francis
Thank you to my family for all their help over the years, my wife Julie, my children Adam, Chloë, and Jake, my parents Roy and Pauline, my brother and sister Martin and Sue and their families. I would also like to make special mention to my mother-in-law Gillian Willson who passed away during the writing of this book. You're with Lawrie now. Rest in peace.

Gerry and Chris would both like to thank everyone who agreed to be interviewed for this book: the players; Darren Anderton; Dean Austin; Sol Campbell; Micky Hazard; David Howells; Jürgen Klinsmann; Gary Mabbutt; Stuart Nethercott and Teddy Sheringham; kit man Roy Reyland; head of PR Nick Hewer; former Notts County manager Russell Slade; former Manchester City player Steve Lomas; BBC commentator Jonathan Pearce and Tottenham supporter Daniel Wynne.

About the authors

Gerry Francis has enjoyed more than 50 years working in elite football since signing schoolboy terms with QPR. At the age of 23 he was made England captain and in 1976 he skippered QPR to within a whisker of being crowned champions when they finished runners-up to Liverpool.

Francis is a rare example of an Englishman to reach the very top as a player and then as a manager. He is the only manager during the Premier League era to have taken two clubs to the position of top London team, doing so with QPR in 1992/93 and Tottenham during the season which is the subject of this book.

On being appointed Tottenham manager in November 1994 he was struck by the size of the club and found himself inspired to write about his first few months in charge. They are writings which offer real insight into the life of a Premier League manager and they have been included in this book. After leaving Tottenham in 1997 he again managed QPR (1998–2001) and Bristol Rovers (2001). More recently he has worked as assistant manager to Tony Pulis at Premier League clubs Stoke City, Crystal Palace, and West Bromwich Albion, helping the latter to mid-table finishes in 2015/16 and 2016/17.

Chris Slegg is a writer and sports journalist at the BBC where he has reported live on football at all levels from non-league to the Champions League Final. He has worked at major events including the World Cup and European Championship as well as the Olympic and Paralympic Games at London 2012 and Rio 2016.

As a schoolboy in 1994/95, his love of football saw him attend nearly every Tottenham home game as well as many of their away fixtures. With aspirations of a future career in journalism he wrote his own reports on the games he attended and kept newspaper clippings and match programmes from that season. All have proved to be valuable research tools as he set about putting this book together; a book which tells the story of a season he, and many football fans, will never forget.

What Happened in 1994 and 1995

1994

20 January: Sir Matt Busby, the legendary former Manchester United manager, dies aged 84.

12–27 February: Team GB win two medals, both bronze, at the Winter Olympics in Lillehammer, Norway.

12 March: The first women are ordained as priests in the Church of England.

1 May: Brazilian F1 driver Ayrton Senna, 34, is killed in the San Marino Grand Prix.

2 May: Blackburn Rovers lose 2-1 at Coventry City, a result which officially crowns Manchester United (who won 2-1 at Ipswich the previous day), as Premiership champions.

6 May: The Channel Tunnel officially opens.

12 May: Serving Labour Party leader John Smith dies of a heart attack at the age of 55.

13 May: Film *Four Weddings and a Funeral* released in the UK.

14 May: Manchester United win the FA Cup, beating Chelsea 4-0 in the final at Wembley to complete the Double for the first time in the club's history.

25 May: The Camelot Group consortium wins the bid to run the UK's first National Lottery.

29 May: Scottish group Wet Wet Wet's cover of 'Love Is All Around', which is featured in the film *Four Weddings and a Funeral*, reaches No.1 in the UK charts. It stays there for 15 weeks – a record for a British act, and second only to Canadian Bryan Adams' '(Everything I Do) I Do It For You' (which spent 16 weeks at No.1 in 1991).

21 July: Tony Blair wins the Labour Party leadership contest, defeating John Prescott and Margaret Beckett.

26 July: A car bomb explodes outside the Israeli Embassy in London, injuring 14 people.

30 July: The main sport story in every newspaper is that Tottenham have sensationally signed former World Cup-winning striker Jürgen Klinsmann.

2 September: Actor and entertainer Roy Castle, best known for his appearances in children's TV programme *Record Breakers*, dies just two days after his 62nd birthday.

3 September: Former Wolves great Billy Wright, who won 105 caps for England, captaining them a record 90 times, dies aged 70.

15 November: The *Daily Telegraph* becomes the first UK newspaper to launch an online edition, the Electronic Telegraph. It's estimated 600,000 people in the UK have access to the internet at home.

19 November: The UK's first National Lottery draw is held. The same day Gerry Francis takes charge as Tottenham manager for the first time in a 4-3 home defeat to Aston Villa.

1995
10 January: British transfer fee record is broken as Andy Cole leaves Newcastle United for Manchester United in a £7m deal (£6m cash plus £1m-rated Keith Gillespie).

25 January: After being sent off in a match at Crystal Palace, Manchester United's Eric Cantona leaps over an advertising hoarding and kicks a spectator who has been verbally abusing him.

15 February: England's friendly match against the Republic of Ireland in Dublin is abandoned in the 27th minute after trouble caused by far-right activists in the away section.

21 February: Arsenal sack manager George Graham over allegations that he accepted illegal payments from an agent when signing two players in 1992. Graham denies any wrongdoing.

24 February: The Football Association bans Eric Cantona for eight months for his kick on a spectator at Selhurst Park and fines him £10,000.

20 March: The Queen arrives in Cape Town for the first royal visit to South Africa for 50 years.

31 March: Eric Cantona wins his appeal against a two-week prison sentence and will have to serve 120 hours' community service. At a subsequent Manchester United press conference, his only words are: 'When the seagulls follow the trawler, it is because they think sardines will be thrown into the sea. Thank you, very much.' He then walks out.

8 May: The 50th anniversary of VE Day is celebrated across Britain.

10 May: Spanish side Real Zaragoza beat Arsenal 2-1 in the Cup-Winners' Cup Final in Paris. Former Tottenham player Nayim scores the winner from the halfway line in the final minute of extra time.

14 May: Blackburn Rovers become champions of England for the first time since 1914. They lose at Liverpool, but Manchester United can only draw at West Ham meaning Rovers take the title by one point.

20 May: Everton win the FA Cup, beating Manchester United 1-0 in the final at Wembley.

30 May: Former Southampton, Arsenal and England striker Ted Drake dies aged 82. It's also confirmed that at next year's European Championship in England, any drawn matches in the knockout stages will be decided by the first goal scored in extra time – the golden goal. If no goals are scored in the 30 minutes, then it will go to penalties.

20 June: Arsenal manager Bruce Rioch pays a British record transfer fee of £7.5m to Inter Milan to bring Dutch international striker Dennis Bergkamp to Highbury.

22 June: John Major resigns as the leader of the Conservative Party (but not as Prime Minister), triggering a leadership contest.

3 July: The British football record transfer fee is broken for the third time this year as Liverpool pay Nottingham Forest £8.5m for striker Stan Collymore.

4 July: Prime Minister John Major wins the Conservative Party leadership contest, beating John Redwood.

26 August: Newly-promoted Middlesbrough play their first competitive match in their new stadium. The Riverside has replaced Ayresome Park. They lose the Premiership encounter with Chelsea 2-0.

2 September: Frank Bruno finally becomes world champion at the age of 33 when he outpoints Oliver McCall over 12 rounds to win the WBC world heavyweight title.

24 November: *GoldenEye*, the 17th James Bond film, is released with Pierce Brosnan playing the lead role for the first time.

2 December: Nick Leeson is jailed for six and a half years in Singapore on a double fraud charge relating to the collapse of Barings Bank.

PART ONE

June–November 1994

KLINSMANIA

1

Famous Five

'That's part of being a Spurs fan, seeing players who lift you off your seat and excite you.' (David Howells)

IF it wasn't for the handshake which lends it an air of formality, it could be a holiday snap. Clear blue sky to the top left of frame, shimmering blue water to the bottom. In the centre and mid-distance, a yacht and its sail drawing the eye to the hotel-clustered coastline beyond.

In the foreground two figures, both relaxed, smiling and squinting into the sun. One of them just happens to be a celebrated English football club chairman; the other, one of the most famous players in the world. Alan Sugar with his unmistakable curly black-grey hair and beard, attired in a light blue, loose-fitting shirt; right arm outstretched, hand clasped by Jürgen Klinsmann, maroon polo shirt, sunglasses clipped through lowest button hole, blond hair glistening.

Until now Sugar hasn't had much to be cheery about this summer. On 14 June the Football Association fined Spurs £600,000, banned them from the 1994/95 FA Cup and docked them 12 points for the upcoming season after finding the club guilty of financial irregularities committed under former owners. Three weeks later, on appeal, the points deduction was halved, the fine was doubled and the FA Cup ban remained. Tottenham's misdemeanour had been to pay undisclosed loans to players as a way of encouraging them to sign for the club in the late 80s and early 90s.

Under current manager Ossie Ardiles, Tottenham had stayed up by just three points the previous season. Now they were starting on minus six. Sugar vowed to fight the punishment and, in what almost appeared a personal act of defiance, went out and signed Klinsmann. The photo of the two beside Sugar's yacht is a defining image both in the history of Tottenham Hotspur and of English football. 'KLINSMANN COUP' ran the headline in the *Daily Express* on 30 July 1994. 'The brilliant blond striker, 30 today, joined Spurs from Monaco in a £2m deal secretly secured on chairman Alan Sugar's yacht in Monte Carlo.'

Big money, big name signings don't happen like this any more. The expression 'transfer saga' has become a cliché, but that's so often what they are: long and drawn-out, as top players are linked with top clubs over the final year or two of their existing contract before the move finally happens. Klinsmann to Tottenham hadn't even been mentioned in the gossip columns. It had come out of nowhere. Until that picture of the two men standing by Sugar's yacht appeared in the papers few would have considered such a transfer remotely possible.

Before the photo was taken, Sugar met with Klinsmann's agent Andy Gross and his manager at Monaco – a certain Arsène Wenger. Monaco agreed to the £2m fee and, according to Sugar, in his 2010 autobiography *What You See Is What You Get*, Klinsmann accepted that Spurs couldn't go beyond their maximum salary of £8,000 per week. Sugar says that Gross then insisted that because of the problems Tottenham were having with the FA and the possibility of relegation, the two-year contract would have to include a get-out clause at the end of the first year. The Spurs chairman claims that his reading of the demand made by Gross was that it was a get-out clause only in the event of relegation. In his excitement and eagerness to conclude the deal, Sugar agreed to it.

The Spurs supremo was keen to make public the news of the transfer as soon as possible. He says he did so partly out of fear that the deal could yet be scuppered. Although he had an agreement with Monaco and Klinsmann he didn't yet have a legally-binding contract signed. His tactic, he says, was to get a photo of the Klinsmann handshake in the papers so that the player wouldn't then dare back out. Sugar had many contacts at Sky and telephoned them, instructing them to send a film crew to his yacht.

Today Klinsmann lives in California where he served as USA head coach between July 2011 and November 2016, leading the country to one Gold Cup triumph (the equivalent of the European Championship for the Americas and Caribbean region) in 2013. Speaking to me over the phone, he reveals his experiences at Spurs left a great impression on him. 'I had no idea what to expect in London,' says Klinsmann. 'Okay, so

I knew that the English and German cultures looked at each other in a certain way, and I knew that there were some chants that I had heard, but I had no issue with that. Other than that it was all going to be a complete adventure, on and off the pitch. As soon as my wife and I arrived in London, we knew that it was the place for us. It was such a cosmopolitan city, such a diverse place. It is a city where anyone can be themselves. It has its own feel to it. People from all over the world come to live there together and have no problem. Most people are very open-minded. You can just glide into your own lifestyle and enjoy it. There is so much going on culturally.' So how did Sugar persuade him to sign? 'Well, we had a really excellent cappuccino on his yacht,' jokes Klinsmann. 'It was true Italian. Other than that, he was very honest about the situation the club was in, and I thought it would be a real challenge with the six-point deduction to try and help the club.'

Today Nick Hewer is known to millions as a man who for years appeared as one of Sugar's sidekicks on the BBC television programme *The Apprentice*. His frequently-raised eyebrows, straight talking and acerbic wit have made him a popular figure with many viewers. In the 80s and 90s he was Sugar's main PR man at Amstrad and then Tottenham. 'Sugar has a great marketing eye,' says Hewer. 'He knows what he's doing. He knows how to create a buzz. He knows how to be different. It's marketing genius really. To bring in Klinsmann? Bloody hell, he knew that would be a phenomenal thing. In fact he rang Ossie from his boat and said, "If I can get Klinsmann what would you say?" Ossie said, "He wouldn't want to come to us."

'"But if I could get him, what would you say?"

'"I'd say, fantastic."

'"Good, cos I've just signed him."

'He didn't even consult Ossie in fact. He knew that to bring Klinsmann into the team would just transform people's perceptions of the club, and it did.'

Daniel Wynne has been a Tottenham season-ticket holder since just before his fifth birthday in 1975. Today he is the club's in-house match commentator. Speaking as a fan, he says: 'There was no build-up to the signing. It was a complete surprise. They were different times. That couldn't happen now. I was sitting at work when I heard Klinsmann had signed for Tottenham. The first thing that came to mind was the newspaper headline in 1978 when we signed Ardiles and Ricky Villa: "SPURS SCOOP THE WORLD". That's what it felt like again.'

While Oleg Salenko of Russia and Hristo Stoichkov of Bulgaria had shared the Golden Boot at USA 94 with six goals each, Klinsmann had been the true star striker of the World Cup. Germany had been surprisingly beaten by Stoichkov's Bulgaria in the quarter-finals, but Klinsmann had lit up the tournament with five goals, all of them of the highest quality. A World Cup winner with West Germany in 1990, Klinsmann had spent the last five years playing for two of Europe's richest and most glamorous clubs. First, Internazionale of Italy, with whom he won the UEFA Cup in 1991, then on to Monaco where he made it to the Champions League semi-finals in 1994.

Now he was coming to Tottenham, reduced, since the turn of the decade, to the role of a mid-ranking team at the best of times and now seriously in the doldrums, having been hit by the damning FA sanctions. In the summer of 1994, Klinsmann had his pick of clubs. However, you look at that photo more closely today and you notice that Klinsmann is pulling Sugar's arm towards him, perhaps desperate to seize the opportunity he's been offered.

Bigger clubs in Europe had been chasing his signature, but the only two English clubs firmly linked with him were Aston Villa and Everton, both on a par with Tottenham in terms of profile, and both having won the game's biggest prizes far more recently than Spurs. Villa had been champions in 1981 and European Cup winners the following year. Everton had won two league titles, one FA Cup and the Cup-Winners' Cup in the 1980s. Who knows what else they might have achieved in Europe, but for the ban on English clubs after the Heysel disaster in 1985? The most recent of Tottenham's two league titles had of course been achieved way back in 1961, although the 60s, 70s and 80s had been littered with cup successes.

Two factors might have put off other English suitors. Firstly, Klinsmann's age. Secondly, his reputation. If there had been magic in his performances at USA 94, there had been menace four years previously at Italia 90. West Germany had won perhaps the ugliest World Cup tournament of all time – beating Argentina 1-0 in a final in which their opponents had two men sent off.

In 1990 the tactics employed by defenders could be brutal. Argentina themselves had been the victims of some roughhouse play from Cameroon in the opening game; the West African side were also reduced to nine men, but still caused a huge shock with a 1-0 win over the defending champions. As such, the forwards had to resort to sometimes devious means. Klinsmann had become infamous as the greatest exponent of the dive. His antics, and those of others, in a World Cup full of cheating, simulation and dangerous tackling, coincided with England's best-ever World Cup showing on foreign soil.

In the semi-finals England met West Germany. The Germans prevailed on penalties after a thrilling match. Andreas Brehme's free kick took a huge deflection off Paul Parker, and looped over goalkeeper Peter Shilton to give West Germany an early second-half lead. Gary Lineker equalised with an unerring shot nine minutes from time. In extra time both teams hit the post, and of course Paul Gascoigne's World Cup fell apart when he received his second booking of the tournament for a foul on Thomas Berthold. The 'Tears in Turin' rolled down Gazza's cheeks as he realised he would be banned from the final. His friend and Spurs team-mate Lineker turned to manager Bobby Robson to warn him to 'have a word' with the England maestro, who was now an emotional wreck. The match finished 1-1, and then England had their first experience of their now all-too-familiar penalty shoot-out pain as Stuart Pearce and Chris Waddle missed while West Germany scored all theirs. In the eyes of England fans, the emotion of the occasion and their team's defiance in the face of adversity meant they were the moral victors, and that merely served to enhance the image of Klinsmann and his team-mates as pantomime villains.

Four years on, Klinsmann had now arrived in England with a sullied reputation to restore. Klinsmann was the second high-profile arrival at Spurs in as many days. Ilie Dumitrescu had also shone at USA 94, with some eye-catching displays in midfield as he helped guide Romania to the quarter-finals. In the round of 16 he scored twice in a 3-2 win over Argentina, one of the most entertaining games in World Cup history. The signing of 25-year-old Dumitrescu was in itself big news, but the capture of Klinsmann took things to another level. If Spurs fans were ecstatic, how did the players feel?

Darren Anderton was 22 then. He'd joined for the same £2m fee as Klinsmann two years previously, a hefty sum at the start of the 90s. In Anderton, Spurs were signing raw potential, in Klinsmann, proven quality. More than two decades on, Anderton has agreed to meet at The Grove in Hertfordshire to discuss his memories of 1994/95. Set in a stunning 300-acre country estate, the hotel which describes itself as 'more than five star' has often been used by the England team. The 18-hole golf course is popular with current and former footballers. Over a pot of tea in the restaurant off the main lobby, Anderton recalls the whirlwind summer of 1994 and the season that followed as clearly as if it was yesterday. He can remember the sequence of games and major events as accurately as most passionate supporters. For Anderton, who was about to start his third season in a Spurs shirt, the first feeling was one of shock that one of his new team-mates would be a former World Cup winner.

'I was out in America watching the World Cup with friends when I found out we'd signed him. It was almost unbelievable. I saw that picture of him on the boat, and I thought it was a wind-up,' says Anderton. 'Speaking to the boys we were all saying, "Surely not?" and "How good are we going to be this year?"

'We'd had a really terrible season the year before. Teddy [Sheringham] had been out injured. It had been Ossie's first year and it had been a nightmare as we only just stayed up. Then all of a sudden – fair play to the chairman – he'd gone out and done this, he'd seen what was going on at the World Cup and sprung into action to sign the best players.'

Anderton's former team-mate Sheringham, who is also happy to reminisce about 1994/95 in a separate interview, agrees. 'I felt we already had the basis of a good side there at Spurs, but to give us that little bit extra, a real top quality player, someone who could do something special in the blink of an eye, that made a real difference. Bringing in Jürgen was a masterstoke,' he says.

Football transfer deals have to be seismic to make the network news. The fee either needs to be astronomical – which this wasn't – or the player has to be a household name. Jürgen Klinsmann – thanks to his brilliance at USA 94 and his histrionics at Italia 90 – was exactly that. Sure enough, Klinsmann's arrival at Spurs featured on the BBC One O'clock and Six O'clock News. Over pictures of Klinsmann in action for Germany against Bolivia at USA 94, newsreader Jennie Bond told the afternoon audience: 'Tottenham Hotspur have signed the German striker Jürgen Klinsmann for a transfer fee of £2m. Klinsmann, who's 30, was Germany's leading scorer at the last World Cup. He'll join Spurs on a two-year contract from the French League club Monaco.' Her colleague Martyn Lewis then introduced the next item, which was that the date had been confirmed for the first UK National Lottery draw – 19 November 1994. Spurs fans, though, felt as if they'd already hit the jackpot.

With this signing, Tottenham had positioned themselves at the centre of the football universe. Everyone wanted a piece of them. In the Premier League era, perhaps only Newcastle's failed title challenge in 1995/96 and Leicester's fairy-tale triumph in 2015/16 have garnered a greater level of interest from the football neutral and the wider public.

In the summer of 1994, midfielder David Howells was about to start his tenth season at Spurs. As one of Tottenham's longest-serving players at the time, he had played alongside greats including Gary Lineker and Paul Gascoigne as well as Ossie Ardiles and Steve Perryman, who were now his manager and assistant manager respectively. Like Anderton, Howells can also remember his feelings when he learnt of Klinsmann's arrival: 'I was at White Hart Lane when I heard the news. I was just leaving the ground and it was on the radio. It was one of those that you're not sure whether to believe straight away, even as a player. What made it better was that the newspapers were almost ridiculing Spurs at the time.

'There were rumours of signing maybe Ruud Gullit; big names like that were coming up and it was always "Oh, Spurs are after that one again. It's folly, it's not gonna happen." And then we got Klinsmann. Wow. Dumitrescu was a real coup anyway cos he'd had a great World Cup, so that whetted everyone's appetite, but then to pull off the Klinsmann one, to get home and actually see it on the news with Sugar on the yacht with Klinsmann in Monaco, was barely believable.

'The players were so excited. Signings at any level give you a buzz because you want to know what the individual is like, but when it's someone as well-known as a Klinsmann, when you sign a Klinsmann and you know what a great player he is, you know he's only going to improve you. You then start to think about what he will be like as a person and what else he will bring to the set-up aside from his undoubted quality on the pitch.'

London is perhaps the most beautifully strange football city in the world, certainly in Europe. Big cities tend to have big clubs bearing their names. Barcelona. Roma. Paris St Germain. Bayern and 1860 Munich. Real and Atletico Madrid. But there is no London United. No London City. No London anything. It is a capital city with no combined football identity, but instead a myriad of colours, of chants, songs, and superstitions: a football frenzy of rituals, histories and traditions. Pitches that are patches of green in a concrete jungle. Chelsea, Brentford, Fulham, Millwall. Splendidly simple place-names with no need of a suffix. Then there are names which carry a certain mystique: Queens Park Rangers, Crystal Palace, Leyton Orient and – surely the finest football name of them all – Tottenham Hotspur.

Klinsmann wasn't just Tottenham's first true superstar player since the departure of Paul Gascoigne, but London's too. Gazza's final Spurs appearance had been the 1991 FA Cup Final, when his self-inflicted injury saw him stretchered off and sidelined for a year before completing his £5.5m move to Lazio in Italy's Serie A. In the meantime Spurs had become functional, Chelsea were a mid-table team and even though Arsenal were still winning trophies, (adding the FA Cup and League Cup in 1993 and the Cup-Winners' Cup in 1994 to the league titles of 1989 and 1991), they now played ultra-defensive football under George Graham. Where Manchester had Eric Cantona, London football needed something, someone, to love.

The arrival of Klinsmann was that aphrodisiac. It sent white and blue blood coursing through the veins again. Tottenham was perfect for Klinsmann; Klinsmann was perfect for Tottenham. The cockerel could crow again. Every blade of the White Hart Lane turf appeared touched by magic. Every square inch bounded by those white lines seemed to awaken to infinite possibility.

There has never been a pre-season at Tottenham, or perhaps at any club, like the one in 1994. Klinsmann was ready for a hostile reception at the press conference to announce his arrival. Since the news of his signing had broken, television viewers in England had seen endless replays of what many considered to be an outrageous dive in the 1990 World Cup Final. The challenge by Argentina's Pedro Monzon was quite clearly a foul, and one for which he was rightly shown a straight red card, becoming the first player to be sent off in a World Cup Final. It was also a foul which is quite clearly strong enough to knock Klinsmann off his feet. It was the way in which he fell, though, that Klinsmann has long been derided for. If you watch a slow motion replay there are four distinct stages to it. A fraction of a second after becoming airborne, Klinsmann twists the whole of his body, as if to add emphasis to the fact he's been impeded. Then he hits the turf almost vertically – not quite head first, but shoulders first – as he holds his head in his hands and then propels himself straight back upwards as though he's detonated a landmine on impact. Then come two sideways rolls to his left before he settles face down and motionless. The referee sprints across to Monzon to show him the red card, then beckons for the stretcher. There's little doubting the histrionics of Klinsmann's tumble.

His other most replayed fall occurred in the 1994 Champions League semi-final, when Monaco were beaten by Milan in one of the last games Klinsmann played for Wenger's side. Milan defender Alessandro Costacurta appeared to make minimal contact, sending Klinsmann into a series of sideways rolls along the turf. Costacurta received a second yellow card, was sent off and banned from the Champions League Final.

On arrival in England, there was also another barrier for Klinsmann to overcome: xenophobia. It may have been half a century since the countries were at war, but England's mainstream media was seemingly incapable of passing comment on a match against Germany or a German player without reference to the conflict. It was perhaps only the outrage caused by the *Daily Mirror*'s ridiculous 'ACHTUNG! SURRENDER' headline, when previewing the Euro 96 semi-final, that forced a greater awareness of just how distasteful this was. Their front page included mocked-up pictures of Stuart Pearce and Gazza wearing tin hats and warned: 'For you Fritz, ze European Championship is over'.

The day after Klinsmann's transfer to Spurs was confirmed, one newspaper ran the headline 'DIVE BOMBER'. The war reference was unnecessary, though the copy itself was compelling: a warning to Klinsmann from one of England's most prominent referees, Keith Hackett, who had just retired. 'The message to Klinsmann must be that it will not be stood for here. He'll be playing with the world's best referees and won't get away with any nonsense. Nobody can fail to be aware of the reputation Klinsmann has got for himself.' England and Manchester United defender Paul Parker had been sought out for quotes too. He was still scarred by the experience of marking Klinsmann in the 1990 World Cup semi-final. 'Normal precautions are no use against Klinsmann,' he warned. 'You simply cannot mark him tight as you would do most attackers. And the closer he gets to the penalty box, the more he is ready for one of his tricks. Go in hard on him at your peril. I reckon the new laws on tackling from behind were absolutely made to measure for Klinsmann.'

Klinsmann knew exactly what to expect at his first press conference, which took place on Thursday 4 August. Flanked by Ardiles and Sugar, who had interrupted his family holiday to be there, Klinsmann surprised everyone: 'Maybe I can ask you the first question,' he said, beating the journalists to it. 'Are there any diving schools in London?' There was laughter throughout the room. When it died down Klinsmann continued: 'It is no problem. I just laugh about it. If people are serious, then maybe we can discuss it over a couple of beers and they can show me tapes of it – because I don't remember the incidents. Perhaps the fans will try to provoke me, but I will just try to play good football.'

Klinsmann had struck the first blow. His self-deprecating sense of humour had the press onside straight away. Gary Mabbutt – Tottenham's captain at the time – says Klinsmann had initially intended to take the joke even further: 'When Jürgen arrived he was frustrated that one newspaper did a big spread titled: "How to do the Klinsmann dive". I was sharing a room with Jürgen and he said, "Listen, this is not true, I have never dived, I have never cheated, I have never done it on purpose in my life." He was really upset at how the British media portrayed him. Basically we agreed he had to laugh at himself, he had to find a way of turning it around.' Mabbutt chuckles at the memory of what they came up with. 'There was a thought that for the first press conference we could try to hire one of those old-fashioned massive diving suits with the massive masks, the big head, and Jürgen could walk in with this big metal suit on. We looked into it but you couldn't hire one anywhere, it was impossible.'

'I quickly learnt in England that you have to laugh at yourself,' says Klinsmann. 'The dressing room was full of jokers, they all made me laugh. Two people who were especially funny were Teddy Sheringham and Colin Calderwood. It was a different experience from in Germany,

Italy or France. I realised that you can't afford to take yourself too seriously. You can't be offended. Teddy and Colin were always ready to hit you with something, but they expected you to hit them straight back. What that kind of humour means, is that you accept people for who they are. You give as good as you get. That was a wonderful experience for me. You respect people on the field and off it. The tricky thing with Colin was that it took me half a year to get to know his Scottish dialect, so for a while I really didn't know what he was saying. Playing with characters like that though made my Tottenham career really entertaining.'

Two days after that press conference it was Klinsmann's debut. Watford v Tottenham remains probably the most-hyped friendly Spurs have ever played. The match had been arranged as part of the deal which saw Steve Perryman leave Vicarage Road in 1993 to become assistant manager to Ardiles. Watford would have been pleased enough to secure the high-profile friendly even then, but now – with Klinsmann in town – the gate would be more than doubled. 'JOIN SPURS AND SEE THE A406' was the headline in the *Evening Standard*. Their reporter Mick Dennis asked whether Klinsmann, 'a fine footballer, a civilised person, and very much a man of the world' would be 'prepared for the horrible reality of a wet Wednesday on the A406?'

On the day of the match local traders showed the kind of entrepreneurial spirit a modern-day Lord Sugar would seek in an apprentice. En route to the ground, in the shopping precinct a little way down Vicarage Road, you could buy a Klinsmann T-shirt for £9.99, or two for £15. Watford had been expecting a crowd of around 6,000 prior to Klinsmann's signing. Press reports note that 4,000 were waiting outside Vicarage Road two hours before kick-off. The crowd in the end was a capacity 14,000 – a late surge forcing ground staff to take the decision at 2.45pm to push the kick-off back by 15 minutes to 3.15pm. No fewer than eight television camera crews were in attendance.

Stuart Nethercott, one of Tottenham's first-choice centre-backs at the start of 1994/95, remembers the frenzy well. 'You felt the buzz,' he says. 'I think the feeling among a lot of the supporters – because of the FA punishment – was that everyone was against us. The feeling was, "Right, let's stick together." It fostered a camaraderie. It was all backs against the wall.'

Darren Anderton agrees: 'From the moment Jürgen arrived you felt something special was going to happen – even in the pre-season games. Watford away, I'll never forget it. Thousands of fans there, kick-off delayed, the news crews everywhere. Trying to get off the pitch after the warm-up to get to the changing room and get ready for the game took forever, because hundreds of people were waiting to get his autograph. It was madness and it was great to be a part of.'

The pre-season interest in Spurs also made an impression on Howells: 'It was just a carnival,' he says. 'I played in all the pre-season games. I was captain for a few as well. Spurs fans were desperate to get in at Watford. There were thousands of people outside, who were struggling to get in for a pre-season friendly which three or four weeks earlier would have been a total non-event. All of a sudden it was a massive news event as well as a sports event. It was handy for me too having Jürgen there, because funnily enough I was due to head straight to Heathrow after the Watford game to fly out to Berlin to stay with friends there for a couple of nights. I was speaking with Jürgen about what to do when I was there, and it was great to have some inside info from him. He really looked after me. He was such a great bloke and everyone got to know him really well. He was so approachable, just a decent, decent man.'

Saturday 6 August, 1994
Pre-season Friendly
Watford 1-1 Tottenham Hotspur
Johnson 35
Sheringham 65

A furry creature, either a stoat or a ferret – the various sports hacks come to different conclusions – scuttles across the pitch before kick-off and has to be chased away by Watford's mascot. It seems every living being in Hertfordshire wants to sample what's been dubbed 'Klinsmania'.

Klinsmann himself takes to the pitch in a No.18 shirt. In the press conference to announce his signing earlier in the week he had been wearing Sheringham's No.10. Watford go ahead ten minutes before half-time with a goal Klinsmann would have been proud of. Richard Johnson – a young Australian once rejected by Spurs after a trial – smacks one in off the bar from 30 yards.

Midway through the second half Sheringham nets Tottenham's equaliser. Klinsmann has had a quiet debut; his best chances come in the final ten minutes. First Nicky Barmby plays him through but he drags his shot wide. Then a fine header looks like it is creeping in at the near post but is well saved by Watford keeper Kevin Miller, a £250,000 summer signing from Birmingham. When the final whistle blows Klinsmann is mobbed by Spurs fans as he leaves the pitch.

'It was like the Gazza days where crowds followed us everywhere because of Gazza, and to a lesser extent Gary Lineker,' says Howells. 'With

Gareth Bale, a long time after I'd left, you had that too – somebody extraordinary. That's what we do as a club, produce extraordinary individuals, going back to Ossie and Glenn Hoddle. Martin Chivers was probably my first hero, before that Jimmy Greaves – more recently there's been Chris Waddle, David Ginola and then Bale.

'That's part of being a Spurs fan, seeing players who lift you off your seat and excite you. Hopefully Tottenham will always have that and always be that. It's about every now and again seeing something you're not going to see anywhere else.

'I know we didn't produce Gareth Bale as such, but we brought him on from what he was at Southampton and turned him into what he has become. With Luka Modric, it was the same sort of thing. I watched him play for Real Madrid recently – just a magical, magical player, and I think Spurs take a lot of credit for what he's become. It's just disappointing we can't hold on to them.'

Tottenham right-back Dean Austin agrees that the size of the crowd for a pre-season friendly at Watford emphasised how big the Klinsmann signing was. 'It was just a feeling of, "Crikey, we're getting a world-class player here, a World Cup winner." What struck me more than anything was just what a normal, down-to-earth top fella he was. So normal and down-to-earth it was incredible, really. Obviously there was an aura that came with him, but we had a fantastic set of players at that time and there was an incredible spirit as well among the group. There was a core of us who would go on nights out. We did it at the right time, we weren't going out every night of the week. There was Ian Walker, Stuart Nethercott, me, Darren Anderton, David Howells, Teddy Sheringham, Cask [Darren Caskey], Justin Edinburgh. You know, we had a good group. I think for any player Klinsmann was the perfect role model. How he prepared himself, how he carried himself on a daily basis. No ego, none of this "I'll do what I want," he was just one of the lads. He's a credit to the profession, really.'

Anderton, though, remembers something about the Watford game which doesn't quite fit in with that image of Klinsmann as the model professional, although admittedly it's notable probably because it was his only transgression, and a minor one at that. 'A funny thing was that before the game Jürgen had half a glass of red wine. He never did it again, but for some reason he did it that day,' says Anderton. 'He was relaxed. Obviously he'd been at the World Cup and hadn't done any sort of proper pre-season. He was clever, using the friendlies as his pre-season, so he wasn't running around like a madman. He was just easing his way back into it really.'

Tuesday 9 August, 1994
Pre-season Friendly
Shelbourne 0-1 Tottenham Hotspur
Klinsmann 65

Spurs head to Ireland for another friendly. Ilie Dumitrescu can't play at Tolka Park because he is still awaiting a work permit, so once more all the attention is on Klinsmann, who is partnered up front by Teddy Sheringham.

Darren Anderton starts, but he is stretchered off with two minutes to go with an ankle injury. Nicky Barmby is on the bench and comes on for Jason Dozzell.

Klinsmann scores his first goal in a Tottenham shirt. It comes 20 minutes into the second half and is enough to win the game.

'From memory, it was in Ireland that we first discussed the idea of Klinsmann doing the dive celebration,' says Anderton, who fortunately went on to recover from that ankle knock in time for the first game of the season. 'We were on the coach to the game for the Shelbourne match. I think it was David Kerslake who had the idea. Luckily Klinsmann didn't do it in Ireland. It would have been wasted in a friendly.

'The whole pre-season was unbelievable, it was madness. It's quite funny 'cos the overseas boys can have a different approach to us, but the way Jürgen was, the minute he walked on to the training pitch he was the most humble, nicest guy you could ever meet. You have to think he could have played for anyone in the world. Then again, London's a pretty good draw for anyone. I've been fortunate enough to live there for many years and I love it. It certainly helps clubs get players to come and play for you. It's still my favourite season as a professional footballer to be part of that. Everybody clicked.'

Klinsmann says: 'I'd never experienced what I saw in Ireland. Ossie came into the dressing room after the game and handed us £20 or £30 each. He just said, "Go out and have a good time." So we all went to the pub. Okay, in Italy sometimes we would go for a club meal after training and maybe have some wine, but this was a different culture. The players took me out to a club and we had a beer late at night. That spirit helped us. It showed we were all the same. I knew that they would be there for me and they knew that I would be there for them.'

Saturday 20 August, 1994
Tottenham will kick off their Premiership campaign away to Sheffield Wednesday this afternoon. All the talk in the football media has been about Spurs and their new striker, so it's no surprise that one of the main

features on this lunchtime's *Football Focus* on BBC One is an interview with Klinsmann recorded earlier in the week.

Reporter Clive Tyldesley sits with Klinsmann inside an executive box in the West Stand at White Hart Lane. The pitch on which Klinsmann will become a cult hero is visible behind him. Sporting a blue cardigan with red, yellow and white stripes and a white T-shirt underneath it, Klinsmann smiles from his piercing blue eyes throughout the interview as he explains why he decided to leave Monaco for North London.

The piece starts by showing Klinsmann scoring a goal for Germany against the Netherlands. His team-mate Guido Buchwald beats Aron Winter on the left and whips in a lovely low cross to the edge of the six-yard box, where Klinsmann, who has been lurking behind his marker, surges ahead of him and dispatches a delicious left-foot volley. His celebration – shown in slow motion – involves pogo-ing four times off both feet and circling both arms in a windmill motion as Tyldesley's script begins: 'He's a world champion, a European Footballer of the Year and a proven goalscorer with Inter Milan, Monaco and Germany, one of the world's great forwards. And now he's Jürgen Klinsmann of Tottenham Hotspur.'

The piece then cuts to Klinsmann sitting in that box in the West Stand at White Hart Lane, with the old wooden seats of the Paxton Road upper tier behind him over his right shoulder. 'Five years ago I left Germany, and everybody felt I should stay in Germany because I had everything I needed in Germany,' says Klinsmann. 'But I said, "No, I have to go to Italy because I need a new experience." And so all the people said, "Will he make it?" Because you have to change your mentality, you have to learn the language and all that stuff, and I made it in Italy, I made it in France and now I try to give my best in England.'

'Is this the biggest challenge, though?' interjects Tyldesley. Klinsmann pauses. 'Erm … It's … Yeah, you can compare it to the challenge of Italy in the same way when I went to Inter Milan.'

'What turns you on about football? What do you want to get out of football most?' Klinsmann's face lights up at the question. 'Oh you know, it's just to play the game, I mean every time I have a ball around, I enjoy playing a lot. I enjoy every day when I train, every little game that we play, even if you play maybe in a park or somewhere, it's just the game that pushes me all the time. And I think here in England you can see it all over, all over in London and everywhere, they play, the kids they walk around, they run around in their football shirts and I think that's the wonderful part.'

To the accompaniment of some music the piece then shows the viewer two of Klinsmann's goals from USA 94, his arrowed low finish against Belgium, and his flick, pivot and left-foot volley against South Korea, before the music fades out and Tyldesley picks up the voiceover: 'Five goals during the summer's World Cup finals confirmed Klinsmann's standing in the game. Interestingly, he's a great defender of England's standing, challenging the view that we've slipped into the second division of world football.'

'I mean the faster a game gets, you know, the more difficult it gets,' says Klinsmann. 'And if you play as fast as you play here in England it's normal that you are making more mistakes in a game, and the more you have space, the more you have time to control the ball, to pass it or to look around. It looks maybe nicer in the first moment, but it's no big deal when you have the time for it. And here it's more difficult because everything goes so fast and I enjoy that.'

The piece then treats Tottenham fans to a first teasing glimpse of Klinsmann in a Spurs shirt: 15 seconds or so of action from the Watford friendly as he picks up the ball, sprints forward, bemuses two defenders but then curls his shot too close to the Hornets keeper.

Klinsmann's interview continues: 'I just wanted to do something new. I mean I'd played three years in Italy, two years in France and so suddenly there came this possibility with Tottenham and it was a big, big challenge for me, and the more I was thinking about it I thought, "Yeah I should do it, I should try it. I should come over to England." Now I'm here and it's going to be a totally new experience for me, and I'm looking forward now to the first real game in the championship.'

The viewer then sees a shot of the entire Spurs team modelling the new strip for the official team photo. The camera closes in on Klinsmann standing between David Howells to his left and Justin Edinburgh to his right as Tyldesley's script continues: 'In midsummer Tottenham's very championship survival was on the line. They'll now carry a six-point handicap, and at present there's no prospect of Klinsmann's first season featuring an FA Cup run.' The camera pans to the left of Howells, where it stops on another key signing. 'But his arrival, along with the Romanian World Cup forward Ilie Dumitrescu, has lifted the cloud above White Hart Lane.'

As a respected journalist, Tyldesley of course has to get in the question that every non-Spurs fan wants to hear answered. As Klinsmann is shown in close-up taking what most would agree was an exaggerated tumble in a Germany match as an opponent's boot makes the slightest contact with his own, the voiceover continues: 'The only cloud on Klinsmann's horizon is his reputation as a diver for free kicks and penalties. He's surprised at the media attention given to the odd slip and stumble in his international past. To any charge of cheating he pleads innocent.'

Klinsmann says: 'I never heard about this story, never, never, never. Not in Italy, in France, in Germany. And, er, I just try to find out how they can talk in this way about you, so maybe I thought they just invented this stuff to provoke you a bit before you come over to England. Maybe they expected you to answer in a kind of aggressive way, and I just made a joke about it and so the whole story was over.'

Tyldesley hits Klinsmann with a follow-up question: 'Are you worried that it will be in the minds of referees, that referees will be looking for it now that it has been talked about?' A body language expert might note the slightest frustration from Klinsmann at being pressed on the matter. As the question comes in he purses his lips, pushes his tongue forward just slightly to rest between them. His eyes narrow a millimetre, before an extended blink and a triple shake of the head as he replies shortly, yet calmly, 'No … no. Because I don't do it.' And that is how the report ends.

The locals in Sheffield are unconvinced. As Tottenham's team coach arrives at Hillsborough, Owls fans are there to welcome Klinsmann with home-made diving scorecards: 5.9, 5.9, 5.9.

FA Carling Premiership
Sheffield Wednesday 3-4 Tottenham Hotspur

Petrescu 54, Calderwood (og) 64, Hirst 83
Sheringham 19, Anderton 30, Barmby 71, Klinsmann 82

The long summer wait is over. The moment every football fan has been holding out for. The season starts here. Sure, the World Cup was good, but it lacked intensity because England weren't there. It's been months since there was anything to get worked up about. Opening day is always a mixture of nerves, excitement and optimism.

For Spurs fans there's even more than usual to talk about: two World Cup players in the line-up, a desperate need to start hauling back the six points that have been docked, and, at kick-off, a formation which has the journalists and commentators in South Yorkshire aghast in expectation.

Ossie Ardiles has fielded five attackers. Captain Teddy Sheringham plays just off Jürgen Klinsmann. Nicky Barmby is in the hole behind them. Darren Anderton lines up on the right, Ilie Dumitrescu on the left. The media quickly christen the forward line employed by Ardiles the 'Famous Five'.

Is it bold attacking play or reckless foolishness? Colin Calderwood is Tottenham's sole man in midfield. At the back Sol Campbell and Stuart Nethercott are in the centre, David Kerslake on the right and Justin Edinburgh on the left. Ian Walker, just 22, gets the nod in goal with Norwegian Erik Thorstvedt having returned from the World Cup injured.

It starts well for Spurs. Sheringham breaks the deadlock in the 19th minute. Anderton sends in a cross from the right that is just too high for Wednesday's own Romanian debutant, Dan Petrescu. It drops over his head to Sheringham who collects it where the 'D' meets the area on the left-hand side of the box. Petrescu's inability to cut it out leaves Sheringham slightly surprised to find the ball at his feet. It gets caught under his right foot, but he recovers brilliantly to knock it forward with his left and then get a shot away off the outside of his right to send it bending beyond the goalkeeper, Kevin Pressman, from about 15 yards. He doesn't have the momentum to get any real power on it, but the accuracy of the shot is perfection.

Sheringham celebrates Tottenham's first goal of the season by charging towards the Spurs fans to the left of the goal. He sways his hips from side to side and pumps both arms up and down with the second and third fingers on each hand pointed outward together like pistols. As he does so Klinsmann grabs him from behind with both arms around his waist. The two different shades of blond, flaxen hair – Sheringham's chocolate, Klinsmann's golden – sparkle in the Yorkshire sun. Left-back Edinburgh is next to join the celebrations, jumping on Klinsmann's back and saluting with his left hand towards the Spurs fans.

'The away fans that day were tremendous, they always were,' says Nethercott. 'Spurs fans always travelled in their numbers, still do today. The away fans were always right behind you. Sometimes at White Hart Lane, they could be a bit moany even if you were 4-0 up. But away they were brilliant.'

Sheringham agrees that the Tottenham travelling contingent were usually a delight to play in front of. 'That day, there was just a real sense that this wasn't going to be any old season. The away fans always create a great atmosphere, but there was a feeling in the air that something special was about to happen at the club. The way the game panned out was just incredible.'

It's utter delirium in the away section at Hillsborough, and on the half-hour mark Spurs again score from nowhere. Nethercott pumps a fairly aimless ball forward from just inside the Spurs half. Wednesday centre-back Des Walker has more time than he realises on the edge of the box but misjudges his headed clearance. It drops about 25 yards out to Klinsmann, who – with his back to goal – plucks it out of the air with his right boot, controls it and lays it back to the onrushing Anderton who has already mapped out his route to goal. He takes one touch to bring it under control and then sends a slide-rule pass forward to Sheringham, who plays it straight back into Anderton's path with his first touch. Anderton knocks it on into the area with his right foot, and stretches to get there again before two Owls defenders close in. He toe-pokes it beyond Pressman from virtually on the penalty spot. 2-0 to Spurs. Like Sheringham's goal, the slightly unorthodox nature of the finish adds to the goal's aesthetic appeal. In both cases the chance seems to have gone before it's converted with subtlety rather than strength.

'The Sheffield Wednesday game remains one of my favourite memories of the season,' says Anderton. 'It was amazing up in the bar afterwards. Even in those days you would have a little night out on the Saturday. We had another game on the Wednesday, but we were just enjoying it, thinking, "We're flying here, we've got a really good team – we've got a chance." Just buzzing.'

Within the first 20 minutes of the second half, Spurs have blown their two-goal lead. Petrescu, a £1.3m signing from Genoa, pulls one back for Wednesday in the 54th minute. There's an element of fortune about the goal. Wednesday's highly-rated 20-year-old midfielder Chris Bart-Williams takes a corner from the left. Campbell cuts it out at the near post and gets real distance on his header. It drops about 25 yards out to John Sheridan, whose wild volley crashes into his own team-mate Petrescu on the edge of the box. Petrescu knocks it on to himself and then side-foots it beyond Walker at the near post. Spurs still lead, but it's now 2-1.

Then disaster for Calderwood, who has surprisingly been given the nod by Ardiles to start in the holding midfield position in preference to David Howells. Bart-Williams charges into the box from the right-hand side, deceives Campbell and plays a one-two with Mark Bright. Before Bart-Williams can get his shot away Calderwood flies in and whips it off his toes with his right foot, only succeeding in sweeping it into the back of his own net. 2-2.

'It was a rollercoaster of a game,' says Nethercott. '2-0 up, then 2-2. And I think we knew from the moment Ossie named the team that that was how it was going to be. The philosophy was: you score three, we'll score four.'

Sheringham adds: 'I think we always had the confidence to know that we could get another goal. So, obviously it's disappointing to throw away a two-goal lead, but it never worried us. We knew we had the quality in the team to get goals from anywhere. That gives you major belief.'

Hillsborough is rocking now. Sheffield Wednesday have been a force over the last few seasons under manager Trevor Francis. As a second-tier side they beat Manchester United in the League Cup Final in 1991. Since they returned to the top flight for the 1991/92 season, Spurs have failed to beat them in six meetings and have finished behind them every year. Francis has strengthened his line-up this summer by spending £4.6m on four new players including Petrescu, full-back Ian Nolan and midfielder Ian Taylor.

Bart-Williams comes close to putting the home side 3-2 up but hoists his effort over the bar when he should do better. For Spurs, Campbell has acquitted himself well in the heart of defence alongside Nethercott, but with 21 minutes to go Ardiles replaces him with veteran defender and club captain Gary Mabbutt who helps steady the ship. Moments later Tottenham have the lead again.

Sheringham wins a header just inside the Wednesday half. He directs it beautifully, almost ducking under it to make sure he gets exactly the right pace and direction on it to glance it behind himself and into the path of Barmby. With Klinsmann on his left, Barmby continues his run towards the Wednesday box. All the time the Wednesday defence is wondering: will Barmby square it to Klinsmann or go it alone? He goes it alone, enters the box, and crashes a right-footed shot rising beyond Pressman across goal into the far top corner. 3-2 to Spurs.

With eight minutes to go it gets even better for them. It's the moment the travelling fans and the press have been waiting for, a debut goal for Klinsmann. It's a slick passing move which leads to the goal, with Spurs keeping possession for a good 20 seconds in the build-up. It starts when the referee blows for a foul on Klinsmann midway into the Wednesday half, out near the right-hand touchline. It's taken short to Kerslake who plays it infield to Micky Hazard, on for the substituted Dumitrescu five minutes earlier.

As Taylor closes him down Hazard plays a composed pass back to Mabbutt inside the centre circle, just inside the Spurs half. He then trots back to join him, beckoning for Mabbutt to return it. Mabbutt accepts the invite. Hazard still has Taylor on him, but has complete control of the ball and his surroundings. He pirouettes and plays it short to Calderwood, who is also inside the centre circle, but is in space and can jog forward 15 yards towards the Wednesday box and then play it directly forward to Klinsmann. Klinsmann, with his back to goal, lays it ten yards to his left to Barmby who, also with his back to goal, controls it with his left and then knocks it back towards Hazard with his right.

Hazard's cushioned first-time pass out to the right is perfect for Anderton. He controls it with his left, wraps the outside of his right boot around it to knock it away from himself and open up some space, and then sends in a sumptuous teasing cross, dropping it over the heads of two Wednesday defenders to Klinsmann waiting at the far post, eight yards out.

Klinsmann's execution is textbook. He gets side on to the ball, takes a running jump at it and crashes his header into the net. The term 'bullet header' was made for this. 4-2 to Spurs.

Then comes one of the most original goal celebrations in football history, as he peels away to the left with his team-mates in pursuit. He spreads both arms wide, runs eight more steps and then brings them together as he hurls himself to the turf. A comical dive to mock his detractors. Three of the team-mates following in his slipstream do likewise, Sheringham, Calderwood and then Barmby who squeezes himself between Sheringham and Klinsmann as he hits the ground. The late arrivals jump on top. Spurs celebrate en masse.

'When we arrived at the stadium and saw the diving signs, we all laughed about it,' says Klinsmann. 'The idea to do the dive was a brilliant idea. The wonderful thing was that some of the opposition fans were laughing about it too.'

Kit man Roy Reyland, who worked at Tottenham for 29 years before leaving in 2005, says the celebration summed up the special feeling at the club in 1994/95. 'There was an amazing team spirit,' he says. 'I remember us playing that day in that ridiculous purple kit, and the hype was all centred around Jürgen's diving and what he'd done in the World Cup. I never really looked at him in that way, I'd seen him throw himself about a couple of times but he wasn't really any different to numerous other players that had done it. It was a big first game of the season, we were all keyed up, thinking "Let's go there and prove everyone wrong." To have a 4-3 thriller with everything that went on within that game with the highs and lows, and Jürgen eventually scoring the winner and celebrating like that was magical really.

'It's not often you get ex-players coming back to a club and managing the team, so to have Ossie Ardiles, Stevie Perryman and Chrissy Hughton all there on the coaching staff was exceptional. Tottenham have got this culture, bonding, team orientation that goes on, and Ossie instilled that. He liked socials, he liked everyone eating together, he wouldn't have a management table separate from the players. Everybody ate together and I think the camaraderie – and we had some big jokers in that team as well – made the team what it was.'

It's not over yet, though. Within a minute Wednesday have made it 4-3, and there are still seven minutes plus injury time to play. It's a spectacular goal, arguably the best of the game. Bart-Williams drifts in a cross from the right and Taylor has got himself between Nethercott and Kerslake on the penalty spot. He outjumps Kerslake and heads it back to David Hirst, who rifles a ferocious volley from right on the edge of the box, dipping beyond Walker into the top corner. Spurs still lead, but only by one goal.

Wednesday fans sense their team can still do this, and moments later they get an extra boost as Spurs are forced to play out the game with ten men. Klinsmann and Des Walker jump for the same ball and clash heads. Klinsmann falls to the ground, blood gushing from his head. He appears motionless as he's stretchered off. Spurs have used both their substitutes so are a man down. Wednesday have little time to make the numerical advantage count, though, and Spurs hold on for what has been a thrilling 4-3 win. Three points on the opening day of the season means Spurs are occupying a place near the top of the table and bottom of it at the same time, since the six-point deduction effectively leaves them with minus three.

After the press conference with Ardiles, one journalist asks the Spurs boss if Klinsmann is well enough to give an interview. Ardiles leads the journalists down to the pitch where, quite some time later, Tottenham's match-winner emerges from the dressing room with blood still seeping from his mouth.

'I'm fine,' he says. 'There are seven or eight stitches inside the mouth, but I'm very happy to have started with a victory, especially away from home. I can't remember being carried off because I was unconscious, but I'm okay now. English football is famous for being fast and I enjoyed it. It's good that over here both teams go for victory – it makes it a very exciting type of football.'

Klinsmann is then asked about his cheeky celebration. 'Yes, I did make a joke of the celebrations. Teddy Sheringham suggested that I should dive when I scored my first goal in England. I saw him starting to do it when I hit my goal, so I dived too. It was a one-off. You won't see me diving like that again this season. But it just shows the spirit that exists here. I'm a simple guy who feels he has been accepted. I'm one of the lads.'

Ardiles tells the press that Klinsmann was unconscious when he reached the dressing room. 'I was there when he woke up. He said,

"That's funny, where am I?" He asked if we had won and when we told him we had, by 4-3, he said, "That's good, I'll go back to sleep!" He's a wonderful character.'

Reyland remembers there was initially real concern in the dressing room for Klinsmann. 'He'd taken a battering, but he knew the English game was going to be tough, and he wouldn't let it deter him. As the season went on he was brilliant, absolutely brilliant. When he captained his country for the first time he came back and gave me his shirt and his captain's armband and said, "That's for you." I've never collected shirts in my life, because I'm a kit man – it's a bit like working in a sweet shop. You go through a million shirts. But that was just something else.

'I think I've got seven or eight shirts from when people have left and signed them personally to me. Like Sol Campbell, for all that went on, he did it, and Steffen Freund. Those little personal things I've kept. But apart from that I've never kept anything.' Even those who didn't receive a physical memento from Klinsmann like Reyland did were given plenty to treasure by the German. All those who watched him play or played alongside him have been left with so many standout memories.

'When you think about seasons in which you don't win anything, but that you will never forget, I think there are four that spring to mind in my lifetime as a Spurs fan,' says Daniel Wynne. 'There was 84/85, when we went hammer and tongs with Everton to try and win the league. It came down to basically whoever won at White Hart Lane when they met in April would go on to win the title. We lost 2-1, Everton romped it in the end and we finished third, behind them and Liverpool.

'Then there was 86/87. That was so special for Clive Allen's 49 goals and the excitement of reaching the FA Cup Final, the League Cup semis and finishing third. What we have just witnessed in 2016/17, finishing second for the first time since 1963 and going a whole season unbeaten at The Lane, also has to be on that list. And then there's 94/95. Now 94/95 is actually far less successful than 84/85, 86/87 or 2016/17, and yet somehow it's still special – and Klinsmann is the main reason for that.'

As the Tottenham team coach, with 'Famous Five & Co.' on board, made its way back from South Yorkshire, football fans throughout the land were looking forward to that evening's *Match of the Day*. Spurs fans of course would enjoy the result, but there would be plenty for the neutral too: a five-man attacking line-up; seven goals, many of them spectacular; the winner scored by World Cup star Klinsmann; and an amusing goal celebration to boot. The first seeds of Klinsmania had been sown. In three days' time they would really start to take root.

2

Overhead Kick

'You could see him going up in slow motion.
It was almost like everything was written.
Like it was meant to be.' (Darren Anderton)

I F YOU were to choose just one single freeze-frame from Tottenham's
entire 1994/95 season that would best represent it as a whole, it would
be Jürgen Klinsmann, airborne and horizontal, right foot above
his head and connecting with the ball to send it on its way into the net
against Everton. An image as geometrically beautiful as it is aesthetically
so. That moment happened at 8.05pm on Wednesday 24 August, 1994.
What a way to mark your home debut, what a way to score your first
home goal. Now, anything felt possible. Tottenham had a goalscorer
who could push new boundaries and a team prepared to help him do so.

The glory of that moment began a fraction of a second before
Klinsmann launched himself skyward, when every supporter inside
White Hart Lane instinctively knew what he was about to attempt and
somehow understood it could only end one way. It was a premonition.
The sound of a sharp intake of breath, and 24,000-odd seats clattering
upwards as their occupants rose to their feet, signified the collective
awareness of the magic spell Klinsmann was about to cast.

In playgrounds, children called this type of goal 'a Pelé'. That's
because the first time many had ever seen a goal like it was when the great
man himself enacted one during the film *Escape to Victory*. An overhead
kick seems an almost superfluous means by which to propel a ball into
the net, a move which belongs in a gymnastics routine rather than on a

football pitch. Youngsters would spend hours trying to perfect one on the playing fields and in the garden, most often failing even to connect with the ball, let alone send it in the right direction.

As the well-known saying goes: 'They're all worth one point.' It's true; but if goals were marked on artistic merit, Klinsmann's stats for 1994/95 would be even more impressive than they already are: 20 league goals and 29 in all competitions. Partly this was down to his physique. His body moved as precisely as an animated player on a computer game. He played the game in angles, in delightful straight lines and delicious curves. Whenever the ball left his foot or his head it appeared pre-programmed to find its way into the net, as though it had been dispatched on the only possible course to its intended destination. In one interview Klinsmann gave during the season he explained that when he had been younger, when he found himself with a scoring chance, all the different ways to beat the keeper would flood through his mind, and he would sometimes fluff it because of that. He had learnt, he said, to make one decision and to stick with it; after that his strike rate improved dramatically. You could see this in his game. Every action was definite.

It was Darren Anderton who provided the cross from which Klinsmann's home debut overhead kick goal was scored. 'I chopped and weaved a couple of times and then floated it to the far post. Teddy headed it back to him. You could see him going up in slow motion. It was almost like everything was written. Like it was meant to be,' remembers Anderton some two decades on.

Anderton's cross found Sheringham, who did well to beat his man on the corner of the six-yard box and head the ball downwards to Klinsmann a couple of yards away. The ball dropped behind Klinsmann, who flicked out a boot and got a touch on it, sending it skywards again. Young centre-back Stuart Nethercott had come charging up and won the header to nod it back to Klinsmann. From the moment Nethercott headed it, Klinsmann's body shape defined exactly what he was about to attempt. Spectacular though the goal remains when viewing it on TV or online today, it can't compare with seeing it live. Klinsmann's pivot through the air appeared almost perfectly circular, like turning a dial. From leaving the ground, to connecting with the ball, to returning to earth, all done in one sweeping motion.

What followed next was perhaps the most joyous goal celebration ever witnessed at White Hart Lane. In the history of Tottenham Hotspur Football Club goals of even greater quality, and indeed goals of far greater importance, than this one have been scored. None, though, has been celebrated so exuberantly. Just like at Hillsborough, Klinsmann ran to the touchline to the left-hand side of the goal and pulled out the dive celebration. This time, though, every single Tottenham player joined in with a dive of their own. One by one they dived over him, around him or straight on to him. Even Ian Walker, Tottenham's goalkeeper, came sprinting out of his goal across three-quarters of the length of the White Hart Lane turf and propelled himself across the pitch towards the pile consisting of his ten team-mates.

Walker's father Mike was the opposition manager that night, and can't have imagined before the match that he would be seeing his son inside Everton's half at any point. This goal celebration represented Klinsmania in all its glory: a heaving, massed bundle of Spursness. It looked like a Tottenham Hotspur united. A team in love with the game, a team playing for one another. 'The atmosphere was just electric,' remembers Anderton. 'We had a close-knit bunch of lads. We would go out together on a Tuesday or a Wednesday night. You have to have that social time together, as opposed to coming into the training ground and leaving on your own and doing your own thing. It came across on the pitch, and the fact that we were allowed to play for joy fostered that team spirit too.'

Klinsmann had said after the Sheffield Wednesday game that the dive celebration would be a one-off, but it turned out Teddy Sheringham's young son Charlie had enjoyed it so much he'd pleaded with his dad to ensure it was repeated. Such a plea could not be ignored. 'Charlie loved what he had seen on TV,' says Sheringham. 'He told me that I had to make sure Jürgen did it again when he got his next goal. He thought it was really funny.'

Thanks to Charlie, every Spurs fan at The Lane had a moment to treasure. To the fans in the stands this celebration felt almost as exciting as the goal. There was a momentary fear, though, that with every Spurs player celebrating in the Everton half the Merseysiders might simply kick off quickly and walk the ball into the net Walker had vacated, and that a schoolmasterly referee might somehow allow the goal to stand as if to teach Tottenham a lesson for getting carried away.

'Initially I hadn't intended to do it again, but there was no way I was going to let my team-mate's son down,' says Klinsmann. 'There was so much energy in the stadium that night, indeed throughout the whole season. At White Hart Lane, the fans were very sophisticated. They are very knowledgeable about their football. They sense when things are happening and when they need to make themselves heard. It doesn't really matter if the stadium holds 70,000 or 35,000 if you have fans like that. They carried me in many games. Not so much on this night when we were ahead, but on other occasions when we were behind, or when we needed a goal, the stadium would come alive and they would give you so much energy, that it would just lift you. That year it was impossible for me to stop running. Probably if the game had been over and the fans had still been there, I would have still been running. When my mum and dad came over to watch games, the first thing they said was that they had never, ever experienced anything like that. And they went to big games. I mean, they came to Inter Milan when we played AC Milan in front of 86,000 people and the San Siro was rocking, but they said that the energy they felt at White Hart Lane was unique. It is the people that make it unique. I was there quite recently to watch a game with Gary Mabbutt and you start to feel it when you drive up towards the stadium – it is just pure energy.'

In the days after this match, the FA gave Klinsmann tacit permission to continue with the celebration, but hinted at concern over the whole team joining in. Colin Downey, referees' secretary at what was then the FA's Lancaster Gate headquarters, told the media: 'He's not doing it in front of the visiting supporters, so there is no intent to incite anyone. Once he has done it a few times it will become old hat and he might stop. At the moment I don't see it as a problem, but if he keeps doing it I'm sure the referee in charge will have a quiet word with him. But we all appreciate scoring goals is an exciting time and players like to enjoy themselves, and we don't want to stop all that. If it gets to the point where the whole team joins in and it delays the restart, then the FA might decide to have a word with the club about it.' Since the whole team was already joining in, Downey's comments felt like an informal warning for them to stop.

The fact that Nethercott provided the assist for this goal says much about how Spurs were playing under manager Ossie Ardiles. This was a centre-back joining in with an attack 20 minutes into a game which was still goalless, and in which Spurs already had five forwards on the pitch. It had been a breathless opening quarter, and Spurs should already have been ahead even before Klinsmann struck. Nethercott himself was just 21, and had made his debut some 17 months earlier in a 1-1 draw against Chelsea at Stamford Bridge. On this occasion against Everton he was starting a league match for only the 14th time in his career, and this would prove to be his first season as a regular.

Today Nethercott is a PE teacher in Braintree, Essex, where he also runs coaching schools. He remembers the start of 1994/95 with fondness: 'I'd been with the England Under-21s with Sol Campbell at the Toulon tournament in the summer, and I think Ossie was quite impressed with that. So we started as the first-choice defenders. The team went off like a house on fire against Everton. It was a special night, the plan was to go out and attack and beat teams; if we conceded, we conceded.'

Tall, stocky and flame-haired, Nethercott was an unmistakable figure on the pitch. He was with the club for seven years before leaving for Millwall in 1998. To most observers he looked as if he was playing a level above his true standard, and he coped admirably with criticism from some Spurs fans throughout his career. When you're on the same pitch as Sheringham, Anderton, Barmby and now Klinsmann and Dumitrescu too, it's not hard to stand out for the wrong reasons if you are not a naturally-gifted player. What must it have been like for the Spurs defence at the start of that season? They took the flak, but what chance did they have? This, though, was one of Nethercott's best games for the club. He beams at the memory of setting up Klinsmann's first White Hart Lane goal: 'All I was trying to do was keep the ball alive in the box,' he says. 'When he's put an overhead kick in I'm just thinking "Wow".'

Rarely the most composed player, there was even something comical about Nethercott's involvement in the dive celebration. Klinsmann's dive was the most graceful, Nethercott's the least. He sprinted towards the assembled mass but then slowed as he approached, as if fearing he might get hurt. Then he flopped himself rather gently to the ground instead of diving with arms outstretched. If these days Klinsmann's dive could be compared to one of Olympic medal winner Tom Daley's, Nethercott's would be the comedian Peter Kay's running bomb in the famous John Smith's Bitter adverts of the mid-noughties.

'My dive wasn't too great,' laughs Nethercott. 'It was awful. I still get stick now when I meet up with the boys. I think I was more worried about my shoulder than anything. I was a bit late arriving on the scene as well. I get hammered for it, absolutely hammered for it. I still carry that one around with me. What a celebration though! Ian Walker has run from his goal, slid in and, you know, that shows the spirit was great. Sheffield Wednesday away and Everton at home were great games to play in, and when you look at the results they made it even more special.'

Tottenham were making the game look easy and running Everton ragged. Every time Tottenham had the ball there was the sense that something would happen. Klinsmann was the embodiment of a shard of light, straight lines and all gold. He was a solar beam. Player and ball seemed magnetised, drawn together and then forced apart with energy. The team fizzed whenever its talisman was on the move. He was football's equivalent of Da Vinci's *Vitruvian Man*: the perfect proportions between player, ball and goal, always calculating the correct angle to find the line to propel source to target. Tottenham's kit that season lent itself perfectly to Klinsmann's style of play. The numbers were displayed in digital font. All straight lines. Like the straight lines Klinsmann so beautifully played in, and the straight lines he so beautifully scored his goals in.

That summer one of the five he notched for Germany at the World Cup was replayed endlessly on TV: a searing shot across goal and into the bottom corner, to put his country 2-1 up in what was eventually a 3-2 win over Belgium in the last 16. Klinsmann struck from the edge of the area to send the ball flying into the bottom corner. As it hit the net, it crashed into a water bottle which went spinning through the air towards the television camera behind the goal, spraying its contents as it did so. Klinsmann appeared to enact William Tell, aiming for a target within a target and proving accurate. If, in some imaginary fifth dimension, there existed a predetermined route by which an object could always map its way unfailingly to its intended destination, Klinsmann had the supernatural power to find it.

The quality of Klinsmann's overhead kick against Everton, and the humour in Nethercott's part of the celebration, have stayed with kit man Roy Reyland to this day: 'Nethers, bless him. He comes in like a wounded animal and falls on top. But the execution of the goal from Klinsmann? Wow. There must have been pressure on his home debut, and this was pure instinct. One of the best goals ever at The Lane.'

For the football romantic Tottenham have always been easy to fall in love with. There is magic in the names Hotspur and the now demolished White Hart Lane. There is magic too in the achievements: the only non-league team to win the FA Cup; the first team of the 20th century to win the Double; the first British team to win a European trophy. In the 20th century, the habit of nearly always winning a trophy in a year ending in '1' also made it feel as though a greater power was the guiding force behind the team. It's a team that has, for almost its entire history, played in white shirts as dazzling as the skills of so many of its players. Now Klinsmann's talents dazzled too.

In more than 40 years as a season-ticket holder, Daniel Wynne has seen it all. Klinsmann's overhead kick and dive celebration is one of his most treasured memories. 'When he got that overhead kick literally the whole place erupted. It went as crazy as I've seen it,' says Wynne. 'For me, you can put it in the same bracket as three other occasions at White Hart Lane when the place went berserk. Firstly, winning the UEFA Cup Final on penalties in the second leg at home in 1984, then the reception Gascoigne and Lineker got when they came back from the World Cup in 1990, and of course the finale, the scenes after the last-ever match at The Lane against Manchester United in 2017. It was as special as that when Klinsmann scored against Everton. It was a celebration that caught the imagination. The way the players all responded to him, and he responded to them too, showed he had the power to bring the whole place together. To see someone of Jürgen's status responding to Stuart Nethercott – no disrespect to Stuart Nethercott who I've met and who is a lovely bloke – it showed the two ends of the spectrum. They were special days.'

'Jürgen was probably the best player I ever played with,' says Nethercott. 'To play alongside him in that team means a lot, he was brilliant to me. He was even brilliant to me the second time round, when he came back to the club (in 1997/98) as I was on my way out. He remembered my name, he helped me just to keep my head down, and you know, keep my spirits up by telling me, "The time will come when you get your move," and that sort of thing. That was a nice thing to do. I was still only 24 at the time. He was a great bloke.'

Those inside White Hart Lane for Tottenham v Everton were especially privileged to bear witness to everything that night. To comply with the post-Hillsborough Taylor Report that insisted on all-seater stadiums – and to raise its capacity from 5,400 to 8,400 – the South Stand was being rebuilt and was, for the start of the season, completely closed. For now this brought the White Hart Lane capacity down by around 6,000, which meant many missed out on seeing Klinsmann's home debut. Just 24,553 fans were present against Everton, packing out the North, East and West Stands and looking towards a building site at the southern end. With work having started over the summer, the main girder – weighing some 300 tonnes and which would eventually support the new structure – was already in its final position. It wouldn't be until the match against QPR on 8 October 1994 that even some of the lower seats in the South Stand could be occupied, with a full lower-tier capacity planned for early January, 1995. The new South Stand was scheduled to re-open in its entirety in March. So many Tottenham fans missed out on the pleasures of 1994/95 at first hand because they couldn't get tickets to be there.

Supporters making their way into White Hart Lane for the match against Everton did so with a keen sense of anticipation, given what had happened away to Sheffield Wednesday just four days earlier. This was a first chance for those who had not been able to travel to South Yorkshire to see Klinsmann and Dumitrescu and the 'Famous Five' up front: a first chance to experience the phenomenon that was Klinsmania. As fans gathered in the stadium, many wore shirts adorned with 'KLINSMANN 18'. Kay Lyons, who ran the supporters' shop, told journalist Harry Harris in his book *Klinsmann* (which offers a contemporaneous account of the first half of the 1994/95 season) that she couldn't get enough number 18 shirts with Klinsmann's name on them. She kept running out of Ns. Later in the season, Spurs opened a special print shop halfway up the High Road to help with the demand to print his name. Shop manager Andy Leadbitter told Harris that nine out of ten requests were for Klinsmann and that they couldn't cope with demand on matchdays. It wasn't just the shirts; posters, T-shirts, photos and anything with his name on were flying off the shelves. Back then you paid by the letter. Klinsmann's name cost £12.25, with the shirt itself setting you back £35. In the run-up to Christmas the club had 30 people working overtime to cope with demand in the mail-order shop. Lyons admitted that the kit manufacturers had underestimated the demand for Spurs shirts, and that they simply hadn't supplied them with enough. Business had gone through the roof since Klinsmann signed. The shop had sold 12,500 of the new purple away shirts, and more than 6,000 home shirts of which they were down to their last few. Lyons described the queues outside the door as 'unbelievable' and estimated that merchandising turnover had increased by a third, with orders coming in from all over the world and a huge amount of interest from Germany.

Perhaps there wasn't quite so much demand for the training tracksuit the up-and-coming Sol Campbell was modelling in the programme for the Everton game. Tracksuits and shell suits were popular evening and weekend wear for pre-teenagers of the 90s, and for many had replaced denim as the preferred choice of casual wear. In this advert Campbell stood square on, forced smile, hands in pockets, sporting an ill-fitting Tottenham training tracksuit. The navy blue number made by Umbro wasn't cheap at £59.99. Few opponents ever made Campbell look as uncomfortable as he does in this picture.

Many Spurs fans will never forgive Campbell for the manner and destination of his departure. At the start of the 1994/95 campaign, three weeks shy of his 20th birthday, the 6ft 2in, 14st 2lb centre-back was in the early stages of a season which helped shape him into one of England's best defenders. Sulzeer Jeremiah Campbell, as he was named when he was born in 1974 in Plaistow, East London, had made his first-team debut up front, coming off the bench to score a last-minute consolation goal in a 2-1 home defeat to Chelsea in December 1992. He didn't play again that season and was then used in a variety of positions, at left-back, centre-back and up front in 1993/94.

Now, with Gary Mabbutt approaching the end of his career and largely restricted to a place on the bench for the first part of this season under Ardiles, Campbell was establishing himself as his team's first-choice defender and, in a season where the team's emphasis was to be so much on attack leaving him often exposed at the back, he would certainly have plenty of opportunity to hone the skills which eventually saw him win 73 caps for England. By the time Campbell retired in 2012 he had an impressive haul of honours: the 1999 League Cup as captain of Tottenham; the 2008 FA Cup as captain of Portsmouth; and of course three FA Cups and two Premier League titles – including the 2001/02 Double – in another corner of North London.

Everton, so mercilessly cut asunder in the first half of this match, would become opponents who would in part define Tottenham's, and Campbell's, season. When they met again at Goodison Park in December new managers would occupy both dugouts. Everton would sack Mike Walker in early November, soon after Spurs had disposed of Ardiles. In Walker's place would come Joe Royle, who perfected a game plan that was the very antithesis of that on show by Spurs tonight, but which would prove sufficient to win them silverware at Tottenham's expense as they came out on top in April's FA Cup semi-final meeting – when Campbell was out injured – and went on to lift the trophy.

This first meeting of the season at The Lane, though, was Tottenham's night. In the build-up to the match Klinsmann had told the press that this was the most attacking team he had ever played in: 'It is a very offensive style,' he said. 'I have played with three or four forwards but never five. It is a pleasure to play in this style. It puts responsibility on the front two to work hard defensively. The defence starts at the front.'

It had been a while since there had been reason for optimism at The Lane. The previous season had been a real slog for Spurs. A long-term injury to Sheringham left them without enough firepower, as they were dragged down into a desperate fight against relegation. Safety was only secured in the penultimate game. The Sky cameras were there for a rescheduled Thursday night match (rain had seen the original game postponed) as Spurs took on Oldham at Boundary Park. Spurs won 2-0 through late goals from David Howells and Vinny Samways, preserving their own top-flight status and as good as sealing Oldham's relegation.

Those at The Lane to witness Klinsmann's home debut against Everton had seen their team win just one league match here since the Toffees had last visited ten months previously. On that occasion in October 1993, Everton led 2-1 with just one minute to play before late goals from Sheringham and Darren Caskey turned it into a 3-2 win for Spurs. That breathless finish gave Spurs fans much cheer, but it seemed they had used up all their celebrations for the 1993/94 season in those frantic minutes. Their team won just once more at home in the league that season, when relegation rivals Southampton visited in April.

As 1993/94 unravelled, it began to feel as though Tottenham might leave the Premiership party early and be relegated into the second tier. Manchester United had quickly established themselves as the giants of the Premiership's dawn. In 1992/93 – the first season of the Premier League – an unlikely duo of Aston Villa and Norwich pushed them all the way in a three-way title battle. United prevailed. Then in 1993/94 the challengers to United were big-spending Blackburn, and also Newcastle who had just come up from Division One. Again United took the title. With these clubs attracting the headlines, there wasn't much joy to be had in N17.

For Spurs the 90s was a decade that would be bookended by trophies: the glorious Gazza-inspired 1991 FA Cup triumph under Terry Venables, and the rather more prosaic 1999 League Cup win under George Graham. Looking back now, the joy of 1994/95 was a welcome aberration in the wilderness years sandwiched between those cup finals. What Tottenham fans were about to witness in 1994/95 would excite them as much as 1991 and, some would say, even more so.

In the distance, the light atop One Canada Square, the tallest building in Canary Wharf, had always been visible to those seated towards the eastern side of the Paxton Road end, blinking away in the gap between the East Stand and the Park Lane end at the South. Tonight, with an open hole where the Park Lane end was being rebuilt, that symbol of the financial district which had sprung up in the regenerated Docklands was clear for everyone to see. The relationship between football and money was likewise becoming clearer with each passing Premier League season.

Twenty years on, Lord Sugar, as he is now, is more closely associated in the minds of the public with that financial district of Canary Wharf than he is with football. In truth the sweeping aerial shots used in the title sequence of *The Apprentice* have little to do with where or how Alan Michael Sugar made his money. How he spent it as Tottenham chairman in the summer of 1994 didn't find much fault with Tottenham fans, even though his overall near-ten-year reign is viewed unfavourably by many.

When he was just 19 years old, Sugar was earning the equivalent of £2,000 a week in today's money selling radios. He went on to form Alan Michael Sugar Trading – Amstrad – which floated on the Stock Exchange at £8m in 1980. That netted him a personal profit of £2m at the age of 33. Six years later when he launched Amstrad's new computer, the PC1512, the share price rose to a level where the company had a market capitalisation of £1.2 billion. With Sugar holding 45% of the shares, theoretically at that point he was worth £540m. The business of football never came so easily to him, but he must have felt he had cracked it with the signing of Klinsmann. Sugar has spoken fondly of witnessing two fans with 'SUGAR' on their replica shirts making their way into the Everton home game, and admits they may be the only two fans ever to have felt moved to emblazon their kit with his name.

Sugar has since declared it was largely a mistake to have got involved in football. He has said there were no highlights from his decade in charge, and that his involvement with Spurs was to the detriment of Amstrad. So why did he do it? His former PR man Nick Hewer says: 'I think he got involved very simply because Spurs was a family tradition, it was a local club. I think he would admit that he quite liked the profile, and it was a challenge. It really was a challenge. He said to me, "I don't get any credit." And I said to him, "It's very simple; when the team's doing well the manager's a hero and when the team's doing rubbish the chairman is the villain. Jack Walker is about the only chairman who was ever popular because he bought the league at Blackburn."

'Alan absolutely worked himself to a standstill, and he admits he took his eye off Amstrad. He was working day and night on his football and not getting any credit for it. But when he left he made £20m which was pretty unusual; not many people came out of football with a profit, and that wasn't why he went in. Nobody cared about him and he thought that was poor. Recognition or acknowledgement for what he had done would have been nice. He actually reshaped football to a considerable extent, but the money men don't matter in the eyes of the fans.'

As Tottenham took on Everton in their first home game of 1994/95, Sugar was at the height of his popularity. At the beginning of what was the third season of the Premier League, football's new-found riches were beginning to bear fruit. The first club to gamble that wealth on the signing of overseas players in their prime was Tottenham. In many ways it wasn't a gamble at all. The wider public was ready to embrace football again and wanted players and teams to entertain them. Riding high in the charts in August 1994 was Wet Wet Wet's cover of 'Love Is All Around'. It would be in the No.1 position for 15 weeks from June to September, much to the annoyance of many. It wasn't just the soundtrack to the summer, but the soundtrack to *Four Weddings and a Funeral*, the romantic comedy written by Richard Curtis and starring Hugh Grant, which proved a huge hit on both sides of the Atlantic. While the era of Britpop and what felt like the genuine political revolution of Tony Blair and New Labour riding to power were both still three years away, this was a Britain that was slowly learning to have fun again after the dark days of the 1980s. On the football pitch, Tottenham were about to have more fun than most.

Spurs had of course famously brought top overseas players to these shores on a previous occasion. Immediately after Argentina had won the 1978 World Cup, Spurs had swooped on two of their players: Ossie Ardiles and Ricky Villa. Overseas signings then became more commonplace, but the floodgates didn't exactly open. Even 16 years on, in 1994, clubs could only name three players from outside the Home Nations and the Republic of Ireland in a Premiership squad. It was still a novelty for the likes of Jürgen Klinsmann and Ilie Dumitrescu to arrive in England. Televised football was relatively rare compared to today. Sky showed two live games a week. Live terrestrial coverage remained limited to the FA Cup, England games, the European Championship and the World Cup, with Premiership highlights also available on the BBC's *Match of the Day*. It was only in those major international tournaments that armchair supporters really got to see overseas players of the calibre of Klinsmann and Dumitrescu. There was nothing like the fascination with European club football that there is today. The now defunct Cup-Winners' Cup, the UEFA Cup (the previous name for the modern-day Europa League) and even the Champions League which, like the Premier League, was also in its third season in 1994/95, were very much an afterthought for most fans.

More than 20 years on, Anderton laughs warmly as he describes the start to that season: 'Ossie was so relaxed, he used to smoke all the time in the dressing room. In training he would say, "When we win the ball, when we get the ball back – we go!" and wave both his arms forward. "Kers [David Kerslake], Justin Edinburgh – go!" It wasn't just the five attackers, it was the seven, so Colin Calderwood had to sit there at the front of Stuart Nethercott and Sol Campbell. It was suicide against better teams.'

Former Spurs player Steve Perryman was assistant to Ardiles. Perryman made a club record 854 appearances for Spurs between 1969 and 86, and is one of their finest-ever defenders. Anderton considers his role: 'Stevie P, who was a legend at the club defensively, a captain himself, would have conversations with Ossie saying, "We've got to defend more." The boys would say, "What do we do when we lose the ball, do we need a shape?" Ossie would say, "No, no, you're good players – you shouldn't lose the ball." He was so laid back and so much fun to play for, but in terms of winning things you've got to be very good defensively as well and, unfortunately for us, we weren't. It wasn't just because of the defenders but the whole team; it could never work long-term. Teams worked us out.'

Anderton had found himself nicknamed Shaggy after the gangly character in the *Scooby-Doo* cartoon. He was named this affectionately by Tottenham's players and fans. It was down to his physique. It belied his talent. He was a quite brilliant football player. Over the next few years, both he and Teddy Sheringham would find themselves oft-criticised by fans of other clubs who felt they didn't merit their place in the England set-up. With Spurs not having quite the cachet of Manchester United, Liverpool or Arsenal, their England selection – however well they played – was always questioned by the critics in the press, the workplace and the playgrounds.

Both players were supremely gifted. Anderton's end product could hardly ever be faulted, certainly by comparison with modern-day wide players whose pace takes priority over their passing and crossing. As well as creating chances he was a fine finisher. Of the members of the 'Famous Five' it was also he who was the most disciplined, he who offered the most protection to Tottenham's exposed defence. He was also unlucky. Unlucky with injuries, unlucky to be labelled 'Sicknote' by the press – a tag he could never rid himself of – and unlucky in semi-finals. Anderton lost five of them in his career. The first was in 1992 for Portsmouth against Liverpool, when Pompey became the first club to lose an FA Cup semi-final on penalties.

He had been the star of Pompey's run to the last four. It was his fine goal which gave Second Division Portsmouth the lead, with just nine minutes of extra time remaining, against top-flight Liverpool in the original semi-final at Highbury. Ronnie Whelan equalised five minutes later for a 1-1 draw. In those days the semi-finals went to a replay, and when Pompey again held Liverpool to a draw – this time 0-0 at Villa Park – it meant a penalty shoot-out. Liverpool won it 3-1. Anderton, then aged just 20, would have taken Portsmouth's fifth penalty – but he never got the chance.

Anderton's exploits throughout the 1991/92 FA Cup run brought him to the attention of Spurs, who signed him for £2m that summer. His first season at The Lane featured another FA Cup semi-final defeat, as Spurs lost 1-0 to Arsenal at Wembley. Again the luck was against Anderton, who looked like he had won Spurs a certain penalty when he was brought down by Andy Linighan early on. The referee failed to give a penalty and allowed Linighan to stay on when others would have shown him a red card.

Tony Adams scored the winner for Arsenal ten minutes from time. Anderton played in two more FA Cup semi-final defeats with Spurs, to Everton in 1995 and Newcastle in 1999. The most painful semi-final setback of his career was at Euro 96, when England lost to Germany on penalties at Wembley. In golden-goal extra time Anderton hit the post from six yards, moments before Paul Gascoigne's even more gut-wrenching failure to connect with Alan Shearer's cross in front of an open goal.

Anderton ended 1994/95 by turning down a move to Manchester United, and stayed with Spurs for another nine seasons. A 1999 League Cup winner's medal provided the only silverware, but for him 1994/95 stands out. 'I just felt we were always on the cusp of something special, several times during my time at Tottenham – but this season more than any other.'

Dumitrescu's arrival – for a then club record £2.6m – had been confirmed the day before Klinsmann's. While Klinsmann was already a fully-fledged superstar, Dumitrescu had only become known to most English fans thanks to his magnificent performances at the 1994 World Cup in the USA. Speaking through a translator for the Tottenham v Everton programme feature, Dumitrescu said he wanted to inject some 'Latin fantasy' into Tottenham's play. Fantasy he did surely provide.

At the World Cup, Dumitrescu and Romania had indulged in fantasy football throughout a tournament in which they reached the quarter-finals before losing to Sweden on penalties. Their most notable performance came in the last 16 under the scorching sun of the Pasadena Rose Bowl in California, where they blew away the 1986 winners and 1990 runners-up Argentina with a surprise 3-2 win in front of more than 90,000 fans. Dumitrescu it was who opened the scoring with a direct free kick from an almost impossible angle. His delivery, from deep on the left-hand side of the field and a few yards closer to goal than the top of the area, flummoxed Luis Islas. The Argentina goalkeeper didn't know whether to come for the cross or stay on his line for a shot. In the end he did neither, and Dumitrescu's delivery sailed over the keeper's head and into the net to give his country an 11th-minute lead. Whether he meant that goal or not, there was no doubt about the intent with which Dumitrescu and Romania took the game to Argentina.

With the great Diego Maradona looking on from the stands, having been kicked out of the tournament for a positive drugs test, Argentina equalised from the penalty spot five minutes later through Gabriel Batistuta. In a breathtaking start to the match Dumitrescu put Romania 2-1 up in the 18th minute. This time he latched on to a sumptuous pass from the magisterial Gheorghe Hagi and dispatched a delicately-tapped finish off the instep of his left boot, when it had momentarily looked as though he would hit it with his right. Islas, like most inside the stadium, was deceived as Dumitrescu found the tiny gap between him and the near post.

In the second half Dumitrescu returned the favour to Hagi for what proved to be the winner. It was a build-up which had echoes of the Pelé–Carlos Alberto combination for Brazil against Italy in 1970, widely regarded as the greatest goal ever scored in a World Cup Final. Dumitrescu, like Pelé, caressed the ball as he received it, allowed it to move across his body, and then delayed his pass until the perfect moment before spraying it out to the right. There Hagi, as Carlos Alberto, ghosted in and veritably smashed it into the net. It didn't have the significance of the Carlos Alberto goal which helped Brazil to a 4-1 win and their third Jules Rimet trophy, nor indeed the panache of the white puff of chalk from the goal line rising into the air, but it was almost its equal in quality. Abel Balbo pulled one back for Argentina with 15 minutes to go, but Romania were deserved 3-2 winners and should really have scored more goals. Dumitrescu, Hagi and Florin Raducioiu were the stars of the show in a team which took the country further than it had ever gone before – or has ever since – in a World Cup.

If you were to arrange Tottenham's 'Famous Five' on a fantasy football spectrum, there would be no doubting Dumitrescu's position at the extreme end of it. During those first magical weeks his play was a joy to behold. In style of play Dumitrescu was also probably the closest fit to his manager. If anyone was going to regard him as a luxury it certainly wouldn't be Ardiles, who had been aware of his talents well before they helped knock his own Argentina out of the 1994 World Cup. The previous season Ardiles had dispatched his assistant Steve Perryman to Northern Ireland to assess Dumitrescu in a friendly, and then to Wales for a World Cup qualifier. The Tottenham programme article notes that Perryman was particularly impressed by Dumitrescu's 'calm contribution in a volatile match' in Wales. It was he who set up Raducioiu for the late winner with which Romania booked their place at USA 94. In the interview Dumitrescu goes on to say that he hopes to be able to speak without a translator soon, and his team-mates remember him as someone who worked hard to fit in even if he didn't always work hard on the pitch.

'Dumi's in coaching now,' chuckles Anderton. 'God knows how! He was a character. He used to turn up in some clobber. He loved London – absolutely loved it, always wanting to go into town. He would make us laugh. We would go to Faces nightclub. We'd want to get the beers in, he would be saying, "No, no, get champagne!" He must have been on a fair whack.' Indeed, he probably was. While Sugar maintains Klinsmann was on £8,000 a week, the press at the time reported him to be on anything between £15,000–£23,000. It's likely the higher figures included a signing-on fee and generous London living allowance. Dumitrescu would probably have been earning not much less than Klinsmann.

Kit man Roy Reyland came across many quirks with the hundreds of players he worked with, but Dumitrescu had one of the strangest. 'He used to have this thing where he'd cut the bottom off his socks, he'd take the inner sole out of his boot and he'd put his bare foot into his boot with no inner sole and then sit in the bath so that the boot shrunk to his foot. He never wore socks in training or matches. He said he could feel the ball better. These days the boots are like carpet slippers, and they weren't bad then to be fair, but they were still soft and supple. They used to have inserts in the bottom of the boot, whereas now it's like a sole unit and if you snap a stud it's gone. You used to be able to change the inserts. So his feet would be on top of the six metal inserts, bare. But that was Ilie.'

Wednesday 24 August, 1994
FA Carling Premiership
Tottenham Hotspur 2-1 Everton
Klinsmann 21, 36
Rideout 46
Sheringham missed pen 45

Dumitrescu had been the only one of the 'Famous Five' not to have scored in the season's opening game at Hillsborough, but as he and Klinsmann make their home debuts tonight he almost beats his team-mate on to the scoresheet. With just eight minutes gone Barmby centres a low drive, which Dumitrescu battles to reach before swivelling to get an eight-yard shot away. Everton keeper Neville Southall somehow tips it on to the bar. Moments later, Barmby is again the provider as he pulls the ball back from the corner to the penalty spot and Dumitrescu comes charging in, only to see his shot crash off David Unsworth and over the bar.

All that comes before Klinsmann's acrobatic overhead kick with which he opens the scoring in the 21st minute. The crowd have barely recovered from that, and the excitement of the dive celebration, when a quarter of an hour later Klinsmann doubles the lead. This time it's Kerslake down the right; his cross is glanced on by Barmby and Klinsmann is there again. So in control of the moment is he that he stands still and simply lets the ball hit his head, caressing it into the net as it does so. It all looks so easy.

There is no extravagant dive to celebrate. Klinsmann mirrors the simplicity of his goal with the celebration. He stands rooted to the spot, raises both hands to the heavens and receives the adulation of his fellow players and fans.

Spurs should be 3-0 up by half-time after Barmby's pass hits Unsworth's hand and the defender is harshly pulled up for a penalty. Will there be the opportunity for a first-half hat-trick for Klinsmann? No. Sheringham is captain and his manager's nominated penalty taker, but he blazes his spot-kick over the bar with virtually the last kick of the half.

'I didn't concentrate on the job in hand,' admits Sheringham. 'It was such an emotional night, with it being Jürgen's home debut, and that wave of emotion was coursing down from the terraces. Some of the crowd were chanting "Jürgen, Jürgen," because they wanted him to take it and get the hat-trick. But it was my job to take it.'

Some of the following day's newspapers suggested Sheringham's nose had been put out of joint by the arrival of Klinsmann. 'Nothing could be further from the truth,' says Sheringham. 'Having Jürgen there was brilliant for me. Instead of each of us having a centre-half on us, we would often get games where both of them tried to mark Jürgen. That gave me extra space and meant I was able to do a lot more damage.

'It was just fantastic when he joined. Playing with him was a revelation. It was a dream to have a player like him alongside me. He didn't know what to expect either. He was willing to learn and was open to new ideas. He didn't know what he was coming in to. I wanted to accommodate anyone, whoever arrived I would have been looking to create a good partnership with them. A lot of people thought I might feel I was being knocked down the pecking order, but it couldn't have been any better for me. It improved me as a player.'

Tottenham's players appear to glide across the pitch. It looks like they are playing by their own rules, that they can go on to score as many goals as they want. Every defender in turn joins in with an attack at some point during the game. Spurs, though, experience a dreadful few seconds either side of half-time. The penalty miss just before the break starts the reality check, then it continues 32 seconds after the restart when Paul Rideout is left with the freedom of the Paxton Road penalty box and ghosts between Edinburgh and Campbell to pull one back.

Tottenham have been a class above their opponents, but the margin is now just one goal. 2-1, with an entire half to play. That's part of the beauty of football. What it giveth with one hand it so often taketh away with the other. Whatever flights of fancy Spurs have indulged in, whatever heights they have reached in their attacking play, they are only ever a moment from disaster. With just four minutes to go, Everton should equalise when Matt Jackson's shot rockets goalwards only to crash off Edinburgh, who is lying injured in front of goal, and bounce up over the bar.

Tottenham hang on for what is only their second home win so far in the calendar year of 1994. It is the first time since 1980 that they have won their opening two league matches. A club which had survived relegation by just three points the previous season is suddenly being talked about as an outside bet for the league title. As Klinsmann notes in his post-match interviews, Tottenham have immediately clawed back the six points they've been docked. 'We are now equal with everyone else,' he tells the assembled press. 'As everything is possible in football, we can start for the championship. I am excited by that. There is a lot to play for.' Tottenham's title odds – 500/1 in pre-season – are slashed to 14/1.

The *Guardian* ran the headline 'SPURS ON SONG WITH NUL POINTS'. David Lacey wrote: 'Jürgen Klinsmann continues to clean up the Premiership, but by now he will have realised that he is not playing in front of the Siegfried Line, just a line of washing which threatens to peg out now and then.'

The *Evening Standard* went with 'NO STOPPING THE SPURS JURGERNAUT'. 'Two goals on his home debut is the stuff of Bavarian fairytales,' wrote Michael Hart. The frequency with which the media made reference to Klinsmann's nationality, with puns in headlines and prose, highlights how it was still a relative novelty for an overseas player to be lighting up the English game.

For most of Sugar's tenure as chairman the commonest accusation levelled at him was that he wasn't willing to speculate in order to accumulate. He did in 1994 though, and he immediately reaped the rewards. The day after beating Everton, Tottenham's share price shot up by 14p, adding £1.6m to the club's Stock Market value to push it beyond £20m. The City liked what it was seeing off the pitch and the supporters liked what they were seeing on it.

There was, though, one Tottenham fan in the stadium for the Everton match for whom the magic of the moment was proving bitter-sweet – David Howells. He grew up supporting the club and then made his debut for them in 1986. By 1994 Howells was one of the longest-serving players at Spurs. Only Gary Mabbutt and Micky Hazard (who was now in his second spell at White Hart Lane) had a longer association with Tottenham. As Klinsmann hit his first goal and Spurs celebrated *en masse*, Howells had mixed feelings: 'It was brilliant and I was just gutted not to be part of it. I wasn't even on the bench. I was buzzing and jumping up and down celebrating in the stands. I always, always want to see Tottenham win and it was a great goal. It was exciting, but part of me was thinking I should be down there doing that as well. That feeling was really strong in my mind.'

Howells had been as excited as anyone in pre-season, and had fully expected to be involved in midfield during the Ardiles revolution. 'Pre-season I played every game, was captain for a few, then it gets to the first league game and Ossie dropped me. He played Colin Calderwood as a holding midfield player instead of me, which was …' Howells tails off and shrugs. He says he still can't understand the decision. 'Colin was a decent centre-half and a great lad, but hadn't really played as a holding midfield player. Ossie hadn't tried him there pre-season, and then we got to that first game and he decided to go with Colin in there.'

Howells says Ardiles didn't explain his decision to him at the time. 'I've spoken to Ossie since, I still get on very well with him – I see him every time we work at the ground together, that's just football – and it's what he thought at the time. He's the manager. But it was difficult for me, having played in all the pre-season games. Especially as there was all this hype around the team and I wanted to be part of that, so to miss the first game at Sheffield Wednesday was tough. I remember sitting on the bus on the way to the game, sat in a four with me, Teddy, Jürgen and – probably Colin [Calderwood] actually – and we were talking about doing the dive after scoring, and Jürgen said: "Yeah, I think I will." So I was part of that little joke. And then I wasn't involved.'

It was only on arrival at Hillsborough, says Howells, that Ardiles told him he had been left out. It was a ground which had happy memories for a player who had made a surprise debut there for Spurs eight years previously. In February 1986, then aged 18 and enjoying a successful spell as a central striker for the youth team, Howells was called up in place of Clive Allen, who was dropped as he and the team endured a wretched run of form in front of goal. On a snow-covered pitch Howells did what his boyhood hero Martin Chivers had done in January 1968 (a month after Howells was born) – made his Tottenham debut at Hillsborough and scored. At 18 years 69 days old, he remains the youngest player to score on his competitive debut for Spurs.

'The manager, Peter Shreeves, was having a shocker,' says Howells of his debut. 'We hadn't scored in six league games and Clive Allen was dropped. I was scoring goals for fun in the youth team. I'd been in the squad a couple of times, and on the way to Sheffield Shreeves said, "You're playing today, son." I think he'd already told my dad, because my dad was already on the way up there – this was before mobile phone days so they'd let them know in advance.

'The pitch was covered in snow. It was an orange ball, back in the days when they literally would just clear the lines and play. We were losing at half-time and Steve Perryman was captain and was badgering them to call it off, because we were literally playing on snow and it was getting a little crust on the top as well, and it was very difficult to play on. We got an equaliser quite quickly in the second half, and I got the winner with 15–20 minutes to go. Paul Allen crossed it and I slid in about level with the penalty spot and side-footed it in. It was just, I mean, surreal really because I'd never played in front of a big crowd before.' Howells didn't have many games as a centre-forward. He went on to blossom into a fine midfielder, stable and solid defensively but also with a range of passing to bring others into the game and the ability to get among the goals himself.

The start of the 1994/95 campaign, though, was his toughest spell at the club. Where he had benefited from Clive Allen's misfortune back in

1986, Calderwood was to benefit from that of Howells for the remainder of the Ardiles era. 'Even on the bus to Sheffield I thought I was playing, so to not even be on the bench was very disappointing. I didn't get a look in really until Ossie got sacked,' he says. Jürgen Klinsmann had now followed Chivers and Howells in making his Spurs debut at Hillsborough and scoring. For Howells that moment, and the next few weeks, would have to be endured as a frustrated spectator.

As both Klinsmann goals went in against Everton, the recently installed scoreboard at White Hart Lane flashed up 'Wunderbar Jürgen'. Spurs had proudly unveiled this – what seemed huge at the time – animated scoreboard during the previous season. It was later moved and incorporated into the side of one of the giant Jumbotron screens, continuing to deliver its pixellated messages until White Hart Lane was knocked down. Ticket office manager Chris Belt told the press that season tickets – which cost between £338 and £494 – were in high demand: 'We have put on £500,000 in season-ticket sales since the signings of Klinsmann and Dumitrescu, and they are still coming in. This evening's game against Everton was a sell-out, and we could have sold out Wembley for Saturday's game against Manchester United,' he said.

Manchester United it was who were due in North London next. Having beaten Sheffield Wednesday and Everton, now manager Ossie Ardiles, his new talisman Jürgen Klinsmann, and the rest of Tottenham Hotspur's 'Famous Five' would face the ultimate test against the team that had been crowned champions of England for the last two seasons.

3

'Never Offside, Lino'

*'It was never offside, not even close. That
would have been three wins out of three
and victory over the reigning champions.'
(Darren Anderton)*

OVER the first two seasons of the Premier League era, one team
had emerged as its leading force – Manchester United. League
champions in 1992/93, league title and FA Cup Double winners
in 1993/94. They played with style and a swagger, but a snarl too. If you
weren't a fan of United, by the summer of 1994 you really weren't a fan.
Kids of the 80s had grown up either loving or hating Liverpool. Now
they did likewise with Man U.

Everything seemed to go United's way: seven minutes of injury time
to score the winner against Sheffield Wednesday in a vital match during
the 1993 title run-in; two penalties against Chelsea in the 1994 FA Cup
Final. 'Biased refs', 'Lucky United', came the envious cries from anyone
not wearing a United shirt while kicking a ball around on parks and
playing fields throughout the country. That match against Sheffield
Wednesday on 10 April 1993 had been key to United finally ending their
26-year wait for the title. They trailed 1-0 at Old Trafford until the 86th
minute, when centre-back and captain Steve Bruce thumped a towering
header beyond Owls keeper Chris Woods. The winner came six minutes
into injury time as Bruce again leapt to head home.

The wild celebrations, which included manager Alex Ferguson running on to the pitch and his assistant Brian Kidd doing likewise before dropping to his knees in disbelief, have become one of the most replayed moments in Premier League history. It was probably the first instance of what became known many years later as 'Fergie time' – a sarcastic suggestion by rival fans that referees seemed to allow Ferguson's United to play for as long as required to get their necessary winner or equaliser.

United's 2-1 victory that afternoon wrested control of the title race back from Aston Villa. It's hard to believe that United had gone more than a quarter of a century without the title before Alex Ferguson, then just plain old Alex Ferguson in his pre-knighthood days, led them to glory in that inaugural season of the Premier League. It was a triumph which proved the catalyst to an unprecedented era of dominance in the English game: league title and FA Cup Doubles in 1994 and 1996; the unrivalled Treble of Champions League, league title and FA Cup in 1999; and a total of 13 league titles, two Champions League titles and four more FA Cups – added to the one he had lifted in 1990 – all by the time Ferguson left in 2013.

The previous season, on the penultimate weekend of the 1991/92 campaign, Leeds United knew they would pip Manchester United to the Division One title if they could beat Sheffield United and Manchester United failed to take maximum points at Liverpool later that day. The broadcast rights holders back then were ITV. Their programme *The Match* showed the last top-flight league matches ever to be broadcast on terrestrial TV, as Leeds won 3-2 at Bramall Lane before Manchester United were toppled 2-0 at Anfield. Leeds were champions. Their manager Howard Wilkinson remains, at the time of this book's publication, the last English manager ever to win the league. Leeds top-flight champions in 1992, Manchester United in 1993: yet the year between their respective achievements feels like a decade, given the changes to football and the way it was broadcast.

The dawn of the Premier League, in many ways Sky's Premier League, was a television revolution on a par with the 1970 World Cup when many were able to watch football in colour for the very first time. As Brazil – the greatest exponents of the beautiful game – lifted the Jules Rimet trophy in glorious technicolor, they won an army of new admirers and fans right across the globe. Manchester United did likewise as they strutted their way to the title in 1992/93, with those who could afford the Sky subscription able to follow their progress and watch their matches regularly throughout the season. Thus, when they arrived at White Hart Lane on that Saturday afternoon in August 1994, they did so as easily the standout team in English football. The reigning league champions and FA Cup holders had only just missed out on an unprecedented domestic Treble earlier in the year, when they were beaten by Aston Villa in the League Cup Final at the end of March.

On Saturday 27 August 1994, the team everyone loved to hate arrived in North London to take on the team everyone was talking about. Having seen his bold attacking tactics pay off with a return of maximum points against Sheffield Wednesday and Everton, Ardiles was about to unleash Tottenham's 'Famous Five' on United.

The very personification of that swagger and snarl with which United played was their talismanic forward Eric Cantona, who had been a league champion in each of the three previous seasons, with Leeds in 1992 then twice with Manchester United. He of the upturned collar and the upturned nose looked down with affected arrogance on every opponent, the mere mortals attempting – and usually failing – to thwart his genius. But United stepped off the team bus at White Hart Lane without him. Cantona was banned for the first three league games of 1994/95, having been sent off in a pre-season friendly at Rangers. After replacing Dion Dublin at half-time at Ibrox he was booked in the 81st minute for walking away from the referee, and then again one minute later for a foul on Steven Pressley.

Whenever Cantona entered the pitch, he looked as though he owned the place. No one would get in his way; he would walk all over his opponents – quite literally in the case of Swindon Town's John Moncur. In a match at the County Ground in March 1994, Cantona viciously stamped on the former Spurs midfielder's head as he lay prostrate on the turf. The Frenchman was rightly sent off, and just four days later he received another red card for two bookable offences in a match at Arsenal. His most outrageous moment of ill-discipline was yet to come: the kung-fu kick on a Crystal Palace fan in January 1995. His subsequent nine-month ban would ultimately derail United's title bid, and no doubt helped Blackburn steal in to win it by one point. In the eyes of many, though, Cantona's artistry outweighed his aggression. It was an artistry which swept across the red half of Manchester, and helped reawaken a sleeping giant while rival clubs slumbered through the early and mid-90s.

At the dawn of the Premier League, there existed within English football an established so-called 'Big Five' of clubs: Manchester United, Liverpool, Everton, Arsenal and Tottenham. One theory goes that whichever of them won that first Premier League title would be well placed to embark on a period of dominance. Each had a huge existing fan base built up through decades of success. When the Premier League began, no team had won the league more often than Liverpool – 18 times. No team had won the FA Cup more than Spurs – eight times. The only clubs to have won the Double of league title and FA Cup in the 20th century had been Tottenham in 1961, Arsenal in 1971 and Liverpool in 1986. Liverpool were the most decorated team in terms of European silverware with four European Cups to their name, but every club in the 'Big Five' had won a European trophy. All five had history, tradition and plenty of support. This, coupled with the increased exposure provided by satellite TV and all the riches it would bring, would give any of them huge added impetus if they could win the first Premier League title.

So could it have been Tottenham? Unfortunately, they weren't even close. In the summer of 1992 Doug Livermore, assisted by Ray Clemence, had been put in charge of first-team affairs by chief executive Terry Venables. Weeks after managing Tottenham to their 1991 FA Cup triumph, Venables became the club's joint owner alongside Alan Sugar. The idea was that Sugar would take care of business and Venables of team affairs. Venables moved upstairs and appointed Peter Shreeves as manager for 1991/92, but a hugely disappointing 15th-place finish led to a shake-up with Shreeves axed and Livermore and Clemence coming in.

Both were well-liked, respected figures but with no real managerial experience to their names. Livermore's playing career began as a midfielder at Liverpool, where he made his debut in 1968 and chalked up 18 appearances before leaving for Norwich in 1970. He had a brief loan spell at Bournemouth and also represented Cardiff and Chester, where he retired in 1980. As manager he had two months in caretaker charge of Swansea in 1983 following John Toshack's departure, and a month at Tottenham in 1987 as then chairman Irving Scholar waited to install Venables.

Clemence had enjoyed far greater success as a player. By the time he left Liverpool for Spurs at the age of 33 in August 1981, he was already a winner of five league titles, three European Cups, two UEFA Cups, the FA Cup and the League Cup. He then won the FA Cup with Spurs in 1982, but injury meant he missed out on the UEFA Cup triumph two years later. A knee injury sustained against Norwich in October 1987 forced him to retire and take up the post of goalkeeping coach at White Hart Lane. He also had a spell in charge of Tottenham's reserves before he stepped up to assist Livermore with the first team.

Both softly-spoken figures, it seemed to the outside world that Livermore and Clemence went about their business in a low-key way; it was hard to imagine them having the strength of character or personality to inspire the dressing room, certainly not to the extent of someone with such revered man-management skills as Terry Venables. However, it was to Clemence and Livermore that first-team duties fell, and the club was willing to spend to boost their chances of success in the first Premier League season. Centre-back Neil Ruddock, who had previously been with the club before leaving for Millwall in 1988, had arrived back via Southampton for £750,000. The fee for the 24-year-old was set by a tribunal with the south coast club, who valued him far more highly, labelling it 'ridiculous'. Dean Austin, just 22 and an emerging talent at right-back, cost £375,000 from Southend.

Then there were two big-money, high-profile signings: Darren Anderton for £2m from Portsmouth and Teddy Sheringham for £2.1m from Nottingham Forest. Anderton signed a four-year contract worth £3,000 a week, rising by £1,000 a year, with a BMW chucked in for good measure. His ability to whip in a menacing cross found the perfect foil in Sheringham. Edward – as the late great Brian Clough, his manager at Nottingham Forest, insisted on calling him – began the season by scoring the first-ever goal in a live televised Premier League match as Forest beat Liverpool 1-0 at the City Ground. Scot Gemmill played him in down the left and Sheringham cut into the side of the penalty box, beat right-back Rob Jones and sent a searing drive beyond goalkeeper David James into the far right-hand top corner. Sheringham was delighted with that goal. 'It was an absolute blinder,' he says. 'I was immensely pleased to have scored the first-ever live televised Premier League goal. It will always be the first.'

It was the sort of goal Tottenham were willing to pay big money for, and by the end of the month he was a Spurs player. He would go on to net a further 21 goals for his new club in 1992/93, finishing on 22 as the top goalscorer in the inaugural Premier League season.

As well as Sheringham and Anderton there was more talent in the 1992/93 team. With established midfielders Paul Allen, Vinny Samways and Steve Sedgley still on the scene, Nicky Barmby just emerging from the youth team and the usually reliable Erik Thorstvedt in goal, Livermore and Clemence had a decent squad at their disposal. Not good enough, though. At the end of the season they were a huge 25 points behind the eventual champions Man United, back in eighth place. An entertaining run to the FA Cup semi-final finished in a gut-wrenching 1-0 defeat to Arsenal at Wembley, as the Gunners gained revenge for Tottenham's Paul Gascoigne-inspired 3-1 win at the same stage of the competition two years previously. Defeat to the old enemy was hard to take, but the season did at least provide the consolation of a league double over them. Paul Allen scored the only goal at White Hart Lane in a game which took place a couple of weeks before Christmas, while the return fixture at Highbury in the final match of 1992/93 saw Spurs run out 3-1 winners. Sheringham notched his final goal of the campaign, and

Scottish striker John Hendry enjoyed his best-ever game in a Tottenham career which amounted to just 17 league appearances as he twice beat David Seaman.

It was a disappointing season, but Tottenham's eighth-place finish of 1992/93 doesn't look so bad when set against the rest of the 'Big Five', who appeared a fading force. United were deserved champions, but they took advantage of a power vacuum within the English game. Liverpool were sixth, Arsenal tenth and Everton 13th. All had their distractions.

Liverpool and Everton were still trying to recover from the departure of great managers, leaders of the calibre whose achievements Ferguson would go on to equal and surpass. At Anfield, off the pitch Liverpool were emerging from the horrors of Heysel and Hillsborough, and on it from the departure of Kenny Dalglish in 1991. His achievements in winning three league titles and two FA Cups, including the 1986 Double, were always going to be a tough act for Graeme Souness to follow. Souness lasted three years, with just the 1992 FA Cup triumph to show for his efforts.

Across Stanley Park at Goodison, Howard Kendall had left in 1987 after becoming the most successful manager in the club's history by winning two league titles, the FA Cup and the European Cup-Winners' Cup. His successor Colin Harvey lasted a trophyless three years. Now, at the launch of the Premier League, Kendall was midway through his second spell in charge. The old football adage 'never go back' held true. By December 1993, having failed to restore former glories, Kendall was gone again.

In North London, Tottenham and more pertinently Arsenal, who still had the architect of their 1989 and 1991 title triumphs George Graham at the helm, should have been well placed to step into the void and challenge United. Graham, though, became entrenched in an overly-defensive game plan, while down the Seven Sisters High Road, Tottenham were creating many of their own problems.

Simmering throughout 1991 to 1993 was a bitter feud between the new owners – Sugar and Venables. It was a falling-out that would go on to have major repercussions for Tottenham and English football well into the mid-90s. It's now clear the pair didn't get on from the moment they went into business together, even before their joint takeover of the club was complete. Their battle ended up in the High Court, and also led indirectly to the downfall of Graham at Arsenal.

The Sugar and Venables takeover happened in June 1991, just weeks after the FA Cup triumph. With the club in a financial mess, the pair combined to buy out Irving Scholar's shares for £6m. At the time their takeover was widely regarded to have saved Spurs from going bust, though many now believe that the club's position, though not healthy, wasn't quite as precarious as initially thought. Sugar claims in his 2010 autobiography *What You See Is What You Get* that once the takeover was complete, he immediately set about prioritising the reduction of the club's £11m debt, but that Venables was intent on signing players and that he bought Gordon Durie from Chelsea in the summer of 1991 without Sugar's permission.

The next flashpoint between the pair came in the summer of 1992, when Venables told Sugar he wanted to sign Sheringham. Sugar claims in that autobiography that Venables suggested during the conversation that the player's manager at Forest, Brian Clough, was insisting on a bung to enable the transfer to go through. Sugar says he instructed Venables to ensure the deal was 'done in the conventional manner', and while there is no evidence that Venables did anything wrong, it was Sugar's unease over the deal – which he claims saw agent Frank McLintock paid his £50,000 fee in cash – and several other disagreements, that convinced him he wanted to dismiss Venables as chief executive. That's exactly what he did at a board meeting on Friday 14 May, 1993, almost two years to the day since Tottenham's FA Cup win.

Many Tottenham fans were outraged that the popular Venables had been ousted and threatened not to renew their season tickets. Players too were upset. Neil Ruddock was the most outspoken. He had been in the process of negotiating a new deal with Venables and left for Liverpool after just a year with the club, a year in which his commanding performances at the heart of defence had been among the real high points of the Livermore/Clemence tenure. Of course Venables fought against his dismissal, and a bitter High Court battle ensued. It was during this court case that Venables' barrister read out the section of Sugar's witness statement which made public the allegations surrounding Clough. Sugar says he did not expect these allegations to be brought up during the court case. After a two-day hearing the judge upheld Sugar's decision to sack Venables, who then set about suing Spurs until eventually deciding to walk away. Sugar admits he became 'obsessed' with the legal battle and 'devoted seven days a week to fighting it'. Set against this backdrop it's perhaps not surprising that Spurs struggled to fulfil their potential in the early years of the Premier League.

Sheringham also feels he was unfairly tainted by the controversy. In his autobiography published in 1998, he talks of a meeting with McLintock and Clough's assistant Ronnie Fenton at Luton services (chosen because it was halfway between Tottenham and Nottingham) on the day the deal was completed. It was at this meeting that the bung was alleged to have been taken. In his book, Sheringham says he never saw any money change hands, then or at any time afterwards. He was clearly affected by the allegations for a long time, adding that although nobody ever claimed he might personally have benefited from anything that might have gone on it was daunting to have to go in front of an inquiry and be interrogated about what he did or did not do and about what he did or did not see. The allegations surrounding Clough led to the FA's attempt to clean up the game, as they launched an inquiry into illegal payments. The only manager found guilty of wrongdoing by the FA was Arsenal's George Graham, who was sacked by the club in February 1995 and banned from football for a year.

The Sugar-Venables split had further huge repercussions for Spurs. When Venables was named England head coach at the end of January 1994, the BBC's *Panorama* and Channel Four both ran exposés on him and his companies. Then Granada Television approached Tottenham, saying they'd been handed documents which pointed to a serious breach of football rules regarding payments to players at the club before Sugar took charge. At 5pm on Friday 12 May, 1994, FA chief executive Graham Kelly arranged an emergency press conference on the steps outside their headquarters at Lancaster Gate; he announced to the media that Spurs were about to be charged with illegal loans to players dating back over a decade.

Sugar remains convinced it was a personal act of revenge by Kelly for the embarrassment caused by the fresh TV allegations against Venables following his appointment as England boss. The Spurs chairman couldn't understand how the FA could remain intent on punishing the club for financial misdemeanours committed by a previous regime, when it had also seen fit to appoint someone who had been at the club at that time – Terry Venables – as England coach.

It was this FA hearing, indirectly the result of the feud between Venables and Sugar which began to fester the moment they took charge of the club in 1991, that saw Spurs start 1994/95 facing an FA Cup ban, a six-point deduction and a fine of £1.5m. Whatever the rights and wrongs of the actions taken by both men in the intervening years, it's hard to escape the conclusion that the row took its toll on a club which might otherwise have stood a better chance of stepping into English football's power vacuum and seriously challenging Manchester United in the early Premier League years.

The legal wranglings were still going on in 1996. By then Venables had guided England to the semi-finals of the European Championship as hosts, but had decided before the tournament that he would stand down at its end to concentrate on clearing his name after the controversy surrounding several of his business dealings. He was also facing legal action by Sugar, who sued for libel after Venables published his autobiography in 1995. The case was heard in October 1996, when Sugar won £100,000 in damages which he donated to Great Ormond Street Hospital.

With Tottenham fighting battles off the field, in 1992/93 Aston Villa and Norwich took the fight to Manchester United on it. United were worthy champions, then it was over to Blackburn Rovers to put up a challenge. Rovers finished runners-up in 1993/94 and got the better of United in 1994/95, but it wasn't until the arrival of Arsène Wenger at Arsenal in 1996 that Manchester United had a true, force-to-be-reckoned-with, long-term rival. Spurs and Sugar missed their chance to step into the void.

Spurs had been best placed to become the Manchester United of the South. When it came to silverware they weren't as decorated as United, but their brand was just as strong. For both clubs the glory days had been in the 60s. Prior to their title triumphs of 1993 and 1994, United hadn't won domestic football's biggest prize since 1967; they'd been waiting almost as long as Spurs. Tottenham had announced themselves to the world by becoming British football's first major European trophy winners when they lifted the European Cup-Winners' Cup in 1963. United were crowned English football's first European champions just five years later.

The Premier League changed everything, and Manchester United had immediately taken the competition by storm. Until now Spurs had stuttered, but at the start of 1994/95 the 'Famous Five' had swept them to a maximum return of six points from two games, which in the normal course of events would see them placed second in the embryonic league table. The six-point deduction meant they were effectively sitting third from bottom in a season when four teams would be relegated. Today was a chance to test themselves against the very best.

After winning the Double in 1994, United's opponents in the Charity Shield at Wembley two weeks prior to their visit to White Hart Lane had been Blackburn, the runners-up in the league. United won 2-0. Eric Cantona – whose suspension for his sending off at Ibrox hadn't yet been confirmed – scored from another Wembley penalty and Paul Ince beat Tim Flowers with a spectacular overhead kick. Cantona's three-game ban then began, but his absence didn't appear to affect his team as they started their title defence with a 2-0 win over QPR at Old Trafford. Then came a 1-1 draw away to Nottingham Forest. The hosts were unlucky not to get all three points, with Stan Collymore of Forest giving United's defence a torrid time in a Monday night match live on Sky.

United arrived in North London with a strong recent record against Spurs. They hadn't lost any of the last eight meetings, home or away. But

Spurs, having started the season in fine style and knowing Cantona was absent, sensed a chance. Two youngsters were to continue at the heart of Tottenham's defence: Stuart Nethercott, 21, and Sol Campbell, 19. They were part of a team that had conceded four goals in the opening two games, and were now about to face a United side full of attacking talent. Nethercott and Campbell's respective careers would eventually go on to take vastly different trajectories, but that summer they had formed a solid central defensive partnership for the England Under-21s who won the Toulon tournament. The pair played every game in the competition, keeping clean sheets against Russia and the USA in the group and in the final itself, which ended in a 2-0 win over Portugal. Campbell was on the scoresheet in the semi-final 2-1 victory over Belgium. England's team in the final contained Ray Parlour, Jamie Redknapp and Trevor Sinclair, who would all go on to enjoy distinguished Premier League careers – as would striker Robbie Fowler, who played in all three of the group games.

For Campbell, the 1994/95 season was one which helped shape what was ultimately a hugely successful career. He still endures such hostility from many fans for the manner in which he left the club for Arsenal in 2001. He is a complex character, an introverted individual. That's an impression many would have formed from having watched his television interviews over the years, and from reading his official biography published in 2014.

The make-up of his personality perhaps becomes easier to understand when you discover more about his upbringing. He says in that biography that he and his father Sewell never had any physical contact: no hugs, no handshakes. The first time Sol touched Sewell was when he held his father's hand as he lay dying on a hospital bed. Sewell passed away two days later, the night before Campbell's 29th birthday. After his Tottenham debut as an 18-year-old in December 1992, coming off the bench to play up front and scoring a late consolation goal in a 2-1 defeat to Chelsea at White Hart Lane, he says none of his family asked him a single question about the experience when he returned home that night. Many years later, Sewell only learnt that his son was now the captain of Tottenham when someone happened to mention it to him down the pub. The pub, according to Sol, is where Sewell spent the majority of his time. In the epilogue to his biography Campbell says he forgives Sewell for being hard on him and his brothers. He also says he forgives his brothers for being tough on him too. Sol was the youngest of 12 siblings, and five years separated him from the next youngest, John.

It's not just that Campbell left for Arsenal that upsets many Spurs fans, but the manner in which he did so: giving public assurances that he wouldn't cross the North London divide, and allowing his contract to run down so that he could leave on a Bosman. It meant Tottenham didn't get a single penny for the talent they had nurtured through their youth academy. That was considered unforgivable.

Of the entire 1994/95 Tottenham team, only Teddy Sheringham ended his career with a club honours list more impressive than Campbell's. Sheringham's final tally included the 1999 Treble of Champions League, Premier League and FA Cup plus two further Premier League titles, all with Manchester United. It just about eclipses Campbell's medal haul in terms of prestige. At Arsenal Campbell won two league titles and three FA Cups including the Double in 2001/02. He didn't play in two of those FA Cup finals (suspended in 2003 and left on the bench in 2005); but perhaps extra weight should be added to the 2003/04 league triumph, since he was part of the 'Invincibles' team which achieved the unprecedented feat of completing an entire 38-game league season undefeated. He also captained Tottenham to League Cup glory in 1999, and was skipper again when Portsmouth claimed the FA Cup in 2008.

Jürgen Klinsmann and Gica Popescu are the only members of the 1994/95 team who can be put in the same bracket as Sheringham and Campbell regarding club honours. Of course Klinsmann was a World Cup and European Championship winner at international level, but his club prizes were few and far between. He was limited to UEFA Cup wins with Inter and with Bayern Munich, where he also won one Bundesliga title. Popescu's most noteworthy prizes were the Copa Del Rey and European Cup-Winners' Cup with Barcelona and the UEFA Cup with Galatasaray. He also won a host of league titles and cups in the less competitive leagues of Romania, the Netherlands and Turkey.

So, given the measure of Campbell's success after leaving Spurs, would 1994/95 still mean anything at all to him? Well, it appears it did; quite a lot, in fact. Campbell has agreed to a telephone interview. On the phone he sounds very much as he does in TV interviews: thoughtful to the extent of being hesitant, articulate in the way he delivers every single word with emphasis, and measured in the way he makes clear exactly what he means. His voice is a loud whisper.

Campbell agrees with Nethercott that it was their performances for the England Under-21s in the summer of 1994 which elevated them to first-choice starters for Spurs. 'We beat Portugal in the final to win the whole tournament, and it kind of went from there really,' he says. 'All of a sudden Spurs said, "Well, why don't you guys who have really done well with England go on and play for us?" As a youngster you learn a hell of a lot at that tournament – so many players have gone on to play for their senior international teams. But if you've got two young guys learning on the job, as Spurs had with me and Stuart, then it's quite difficult because you need a lot of protection around the game. If you're both in the team too much you've got a hell of a lot to think about and you've got to make the right decisions.'

While Campbell and Nethercott, with young goalkeeper Ian Walker behind them, set about concentrating on trying to keep United at bay, the excitement of the home fans and the neutrals again centred around the exploits of the 'Famous Five' and what they might be able to do against United. Ilie Dumitrescu was pictured on the front page of the match programme which cost £1.50. The fans' letters page inside clearly captured the mood. 'Even with the full media spotlight on him when he arrived at White Hart Lane for the first time, Jürgen Klinsmann left his press conference to meet the fans, many of whom had been waiting outside the gates for much of the morning,' wrote a Mrs L. Maybank from Buckhurst Hill in Essex. 'I was amongst them and was delighted just to see him sign for Spurs. But then to take time out to sign autographs in the car park was just tremendous. To my mind, the man is a superstar who could have gone to any club, literally in the world.'

Another letter from N. Prior in Walthamstow read: 'While Jürgen Klinsmann has grabbed the headlines, Ilie Dumitrescu appears to have slipped in quietly; yet his World Cup form suggests that Ossie has a real pearl on his hands. He has shown real commitment to our future by signing a four-year contract, and I am convinced that his presence, even on the training field, will do so much for the education of our talented young players. So welcome to both – just having them here is a boost for all Spurs fans.'

As Spurs and United took to the field, many of the home fans in the crowd of 24,502 – an attendance restricted by the works continuing on the South Stand – sensed this might just be the day their team finally got the better of United again. Their last victories had come in 1989/90, when Spurs had beaten United three times in the same season, doing the double in the league and also winning a League Cup third-round tie.

Saturday 27 August, 1994
FA Carling Premiership
Tottenham Hotspur 0-1 Manchester United
Bruce 49
Sheringham pen (80) saved by Schmeichel
Straight from kick-off it's clear Spurs mean business. They dominate the opening exchanges, but Denmark international Peter Schmeichel proves unbeatable. Schmeichel is possibly the only goalkeeper who, when in a one-on-one situation with a forward, is the favourite to win it. His star-jump saves, when he rushes out and makes himself huge

as an opponent bears down on goal, are a hallmark of his game. His distribution is also immense; so often he sparks off a United attack by hurling a throw into the opposition half with pinpoint accuracy. These qualities have been honed by playing handball as a youngster in Denmark.

With just 60 seconds on the clock Sheringham attempts an ambitious volley from the tightest of angles, but the Great Dane reacts sharply to tip it over the bar. Tottenham's next chance falls to Klinsmann. Sheringham spins a beautiful long pass out to Edinburgh on the left, who whips in a teasing cross to Klinsmann. The German leaps for a header but directs it over the bar. Had he got it on target perhaps even the magnificent Schmeichel would not have been able to stop this one.

Next it's Anderton on the charge, riding three challenges and picking out Sheringham with an exquisite cross for the Spurs skipper to head back across goal. The onrushing Barmby and Klinsmann both marginally fail to get on the end of it as the ball bounces harmlessly wide. It's a breathless start by the home team, with United forced to stand back and admire the talents of the 'Famous Five' in full flow. Andrei Kanchelskis has United's only real chance of the first half, as he ends a mazy run by sending his shot across goal and just wide of the far post.

Two minutes before the interval United's back line is finally pierced. Barmby, from just inside the United half, curls a beautiful pass round the outside of the last defender. It's perfectly weighted for Klinsmann to run on to. Klinsmann effectively has possession of it from about 25 yards from goal, but allows the ball to run to exactly where he wants it so that his first touch is actually the one with which he dispatches his shot beyond the advancing Schmeichel from just inside the box. 1-0 to Spurs.

Klinsmann's fourth goal in three games. There's no dive celebration this time, instead he runs to the North Stand directly in front of him and gets down on both knees, clenching both fists in a pumping motion as White Hart Lane erupts. But no, the offside flag is up. Klinsmann realises and climbs to his feet, waving away the linesman's decision with a dismissive flap of his right hand.

'It was never offside,' says Anderton. Indeed, television replays showed Klinsmann had timed his run to perfection. 'Not even close. And it was a crucial decision. The way we were playing we could have gone on to win that game. We should have won it anyway. That would have been three wins out of three, a win over the reigning champions, and what a start that would have been.'

The match is goalless at half-time, but just after the break United take the lead. Tottenham's defence has looked more composed than in the opening two matches against Sheffield Wednesday and Everton. Campbell and Nethercott have coped well with Mark Hughes and Brian McClair. As Hughes enters the area, Campbell gets in a solid challenge and knocks the ball behind for a corner. Giggs whips it in from the right. Walker seems to lose his bearings in the bright sun. With his eyes on the ball he isn't aware of Edinburgh's position. He trips over his own team-mate and is left sprawling embarrassingly on the ground as United captain Steve Bruce simply nods the ball into an empty net. 1-0 to United.

Sixty seconds later United almost double their lead, but Walker goes some way to making amends. Kanchelskis shrugs off Barmby's challenge on the right wing to leave United two-on-one. His pass beats Calderwood and Hughes steams in. He should score. The shot is powerful but central, and Walker blocks it. The ball is in danger of spinning over his head and into the net, but Walker springs to his feet to punch it away. It falls to Ince and he sends a hurried effort over the bar. Relief for Spurs. Still only 1-0 down. Campbell and Nethercott are coping with almost everything United can throw at them.

Campbell says he drew so much inspiration in his early career from a man who was an unused substitute that day against Manchester United – club captain Gary Mabbutt, who had turned 33 earlier in the week. Mabbutt was admired as much by Tottenham fans for his temperament as his talents, and for the fact that it was an achievement in itself to have even broken into the professional game given that he was diagnosed with Type 1 diabetes when he was 17. He had to self-medicate around training and matches.

'Gary is a tremendous gentleman and ambassador for the game,' says Campbell. 'He is a nice man and was a great footballer.' Campbell stretches his voice to add emphasis to the tribulations he saw his mentor endure. 'It's when I used to see what he had to go through just to play football. I used to sit down with him at half-time, and turn and see him getting out his medical kit and testing and seeing if the levels are okay, whether he's got to top this up, or whether it's all fine. Injecting into his groin. I would say to myself, "Wow. That's guts. That's dedication." Being a professional and almost living and breathing the game to the max. To the max. That's amazing to see, someone who goes above and beyond to play football.'

By 1994 Mabbutt had been with the club for 12 years since signing from Bristol Rovers for £120,000 in July 1982. He started out as a midfielder but went on to become a fixture as a central defender, helping Spurs win the UEFA Cup in 1984 and reach the FA Cup Final in 1987, where it was his unfortunate extra time own goal which saw Coventry win 3-2 after a cross deflected off his knee and over goalkeeper Ray Clemence.

In 1991 it was Mabbutt who climbed the 39 steps at the old Wembley to collect the famous trophy from Diana, Princess of Wales, as Spurs overcame Nottingham Forest 2-1 to win a then record eighth FA Cup. On this day against Manchester United Mabbutt wasn't called off the bench, but before too long he would be back in the starting line-up, meaning a change of position for Campbell.

With just over half an hour to go Spurs are relentless in their pursuit of an equaliser against Man U, with Ardiles sending on the ageing yet wonderfully gifted and attack-minded Micky Hazard in place of Calderwood. His well-placed long pass finds Dumitrescu in the area. Dumitrescu nods it back across goal to Klinsmann, who swivels and shoots only to see his effort blocked by Bruce. The ball drops for Sheringham who blasts it goalwards, but Pallister flings himself in front of it. The home crowd have their heads in their hands.

The architect of the move – Hazard – is enjoying a renaissance late in his career. Born in Sunderland, Hazard joined Spurs as an apprentice at the age of 16 in 1976 having been training with them since he was 12. He was part of the 1982 FA Cup-winning team, and set up a goal in each leg of the 1984 UEFA Cup Final triumph against Anderlecht. In 1985 he left for Chelsea. After five years he moved on again to Portsmouth (playing alongside a young Darren Anderton in the reserves), and then Swindon where Ardiles was his manager. In November 1993 he was re-signed by Ardiles for Spurs. The summer of 1994 has been tough – he's endured operations on his knee and Achilles, but appears to be over those problems judging by how well he is playing today.

Hazard, who retired in April 1995, says: 'I was approaching the end then. Every time I think of that team, I feel a little sad because I think it had the potential to become one of the very best Spurs teams. Unfortunately with all the trauma that was going on around the club at the time regarding Venables and Sugar, Ossie and the players got caught in the middle. Everywhere you looked there was quality, wonderful footballers like Darren Anderton, Teddy Sheringham, Klinsmann, Barmby, Popescu, Dumitrescu. If Ossie had stayed, maybe I could have played on for another year, but when Gerry Francis came in, he obviously wasn't going to be building the team around a 34/35-year-old, and I can completely

THE TEAM THAT DARED TO DO

understand that. Everyone has to plan for the future. He had to build his own team. I could live with that, no problem.'

Spurs team-mate Dean Austin regards Hazard as one of the most talented midfielders he ever played with. Austin had grown up cheering on Spurs from the East Stand, where a friend of his dad had season tickets. A midfielder as a kid, he had idolised Glenn Hoddle and Ardiles, but had also recognised the talents of Hazard. When he found himself as a team-mate alongside him in training, he could see Hazard still had it even in his mid-30s. 'My God, I've never seen a guy pass a ball off either foot with such exquisite precision in all my life,' says Austin. 'The ability he had in both his feet was incredible.'

For the match against United, Austin – just as he had done as a boy – was sitting in the White Hart Lane stands again. He had suffered the same fate as David Howells, playing throughout pre-season under Ardiles and then being told by the Argentinian at the last moment before the match with Sheffield Wednesday that he wasn't in his first-team plans.

'Me and Ossie fell out,' says Austin. 'We get on fine now, it was a long time ago. But I disagreed with what he wanted to do, which was to play David Kerslake instead of me at right-back. It was nothing more than that. I'd had the best season I'd ever had in five years in professional football, then played every game in pre-season, every single game, and then just before the season starts Ossie tells me I'm not playing. From my point of view it was the first time I think that I'd really grown up from a boy into a man.

'It was the first time that I stood up for myself. I knew I was the best player for that position, I was upset with the timing that he told me, and there was a bit of anger too.'

Austin is a straight talker. His voice cracks with emotion as he reminisces about the Tottenham days. His protestations to Ardiles fell on deaf ears, as the manager continued to overlook him until he himself was just about to be cast out by the club. Nowadays of course Austin is able to talk with the perspective of an assistant manager having helped Watford win promotion back to the Premier League in 2015 and then comfortably stay up: 'Ossie had to do what he thought was best and I don't bear grudges, but I disagreed with him, I still do.' So was it difficult to enjoy the buzz that was surrounding Tottenham at the start of 1994/95, when he wasn't in the squad? 'No,' he says, 'because Spurs were my club as a player and as a kid, so I still wanted the team to win.' Does he remember much about that match against United? 'I remember the games I played in more, but United were a great team back then, and we pretty much matched them over the course of the season. An unlucky

1-0 defeat at The Lane – Jürgen's goal was never offside – and then 0-0 at Old Trafford in March. I played in that one.'

With just over half an hour to go, United are still leading 1-0. Hazard is trying his best to get Spurs back on level terms. It's the first time this season that Spurs have been behind in a game. Ardiles has shown that his response to such a situation is to effectively transform the 'Famous Five' into a 'Sensational Six' and chuck Hazard on for Calderwood.

Now the whole of White Hart Lane is on its feet as Spurs try to chase down United's lead. United are unmoved. This is a squad of true champions. Goalkeeper Schmeichel, centre-backs Bruce and Gary Pallister and left-back Denis Irwin have been virtual ever-presents in the team throughout the back-to-back title triumphs of 1993 and 1994, missing just six games across the course of those two seasons between them. At right-back is David May, who has been United's only major summer signing, coming in from Blackburn Rovers for a fee of £1.4m. May aside, every other United starter against Spurs has played a key role in the title wins of both 1993 and 1994. The midfield consists of Lee Sharpe, Paul Ince, Andrei Kanchelskis and Ryan Giggs, with Mark Hughes and Brian McClair (in for the suspended Cantona) up front.

With ten minutes to go, Spurs get a perfect opportunity to draw level. Dumitrescu – who has run the United defence ragged all afternoon – shimmies off towards goal from the halfway line, plays a one-two with Klinsmann, rushes into the area for the return and is checked by Bruce. There's no doubt it's a penalty. Referee Keith Burge points to the spot. The crowd is hoping it's Jürgen, but Teddy steps forward. He missed three days ago against Everton, but he's the captain and he's still the nominated penalty taker. This time at least he hits the target. It's low and hard to Schmeichel's right, but too close to him. The keeper gets down to block it.

Sheringham is crestfallen. The white of White Hart Lane is silent, the sea of red roars. Schmeichel's work for the afternoon still isn't done. Twice more he's called into action. First he flings out a boot to deny Klinsmann, who is played in by Dumitrescu after the Romanian has nutmegged Ince. Then he gathers a more straightforward effort from Barmby, who is set up by Klinsmann.

That's the last chance for Spurs. The full-time whistle blows. Spurs 0-1 Manchester United. Ossie's Spurs and his 'Famous Five' are beaten for the first time in their third match of the season. A wrongly disallowed goal and a missed penalty make it feel like a moral victory. A promising performance against the best team in England bodes well for the future, and the home fans leave The Lane in high spirits despite defeat.

Tottenham's back line had played well against United, but of the defensive cracks that opened up in the coming weeks, Nethercott says: 'Me and Sol were young boys and we were probably the youngest partnership in the Premiership, and at the time we were just going with the flow really. If a team played like that now! You look at people like John Terry and they never seem to be stuck out on the channels, they stay in the middle. Our full-backs were 50 yards up the field.' He laughs. 'That was just how we were. So open. I see Ossie now, he joins us in the Legends games and he's still adamant it's the way he wanted to do it. The shame about it is that we had Steve Perryman as his assistant, who's probably the best defender the club's ever seen, and we didn't really get Stevie coaching us. It was all about the "Famous Five". We tried our best. We had Colin Calderwood in front of us, then later in the season Popescu in front of us, but we just got so exposed.' That's certainly how it appeared over the coming weeks, as Ossie's dream fell apart; but on this August afternoon, against the champions at White Hart Lane, it had all looked very promising.

Being a defender under Ardiles must have been tiring and unforgiving, but Campbell feels that given time the manager might actually have got it right: 'It would have worked, but they just needed older players in and around the back line. For me five years later, playing in that team it would not have been a problem, it really wouldn't. You just needed a little bit more experience and then you could have allowed these guys, this "Famous Five", to go off and do their stuff and then at the back the area is solid – and if it flits and the opposition counter-attack, you are all sorted and in the right position.'

'The only reason it didn't work for Ossie was because of a lack of experience at the back. Fast forward five years from there and we'd have been able to handle most of what was thrown at us. I would have been able to say to Stu, or whoever, "Hey hold up, you're not going anywhere," and be able to balance it out with the attack, say the right word at the right time, have a word over someone's shoulder and just wake them up. But as a youngster you just want to get on with the job and you want to impress. You want to stay in the team and sometimes the managing of the game goes by the wayside.'

Asked if Spurs could have gone on to rival Manchester United had Sugar continued to show the sort of ambition he demonstrated in the summer of 94, Campbell concedes it's a possibility. 'I think if people look back now, I mean how I would do it, you almost buy one top player a year and you look at that over five years. I think that's what Tottenham should have implemented. It doesn't help when you have different managers as well. Continuity of style of play is what is required, you need that consistency.

'That was a time when chairmen could keep a manager for maybe four or five years. It's not like today when there's pressure on them to get rid of him after nine months. What was needed was consistency of management and to bring in one or two good players, top bracket, per year and then see where you are in five years. That's the way I thought the planning should have gone.'

Kit man Roy Reyland saw so many players develop at Spurs, and he recognised the talent in Campbell right from the start: 'Until he left he was the perfect Tottenham Hotspur player. He could defend, he could score goals. The size of him too – he was a man mountain. He was dominant in the air, he could play on the floor.

'The best captain I ever worked with was Steve Perryman. He would make decisions on the field without even looking over to the bench, because he knew if he felt it was the right decision, by the time he'd gone across to the bench and asked the question, the incident was over. Sol used to do that too. He made big, bold decisions. He was a great player.'

Reyland, who now works for rugby union club Saracens, also says Campbell was different in personality to your typical football player: 'He was always very polite, always very appreciative of what you'd done for him, always very well spoken, very well-mannered. Always "Please, thank you, may I? Can I?" A bit like a rugby player. That's how every rugby player is. And that was Sol. Whatever you think about him and the cloud under which he left, you can't say he wasn't a great player. He was a rock, an absolute rock and probably one of the best centre-halves, I think, Spurs ever had.'

Three games in to 1994/95, reputations were being built, Spurs were playing well, confidence was soaring. 'We should have beaten United,' says Anderton. 'Missing the penalty and having the goal disallowed was tough. Jürgen was never offside. After that result, people were already saying, "Oh, the bubble's burst." But then we went to Ipswich.'

4

Portman Perfection

*'It was some of the purest football I have ever
seen from a club side – the sort of football I
dream about.' (Ossie Ardiles)*

TUESDAY 30 August, 1994: Ipswich Town 1-3 Tottenham
Hotspur. Flick through the record books and nothing leaps off
the page about this match; there's nothing outrageous about the
scoreline, it's a run-of-the-mill league fixture, four games into the season
– as such nothing decided by the outcome, no one crowned champions,
no one relegated or qualifying for Europe. The result, though, should
have an asterisk against it, denoting that from Tottenham this was a
performance of sheer beauty. Ask any Spurs fan who was in the 22,559
crowd on that late summer's night, and most would tell you it was one
of the best footballing displays they've ever witnessed from their team.

The stakes may not have been as high, or the occasion so grand, but
the way Tottenham strutted their stuff in Suffolk that evening drew
from the national press comparisons with the Dutch 'Total Football'
teams of the 1970 and 1974 World Cup tournaments. Spurs boss Ardiles
had long hailed that '74 team as the one whose standards he aspired to
reach.

Unlike with the Dutch, the Jules Rimet trophy wasn't on offer for
Spurs, just three points. The world wasn't watching. It wasn't live on
TV. There wasn't even a *Match of the Day* highlights programme that
night. Tottenham's offering was exclusive to those who had paid for their
tickets and made the trip to East Anglia. And what an offering it was.

The Portman Road pitch could have been made of velvet but it would not have been creased, so delicate was every Spurs touch, so smooth their every pass. Manchester United may have halted their progress three days earlier, but there had been a maturity about Tottenham's performance against the champions. If they could align that with the attacking prowess and goalscoring verve demonstrated in the victories against Sheffield Wednesday and Everton, there was every reason to hope Spurs could get back to winning ways.

However, at this moment, this was a stubborn and defensive Ipswich side. Under John Lyall – a manager who guided West Ham to FA Cup success in 1975 and 1980 and to the European Cup-Winners' Cup Final in 1976 – Ipswich had done what they needed to do to stay in the Premiership. Just. A goalless draw at Blackburn on the final day of 1993/94 kept them up by a point. Lyall would actually miss this game against Spurs, leaving his coach Paul Goddard to take care of team affairs while he concentrated on trying to sign a new player for the club. Spurs had failed to get the better of Ipswich in their four meetings since the launch of the Premier League, drawing three and losing one. Tottenham, under Ardiles, had also been humiliated by Ipswich in the previous season's FA Cup; they lost 3-0 at Portman Road in the fourth round.

Ipswich had no shortage of experience in defence, with 37-year-old former Scotland international John Wark – who had starred alongside Ardiles in the 1981 film *Escape to Victory* – as their captain. Up front, 24-year-old striker Chris Kiwomya had a burgeoning reputation that would see him go on to seal a £1.25m move to Arsenal in February 1995 as one of George Graham's last signings. In midfield Bulgaria international Bontcho Guentchev already had cult hero status among Town fans. They would chant his name to the tune of the 1993 UK No.1 'No Limit' by 2 Unlimited. The eurodance anthem had these lyrics:

No, no.
No, no, no, no.
No, no, no, no.
No, no, there's no limit

which Town fans changed to:

Bontcho.
Bontcho, Bontcho.
Bontcho, Bontcho.
Bontcho, Bontcho, Guentchev!

Aged 30, he had played against Klinsmann's Germany in the summer's World Cup quarter-finals, coming on in the final minute at Giants Stadium in New York as Bulgaria caused a huge shock. With 15 minutes to go they were still trailing to a Lothar Matthäus penalty before goals from Hristo Stoichkov and Yordan Letchkov turned the match on its head as they won 2-1 to reach the semi-finals. Guentchev was sent on so late in that game that he can't claim to have had much bearing on the result, but he had played a key role in the last 16, successfully scoring from the spot in a shoot-out as Bulgaria beat Mexico 3-1 on penalties after a 1-1 draw.

For the fourth match in succession, Tottenham's starting line-up was unchanged: Walker; Kerslake, Campbell, Nethercott, Edinburgh; Calderwood; Anderton, Barmby, Dumitrescu, Sheringham, Klinsmann. As a player, 'Ossie's Dream' was fulfilled by winning the 1981 FA Cup. Tonight these 11 men would help him achieve his managerial dream as his footballing philosophy reached its zenith.

Break these players in half and you'd have found the words of Tottenham's Double-winning captain Danny Blanchflower's famous quote writ through them like a stick of rock. 'The game is about glory. It's about doing things in style, with a flourish, about going out and beating the other lot, not waiting for them to die of boredom.' It was as though Ardiles had made them each write it out 100 times on the dressing-room walls before taking to the pitch; as though he had forced them to stand in front of the mirror and contemplate the motto scribed beneath the cockerel on their shirts: *Audere est Facere.* To Dare Is To Do.

For fans who hadn't been alive to watch Tottenham's two title-winning teams, this felt like a brief glimpse into the legend of the Push and Run team of 1951 and the glory of the Double ten years later. Tonight those supporters were housed in the upper tier of the Cobbold Stand. Their heroes danced and darted beneath them, the lightning white flashes of their shirts criss-crossing a lush green August turf. It was Brian Clough who said, 'If God had wanted football played in the sky he would have put grass there.' Clough – and no doubt the Supreme Being too if he was watching – would both have enjoyed this game. Spurs kept the ball exactly where the grass had been put.

Ardiles has often spoken of being a firm believer that one moment, one split second, can shape a career. He's described how for his own career, his own life, that moment happened as a player in an international for Argentina against Peru. It wasn't a great goal, or even one of his trademark mazy runs, but a nutmeg: a moment of showboating, of entertainment. The fact that it came against one of the legends of his era, Peru midfielder Teofilio Cubillas, he says made it extra special. The ball was deep in Argentina's half and Ardiles admits he was taking a huge gamble; if he had been dispossessed by Cubillas, his opponent could well have scored for Peru. If that had happened, says Ardiles, he wouldn't have played in and won the World Cup, and he wouldn't have ended up being signed by Tottenham. He pulled off the trick successfully, and that got everyone talking about his talents.

His football philosophy was moulded by his 1978 World Cup-winning manager César Menotti. In his homeland it's called *La Nuestra*; it's all about playing beautiful football, it prioritises touch and keeping possession. In his 2009 autobiography, *Ossie's Dream*, he explains that Menotti was insistent on winning the ball as quickly as possible. When the team didn't have the ball they had to make it as difficult as possible for the opposition and try to get it back as soon as they could. They did this by playing *al achique*, which basically means pressing, but pressing in a way that reduces the size of the pitch and makes the playing area as small as possible. When the team has the ball they have to try to open up the pitch as much as they can. When the opponents have it, they must close it down as much as possible.

Ardiles says this is exactly what the Netherlands team of 1974 did. 'One of the best teams I've seen in my life,' he says. 'For this to work,' adds Ardiles, 'you need intelligent players, players who know how to make decisions and play each and every ball with that intelligence.' On this occasion, particularly in the first half against Ipswich, so many of his Tottenham players exhibited that intelligence. The 'Famous Five' were at their fluid best. The orchestrator of so much of their good work was Ilie Dumitrescu, who enjoyed what would prove to be his most impressive game in a Tottenham shirt.

Tuesday 30 August, 1994
FA Carling Premiership
Ipswich Town 1-3 Tottenham Hotspur
Kiwomya 86
Klinsmann 14, 38, Dumitrescu 28
Just five minutes in Dumitrescu comes close to scoring. Deep in Spurs territory, Stuart Nethercott takes on his man and beats him before spraying a beautiful pass out to the Romanian on the left. Okay, Nethercott might not have performed a nutmeg, and his opponent isn't of the calibre of Peru's Cubillas, but Ardiles is no doubt proud of the confidence displayed by his young charge.

As Nethercott's pass finds Dumitrescu, he cushions it dead, pushes it forward and charges into the box. He then ups and slows the tempo, changing the gears three or four times: changing direction too, dipping to the left and to the right, then to the left again, and so on; he's like Muhammad Ali with an opponent on the ropes, just waiting for the perfect moment to deliver the knockout blow. Toying with the Town defence, no one knows what Dumitrescu will do next. Then, when the space is there, suddenly he unleashes a vicious curling shot. As it heads towards Craig Forrest's goal it looks like it has the beating of the Canada international. It spins just wide of the post. Dumitrescu is inches away from a spectacular first goal for his new club.

Minutes later he comes even closer. Again he has the Ipswich defence in a trance, hypnotised by his dancing feet, mesmerised by his bobs and weaves. This time there is definitely nothing Forrest can do as the shot comes in, but Dumitrescu's effort cannons off the crossbar and away to safety. They should already be 2-0 up and in the 14th minute Tottenham do take the lead. Nicky Barmby is the instigator this time. He chips an exquisite pass forward to Teddy Sheringham, who has timed his run to perfection. Ipswich's defenders are caught flat-footed as they appeal in vain for offside. Sheringham now has time, space and options.

Earlier in the day he has been able to celebrate a recall to the England squad for the following week's friendly against the USA at Wembley, the news providing a timely boost for a striker whose confidence may well have been dented by penalty misses in his last two Tottenham games.

As Sheringham bears down on goal from a tight angle on the right, he has just Forrest to beat from six yards. He could take the shot on, but unselfishly he slides it across to Jürgen Klinsmann, who is lurking to tap in his fourth goal for Spurs. Klinsmann runs towards the Spurs fans to his left and pumps both fists in delight. One by one Sheringham, Barmby and then Darren Anderton stream over to join him and offer a congratulatory hug.

Having been run ragged for the opening quarter of an hour, Ipswich almost haul themselves back into the game immediately. Guentchev gives the Town fans their first opportunity to chant his name, as he crashes in a 20-yarder which Ian Walker splendidly palms away.

By the half-hour mark Spurs have doubled their lead with a move which starts in their own six-yard box. Justin Edinburgh intercepts a cross deep inside Tottenham's area and calmly clears the ball. A few passes later it's with Sheringham, still deep inside the Spurs half on the right-hand side of the pitch. He moves into opposition territory and then plays the ball directly ahead of him to Klinsmann, who takes a touch, looks up and sees Dumitrescu charging down the left and into the area. Klinsmann's delivery is brilliant. He hits the kind of pinpoint cross-field pass which will one day become a trademark of David Beckham's latter years, a sweeping 40-yarder into the area which drops perfectly for Dumitrescu to fling himself at and send a diving header beyond the helpless Forrest. 2-0 Spurs.

Dumitrescu has his first goal for Spurs: one thoroughly deserved after a magnificent start to this game. He charges across to the stand where the Spurs fans are seated, and raises his arms towards the upper tier. Sheringham is the first to catch him, grabbing him from behind. Klinsmann, Colin Calderwood, Anderton and Barmby are next on the scene in that order. Tonight Dumitrescu's team-mates are revelling in his talents.

Ten minutes later it's 3-0. There's an element of fortune for Spurs. They take a quick corner on the left with Ipswich immediately regaining possession, but referee Rodger Gifford orders Spurs to retake it. This time Anderton knocks it long, curling an inswinger with his right boot towards the near post. There Nethercott leaps to glance a back-header across goal to the far post, where from about three yards out Klinsmann volleys home. Klinsmann wheels away to his right to celebrate, high-fiving with Sheringham, then Barmby, before a two-handed high-five with David Kerslake. He then trots back across towards the side of the pitch from which the corner was taken and engulfs Nethercott in a bear hug. It's the second time in three games that Nethercott has laid on a goal for Klinsmann with a header.

'I can't remember that goal as clearly as the Everton one,' says Stuart Nethercott. 'But I do remember how well we played that night. Some of our stuff, particularly in the first half, was beautiful. If we could have bottled that and delivered it every week then we'd have won the league, and won it in some style too. It was a night when everything clicked. Ossie was purring afterwards. We should have scored far more, really.'

One man who followed Tottenham closely in 1994/95 was commentator Jonathan Pearce. He worked on 24 Spurs matches that season. Today he is one of the BBC's leading commentators on *Match of the Day*. He has commentated on pretty much every showpiece occasion the sport has to offer, including European Championships and World Cups. He first came to prominence in the 1990s on London radio station Capital Gold, where he had a style all of his own. He understood that every match meant something to the fans, and brought every occasion to life with his impassioned commentary.

'My overall memory of what it was like to follow Spurs that season? The word I would choose would be very simple – it was fun. It was great fun commentating on them,' he says. 'It was just a joyous expression of football and the way you believed it should be played. You've got to remember the whole Gullit, Zola, Bergkamp, Henry explosion hadn't happened yet. We've become blasé about these great players. You felt watching Spurs that season that, "Wow, this is what it can be like from here on in. This is what the Premier League can become." It was thrilling. We always got stick at Capital because when we started out Arsenal had won the league and everyone accused us of being an Arsenal station. Then Tottenham won the FA Cup in 1991 and everyone accused us of being Spurs. Then we had the Chelsea revolution in the mid to late 90s and everyone said we were biased towards them. We couldn't win.

'I've felt close to a lot of London clubs at times: close to Arsenal, close to West Ham, close to Chelsea, close to Spurs, close to Palace – where I had a season ticket because my now wife is a Palace fan and so are my in-laws. I've never supported any of those clubs. I've never supported Spurs, yet in 1994/95 I felt my job let me be among the Spurs fans and share in the fun of it all. And that really is the word, it was great fun.'

As the players celebrate the third while the clock ticks over into the 40th minute, it seems highly unlikely that Tottenham's scoring for the night is now complete. It's no exaggeration to say that by the final whistle they should be in double figures. Klinsmann should have six, Dumitrescu three, and Barmby, Anderton and Sheringham should all be on the scoresheet. However, Tottenham's finishing fails to match their passing and build-up play in the second half. Sheringham and Klinsmann both miss one-on-ones, with Anderton hitting the post.

So fluid is Tottenham's performance that every single outfield player has a role in at least one of the attacking moves. At times it seems like Tottenham are giving themselves too many options. One move, sparked when Sheringham intercepts and works his way into the box, ends with the Spurs skipper being joined by Anderton, Klinsmann, Barmby and Dumitrescu in the area: the entire 'Famous Five' queuing up for a shot. The duty falls to Dumitrescu, but he can't beat Forrest to make it 4-0.

Ipswich, to their credit, refuse to be completely overawed. They force Walker into several fine saves and keep the pressure on Campbell and Nethercott, who impress onlookers to the extent that they are being talked about by some in the press as a possible future centre-back pairing for England. As well as the failure to add to the goal tally in the second half, the other disappointment is that Spurs fail to keep their first clean sheet of the season. With just over four minutes to go Kiwomya strikes for Ipswich. Either side of the goal Walker has to make sharp reaction saves, another reminder that despite Tottenham's breathtaking football, they remain so fragile.

The final whistle blows. 3-1 to Spurs. Even with the six-point deduction, three wins from the first four games means Spurs are now finally in credit on the league table. They are in plenty of credit too with the media, sports writers and broadcasters left wowed by what they've seen at Portman Road. Portman perfection. Ardiles tells the press, 'It was some of the purest football I have ever seen from a club side – the sort of football I dream about. We are a beautiful team going forward. I see no reason why we can't go out and entertain like this every week.'

The headline in *The Independent* tomorrow will read: 'KLINSMANN DOUBLES THE DAMAGE; TOTTENHAM'S IMPORTS WORK WONDERS'. Mark Burton says: 'Tottenham's insistence on accentuating the positive put their effective points tally above zero last night, courtesy of a devastating first-half display of attacking football. Accountants of the smaller clubs might rub their hands at the sight of Tottenham charabancs full of charismatics heading into town to pack their ground to the rafters, but they do not have to take into account the effect the five-man Spurs attack can have on opposing defenders. They tend to swoon.'

The Guardian will go with 'ALL KLINSMANN ON THE EASTERN FRONT'. Russell Thomas hails a 'refreshing attack-orientated approach with which Tottenham are enriching the English game.' In the *Daily Mail*, under the headline 'HAPPY ARDILES HAILS HIS BEAUTIFUL SPURS AFTER A FOOTBALL MASTERCLASS', Brian Scovell pens the following: 'The whole team played brilliantly, rotating around like the great Dutch teams of the 1970s.'

Ipswich's Guentchev tells the press: 'Spurs are not only the most exciting team in the country, they are the best. Sure, they can be champions, why not? United are not as good as they were last season. Right now Tottenham are the best in the Premiership. Jürgen Klinsmann was magnificent, but I also admired Teddy Sheringham, Ilie Dumitrescu and Darren Anderton.'

With hindsight though, was everyone getting carried away? At the end of the season Ipswich would be relegated, having finished bottom of the table and endured a series of thrashings. There were no fewer than five 4-1 defeats to Nottingham Forest, Everton, Blackburn, Arsenal and Sheffield Wednesday. There was a 4-0 reverse at Leeds, and of course the humiliating 9-0 loss at Old Trafford in March 1995 – still a Premier League record defeat.

And yet this was a team that was also capable of a 3-2 win over Manchester United at Portman Road, just three weeks after Spurs visited. In January they would also become the first team all season to win at Anfield as they beat Liverpool 1-0. Before Spurs arrived in East Anglia, Ipswich's form was more than respectable. They had lost 1-0 at home to a very good Nottingham Forest side on the opening day of the season, but had then picked up four points on the road, courtesy of a 1-1 draw at Wimbledon and a 2-1 win at QPR.

Ipswich didn't play all that badly against Spurs; it was more a case of Spurs playing extremely well. Looking back on that night, Darren Anderton says: 'We should have won by nine or ten. The first half was the best football I think I have ever been part of. We just kept going. It was absolute madness. Obviously it worked out that they weren't a good team over the course of the season, but to do what we did to them in that first half was still something. We should have been 6-0 up in that first 20 minutes. It was just ruthless, we absolutely annihilated them.'

David Howells – still being overlooked by Ardiles – had travelled with the team even though he wasn't in the squad. 'One game I do remember watching very well is Ipswich away, which was probably the best performance for a long time,' he says. 'Dumitrescu was outstanding and we won comfortably. It was like a team from a different world playing. I was thinking, I want to be playing in that, that's how football should be played.'

Tottenham's performance that night may also have been aided by the new rules brought in at the summer's World Cup clamping down on tackling from behind. Teddy Sheringham told the press after the game that he definitely thought it was having a bearing on English football: 'It has been good news for a team like us, who want to play an attacking, passing game,' he said. 'It encourages positive play. Defenders can't just clatter front players now. And the benefits for a team like us will be immense. I am sure, for instance, that we will pick up fewer injuries. And it means our game can flow.' The new rules helped Klinsmann to shed his reputation as a diver, because there was no longer such a need for forward players to accentuate when they had been fouled. Defenders couldn't get away with so much and with less rough treatment being handed out, forwards felt they didn't have to overemphasise every challenge on them to make sure that referees took action before they got hurt.

Everything seemed to be coming together at just the right time for Spurs, and for the supporters who had made the trip along the A12 to East Anglia this was a night to savour. The away contingent at Portman Road were vociferous throughout. Tottenham had hit their stride straight from kick-off and were relentless for the entirety of the first half. The supporters were equally consistent. The noise never let up.

It ended in heartbreak, and many Spurs fans will never forgive him for the way he left, but Sol Campbell insists the abuse that he gets from some today doesn't detract from his memory of the bond between Spurs players and fans, particularly in that season of 1994/95. As the entire team made its way over to the Spurs fans at Ipswich, saluting their presence, applauding their support, grabbing and kissing the cockerel crests on their shirts and pounding their chests, players and supporters knew they had been united in something special.

'That season was all about excitement,' says Campbell. 'It was about bringing back the good old days of football, proper football. That was the key. You need to engage with the fans and vice versa. Buying those players showed the ambition. The fans could see that ambition. It was a great time. It was fun. It was fun to be around the ground and the training ground and know that you could compete football-wise with the top teams.'

Campbell feels that the atmosphere at most grounds today has deteriorated. In the early to mid-90s venues were continuing their transformation into the all-seater stadiums of the modern day, grounds which to many now feel soulless. 'One of the main things today is that standing has gone,' says Campbell. 'Celtic have brought back a little bit of standing. I honestly feel that's a good thing. If it's all done right, and also there is no more fencing now to crush people, fans can spill on to the pitch if, God forbid, there is something going on. I think in ten years' time that's gonna come back in the Premier League at all clubs. It will add atmosphere; you can have a cheaper ticket too, it will help supporters if they can't spend so much. I think just some home fans standing would be a good thing.'

At Ipswich, the Tottenham travelling contingent had been in a seated section, but most were on their feet throughout. Away fans generally create more atmosphere than those at home. Those who make the trip, especially on a weekday evening, tend to be the more dedicated supporters; having committed to an away day they will be determined to sing and enjoy themselves no matter what their team does on the pitch. A good performance, never mind a win, is a bonus.

These days, as club commentator, Daniel Wynne is at nearly every game, and even before taking on that role – as a lifelong fan – he rarely missed a match home or away, but he had good reason not to be at Portman Road: 'My son was born on the morning of the Ipswich game. He was our first child and I wasn't allowed to go,' he says. 'My friend turned up in the hospital that afternoon with a teddy bear, and we called it Jürgen. Years later, when Klinsmann came back for the Tribute Trust game against DC United in October 2002, I was invited to be one of the trustees of the Tribute Trust, which was set up to help former players. He came over the day before and there were some opportunities for photos;

I managed to get one with him and my son holding that teddy bear as well. That was quite a special moment. I had a chance to meet him and have a quick chat. He was genuine, it was clear what Tottenham meant to him. I've got the programme from the Ipswich game and know that it was one of the most complete performances, certainly away from The Lane, that we had seen for quite some time. The first half we absolutely destroyed them, but Tottenham being Tottenham didn't actually finish it off by keeping a clean sheet – that would be too much to ask.'

It wasn't just with his goals that Klinsmann was winning over the public and the media. His jokes at his first press conference and his dive celebration had played a part, and many were also impressed by seeing him pootle round London in a 1967 VW Beetle – not your average Premier League footballer's choice of wheels.

'Jürgen was just brilliant for Tottenham and brilliant for English football,' says Jonathan Pearce. 'When he was manager of Germany in 2006, nearly ten years after he had last been in England, we went out there to do a feature for the BBC before the World Cup. At the time the German press didn't like how he was running the team. Some of the fans even had "Klinsmann Out" banners on the day of the game – it was a friendly against USA in Dortmund. We didn't have an interview booked with him, but he saw me and he still remembered me from covering Spurs in the 90s. He came over and said hello. I think he is a really approachable, open man. He is just in love with the game. I don't think he's so in love with the politics of the game, but he's in love with the game. He just loves the thrill of it all.

'In interviews you could talk to him about things outside of football. You could talk to him about his Beetle. I think he was off to do a trek around America in it. He would let you get to know him as a person. That doesn't happen so much in football these days. He was genuine. He won the Capital Gold London Player of the Year, which was voted for by fans. Every season with that award it would be close. You would get a leading West Ham player, a leading Arsenal player, a leading Tottenham player and it would split the vote. With Klinsmann though, he united the voters. He was way clear. I remember giving him the trophy; this is a man who had lifted the World Cup for his country five years earlier, and when I gave him it, honestly, genuinely, he treated it almost like I was giving him the World Cup again. He was so pleased to get an award from London football fans. He was truly grateful.

'The fact that he remembered me so many years later really stood out to me. I'm not sure any of the Spurs players would know me from Adam today, except perhaps Harry Kane. There is something of Klinsmann's temperament in him. I think Harry Kane has that rapport. I think he understands it, he gets it because he is one of their own. He doesn't walk past you, he says hello. And it's just a little thing, just a tiny, minuscule thing. If you're in the stadium waiting to go on air beforehand and the players walk around the pitch, most of them will just walk past you. Harry, though, will always say hello. He is a throwback.'

Yes, a throwback to the joys of 1994/95. As the Tottenham fans filtered out of Portman Road that night few could wait to see their team play again. There followed, though, the frustration of a 13-day break for international fixtures before Tottenham's next game. Anderton and the recalled Sheringham would be joining up with Terry Venables and England for a friendly with the USA, while Klinsmann would be leaving the morning after the Ipswich match to play for Germany in a friendly against Russia in Moscow.

Spirits were soaring at Spurs, and the share price was too. Following Klinsmann's two goals against Ipswich it rose by 19p. Klinsmann was said to have added £9m to the value of Spurs in the 34 days since he signed. The club was now valued at £24m on the Stock Exchange, with shares at an all-time high of £1.51. Two days after the Ipswich game they rose again to £1.58. Had Ardiles set up his own company at this point, and perhaps called it *La Nuestra Inc.*, its profits would have been soaring too. Whatever it sold, perhaps Liquid Football smoothies, the queues would have streamed around the block – so willing were many right now to buy into his philosophy after what they had witnessed at Ipswich.

The 'Famous Five' could do no wrong, and at its apex was a new Tottenham hero who just couldn't stop scoring. Jürgen Klinsmann now had five goals in four games; it would have been six but for the wrongful offside flag against Manchester United. Perhaps it would have been eight if he'd been taking the penalties instead of Sheringham.

On a summer night in Suffolk, Spurs supporters had seen their team reach footballing nirvana. As the sun set behind the stadium during the match, the glow of the floodlights captured Ipswich defenders chasing the Spurs shadows in desperation. It was a beautifully still evening, perfect for football. A sunset of pink, orange and red hues dappled the East Anglian skyline. For Spurs it had been Portman perfection. For 90 minutes at least, Ardiles' philosophy of *La Nuestra* had been a reality in the rarefied confines of England's top division. The future looked bright. But for one member of the 'Famous Five' – Ilie Dumitrescu – and for Ardiles himself, it would never be quite this good again.

5

On the Slide

'Winning breeds confidence. When you're on a run, you just feel like you can win every week. Unfortunately it works the other way too.' (Darren Anderton)

O N that night at Portman Road, Tottenham fans had seen fantasy football. Ossie's dream appeared close to becoming a reality. In the season's first game Sheffield Wednesday had scored three, so Spurs had gone and scored four. Everton had then been played off the park and Jürgen had hit a goal from another planet. Tottenham had been unlucky to lose to Manchester United, and then came Portman perfection. Spurs were on a roll. But now it was time for an international break.

Wednesday 7 September, 1994
International Friendly
England 2-0 USA
Shearer 33, 40
Terry Venables plays Tottenham pair Darren Anderton and Teddy Sheringham from the start. Anderton lasts the full 90 minutes on the right of midfield. Sheringham, up top alongside Blackburn's Alan Shearer, is replaced by Arsenal's Ian Wright with ten minutes to go. Shearer gets both goals as England's preparations for Euro 96 continue with a comfortable win.

A host of players are away with their respective countries, so Ossie Ardiles is virtually alone on the Spurs training ground. Klinsmann is with

Germany in Moscow. He sets up his country's only goal in a 1-0 friendly win over Russia. Stefan Kuntz is the scorer. During the international break Klinsmann receives Germany's Footballer of the Year award, finishing ahead of Lothar Matthäus who is second and Matthias Sammer who's third. It's the second time he's won the award, the previous occasion being in 1988 when he was with VfB Stuttgart.

Even in Klinsmann's absence, Spurs are still reaping the rewards. Tottenham merchandising manager Kay Lyons is quoted in the press, saying that the last time Spurs experienced anything like this demand for shirts was when Gazza and Gary Lineker returned from the 1990 World Cup. She says Klinsmann is outselling those two put together, and that shirts are being sold as soon as they are put on the shelves.

Friday 9 September, 1994

A third World Cup star signs for Tottenham. Alan Sugar has paid Dutch club PSV Eindhoven £2.9m for Ilie Dumitrescu's Romania team-mate Gheorghe Popescu. Gica Popescu, as he's more commonly known, plays in central defence for his country but is likely to be used in midfield by Spurs. The Spurs chairman – who has now shelled out £7.6m on his three big names – is determined that the news of the signing again creates maximum impact.

In Monaco he made sure the camera crews and photographers were tipped off about Klinsmann. They were at the harbour in time to capture the now famous picture of the chairman and his World Cup star striker beside his yacht. This time Sugar tells the media he's sent his private jet to collect Popescu from Eindhoven. The player will be landing within the hour. By the time the jet touches down, the press have gathered by the runway. Popescu walks down the steps and conducts his first interview the moment he touches the tarmac.

The skies are grey and threatening. Popescu's curly mop of hair is blowing in a fierce wind, which is picked up by the cameraman's microphone as he says in faltering English: 'I think that Tottenham are very good. They are a very big club. Dumitrescu, my friend, plays at Tottenham and I come here to play very good football. I try to play very good football with the players.' Stony-faced throughout the interview, he doesn't exactly look pleased to be here. Perhaps Spurs need some of that meanness, though, whether it be in midfield or defence. Where Klinsmann and Dumitrescu have brought joy, Popescu can add steel and make the opposition frown.

'Gica Popescu was just a ridiculous footballer,' says Anderton, drawing out the 'rid' in ridiculous to give full emphasis to just how highly he regarded him. 'Some of the things he did on the training ground, and in matches, were unbelievable. He just sat there in the centre of midfield and made everything happen. Of course, with hindsight, it was clear he was only ever going to be there for one year. We were just a stop-gap for him to get to Barcelona. That's how good he was.'

David Howells agrees: 'He was a very good player, you could see that straight away. I always thought he was a centre-half. He wanted to play in centre midfield for Tottenham. When Barcelona come knocking … Well you know, it's Barcelona, simple as that. They saw him as a centre-half too, and he went on there and had a very good career as a centre-half. He was a Rolls-Royce of a footballer. Assured touch, always saw the pass. Much more suited to the English game than Ilie Dumitrescu. He was top drawer.'

Popescu continues his interview on the runway. 'What did Dumitrescu say to you?' one reporter asks Popescu. 'He said Tottenham is a very good club, a very nice club, and Ardiles a very good man. And we played well against the English champions Man United. I feel very good commitment and I decide to come here to play with Dumitrescu and Klinsmann and the other players.'

One newspaper reckons Popescu is the 'final piece in the puzzle' for Ardiles. Tottenham are said to be building a 'foreign legion' that can 'take the league by storm'. He is a quality player, no doubt. He looks older than his 26 years. He's already been voted Romania's Footballer of the Year four times and has won 55 caps for his country. He's been a league champion in his home country, and twice with PSV Eindhoven in the Netherlands.

Saturday 10 September, 1994

With the international break out of the way, Tottenham can look forward to matches against Southampton at home and Leicester away: two teams in the bottom five in a season in which four teams will be going down in order to trim the Premiership from 22 clubs to 20.

Klinsmann is named the Carling Player of the Month for August. It's hardly a surprise. He's scored five goals in his first four games for the club. His personality has made just as big an impact as his goalscoring. He plays with a smile on his face. He's charmed the fans and the press. There's been no diving. The histrionics for which he became infamous with English fans have been notable for their absence.

To mark his achievement as Player of the Month, Klinsmann is given a small trophy bearing the sponsor's name, a magnum of champagne and a cheque for £750. He donates the money to Great Ormond Street

Hospital. It's no wonder the league's title sponsors want to attach their name to a player who has taken the Premiership by storm. Barely a day goes by when Klinsmann isn't in the papers. Everyone wants their say on English football's newest star.

Monday 12 September, 1994
FA Carling Premiership
Tottenham Hotspur 1-2 Southampton
Klinsmann 6
Le Tissier (pen) 75, 89
Campbell sent off 74

Not only does everyone want their say on Klinsmann, everyone wants to see him play. As the building continues on the South Stand, the construction workers appear to be doing some overtime tonight. They're still on site as this game gets under way at 8pm on Sky TV. It's the first time the television audience will get to see Klinsmann in a live game this season. Before kick-off he is handed his Player of the Month award and is heartily applauded by the majority of the 22,387 in attendance at White Hart Lane.

There's no debut for Popescu, who has been forced to return to the Netherlands to await his work permit and international clearance before he is allowed to don the Spurs shirt for the first time.

Whatever happened to Portman perfection? This is so far from perfect. The television audience must be wondering what all the fuss is about regarding the 'Famous Five' and Klinsmann. This is Tottenham's first poor performance of the season. Is the international break to blame? Has it disrupted things on the training ground? Is it complacency? Have Spurs started to believe the hype?

It starts well. Klinsmann puts Spurs ahead in the sixth minute – his sixth goal in five games. Edinburgh hits a long ball out of defence straight down the middle. Klinsmann and Francis Benali give chase. Klinsmann is too strong and too fast. He shrugs Benali off and surges into the box. Saints keeper Bruce Grobbelaar is alert to the danger. He's quick off his line and narrows the angle, blocking Klinsmann's shot on the penalty spot. The ball cannons off Grobbelaar's legs all the way back to Anderton, who is about 25 yards out. He shoots first time and it hits Benali, who is standing just in front of the grounded Grobbelaar. It falls for Klinsmann again, who this time dispatches a fierce first-time shot straight back into the net from about 15 yards out. 1-0 up inside six minutes. It's easy pickings. It looks as if it's going to be like the Ipswich game all over again.

But no, it goes horribly wrong. Spurs are being overrun in midfield. Former Spur Paul Allen is bossing proceedings on his old stomping ground. Allen, Jim Magilton and Neil Maddison take control as Tottenham fail to get themselves into the game.

Matt Le Tissier forces Walker into several fine saves, but somehow, with just over a quarter of an hour remaining, Spurs are still leading. Then referee Alan Wilkie rules that Sol Campbell has fouled Neil Heaney in the box. It looks harsh. Replays appear to show Campbell touched the ball first, and that the incident happened outside the box anyway. Campbell is sent off. Le Tissier – as he always does – scores the penalty. Walker gets a glove to it but can't keep it out. Campbell will now be suspended too.

It gets worse for Spurs two minutes from time. An absolute howler from Nethercott. He swings at Jeff Kenna's cross and completely misses the ball. It drops to Le Tissier six yards out. He doesn't miss those. It finishes 2-1 to the visitors: Southampton's first win of the season.

'Everyone thought it was going to be a party and we were in the role of the patsies,' Saints boss Alan Ball tells the press afterwards. 'That motivated us and we could have been 5-2 ahead at half-time.' A downbeat Ardiles assesses his team's second defeat from their opening five games. 'We didn't look like our normal selves tonight. The sharpness was missing. We can play a lot better than that. It may have been a reaction to the players being away all of last week, but I'm not using that as an excuse.'

It's also the first time Klinsmann's faultless reputation since arriving in England is tarnished by accusations of diving. Klinsmann goes to ground after a tackle by Kenna, whose team-mates are angered by the way in which he hits the turf. They surround Klinsmann and shove and jostle him. Referee Wilkie talks to Klinsmann and Kenna. Sky TV commentator – former Spurs striker Clive Allen – suggests Klinsmann might have dived.

Kenna says in his post-match interview: 'Let's just say I had a little talk with him about it when it happened. I said to Klinsmann, "What are you doing? Don't cheat, don't do that sort of thing." He said he hadn't dived and that it was rubbish to suggest it. But if the referee had given anything we would have felt hard done by.'

Spurs substitute Micky Hazard, who replaces Barmby for the final 26 minutes, defends Klinsmann after the match. 'Players from other teams are over-reacting because of who he is, and I don't think that is right. Yes, the Southampton player played the ball, but he played Jürgen's foot at the same time. It was the same thing that Sol Campbell was told he had done, and not only was a penalty given for Sol's challenge but he was sent off as well. You didn't see any Spurs players around their man accusing him of cheating, did you?'

'We all looked out for each other on the pitch,' says Anderton of the way Klinsmann's team-mates protected him following the diving allegations by Southampton. 'Of course Jürgen would get some harsh treatment at times, because he was a marked man with this reputation of "Oh, he's gonna dive", so referees wouldn't give him certain decisions. Later in my career it happened with David Ginola as well. Especially in those early weeks with Jürgen I think his reputation counted against him, and referees were reluctant to give decisions that they really should have given.'

Having missed the Ipswich game, supporter Daniel Wynne certainly remembers the mistake from Nethercott that gifted Saints their late winner. 'It was my first game back at The Lane after my then wife had our first baby. It was also my birthday. I was ill and I shouldn't have gone, but my wife said, "Just go."

'I went along and in the last minute, Nethercott dropped that clanger and ruined my birthday, so I've never forgiven him for that,' he laughs. 'I've met him, and I told him that – he knows I'm joking. I don't think any player that pulls on a Tottenham shirt isn't trying his hardest. Some make mistakes. Some aren't up to it. I'm not someone who likes to get on the back of your own players. If you look up the definition of the word "support", you are there to help and encourage.'

Saturday 17 September, 1994
FA Carling Premiership
Leicester City 3-1 Tottenham Hotspur

Joachim 45, 90, Lowe 86
Klinsmann 88

Defeat to Southampton, now defeat to Leicester. Spurs have been found out. Plenty of style. No substance. No discipline. No organisation. No chance for the defenders. Popescu still hasn't got international clearance. Spurs need him because they've got no balance in midfield.

Three days shy of his 20th birthday, Leicester striker Julian Joachim is the star of the show. He's been dropped from the starting line-up for the previous two games, but he's back today. What talent he has. His first goal of the afternoon is sheer quality. He wins a 50/50 with Calderwood on the left side of Tottenham's area, charges into the box and curls a right-footed effort around Walker and just inside the far post. Just before half-time. Perfect moment for Leicester to go 1-0 up.

Just as they were against Southampton, Spurs are stretched again. Dumitrescu has gone missing. At the back Nethercott is being given the run-around by Joachim. The visitors are still in it, though, until four minutes before full time when Joachim feeds substitute David Lowe.

He's only been on the field for five minutes. He's been left unmarked on the left. He surges into the box, checks back and whips a beautiful curling shot with his right boot from the corner of the area, across Walker and dropping into the net at the far post.

There's still time for Klinsmann to get his customary goal, and it's another spectacular one. The build-up is almost identical to Gary Lineker's for England against West Germany in the Italia 90 World Cup semi-final. Teddy Sheringham, just as Paul Parker did for England, gets the perfect weight and direction on a lofted pass from the right. Klinsmann – further out than Lineker – takes it down in a similar fashion, allowing it to come across his body to his left. Whereas Lineker waited for it to drop and sent a daisy-cutter across goal into the bottom corner, Klinsmann hits it on the bounce into the far top corner. It's more eye-catching than Lineker's, though of course not as significant.

It keeps up Klinsmann's record of having scored in all but one of Tottenham's games. He's got seven in six now.

There's only one Jürgen Klinsmann,
One Jürgen Klinsmann,
Walking along,
Singing a song,
Walking in a Klinsmann wonderland.

Is a comeback on the cards? Sadly not. Joachim seals it for Leicester in the final minute. Again he is too fast and too sharp for Nethercott. He beats him into the box and sends a low shot beyond Walker at his near post. It finishes 3-1. It's the first time newly-promoted Leicester have won this season. It's their first-ever Premier League win. Last time out Spurs gifted Southampton their first win of the season; this time they gift Leicester theirs.

Leicester boss Brian Little is glowing in his praise of Joachim afterwards: 'Joachim is still only 19. There is nobody in the country who has what he has, apart from perhaps Robbie Fowler. Who knows how good he can become?' he says. 'I dropped him last time because in the previous two games he hadn't had a single shot. I decided it would be better for him to have a little look from the sidelines. He's not the ideal team player. He's more of an individual.'

For Spurs, their brightest individual is starting to show the first signs of frustration. 'We were not aggressive enough,' says Klinsmann, who has been seen clearly remonstrating with some of his team-mates throughout the match at Filbert Street. 'We have to think about fighting for the ball, especially at the beginning of the game, instead of trying to play. We didn't do that against Leicester and that's the reason why we lost the match. We have to remain positive and learn from our mistakes, and against Leicester there were a few.'

Back-to-back defeats to Southampton and Leicester, hardly heavyweights of the Premiership, mean the press are now ready to get stuck into Ardiles. 'We did not earn the right to play against Leicester,' he says. 'I like to see beautiful things but I also like my team to be difficult to play against.' There's been scant evidence of that so far.

'Klinsmann was a true gent, but don't get me wrong – he would get upset if you lost a game,' laughs Sol Campbell. 'If it was a really bad game he used to go into a massive kind of a huff. Rightly so, because we'd lost the game. Sometimes he would just walk straight off into the showers and talk to nobody. For me it was quite a scene to see. I could handle it but managers maybe at the time would think, "What? He's just going into the shower, not talking to anyone." He was upset, understandably; everyone has different characters. He'd seen the best. He'd been around the best. He just wanted to tell us that this is not acceptable. You're better than this. That kind of thing.'

'The Leicester game was the first real sign that it wasn't going to work for Ossie,' says Stuart Nethercott. 'We were totally exposed. We got thumped. Ossie's way of playing was always going to be attack, attack, attack, and if we conceded goals then that was going to be part and parcel of it in his eyes. In some ways he was ahead of his time, with the full-backs bombing on. But there wasn't the balance. The goals we conceded were getting very, very familiar and it was tough. I came out of the side after the Leicester game and Mabbsy [Gary Mabbutt] came back in, and the same thing was happening.'

The Leicester game was the last time Ardiles attempted his 'Famous Five' formation. Having started the first six games together, Darren Anderton, Nicky Barmby, Ilie Dumitrescu, Jürgen Klinsmann and Teddy Sheringham never appeared in the same team again.

Wednesday 21 September, 1994
Coca-Cola League Cup, 2nd Round, 1st Leg
Watford 3-6 Tottenham Hotspur

Ramage 1, Mooney 65, Mabbutt (og) 90
Anderton 4, Klinsmann 17, 34, 45, Sheringham 74, Dumitrescu 87
Porter pen (83) saved by Walker

The FA release a statement hours before kick-off. They've agreed to take the Spurs case to independent arbitration where it will be decided whether the FA Cup ban, the points deduction and the fine are justified. This is good news. Alan Sugar's belligerence is all that has forced it this far. There is a chance now that all the punishments could be overturned.

For now, though, the League Cup remains Tottenham's only realistic route to Europe. Even getting to the third round can't be taken for granted. Recent form means Spurs look ripe for a giant-killing. Beaten by Southampton, beaten by Leicester; now even beating Watford – a team from the Endsleigh League, Division One – over two legs, doesn't seem an easy prospect.

Having fielded an unchanged line-up for the opening six league matches, Ardiles rings the changes for the League Cup. Nicky Barmby is left out so this is the first time Ardiles isn't fielding the 'Famous Five'. Micky Hazard replaces Barmby. Gica Popescu has finally got international clearance and makes his debut, coming in for Calderwood as the holding midfielder. Club captain Gary Mabbutt gets the nod ahead of Stuart Nethercott in central defence and takes the armband from Teddy Sheringham. David Howells is back in the squad for the first time this season, and will have to wait for his chance from the bench.

Popescu is supposed to restore balance to the side; it's hoped he will provide a shield to stem the tide of goals against. He plays well, but the tide keeps lapping against the shore. The underdogs go ahead after just 27 seconds. Sheringham gives the ball away to David Holdsworth, who finds Tommy Mooney down the left. His cross is tucked home by Craig Ramage at the far post. 1-0 Watford.

Darren Anderton quickly equalises. Klinsmann starts the move. He back-heels it to Ilie Dumitrescu, who sets up Anderton to shoot low from outside the box. 1-1 inside four minutes. Then Klinsmann takes control of the game with his first hat-trick in English football. The perfect hat-trick of right foot, left foot and header. All scored within a 28-minute spell to send Spurs into a 4-1 half-time lead. Hazard sets up the first, Klinsmann dispatching it off the outside of his right foot beyond Watford keeper Perry Digweed. The second comes from the head – teed up by David Kerslake's cross. Then it's Dumitrescu with the back-heel, this time to Klinsmann who runs through and fires home with his left. He now has ten goals in his first seven games for Spurs.

Midway through the second half Watford make it 4-2. Sol Campbell chases a long pass with Mooney but loses his footing. Mooney rounds Ian Walker and scores.

Tottenham's nerves are eased when Sheringham restores the three-goal cushion. Nineteen-year-old midfielder Danny Hill, making his first appearance of the season having replaced Hazard ten minutes into the second half, picks out Sheringham, who beats Digweed from the edge of the box. Relief for Sheringham. Only his second goal of the season.

He's missed as many penalties as he's scored goals. 5-2 Spurs. A penalty miss is exactly what happens to Watford next. The home side have a great chance to make it 5-3 when Walker brings down Jamie Moralee with seven minutes to go. The referee opts not to send Walker off. Gary Porter steps up and drills it to Walker's right, but the keeper gets down to block it. Watford fans fume that Walker was allowed to stay on and deny them their opportunity from the spot.

Four minutes later it's 6-2. Klinsmann knocks the ball to Sheringham, who chests it into Dumitrescu's path. The Romanian strides into the box and rounds Digweed for his second goal of the season. Still the scoring isn't over. In the final minute Tottenham's defence is all at sea. Andy Hessenthaler sends the ball across goal as more of a cross than a shot; it hits Mabbutt just in front of the line and goes in. The full-time whistle blows. Spurs have won 6-3.

Klinsmann leaves the Vicarage Road dressing room clutching a match ball signed by all the players. Before he exits the stadium, he conducts a pitch-side interview for ITV's Carlton regional highlights programme, which will air tonight. ITV's lead commentator Brian Moore has been conducting the commentary. The hoopla surrounding Dumitrescu, Popescu and Klinsmann, as well as the possibility of a potential upset, means this was always going to be the headline match. Nine goals is a bonus. Fans stand respectfully behind him as Klinsmann talks to the media.

'People would rather see a 6-3 game than see you win 3-0,' he says. He later shows the written press his match ball, saying: 'This is my first memento from my time in England. It has been signed by all the players and that is very special to me. I don't have a living room full of footballs, because this seems to be an English tradition. It is a great feeling to have scored my first hat-trick in English football.'

In his press conference, Ardiles raves: 'Only the chosen few can inspire us in the way he does. Only people like Eric Cantona can do that. He's got ten goals already and there's no reason why he can't go on and score a lot more.'

Tottenham have a three-goal advantage for the second leg at White Hart Lane in a fortnight's time, but with the open football Ardiles wants his team to play, even against a Division One side, they can't be sure that will be enough.

Saturday 24 September, 1994

The pressure is on in the league. Two consecutive defeats to South-ampton and Leicester means that with the six-point deduction Spurs are second to bottom. Today they will play in-form Nottingham

Forest, who have started their first season back in the top division really well.

Dutch international midfielder Bryan Roy is rivalling Klinsmann as most-talked-about summer signing. Roy was part of the team which prevented Graham Taylor's England from qualifying for USA 94. After the tournament – in which he helped his country reach the quarter-finals – Forest paid a club record £2.9m to bring him to the City Ground from Italian club Foggia. He's only scored twice this season, but his all-round play has been impressive. Forest boss Frank Clark had initially envisaged using him on the left wing as the national team do, but is now playing him through the middle. Striker Stan Collymore is the other danger man in Clark's team. He's been on target three times to lift Forest to third place in the Premiership.

Forest have played exactly the same opponents as Spurs. Their record reads impressively: Ipswich W; Man Utd D; Leicester W; Everton W; Sheff Wed W; Southampton D – unbeaten with 14 points in third place. For Spurs it's Sheff Wed W; Everton W; Man Utd L; Ipswich W; Southampton L; Leicester L – on the slide with nine points in ninth place before the points deduction, and three points and second to bottom when it's taken into account.

Ardiles sticks with the team that beat Watford. No Barmby or Nethercott in the squad; Calderwood is on the bench. So it's Hazard and Popescu – making his Premiership debut – in central midfield. Mabbutt continues alongside Campbell at the heart of defence, flanked by Kerslake to the right and Edinburgh to the left. Up front Anderton and Dumitrescu play out wide in support of Klinsmann and Sheringham. As against Watford, with no Barmby, there's no 'Famous Five'.

FA Carling Premiership
Tottenham Hotspur 1-4 Nottingham Forest

Stone 9, Roy 52, 73, Bohinen 82

Dumitrescu 32

Sheringham pen (45) saved by Crossley

Just as Spurs did against Watford in midweek, they concede early. Collymore does the hard work for 23-year-old Steve Stone. A teasing cross to the corner of the six-yard box, where Stone hits in on the half-volley from a tight angle. 1-0 Forest. Stone, a young man who broke his leg three times before he was 21, is everything his surname proclaims him to be: resilient and sturdy, like his team. They have structure and a concrete base from which to build, but are sculpted with flair and imagination.

Flair and imagination are in plentiful supply in the goal with which Dumitrescu brings Tottenham level, just after the half-hour mark. It's a beautiful, mazy run which ends with a delightful dinked shot beyond keeper Mark Crossley. Like Klinsmann, Dumitrescu also has his own chant from the fans by now. It's not quite so inventive:

Duu-miiiiiiiiii
Duu-miiiiiiiiii

To the untrained ear it's not clear what's being said. The uninitiated ask those next to them, 'Why are they booing him?' It's the same type of chant that was used to serenade former midfielder and 1991 FA Cup winner Nayim, before he left the club for Real Zaragoza last year.

Moments later Dumitrescu is at it again in the final minute of the half. This time he's brought down in the box for a penalty. Sheringham steps up again. He missed against Everton. He missed against Man United. Now he misses against Forest. Crossley, the man who saved from Lineker in the 1991 FA Cup Final, guesses the right way to block his shot.

In the away dressing room at half-time, Frank Clark gives his star player a ticking-off. Roy is told to cut out the flicks and tricks. Stop over-elaborating. Ardiles, judging by what happens in the second half, tells his players to keep going: attack, attack, attack.

With the Spurs defence exposed it turns into a rout. Seven minutes after the break Stone sets up Roy for a brave diving header. Twenty minutes later the pair combine again, and Roy beats Walker with a delicate finish. Lars Bohinen adds flourish to the scoreline for Forest with a sumptuous long-range chip. 4-1 to Forest it finishes. Forest look a good side.

Ardiles rarely loses his temper, but a 4-1 thrashing and three consecutive Premiership defeats mean, for the first time this season, his job is seriously under threat. Angry words are exchanged in the dressing room. Spurs have conceded ten goals in eight days.

The pain of such a comprehensive defeat hovers like an unwanted guest, hangs in the air like an awkward silence. The depression of three league defeats in a row works its way into the deepest cracks between the White Hart Lane fixtures and fittings, sits there, lives there, will not be moved. Impossible to evict for at least a week, until three o'clock on Saturday arrives again and there might be a chance to put things right.

Gary Mabbutt remembers Ardiles losing his rag after the Forest game: 'It was out of character, but to be honest I think it was much needed,' he says. 'It wasn't his usual style to do that. He was usually pretty calm. I was pleased to see it. If anything we could probably have done with hearing that sort of thing from him a bit more the season before.

There were times when things needed to be said. Sometimes you need a rollicking. We'd been conceding so many goals and it had been a bad time defensively.'

Saturday 1 October, 1994

Ardiles is fearing for his job now. Sugar is continuing to fight the good fight with the FA, but if the points deduction doesn't get overturned Spurs really could be going down. The end for Ossie could come today.

If Spurs lose to Wimbledon at Selhurst Park, surely there will be no way back? The press are piling the pressure on, saying he is on his way out of the club. Wimbledon boss Joe Kinnear used to be a Spurs player. No doubt he'd fancy a crack at the job, say the media. The bookies have him priced as the favourite to replace Ardiles.

FA Carling Premiership
Wimbledon 1-2 Tottenham Hotspur

Talboys 29

Sheringham 27, Popescu 63

Ardiles rings the changes to great effect and is rewarded with a much-needed win. He switches formation to a more conventional 4-4-2. Campbell is suspended, so Kevin Scott appears for the first time since May, in the centre of defence alongside Mabbutt. Justin Edinburgh is injured, so Dean Austin makes his first appearance of the season. David Kerslake continues as the other full-back. In midfield, alongside Popescu, forgotten man Jason Dozzell – who hasn't started a game since April – is surprisingly chosen ahead of Hazard, who is on the bench. Barmby is also among the subs, having been left out altogether for the last two games. It seems Ardiles has now abandoned the 'Famous Five' for good.

A virus has swept through the Wimbledon camp. Fortunately for Klinsmann, Dumitrescu and Popescu, there will be no introduction to Vinnie Jones. The midfield hard man, who once famously grabbed Paul Gascoigne by his balls, is among those missing today. However, Wimbledon's first-choice strike pairing of Dean Holdsworth and Mick Harford have recovered in time to start.

Klinsmann takes to the field in his new Reebok Integrity Pro boots. The company has just beaten adidas to his signature. They describe their deal with Klinsmann as 'the biggest in football history', and Klinsmann as 'the most powerful property in world football'. Klinsmann is set to make £2m from Reebok, meaning that over the next two years, including his salary, bonuses and other endorsements, he is in line for a £5m windfall.

Sheringham is a man under almost as much pressure as Ardiles. There are rumours that Ardiles has become frustrated with his drop in form. Three penalty misses are unlikely to have helped his confidence.

Tottenham's cause is aided by an early mishap for Wimbledon. Central defender Alan Reeves is injured. He leaves the pitch for treatment but is desperate to come back on. Kinnear disagrees. On in his place goes 21-year-old Chris Perry for his home Premiership debut. The young man is up against World Cup winner Klinsmann.

Perry does well. Wimbledon join Man United and Forest as the only teams to stop Klinsmann scoring. There are no goals from Jürgen's new boots today. Instead it is Teddy who breaks the deadlock, with his first league goal since the opening day. And how sweetly he breaks it. This is something special. Something inventive. The kind of creativity Spurs are renowned for. Anderton sweeps in his right-side corner a yard above the ground. As it bounces, Sheringham hits it low, sending it straight in at the near post. It's clever, it's crafty, it's clearly something they've worked on. 1-0 to Spurs.

'This was the start of the corner routine that me and Teddy had,' says Anderton. 'It worked three times that season. People always talk about Sheringham and Beckham doing it at Man U, but no, it never quite ended in a goal for them. Mine and Teddy's always worked. Wimbledon was the first one, then Newcastle, then Chelsea. It worked a treat.'

Indeed it did, and the Spurs fans loved it. It was a real novelty to see a creative set piece like this, between the same two players, come off time and time again. It was Tottenham's 'thing'. When it happened a second and third time it felt like an in-joke between the Spurs players and fans, with the opposition left surprised by the routine that had been perfected on the training ground. Anderton knocks the corner low to the near post, Sheringham runs in, hits it low and hard on the bounce and into the bottom corner. Hey presto. Goal to Spurs. Fans go wild.

'It's not an easy one to do,' says Sheringham. 'I tried it as a manager at Stevenage and as a coach at West Ham. A lot of players don't think it is one that can work, but if your movement is right, and your finish is right, then it's a great one, and it's really hard for the opposition to stop. You are the only one who knows the ball is going there, so if you can get half a yard on the opposition and execute it properly, you are fine.

'I wasn't surprised that we managed to make it work three times. The spotlight wasn't on us quite so much back then. Although, when Andy Gray did start analysing it all the time on Sky, people cottoned on to it, so we had to tweak it and try another one where I would come short, and I got a couple of chances from that one too.'

Tottenham can't hold a lead, though. They never can. 1-0 lasts for just two minutes. It's October and they haven't managed to stop any team scoring against them yet. Even Watford got three. Even Steve Talboys gets one today. Talboys was playing for non-league Gloucester two years ago, before Wimbledon signed him for a mere £10,000.

Austin is caught out by Neal Ardley's cross, Peter Fear smashes in a shot, it beats Walker but Scott flings himself at it just in front of the line. He does brilliantly to get a boot on it, but can only send it crashing up on to the underside of the bar. As it comes out Talboys is on hand to convert the rebound. 1-1.

Selhurst Park is the graveyard of champions. It's where non-league tactics meet Premier League. The low stands let in a bloated grey South London sky. The clouds are given solace here. If God had indeed wanted football played in the sky, it's on exactly these South London clouds that he would have put the grass. It is a place where reputations count for nothing. The terraces scream that they do not love you, do not respect you, that you will have to build your reputation again. Klinsmann understands it. Can the World Cup winner do it on a wet and windy afternoon against Wimbledon at Selhurst Park? Yes, he can. He might not score today, but he is again his team's talisman. Nobody works harder. He gives everything for his team. His manager's job is on the line. His team's top-flight status is on the line. A fourth straight league defeat needs to be averted.

Midway through the second half, Tottenham's three World Cup signings combine for the winner. Dumitrescu finds Klinsmann. Klinsmann knocks it square to Popescu. Popescu drills a right-footed first-time shot low and hard from just outside the box, diagonally across goal and in at the far post, for his first Spurs goal. Brutally efficient and effective. 2-1 to Spurs is how it finishes.

After the match Ardiles admits he is aware of the pressure on him. He reveals his good friend Ricky Villa, a former Argentina and Tottenham team-mate, has been on the phone from their homeland offering support. 'The rumours about my future have already made it over there,' he says. 'Ricky was concerned and wanted to wish me good luck. It's at these times when you know who your real friends are.'

Ardiles has won some friends today. He was willing to change his tactics and his team. His players rose to the occasion. They approached one of the most feared fixtures on the calendar – Wimbledon away – with the right attitude. Just when those bloated grey South London skies had seemed ready to swallow him up, Ardiles found himself a tiny patch of blue on the North London horizon.

Tuesday 4 October, 1994
Coca-Cola League Cup, 2nd Round, 2nd Leg
Tottenham Hotspur 2-3 Watford
Barmby 31, Klinsmann 63
Foster 15, Nogan 48, 75
Tottenham win 8-6 on aggregate
Another goal-crazy game. Five more goals at The Lane. A 3-2 defeat
on the night. An 8-6 victory on aggregate. Fourteen goals shared with
a team languishing at the wrong end of the division below them. A
humiliating defeat to a team from the Endsleigh League.

Former West Ham defender Colin Foster outjumps Campbell to
head Watford into a 15th-minute lead. The early autumn chill in the air
is felt more keenly now, in the Paxton and in the Park Lane and on The
Shelf. Spurs couldn't blow it from here, could they? 6-4 up on aggregate
against a team from Division One. It gets worse six minutes later. Darren
Anderton – among the scorers in the first leg – limps off with a groin
injury. It means another chance for young Danny Hill who comes off the
bench to replace him.

Relief all round when Nicky Barmby makes it 1-1 on the night, just
after the half-hour mark. Back in the starting line-up for the first time
since the Leicester defeat, he latches on to a perfectly-executed back-
heel by Klinsmann before smashing home. Reebok waste no time in
celebrating the talents of their newest signing. They've taken out an
advert on the Tottenham scoreboard. As Barmby's shot hits the net,
the scoreboard acclaims Klinsmann's assist, flashing up the message:
'Jürgen Klinsmann sponsored by Reebok'.

Watford of course have no one in their team of the World Cup winner's
calibre, but their team spirit shines as bright as the original Jules Rimet
trophy. Just after half-time they go ahead again. Walker can only palm
Jamie Moralee's shot straight out to Lee Nogan. The glorious horror of
the moment shoots through Nogan's body. The horrible glory of it all. An
almost open goal at White Hart Lane. A chance to put his side ahead. He
tames the passion, controls the panic, and slots home. Spurs 1 Watford 2.

Klinsmann rallies Tottenham after the break. A hat-trick in the first
leg, an assist already tonight. Now he's on target too. Midway through
the second half he combines beautifully with Barmby again. They play
a one-two and as the ball finds its way back to Klinsmann he rifles it
beyond keeper Kevin Miller from the edge of the box for 2-2. As the
White Hart Lane crowd salute their hero, Reebok do likewise again.
'Wunderbar' flashes up on the scoreboard this time.

Tottenham's embarrassment isn't over. With 15 minutes to go Nogan
completes the scoring. Spurs leave him completely unmarked as Tommy

Mooney's lofted cross finds him in acres of space. It finishes Tottenham 2 Watford 3. Tottenham of the Premiership, home of World Cup winners, TWO; Watford of the Endsleigh League, First Division, THREE. Spurs are through 8-6 on aggregate, but this level of performance isn't good enough.

Jeers echo off the stanchions and through the concourses, through the building site at the open South Stand end and out into the Park Lane. Those jeers climb the hunched shoulders and creep into the ears of those who have left early, those who have filtered out into the dark streets, bodies bent, hands in pockets, as though trying to defend themselves against what they've turned their backs on.

'Our defending, both individually and as a team, was unthinkable. We are our own worst enemies,' says Ardiles, who nevertheless appears to be in a state of denial when he adds: 'I am not near breaking point at all. What happened tonight has nothing to do with my attacking principles.'

Saturday 8 October, 1994

The press are talking of a crisis. Ardiles called his players in for extra training on Wednesday. Alan Sugar appears on the BBC's *Football Focus* programme on Saturday lunchtime. The interview was recorded earlier in the week. Despite the recent dip in results, he's bullish about the talent on display in the Spurs team: 'Because of Jürgen Klinsmann and our two Romanian friends, every ground we go to is full. Perhaps at the next Premier League meeting I'll ask every chairman to chip in £50,000!' he says.

In the press the *Daily Mail* claims Klinsmann is on £21,000 a week, twice as much as the pre-tax salaries of Premiership top earners Chris Sutton and Alan Shearer. 'What a load of nonsense,' says Sugar. The story contains quotes from Sugar's head of PR, Nick Hewer. 'We wouldn't have taken Jürgen on if we couldn't afford him. He's brought a tremendous surge of interest in the club and fills away grounds. Our merchandise is doing well. He's box office.' Tottenham are playing QPR today. Just before three o'clock, QPR manager Gerry Francis leaves the away dressing room. Nobody knows it yet, but exactly six weeks from now he'll be coming out of the adjacent door in a Tottenham tracksuit. Parts of the media have already started tipping him as a possible replacement for the under-pressure Ardiles. As he reaches the end of the tunnel he takes his seat in the away dugout. Next time he's here, and for the next three years, he'll be sitting exactly where Ardiles is positioned today.

The future of Ardiles is now being questioned on a daily basis. This match won't be easy, even though QPR haven't won away all season. For Spurs it's no White Hart Lane win since the first home game of the season; Darren Anderton and Gary Mabbutt are injured, Ilie Dumitrescu and Gica Popescu are away with Romania, busy drawing 0-0 with France in a Euro 96 qualifier in St Etienne.

The Spurs boss goes with three at the back: Kevin Scott, Colin Calderwood and Sol Campbell. Justin Edinburgh is on the left as usual. David Kerslake is on the right with Dean Austin left out of the squad altogether. In midfield, Jason Dozzell keeps his place from the last Premier League match alongside Nicky Barmby, and Danny Hill makes only his fourth league start for Spurs. Teddy Sheringham and Jürgen Klinsmann continue together up front.

FA Carling Premiership
Tottenham Hotspur 1-1 QPR
Barmby 79
Impey 45
Scott sent off 38. Ferdinand sent off 38

Under pressure for a result, Ardiles has reined in the attacking instincts. It's the least eventful game of Tottenham's season so far. It affects the crowd, who are quiet today. It's a scrap. A real scrap. A real ugly scrap of a match.

Seven minutes before half-time, both teams are reduced to ten men. It seems harsh on Tottenham's Kevin Scott. QPR striker Les Ferdinand has gone into the book just three minutes earlier, and now reacts to Calderwood's late tackle by lashing out at Scott. There doesn't seem to be much in the way of retaliation from the Spurs man, but referee Peter Jones sends them both to the dressing rooms. With Scott gone, the holes in Tottenham's defence become cavernous. Winger Andy Impey strolls in completely unmarked to head beyond Ian Walker in the final minute of the half. QPR 1-0 up.

Spurs are chasing the game now but the half-time reshuffle by Ardiles still seems strange, given how much his players have struggled defensively today. The more attack-minded Hazard comes on for Calderwood. Spurs are even more exposed now, and Hazard is having his worst-ever game in a Spurs shirt. It looks like the match is getting away from them.

Eleven minutes to go. Hill's cross is headed on by Klinsmann, who has had his quietest game yet for Spurs. Barmby gets to the ball first, just before goalkeeper Tony Roberts. He gets a touch, dinks it over Roberts, looping almost completely vertically up and then dropping straight back down again and into the net. 1-1, and that's how it finishes.

Spurs are tenth in the table with 13 points. But take the six-point deduction into account and they're 17th with just seven points. They're two places above the relegation zone. They still haven't won at The Lane since playing Everton in the first home game.

Wednesday 12 October, 1994
International Friendly
England 1-1 Romania
Lee 45
Dumitrescu 36

World Cup quarter-finalists Romania outclass England at Wembley. Tottenham's Ilie Dumitrescu becomes the first man to score against England since Terry Venables took charge, but at least the new manager remains unbeaten after his first five games.

Dumitrescu's exquisite half-volley puts Romania ahead nine minutes before the break, but England debutant Robert Lee of Newcastle equalises just before half-time when he surges on to Alan Shearer's header to finish well.

Darren Anderton isn't fit to play. David Platt isn't fit to play. Peter Beardsley isn't fit to play. As well as Lee, Southampton's Matt Le Tissier is making his first England start. He's quiet throughout. Arsenal's Ian Wright gets a chance to start instead of Tottenham's Teddy Sheringham, who replaces him with 19 minutes to play.

Man United's Paul Ince is lucky not to be sent off for a reckless tackle on Gica Popescu. The Spurs man is himself fortunate to stay on after hauling down Shearer when through on goal.

There could be a few tired Spurs legs this weekend. Klinsmann has also been away with Germany for a friendly in Budapest. He misses a great chance to grab the winner against Hungary, heading over the bar with four minutes to play. It ends 0-0.

Saturday 15 October, 1994

Take the six-point deduction into account and at kick-off Spurs are only outside the relegation zone on goal difference. Today they're playing Leeds. United's manager Howard Wilkinson has quality at his disposal in midfield: captain Gary McAllister and Wales international Gary Speed. McAllister is not fully fit, but will still play. Spurs fans hoped he might miss this one. He still has the ability to cause them problems.

Ardiles has Dumitrescu and Popescu back from international duty. Popescu has shaken off an injury problem to play which leads to relief all round. Anderton is still out though. It's 4-4-2 again: Walker in goal; Kerslake, Campbell, Scott and Edinburgh across the back; Barmby, Dozzell, Popescu and Dumitrescu in midfield; Klinsmann and Sheringham up front.

FA Carling Premiership
Leeds United 1-1 Tottenham Hotspur
Deane 61
Sheringham 27

Dumitrescu is a real live wire down the wing. He's in the mood today. Just before the half-hour mark he finds himself space in the box. His shot is too hard for Leeds goalkeeper John Lukic, who can only palm it straight back to him. Dumitrescu squares it to Sheringham, who sweeps it into the roof of the net. 1-0 to Spurs. That'll do Sheringham's confidence the world of good – his third Premiership goal of the season.

Walker is playing brilliantly in the Spurs goal. He's had so much practice this season. In first-half injury time he makes a splendid save from Speed's close-range header. There's to be no first clean sheet of the season, though. Midway through the second half Brian Deane fires in an equaliser for Leeds, a rocket right-foot shot on the volley.

It finishes 1-1. With the points deduction taken into account Tottenham are a point and a place above the relegation zone. QPR, Palace, Everton and Ipswich are below them. Ipswich have a game in hand. Even with the points restored Spurs would only be in mid-table, in 13th place with 14 points.

'We're probably a bit low on understanding,' Sheringham tells the press. 'Even though the new players have settled in very well, you still need that understanding. It just takes a bit of time. You have to get used to each other, develop a pattern and mould it into a unit. You won't see the best of Tottenham until after Christmas. There is always going to be pressure on us because of the size of the club and the signings we make.'

Saturday 22 October, 1994
FA Carling Premiership
Manchester City 5-2 Tottenham Hotspur
Walsh 15, 44, Quinn 41, Lomas 52, Flitcroft 79
Dumitrescu (pen) 29, 46

Just when it was beginning to look like Ardiles was slowly rectifying the defensive problems, Tottenham are hammered. They arrive at Maine Road still without a clean sheet all season, but at least having managed to concede only one goal per match in each of the last three.

Isn't it always the way that an old boy comes back to haunt his former club? Paul Walsh was effectively sacked by former Spurs boss Terry Venables, for punching coach Ray Clemence in the face in full view of the crowd when he was substituted in a reserve team match at White Hart Lane a few years back. Today he packs plenty of punch up front for City, scoring two and setting up the other three.

It's back to the cavalier, free-flowing attacking football from Spurs. It should be 5-3 to Tottenham at half-time, but somehow they trail 3-1. Spurs could have been 3-0 up in the first ten minutes. Klinsmann is back to his best. He sets up Barmby who shoots over. He draws a tremendous save out of City goalkeeper Andy Dibble. He forces Garry Flitcroft into a goal-line clearance which knocks the City man off his feet. Then City go ahead. A bright future is expected for 20-year-old midfielder Steve Lomas, who sends in a cross for Niall Quinn. Campbell misjudges it. Quinn knocks it to Walsh, who fires in from ten yards. 1-0 City.

Just before the half-hour mark Spurs equalise. Dibble brings down Klinsmann. Cast-iron penalty. No dive. Referee David Elleray rules that Dibble stays on because Keith Curle was standing on the line to potentially block any shot. After three consecutive misses, Sheringham is no longer on spot-kick duty. Many fans wonder whether Klinsmann will step up. But it's Dumitrescu, who has a good record from the spot. Dumitrescu scores. Fearless shot to Dibble's top right-hand corner. 1-1.

Spurs have played City off the park, but they fall apart in the five minutes before half-time. Walsh reaches Nicky Summerbee's cross first. Walker saves his header, but not convincingly, and it drops to Quinn who heads in the rebound. 2-1 City.

Peter Beagrie surges down the left and plays in Quinn. Walsh is there too. It's Quinn and Walsh against Walker. Quinn tees up Walsh who rattles off the shot. Walker gets a touch on it but palms it down into the ground; it bounces up over him and into the net. 3-1 City. It's Walker's first poor performance of the season.

Spurs need a good start to the second half. They get it. The mesmeric Dumitrescu scores in the first minute. He surges into the City half and feeds Klinsmann. Richard Edghill gets to the ball first, but Klinsmann dispossesses him and back-heels it to Dumitrescu. The Romanian shoots from distance, it hits Curle and spins beyond Dibble for 3-2.

Over the course of the next few minutes Dumitrescu is rampant. Two more surging runs threaten to pull his side back into it. They look certain to get the equaliser. Then City make it 4-2. Walsh plays in Beagrie. His cross is missed by Campbell. Lomas heads in from three yards. Spurs have a mountain to climb, with 38 minutes to play.

The home side are running riot. Eleven minutes from time it becomes even more embarrassing. Walsh works his way beyond three Spurs players and tees up Flitcroft to score from five yards. 5-2 City. Spurs have been thrashed. With the six-point deduction they are now back in the relegation zone.

'It was very satisfying to play so well against my former club,' crows Walsh to the press after the game. 'Walshie was a little devil,' says his manager Brian Horton. 'He's playing better now than at any time in his career. The biggest winners here, though, were the fans. They have seen one of the great games of football.'

Spurs have now conceded 28 goals this season. Ossie surely can't go on like this. The slide is gathering momentum. Tottenham don't look like they are going to be able to turn things round while he remains in charge. The exit is looming.

Steve Lomas made more than 100 appearances for Manchester City, as well as going on to represent West Ham and QPR and winning 45 caps in midfield for Northern Ireland. The goal he scored against Tottenham in City's 5-2 win was one of just eight he managed in his six years at City's former home Maine Road. He'll never forget a match which had it all.

'We could have been three down in the first 20 minutes,' he says. 'Spurs had so many good players: Klinsmann, Sheringham, Barmby, then you had Dumitrescu on the right, and Popescu was supposed to be their anchoring midfielder,' he laughs. 'For us Paul Walsh on the day was absolutely magnificent. He had something to prove. He knew he hadn't done himself justice at Tottenham. He gave Kevin Scott and Sol Campbell an absolute roasting. By Paul's own admission his attitude could have been better at Spurs. I didn't realise how good a player he was until he came to play with us. Paul has regrets about his career in terms of knowing that if he had applied himself when he was with Spurs and Liverpool the way he did at Man City, he would certainly have got more than five England caps.

'I think for the neutral it must have been an incredible game to watch. It truly could have been 7-7. I'm not just plucking that scoreline out the air for effect. There really were that many great chances. I admired what Ossie was doing. He wanted to play attacking football and play the Spurs way. We were an attacking side too. I think we defended with six and they defended with five. They basically had one attacker too many. People don't realise how big a pitch Maine Road was, as well, and I think that added to it because with the amount of attacking players on view it was very much end to end: we attack, you attack, a bit like a gunfight to see who comes out on top. It was a game which said a lot about where the Premier League was going, how it was becoming the most entertaining league in the world. They were exciting times.'

So what does he think about how football has changed, the explosion in wages, the influx of overseas players, the boom in television coverage? 'I think the comparison is that when I was a young player, starting out, I had played maybe 60 or 70 games in the Premier League and I was still driving round in a five-year-old Escort. I do think it has now become an issue in a player's development if they are getting too much too young. You look at the English players who have really had to work for it – coming through from non-league, Jamie Vardy, Charlie Austin – they appreciate everything they have because it hasn't come easy to them.

'Another thing that has changed is the bond between the players and the fans. We had the Junior Blues Club for kids, and we had to turn up at Maine Road on a Sunday and there could be two, two-and-a-half thousand people there. To see what it meant on their faces was great. Now a lot of the interaction is done through social media; it's not the same.'

Jonathan Pearce was commentating on the Manchester City v Spurs game for Capital Gold. 'It was an amazing game to work on,' he says. 'There was something happening every minute. It was breathless. It could have finished anything-anything.

'But also it was the game where we all realised Ossie had to go. They couldn't play football the way they were doing, because the better teams would just carve them open. Forest had done it and now City had too. It was tough, because it had just been a real love affair with Ossie Ardiles, but this was the day we all knew it was over.'

6

Ossie's Nightmare

'Gaffer, can I just stop you there. You're
talking about the "Famous Five" all
the time, what about the "Shit Six?"'
(Colin Calderwood)

Tuesday 25 October, 1994

Doubt and fear infuse every blade of grass at the training ground. Doubt and fear stalk every corridor, work their way round every corner. Doubt and fear have taken up residence in every crevice of the brickwork. It's impossible to see where the next win is coming from. Self-belief has evaporated. Klinsmania feels a long time ago. The bullet-headers, the overhead kicks, the celebratory dives, the TV cameras and the radio commentators; the shirt sales and the No.18s; the goals and the goals and the goals and the goals and the goals.

Tomorrow it's Notts County away in the third round of the Coca-Cola League Cup. Notts County of the Endsleigh League, Division One; Notts County, bottom of the Endsleigh League Division One. Nothing for Spurs to gain and everything to lose.

An FA Cup ban and six points deducted in the league, so the Coca-Cola Cup is the only way to get to Wembley, the only way to get to Europe, perhaps the only way to keep Klinsmann. But Notts County can smell the doubt and the fear. They have got nothing to lose and everything to gain. They haven't won at home in their own division all season. Manager Mick Walker has already gone through everything Ardiles is experiencing now. He has already been put out of his misery, sacked in mid-September with Russell Slade placed in caretaker charge.

This is Slade's first managerial job. He can make a name for himself tonight. He's seen Watford, from the same division, put three past Spurs in each leg of the previous round. He knows his side can take advantage of Tottenham's jitters.

The press say Spurs manager Ossie Ardiles is a dead man walking. If results on the pitch aren't putting enough pressure on him, results in the City surely are. Following Saturday's 5-2 drubbing at Manchester City, shares in Tottenham Hotspur have fallen by 8p to 127p. Those are the sort of league tables Alan Sugar pays particular attention to, the sort of results that really matter to him.

The press ask Ardiles if he will change his approach. 'If someone could guarantee that by playing the long ball and putting in two more defenders we would win - no, I still wouldn't do it!' Will he change his team? Ardiles admits he will shake things up. Three of the back five who shipped five at City will be dropped. Out go goalkeeper Ian Walker, right-back David Kerslake and centre-back Kevin Scott. In come Erik Thorstvedt, Dean Austin and Colin Calderwood in their places with Calderwood set to play in central defence rather than the holding midfield position he has been occupying all season.

'We need to concentrate more,' says Ardiles. 'Especially when we have the ball. When you know you have had a lot of possession and played well and still lost, it is very demoralising. I have made these changes to try and give us more stability.'

Is the Klinsmann honeymoon over too? It's just one goal in six games for him, none in three. A three-game goal drought isn't a long one, but by his own high standards, and after the explosive start to his career in England, it seems like three times as long. 'I did not know it was as long as that,' he says. 'But it does not worry me. We have been creating plenty of chances.'

For so long, everyone had wanted Ardiles to succeed: the fans who worshipped him in his playing days, the current players, many of whom had also idolised him as they grew up, and the chairman who had appointed a fans' favourite to get the supporters back onside following his sacking of Venables. As one of the finest ever to don the Lilywhites' shirt, Sugar had given Ardiles the job on the back of his popularity as a player as much as for anything he had achieved in the dugout.

After leaving Tottenham in 1988, Ardiles' playing career wound down with spells at Blackburn, QPR, Fort Lauderdale Strikers and Swindon, which is where his managerial career began. There was initial success. At the County Ground Ardiles set about trying to combine the best of British and South American football. His methods were christened 'Samba Soccer'. With a diamond midfield and the emphasis on passing, Town fans liked what they saw. He got results too. In 1989/90 Swindon achieved what was then their highest-ever league position of fourth in the second tier. They beat Blackburn in the play-off semi-finals and Sunderland in the final. Under Ardiles Swindon Town were going up to the top division for the first time in their history.

There was to be a bitter twist, though. All his hard work was undone when the FA found Swindon guilty of financial irregularities. The punishment was unprecedented in its severity. Swindon were to be relegated two divisions. They wouldn't be starting life in Division One next season, but Division Three. On appeal the punishment was reduced; Swindon wouldn't go down to Division Three, but neither would they be allowed to go up – they would stay in Division Two. At least all the off-field troubles would give Ardiles some preparation for what was to lie ahead at White Hart Lane.

Two-thirds of the way into the 1990/91 season, Swindon were fighting relegation from Division Two. The football Ardiles had his team playing was proving popular, though, and his methods had not gone unnoticed by other clubs in the division, particularly Newcastle who offered him the chance to become their first-ever overseas manager. It was a tempting proposition for Ardiles – a club with a far bigger fanbase and far greater potential than Swindon, even if they did have their own financial problems. He accepted their offer; but it never worked out for him in the North-East, and within a year he was sacked with Newcastle bottom of Division Two.

West Brom then offered Ardiles the chance to rebuild his career. Even though it meant taking a step down to the third tier, he agreed a deal and replaced Bobby Gould in the summer of 1992. In his first full season he led the Baggies up to the second tier via the play-offs. Then Tottenham came calling, and it was impossible for him to resist the lure of the club where he had enjoyed his finest days as a player.

Tottenham, though, were in turmoil. The bitter feud between Sugar and Venables was far from having run its course. It enveloped the club, and all who worked there, for most of the early to mid-1990s. Ardiles has said that he felt intimidated by Sugar when he first met him, but that he warmed to him. He respected how Sugar probed deeply; he didn't just accept the first answer, but hit you with a follow-up question, says Ardiles.

The majority of the fans were still behind Venables. Players too were angry. Neil Ruddock forced a move to Liverpool, and Ardiles has claimed that Sheringham was upset by the removal of Venables and that he then had a confrontation with Sugar over a pay rise. 'All the stars wanted to leave,' is how Ardiles put it. Those distractions probably didn't help his preparations for his first season in charge – 1993/94. The campaign turned into a disaster. Sheringham was injured for most of the season and Tottenham didn't have an adequate replacement.

As expected, Ardiles insisted on playing the right way. There was neat, passing football, but there was no end product. The team was powderpuff. A relegation battle ensued.

Tottenham won just four home league games in the whole of 1993/94, and none between the start of October and the end of April. As previously mentioned, they were caught in a nerve-wracking relegation battle which went to the penultimate game before a 2-0 win at Oldham secured survival.

The relief of staying up quickly dissipated when it became clear that Spurs would probably be fighting against the drop again the following season. With four teams to be relegated in 1994/95, the FA's decision in June to dock Tottenham 12 points – reduced to six on appeal – meant they were almost certainly destined for relegation, especially as they had only just stayed up by three points.

Then came Sugar's purchase of Dumitrescu and Klinsmann and briefly, oh so briefly, the realisation of Ossie's dream – before it all turned into a nightmare.

Wednesday 26 October, 1994

It's the day of the Coca-Cola Cup third round tie away to Notts County. Klinsmann's 'Wembley Dream' is the main line the papers take. This competition is probably Tottenham's only route to Wembley, their only route to Europe.

'The pitch, the atmosphere, the whole experience of being at Wembley is something special,' says Klinsmann, who has played beneath the Twin Towers just once for Germany against England in a friendly. 'It is world-famous and I would love to go back there with Tottenham.'

The papers are also full of rumours that Klinsmann could return to Germany with Bayern Munich next summer. The Bundesliga club are said to have met with frustration in their attempts to sign Dennis Bergkamp from Inter Milan, and could be prepared to bid £4m for Klinsmann. Bayern president Franz Beckenbauer says: 'We are disappointed not to get Bergkamp, but we will need another big-profile striker and I will now examine another option. We didn't have the money to buy Klinsmann in the summer, which I regret. But it is now possible.'

Klinsmann's response to the press is: 'I want to play abroad and I love London, I really do. It is such a cosmopolitan city, like no other place. And I have no regrets at all about coming here. None.'

He also reiterates the importance of Spurs playing in continental competition. 'A club like Tottenham, with its tradition and its status, has to be in Europe. And it was the prospect of playing in Europe that was one of the reasons why I came to this club. So we really need to do well in the Coca-Cola Cup.'

Coca-Cola League Cup, Third Round
Notts County 3-0 Tottenham Hotspur
Agana 17, McSwegan 20, 72
Dumitrescu sent off 36

The ladies and gentlemen of the press have come to Meadow Lane in search of a cup shock tonight. It's a story with added impetus. It won't just be a cup shock but one which – if it happens – will almost certainly lead to a managerial casualty.

As the teams make their way down the tunnel before kick-off, the County boys are ready to make a name for themselves. Caretaker manager Russell Slade has them primed for the game of their lives. The revamped Meadow Lane is a fine home for football at this level, but the locals haven't had much to cheer here all season – until now. Tonight the changes Ardiles implements at the back make no difference. County's strike force consists of Tony Agana – a club record £685,000 signing from Sheffield United – and Gary McSwegan, a £500,000 arrival from Rangers.

It takes just 17 minutes for County to pierce Tottenham's rearguard. Agana is all arms and legs, strong in the air and toughened by his non-league upbringing with Welling and Weymouth. He packs a fearsome shot too. Richard Walker begins the move with a lofted ball up the left-hand touchline. Agana gets himself between Austin and Campbell, and beats them both in the air for the flick-on.

It drops to Phil Turner on the left-hand corner of the Spurs box. Campbell has tracked back to close him down, but Turner takes it on his chest, draws Campbell out towards the left, spins 180 degrees and plays it back into exactly the space they have vacated. There the onrushing Agana picks it up on the corner of the box. Agana has been left completely free; he takes one touch with his right, then, as Calderwood flies across from the centre of the area, crashes in an incredible left-footed shot from an almost impossible angle. It flies across Thorstvedt and into the far side of the goal, almost ripping the net from its stanchions.

There are 16,952 fans here tonight, and about 14,000 of them go wild. Black and white scarves are twirled in a frenzy. Embraces are offered with outstretched arms, accepted by all, whether family, friend or stranger. Agana peels away to high-five Andy Legg. Their shadows dance beneath the floodlights, shadows Tottenham will continue to chase in vain all night.

The home fans dare to dream. Within a split second, hope is replaced by fear. Have they scored too early? Will the giant now awaken? Hardened fans have seen it all before, these false dawns, early leads which turn to dust. Their worries credit Spurs with far too much character, though.

Within three minutes, before Tottenham know what has hit them, County strike again. Legg plays it forward to Agana, again standing exactly on the left corner of the Spurs box. He is facing away from goal and is backing into Austin behind him. He holds Austin off and then taps a short pass to Legg, who has continued his run. Legg – with Jason Dozzell giving chase – takes it towards the byline and then gets a left-footed cross in. It hits Campbell's outstretched boot, which lends it the perfect trajectory to rise and then drop to McSwegan at the far post. He can't miss with a six-yard header. Tottenham's woeful attempts at defending are comic, with extra slapstick provided by the sight of Popescu tripping over the grounded Thorstvedt on the goal line as the ball finds its way into the net. 2-0 County.

The home side revel in the moment. The celebration has been prepared: a mocking tribute to their visitors' most famous player. They haven't quite got the choreography right, nor has every player remembered what he is supposed to do, but half the team join in with a Klinsmann dive to the turf.

Spurs implode. Dumitrescu loses it. Booked for tripping Legg, 13 minutes later he's sent off for a lunge on Turner. Referee Keith Burge shows him a second yellow, then the red. Dumitrescu pleads with him to reconsider, then accepts his fate and trudges off towards the tunnel. 2-0 down and a man down, with 54 minutes to play.

The Pasadena Rose Bowl must feel like a long time ago now for Dumitrescu. Then he'd had time to weave his magic for Romania against Argentina and reach the World Cup quarter-final; then his talents were admired by every one of the 90,469 spectators who took their seats in the heat of the Los Angeles sun and millions more on TV. The locals haven't come to admire him or his team-mates tonight, though. They've come to bay for blood. They've come to harry and to hassle, as if they are a 12th man on the pitch. And they may as well be on the pitch, so compact is tiny Meadow Lane.

Back in the summer the Pasadena Rose Bowl stretched and yawned upwards and outwards towards the Californian sky, shouting that this was a match for the whole world to see. The players who displayed their talents on its carpet of a pitch could be forgiven for believing they would be spotted by a passing plane, or even an astronaut performing a NASA spacewalk. Tonight, Meadow Lane wants to suffocate you. It wants to jump on top of you, to cage you in, to keep your talents a secret here, hidden from all. It wants to gnarl away at your confidence, at your self-esteem, to make you feel that you are nothing special. And you've fallen for it. Now you do indeed feel like nothing special. You feel stupid.

Ill-discipline is catching. One minute into first-half injury time Klinsmann is booked for the first time in his Spurs career. It's a fairly innocuous challenge, but his unblemished disciplinary record is now tarnished. As the half-time whistle blows, Klinsmann shakes his head at the referee and mutters something under his breath in German.

Tonight, a change in personnel hasn't worked for Ardiles. At half-time he goes for a change in formation. He switches to a back three for the entire second half – Austin, Campbell and Edinburgh. Calderwood has been replaced by Hazard, who will play in midfield. It's a last throw of the dice. Forty-five minutes to save his job. Forty-five minutes to save Tottenham's season. County's fans roar their team back on to the pitch. A sea of fists are clenched and pumped in determination, teeth gritted around elongated cries of 'Come On'. Cries which signify that in this two-club city, for once this is County's night. Forest might be former English and European champions, Forest might be currently third in the Premiership, but tonight – if their side can hold firm for 45 minutes – County are the headline makers.

For Ardiles, initially there are signs of encouragement. Spurs start as though they are a team, a ten-man team, determined to keep their manager in a job. Dozzell's header is hacked off the line, then Barmby comes close, but his shot whistles just wide. Sheringham and Klinsmann barely had a touch in the first half, but in the 65th minute they combine beautifully. Sheringham heads it down to Klinsmann. Klinsmann lays it off to Popescu. Popescu shoots but Paul Reece saves it.

Seven minutes later it's all over. McSwegan again. As a high cross comes into the area, Austin seems to have lost his bearings. Legg beats him in the air and heads it down to Agana on the corner of the six-yard box. Agana holds off Campbell, swivels, and rolls the ball square to McSwegan who simply hammers it into the roof of the net from three yards out. Thorstvedt has been left horribly exposed again. Notts County 3, Tottenham 0.

Newspaper subs are preparing headlines in newsrooms throughout the land. It's not just the press; for the first time the fans are turning on Ardiles too. 'We Want Ossie Out', comes the chant from the terraces: a chant which filters its way across the Meadow Lane turf, hangs like a fog between the dugouts, chases its way down the tunnel, into the dressing room and then the press room. There's a moment of light relief in the post-match press conference when a ringing telephone can be heard. 'If it's Alan Sugar for me, I'm out,' jokes Ardiles to laughter. 'This is the lowest we have reached,' he says. 'The buck stops with me but I haven't considered resigning. I never have in my life and I'm not going to do it now. Everything that could go wrong tonight went wrong. We conceded bad goals and Ilie Dumitrescu was sent off, although I didn't think either of his tackles were particularly malicious. We are trying to sort it out. But we have to keep working to put it right.

'We have a very important game at home to West Ham on Saturday, and it's vital that the fans rally around us. I understand their frustration and I heard what they were chanting tonight, and that's the most difficult thing for me. But we have to sort it out among ourselves.'

Jon Culley writes in *The Independent*: 'This match, Ardiles said, was one that his team dared not lose. In the event, they never looked capable of winning it. They were outplayed so comprehensively that, for the first time, their supporters called for Ardiles to step down.'

Notts County are England's oldest Football League club. They've enjoyed few more glorious nights than this. Bottom of the second tier and thrashing a Premiership team containing three stars of the World Cup. A World Cup winner reduced to not having a single shot on target, a World Cup quarter-finalist frustrated to the point of being sent off.

Their black and white shirts – adopted by Juventus in 1903 – are the perfect symbol of Tottenham's polarised season: sensational Spurs or shambolic Spurs. No middle ground. In the directors' box Alan Sugar is deep in conversation with non-executive director Tony Berry. Between them they decide it is the end of the road for Ardiles – he will have to go.

'I think in Notts County we played a team on the night that were just far, far hungrier and wanted it more and played better than us,' says Dean Austin. 'We conceded two early goals and from that point we were chasing the game. Ossie found out that enjoying yourself is one thing, but you've got to be winning games of football because that's the name of the game. The thing was at that time, with that team, we were either untouchable or very, very bad when we had an off day; there was no in-between.

'As a team sometimes you've got to be able to recognise – this is me talking now with the experience of coaching – you can win games of football with great players, but you can lose games of football with great players. You have to be a team and you have to have some kind of organisation if you're going to be winners on a regular basis. At that time I was a player and a fan, and I had that little bit of a fan in me that made me want Ossie's philosophy to be proved right. I think I honestly felt that because the players were so good, we'd find a way, that – as Ossie seemed to believe – if the other team scored four, we'd score five.'

The man who was Notts County boss that night can still remember the hostility Ardiles had to face from the press after the game. Russell Slade was taking the first tentative steps on what has been a long and distinguished career as a manager throughout the Football League. He was just 34 at the time, and had been in caretaker charge, his first managerial role, for a matter of weeks. He would remain in the role until January when they brought in Howard Kendall and kept Slade on as assistant.

Slade would eventually go on to wind his way through the divisions in managerial posts with Sheffield United, Scarborough, Grimsby, Yeovil, Brighton and Leyton Orient, before finally getting a crack at the comparatively big time with Cardiff in the Championship in 2014. Notts County against Spurs, 26 October 1994, will forever remain one of the most famous results on his CV.

'I saw the pressure he was under after the game. Our press area was absolutely jammed solid, and the first question I got hit with was, "How does it feel to have got Ossie Ardiles the sack?" I was a bit taken aback,' says Slade. 'I didn't think that was very nice. I said, "No, no, no, I've just gone out to win a football match and we've played very well and won."'

'It was an amazing night, one I will never forget. Meadow Lane was a great ground at the time. I think the capacity was 16 or 17,000 but there must have been about 20,000 in there,' laughs Slade. 'I'm not saying anyone was fiddling the gate,' he jokes, 'but somehow people had found a way in. They were even sitting in front of the advertising hoardings by the pitch, which you'd never get away with these days.'

Notts County finished the season where they were when Spurs met them, 24th and bottom of Division One and relegated to Division Two. They had a decent season in the cups though. The win against Spurs set up another tie against Premiership opponents with a trip to Carrow Road where they were narrowly beaten 1-0 by Norwich. In the FA Cup they managed a 2-2 home draw against Manchester City in the third round, but lost the replay 5-2 at Maine Road. Spurs themselves knew exactly how a 5-2 defeat at Maine Road felt. The highlight of the season for the

Magpies was winning the Anglo-Italian Cup by beating Ascoli 2-1 in the final at Wembley on 19 March.

As the coach makes its way out of Meadow Lane, Klinsmann isn't on board. Instead he's staying in Nottingham tonight, then going to Sheffield tomorrow to help the FA promote Euro 96. He's been chosen as an ambassador for host venue Hillsborough, scene of his debut and Tottenham's seven-goal thriller with Sheffield Wednesday on the opening day of the season.

His winning goal and his dive celebration have remained among the most enduring images of the season, and the FA is keen to capitalise. Since that day never has Tottenham's, Ardiles' or Klinsmann's stock been lower than it is right now. Tonight it was Notts County pulling out the dive celebrations. Tonight it was Notts County ending Klinsmann's Wembley dream. For some Tottenham supporters a 3-0 defeat to Notts County is too much to bear. Angry palms clatter against the team coach as it makes its way out of Meadow Lane. Loading the bags into the coach is kit man Roy Reyland. This is one of his lowest moments at the club.

'I don't think the defence ever felt Ossie's methods were too much for them to cope with,' says Reyland. 'But there were games when they were under the cosh for 55, 60 or 65 minutes. Then they would come into the dressing room and think, "God, we could have done with the rest of you doing a bit more." Under Ossie it really was a case of "Put your tin helmets on and go gung-ho. Everyone run forward, and everyone run back." A bit like table football really. Upwards, back, upwards, back. Everyone had a bugle, "Do, do dooh, and everyone charge." It must have been a bit daunting if you were Colin Calderwood, you know, you've got six players in the opposition half and the ball's in your half and you've got four players running at you.

'You back off, back off, back off, but at some stage you've got to go to the ball and if it's two-on-one or three-on-one you're gonna mug yourself off. Some players got criticised more than others. Sometimes it wasn't their fault. We were in a team meeting once and we'd had a couple of good hidings and we were talking about the attackers, and Colin Calderwood says, "Gaffer, gaffer, gaffer, can I just stop you there. You're talking about the 'Famous Five' all the time, what about the 'Shit Six'?" It was brilliant, it just broke the ice. Everyone found it funny.'

Saturday 29 October, 1994
Somehow Ardiles has survived to face another game. It doesn't seem like a stay of execution, though, more a chance to say goodbye. The

die has already been cast. Sugar and Berry have already made their minds up privately. Today Harry Redknapp's West Ham are the visitors. It should be a contest between two evenly-matched sides.

The Hammers are 12th with 14 points. Spurs are 13th with 14 points – but in the relegation zone when you take the six-point deduction into account. West Ham have the greater momentum. They've won three of their last five in the league and won a London derby in midweek, beating Chelsea in the Coca-Cola Cup. Spurs have only won one of their last five in the league, and of course have just been humiliated by Notts County.

It seems Ossie will be gone whatever the result, but can he bid farewell with a win?

FA Carling Premiership
Tottenham Hotspur 3-1 West Ham United
Klinsmann 19, Sheringham 49, Barmby 63
Rush 42

Ardiles has revamped his system and personnel again. In defence right-back Dean Austin, who suffered an injury at Meadow Lane, and centre-back Colin Calderwood, are out, with David Kerslake and Gary Mabbutt respectively recalled in their places. Gica Popescu will be used as a sweeper. Up front Teddy Sheringham has also been dropped to the bench. It's believed Ardiles has become increasingly frustrated with him in recent weeks. Is this a pointed gesture by a manager who knows he is on his way out?

In the dugout Ardiles chews frantically on gum. On the pitch his team are playing well. If they'd put in a performance anywhere near as good as this against Notts County he possibly wouldn't be facing the sack right now.

In the papers before the match Klinsmann has vowed to end his five-game goal drought in the league, and it takes him just over 18 minutes to do so. It's a beautiful move which bears all the hallmarks of the Ardiles philosophy. Klinsmann starts it with a raking long pass from inside Tottenham territory to release Barmby down the wing. Barmby holds it up, then cuts inside to run square along the top of the area, where he surrenders possession to Dumitrescu who is coming in the opposite direction.

Barmby continues his run to the far post and Dumitrescu swivels to deliver a cross towards the penalty spot where Klinsmann is waiting. Klinsmann sells a dummy, ducking under it so that it drops to Barmby, who knocks it back to Klinsmann to tap home from six yards. 1-0 Spurs.

There's only one Jürgen Klinsmann,
One Jürgen Klinsmann,
Walking along,
Singing a song,
Walking in a Klinsmann wonderland.

In the final ten minutes of the first half West Ham assert some pressure of their own for the first time, and Tottenham crack. There won't be a first clean sheet of the season for Tottenham or Ardiles today. Mike Marsh works his way into the Spurs box, and all four defenders, Kerslake, Mabbutt, Calderwood and Edinburgh, appear drawn to him as if magnetised. Marsh knocks in the cross and Matthew Rush steers a left-footed shot beyond Erik Thorstvedt. 1-1. Edinburgh goes off injured at half-time, and Ardiles shakes things up by sending on Sheringham.

Campbell goes to left-back and Popescu drops into the centre of defence. Within four minutes Sheringham puts Spurs back into the lead. Tony Cottee has just missed an absolute sitter for West Ham, steering his header wide. Thorstvedt's goal kick is flicked on by Klinsmann. Sheringham charges in and arrows a left-footed shot across goal and in at the far post. 2-1 to Spurs. What a way for Sheringham to answer his critics – Ardiles possibly amongst them – by scoring a great goal moments after coming off the bench.

Midway through the second half Spurs seal the points. Barmby, the most impressive player on the day, gets the goal. Sheringham flicks on another long ball out of defence. Barmby beats the offside trap just inside the West Ham half. He's 40 yards from goal, but already effectively one-on-one with Hammers keeper Ludek Miklosko. As he enters the box on the left-hand side he crashes an unerring left-footed drive, rising beyond Miklosko and into the nearside top corner. 3-1 to Spurs. And that's how it ends.

Ardiles tells the press afterwards: 'I have to be honest and say this week has been probably the worst of my career. Against Manchester City last week we did not deserve to lose 5-2, but the game against Notts County was the worst. There has been incredible pressure. It has been tough, but it was good to discover that I can handle it.

'We had a meeting with the boys and knew we had reached the very bottom. If you do not have the attitude to win the 50-50 ball and win your own battle it does not matter what formation you play, you are going to be in trouble. It has been missing from some players for some time. Today it was back. I know I am not off the hook. Reports of my funeral have been greatly exaggerated.'

As his words are devoured by tens of hungry dictaphones and scrawled into dog-eared notepads, just down the hallway the Spurs directors are meeting. Moments later Sugar leaves the stadium, refusing to comment to reporters. Non-executive director Tony Berry tells them: 'We will have a board meeting on Thursday, like we always do.' For Ardiles, though, the end will come before that.

West Ham's goal was the 100th Spurs had conceded in 16 months with Ossie Ardiles at the helm. It also proved to be the last time Erik Thorstvedt ever picked the ball out of the net. This appearance, coming just a day after his 32nd birthday, was his final one for Spurs. He had lost his place to Ian Walker at the start of the season after returning from the World Cup injured. Walker took his chance until his dodgy performance at Maine Road, which saw Thorstvedt recalled for the Notts County match. After this game Thorstvedt would be an occasional substitute, but more often left out of the squad altogether until his retirement at the end of 1995/96. His FA Cup winner's medal from 1991 would remain his career highlight.

So did Ossie have to go? 'I think so,' says Anderton. 'Even at Watford, in the League Cup, we're 1-0 down after less than 30 seconds. My groin injury meant I wasn't playing at Man City when we got done for five, or Notts County which proved to be the end for him; but by then it was clear people had worked us out. It was sad to see Ossie go because he was a great manager to play for, and of course an absolute legend as a player.

'Stevie P had tried to get the shape right in training. Every now and then he would be dragging us here and there. Ossie was so funny though, he had such a good way about him. He'd be saying, "For flip's sake Stevie, play, play. We get it, we play. We're better than them."

'We didn't have any shape. Ilie was completely undisciplined. He was attack-minded and that was that. Nicky Barmby was similar to me in that he was more disciplined. But he was really a centre-forward playing in the hole with Teddy who was being asked to play almost as a midfielder, tracking back, which wasn't his game either. So we couldn't get the balance right, which was a real shame.

'I think it was the right decision by the chairman to change the manager. Gerry Francis came in and we 100% needed that. Ossie had come and given me that belief, "You go and get the ball, we want you on the ball." That gives you confidence when you are 21, 22. But we needed a change.'

In his 1998 autobiography, Teddy Sheringham writes 'many people suggested I should have stuck two fingers up' at Ardiles when he came on and scored, but that he himself 'wanted nothing more than for this gentle, sincere man to succeed'. That book was written a long time ago, and today Sheringham says, 'I don't remember being on the bench to be honest, but now with the experience of having been a manager I can quite understand that he had to make whatever decisions he thought were right. Perhaps he would have done it to try and spark something in me. I don't know. What I do know is that I really wanted things to work out for Ossie. He was an absolute legend at the club. I loved playing for him.

'I can see why we needed some sort of stability though. A base to work from. I remember Ossie's first meeting in the canteen when he became Tottenham manager. He said, "I want everyone to pass it and as soon as Teddy has the ball up front, I want everyone to fly forwards." It was a cavalier approach. Fun, but something was missing at the back. Gerry came in eventually and added a certain stability.'

'There is no perfect manager,' says Klinsmann – who since retiring as a player in 1998 has gone on to be head coach of Germany, Bayern Munich and the USA. 'I learnt a bit from all of the managers I played under. Ossie was free-flowing and attack-minded. He took risks, and I have taken a few of them too in my managerial career. Taking a risk was natural to him, because he had done it as such a wonderfully gifted player, with his unbelievable technique. I admired him for that. He was a bit unlucky because we made too many individual mistakes.'

White Hart Lane is quiet now. The fans have long since filtered out of the stadium to the strains of 'Glory, Glory, Tottenham Hotspur', celebrating victory over West Ham, revenge for last season's 4-1 home defeat to the same opponents: a much-needed three points.

Spurs assistant manager Steve Perryman stands with radio reporters at the end of the tunnel. 'There will only be a crisis at Tottenham when the club loses its style on the pitch, but when Ossie's in charge they will certainly not lose that. We've entertained everyone. You must get results as well, but if the man is given long enough, he will provide both.'

Sugar thinks 16 months is long enough. Sugar thinks £12m on new players is enough too.

Sunday 30 October, 1994

David Howells has spoken out in the press. John Dillion of *The People* has the story. 'IT'S YOUR OWN FAULT OSSIE', screams the headline. In the article Howells talks about how difficult it was finding out at the last minute that he wouldn't be involved on the opening day of the season, and says he still hasn't been told why he isn't in the team.

'I regret the newspaper story now,' says Howells. 'Ossie fined me a couple of weeks' wages – it was one of the last things he did. I expected it. I just wanted the article to be about how I was feeling, and the journalist added more in about the team and how we had started to struggle, let a lot of goals in. I didn't want to speak about that. I just wanted to talk about me and what I might be able to bring to the team, and the fact that he hadn't spoken to me and explained things.

'Ossie is a great guy and we get on fine now. He's right up there with the greatest players Spurs have ever had, without a shadow of a doubt. At the time he just wasn't prepared to have a conversation with me about what was going on and that was very frustrating, but we have a laugh about it now.'

Ardiles has since admitted that he realises he didn't show enough respect to players who weren't in his first-team plans. In his 2009 autobiography he explains that he has always had an excellent relationship with his first-team players, but that he didn't know how to handle himself with the reserves. He says he thinks it is because he hardly spent any time on the bench himself as a player. He adds that Keith Burkinshaw, his assistant at West Brom, and Steve Perryman, who did the same role for him at Spurs, were among the many people close to him who pulled him up on this shortcoming.

Stuart Nethercott thinks Ardiles could possibly have won himself more time if he had brought Howells into the team to add balance. 'David was great in the holding midfield position,' he says. 'There were a few that tried out that role, but Ossie had his mind set on what he was going to do and he was going to stick with it. When Gerry Francis came in, he got Howellsy back in, he went 4-4-2, and he got results. He got us fitter too. With Ossie in pre-season there wasn't any running up hills – it was all ball work. Gerry straight away thought he could get us fit. He had us running our nuts off on what we called Terror Tuesday. It worked. It got us fit, he got us organised and the results started to come.

'It would have been great for a legend like Ossie to succeed at the club, but I think deep down we all knew it couldn't continue and we were on a slippery slope. When you get beat 3-0 at Notts County you know your time's virtually up. To be fair, the chairman did the right thing at the time and got the right man in to sort us out.'

Monday 31 October, 1994

Sugar summons Ardiles to his Chigwell mansion and tells him it's over. He'll receive a pay-off of £500,000 to compensate him for the two and a half years remaining on his contract. The 42-year-old accepts his fate and asks whether he can call a press conference for the following day, to get it all over and done with. He says he won't speak to the media after that. Sugar agrees.

It seems Ardiles could have saved himself had he agreed to Sugar's suggestion a few weeks earlier that he bring in defensive guru Don Howe as a coach. The former Arsenal and QPR manager is now part of the England backroom staff under Terry Venables, but Sugar had been keen to employ him to help organise the back line.

Ardiles discussed it with his assistant Steve Perryman, who it's believed said he would be willing to accept the change; but in the end he told Sugar he did not want a new coach working alongside him. It's a decision which may have in part contributed to him losing his job.

Tuesday 1 November, 1994

The farewell press conference takes place at White Hart Lane. Ardiles sits downcast alongside the man who has sacked him. It's like *The Apprentice*, a decade before it first airs, with Sugar explaining why this one isn't the ideal candidate.

Sugar tells the media: 'It was one of the most difficult decisions I have ever had to make. Over the last few days a lot of soul-searching and deep thought has been applied. The difficulty has been compounded by the fact that he is such a delightful person.'

Ardiles says: 'This is the hardest job in football, and I felt I was a pawn in the battle [between Venables and Sugar]. It has been difficult for Alan Sugar as well as me. Privately there is a very strong bond between us, because you get that when things are not going well. Alan Sugar has his critics as I have. People have been suspicious of him because he is a newcomer to the game, but that is very unfair.'

What will you do now? ask the press. With a slight laugh, Ardiles replies: 'You can't play golf all the time, so don't bet against me making a comeback. I won't change my style. I passionately believe that the sort of football I want to play is also what the game needs.' Ardiles admits he disagreed with Sugar's suggestion that he should bring in another coach, saying it would have been 'an indictment' of his work. 'One or two names were suggested, but my answer was always that I do the job my way or not at all,' he says.

The walls are closing in. The room in which hundreds of press conferences have taken place, dozens of them involving this very manager, seems smaller today. The dimensions have changed, along with the parameters of the discourse. No one quite knows the rules now. What do you ask a man who has lost his job? When the team is on the slide, when defeat follows defeat, when the pressure mounts, so long as the manager still has his job there is sport within a sport.

The contest between reporter and under-fire manager continues as the pressure ramps up and up. This is different, though: the manager is already fallen, defeated; the contest is over – and yet there is still a press conference.

Ardiles looks around a room that he will never again survey in the same capacity. In a chequered suit jacket, pink shirt and red tie, he occasionally demonstrates the mental strength to muster a few smiles. At other times he appears close to tears. He feels this to the core, he feels this more intensely than any other sacked Tottenham manager. Tottenham is in his blood. The club he admits he had never heard of before Keith Burkinshaw came to Argentina to sign him is the place where he has built a new life. As a player he must truly have felt that Tottenham was a club made for him: kindred spirits with a shared philosophy.

At the end of the press conference there are sympathetic thank yous and goodbyes from the journalists. But there is still more sport for the media to have. As Ardiles leaves the room, photographers have already moved into the corridor outside to capture his departure. As he comes through the double doors they get him, head slightly bowed; above him, a green sign over the doorway which reads EXIT. It's the picture which will appear in tomorrow's papers.

It seems strange to think of a post-sacking press conference with chairman and manager in attendance. It's unlikely it would happen nowadays. For Ardiles perhaps it was a cathartic experience. Pain and disappointment were etched across his face. Ardiles has since said that only the Falklands War, and the way it affected relationships between Britain and Argentina, has been more difficult for him to deal with than his sacking by Tottenham.

In his autobiography he says that he felt he was destined to manage Tottenham. He speaks of his complete faith in the *al achique* method – of always pressuring the opponent and having the ball all the time and not losing it. Those methods, which he learnt from the man who will always remain his hero – his World Cup-winning Argentina manager César Menotti – he says he's sure he could have implemented at Spurs with more time.

Ardiles speaks of his admiration for Tottenham's mantra: *Audere est Facere* – To Dare Is To Do. He accepts that there may have been 'a certain arrogance' on his part in 'thinking that I could make any player play well beyond his capabilities'. However, he insists he is still convinced it is possible to play with five up front.

At that final press conference he had told the media not to bet against it, but there was to be no managerial comeback for Ardiles, at least not in England. He did go on to coach abroad, the high point coming in Japan. He was named J-League Manager of the Year with Shimizu S-Pulse in 1998, and won the title with Yokohama Marinos in 2000. He also had several other managerial jobs in Japan as well as in Croatia, Mexico, Argentina, Paraguay, Saudi Arabia and Israel. Today he works for Tottenham as a club ambassador.

Steve Perryman conducts an interview with the written press and the broadcast media. Does he have mixed emotions? Is he betraying Ossie by agreeing to Sugar's request to stay on as caretaker manager?

'He gave me his blessing. The first thing I did was to check that out with him. I am saddened for him, he's a wonderful human being,' he says. 'I have benefited from working alongside him. This is a club where I have spent my entire life. The title now is caretaker, but that doesn't matter. I am honoured. Will I play the same way? I have my thoughts about the way the game should be played. What we do need, however, is consistency.'

Wednesday 2 November, 1994

Alan Sugar's first move in his efforts to rebuild following the departure of Ardiles is to try to bring in David Pleat from Luton. He wants Pleat as a director of football, and wants him to have a say in who will be appointed as the head coach. Luton chairman David Kohler gives Sugar permission to speak to his manager, but the two remain miles apart on compensation. Kohler is reported to want £350,000, with Sugar thought to be prepared to offer £75,000.

Town have hardly been pulling up trees under Pleat in Division One. They've won five, drawn four and lost six of their first 15 games in the league. Pleat, though, is still highly respected at White Hart Lane. He had a successful spell as Tottenham manager, halted in 1987 when he resigned following unproven newspaper allegations over his private life.

On the field, many fans had been impressed with what they had seen from Pleat's team in 1986/87. With Clive Allen scoring a record 49 goals, Spurs finished third in the league, reached the semi-finals of the League Cup where they blew a 2-0 aggregate lead and then lost to Arsenal in a replay, and were beaten 3-2 after extra time in the FA Cup Final when Gary Mabbutt's own goal off his knee gave Coventry a shock win.

Pleat has unfinished business at Spurs, but he feels very much as though he still has plenty to offer in the dugout and on the touchline. He has real reservations about becoming Sugar's director of football.

Saturday 5 November, 1994
FA Carling Premiership
Blackburn Rovers 2-0 Tottenham Hotspur
Wilcox 8, Shearer (pen) 49

Perryman sticks with Popescu as sweeper. He makes three changes to the team which beat West Ham last week. Sheringham is recalled up front, with midfielder Hazard dropping to the bench. Thorstvedt is injured, so Ian Walker returns in goal.

Dumitrescu is left out too. The press are told he has a knee injury, but in reality he has had a training-ground argument with Perryman and declined the opportunity to be on the bench having been told he won't be in the starting line-up. His replacement is David Howells, who will occupy the holding midfield role that had been his until Ardiles dropped him for Calderwood without explanation for the first game of the season. This is his first league appearance of 1994/95.

It turned out to be Perryman's only match in caretaker charge, but from this point on, Howells was a virtual ever-present in the starting line-up. 'What was slightly strange from my point of view,' says Howells, 'was that the first thing Stevie P did was put me straight back into the team against Blackburn. Stevie was a great bloke, and I had played with both Stevie and Ossie in my early career at the club. I just thought, well, if Stevie clearly thinks I should be in the team why wouldn't he have spoken to Ossie about it? I've never understood that.

'Ilie was a good lad and a very talented player, and came in fit as a fiddle off the back of the World Cup. He liked London, he liked both sides, the football side and the social side, and he just seemed to lose a bit of sharpness and a bit of fitness as the season went on as opposed to getting stronger. You could play those five players no problem at all if they're all working. You've got tremendous work ethic there, Darren, Nicky Barmby, Teddy Sheringham, Jürgen Klinsmann. Ilie wasn't working. He was the obvious luxury if you like. That's a horrible term, because people who get labelled luxury players are usually the best players – Matt Le Tissier at Southampton was labelled a luxury player. Complete rubbish: he was the best player.

'Ilie though, quite noticeably, wasn't as fit as the others. He wasn't doing both sides of the game, which you have to do, and so he was quite clearly the one who made way.'

The Blackburn programme carries a feature on Klinsmann. 'Jürgen likes to play his football with a smile. The arrival of Jürgen Klinsmann at White Hart Lane was not only an incredible shot in the arm for Tottenham

Hotspur just when they most needed it, but a boost to English football at a time when the game in general is riding high again.

'Football is certainly back in fashion with a bang. Attendances are rising along with standards on and off the field, and when a world-class star such as Klinsmann decided that England was the place to be, it was the icing on the cake. The way the fans have flocked to see him speaks much for the crowd-pulling power of the German international star. And the manner in which he has taken to Premier League football – indeed, his whole attitude – has already endeared him to thousands of new followers.'

Tottenham are well beaten at Ewood Park by the team who will finish the season as champions of England. Rovers boast an £8.3m strike force – Alan Shearer and Chris Sutton – which has become known as the S-A-S. Shearer had joined from Southampton for £3.6m, a record fee paid by an English club, in the summer of 1992. Sutton set that record anew when he signed for £5m from Norwich in July 1994.

Both are involved in the opening goal. Sutton is too strong for Popescu on the right and crosses to Shearer, whose effort crashes off the post and straight into the path of Jason Wilcox. He can't fail to give Rovers an eighth-minute lead from close range.

The home side get a second just after half-time. Klinsmann is furious that referee Terry Holbrook fails to notice a handball by Colin Hendry. Instead of awarding a penalty he waves play on; Rovers break and moments later have a spot-kick of their own when Edinburgh brings down Shearer from behind. Shearer takes the penalty; Walker gets a hand to it but can't keep it out. Rovers win 2-0.

After the match the newspapers seek answers as to who will become Tottenham's new manager. David Pleat of Luton is still one of the favourites, but QPR's Gerry Francis is being hailed as an ever more realistic prospect. Other names mentioned are those of former England manager Bobby Robson, whose contract with FC Porto is due to expire next summer, and former Netherlands, Real Madrid and Ajax coach Leo Beenhakker, who is now with Club America in Mexico. Some of the newspapers even suggest Klinsmann might get the job.

Alan Sugar has been here three years, and the club is now facing its fourth managerial appointment in that time. It's crucial he gets this decision right. It's sad to see Ossie go, but things could get much worse if Sugar brings in the wrong man. Right now, relegation from the Premier League appears a distinct possibility.

PART TWO

November 1994–April 1995

THE FRANCIS REVIVAL

7

Meanwhile at Loftus Road ...

AS THINGS fell apart for Ossie Ardiles at Tottenham in October 1994, across London another man who had become a legend at his club during his playing days was being forced out of his dream managerial job. Unlike Ardiles, Gerry Francis wasn't being shown the door at Loftus Road because of poor results – on the contrary, he had done a magnificent job at a small club. He was being levered out of position because QPR wanted to sell his prime asset Les Ferdinand despite initially promising him that the player wouldn't have to go that season.

At this point Francis's association with Rangers spanned 25 years. He had first become part of the club as a schoolboy in the 1966/67 season when they were in the old Third Division. Alec Stock was the manager and Jim Gregory was the new ambitious chairman. Within a couple of years they had the club back in Division One. Francis signed a two-year apprenticeship in 1967/68 and made his debut while still an apprentice, aged 17 years and 113 days, as a substitute against the mighty Liverpool on 29 March 1969.

In June 1969, he put pen to his first professional contract and made his full debut, still aged just 17, in a Second Division match away to Portsmouth on 13 September that year, scoring in a 3-1 win. He would go on to make 354 league and cup appearances, notching up 65 goals in 13 seasons. In that time he also had the great honour of playing for and captaining his country at both senior and Under-23 level. When he pulled on the senior armband, at the age of just 23, he became the youngest England captain since Bobby Moore. He remains the only QPR player to have captained England. Serious back and knee injuries then forced him out of football for nearly two years.

Francis also captained QPR's most successful side of all time. In 1975/76 he led them to second place in the top flight, scoring 12 goals from 36 appearances in midfield as he did so. Indeed Rangers were top of the table when they had completed all of their fixtures but Liverpool's final game away to Wolves had been postponed because of their European commitments. Rangers had to wait ten days until that match at Molineux. The Reds had the advantage of knowing exactly what they had to do. They came from behind to win 3-1 and take the title by one point. Nowadays of course all the crucial matches on the final day kick off simultaneously.

In 1991/92 Francis returned to Loftus Road as Rangers manager. He maintained a top-half finish every season that he was with the club, (including an impressive fifth place in 1992/93 when they were London's top club in the first Premier League season above Spurs, Arsenal, Chelsea, Wimbledon and Crystal Palace), despite selling over £10m worth of talent. By October 1994, though, it appeared that all of his achievements counted for nothing as far as the owners were concerned.

Relaying those experiences to me as we meet face to face at his family home in Bagshot, Francis describes the turbulent few months which saw him pushed towards the exit doors and led to him taking the job at White Hart Lane. 'The problems had started in 1993/94,' he says. 'Richard Thompson was the QPR chairman. I liked Richard on the whole, but most of the arguments we had were about selling players. He wanted to sell Les Ferdinand, who at the time was one of the most sought-after strikers in the Premier League. Les had struggled to get in the team before I became manager there. He had been sent out on loan to Brentford and Besiktas in Turkey, but I could see how much talent he had.

'I worked so hard to turn him into a player who became one of the most prolific and dangerous strikers in the game, and who of course went on to gain many England caps.

'Les writes in his autobiography about the day, shortly after I became manager, that I told him I thought he had the talent to go on and represent his country. He started laughing. I asked him why he was laughing. "Play for England?" he said. "I can barely get into the QPR team." I told him he had all the attributes and that I could make him a much better player but that most importantly he had to believe in himself, and I made him do that.

'Ultimately it was Les's improvement as a player that caused most of my problems at QPR. I had initially been promised by Richard Thompson that I would not have to sell Les ahead of the 1994/95 season. Now I was being told he would have to go. I'm not stupid. I know a club of QPR's size will have to sell their best players to survive. During my time there Paul Parker, Andy Sinton, Darren Peacock and Roy Wegerle were all sold, bringing in £10m and making the club a great profit. But when you have someone like Les, who will get you 20 Premier League goals a season, it is so important that you hold on to them for as long as you can if you are going to go anywhere as a club. His goals can be the difference between finishing in the top half of the table or being relegated. This is what I told Richard Thompson and QPR at the time. It didn't take them long to find out I was right. The summer after I left, they sold Les to Newcastle, and they were relegated straight away. It took them 15 years to get back to the top flight, a time in which they also spent three seasons in the third tier. I rest my case.

'The club made huge profits from the players I brought through. Les alone went to Newcastle for £6m. In my time there I spent just over £2m; the highest fee I shelled out was £750,000 for Trevor Sinclair from Blackpool. He left for West Ham for £2.3m in 1998.'

With Francis determined to hold on to Ferdinand, it appears the owners began to try to usher the manager towards the exit instead. In March 1994, Francis was upset when Richard Thompson gave second-tier Wolves permission to talk to him about the managerial vacancy at Molineux.

'I got an unexpected phone call from Jonathan Hayward, the chairman at Wolves,' says Francis. 'He said Richard Thompson was happy for us to discuss me taking on the job there. I told him I wanted to speak to Richard first to find out what was going on. I couldn't believe Richard had granted Wolves permission. We were doing so well at QPR, we were eighth in the Premiership with a good chance of qualifying for Europe. Richard said to me that going to Wolves would be a good opportunity for me to manage a club with great potential. He said he felt the size of QPR meant we would be a selling club and I wouldn't be able to keep my best players. I felt totally unwanted by his decision to give Wolves permission to speak to me. I told him if I wasn't wanted then I would go and speak to Wolves, which is what I did.

'Jonathan Hayward was a very ambitious chairman. The owner – his father Jack – was the same. They went out of their way both in financial terms and hospitality to try to convince me to take the Wolves job. But I was happy at QPR. I had spent most of my professional life there. I live close to London and my family, friends and other businesses are all there.

We had just finished fifth in the Premier League and were sitting eighth right now, while Wolves were halfway down Division One. I turned down their offer and the next day Rodney Marsh – my former QPR team-mate – was all over the media saying I should have taken it. He said I had a lack of ambition. I wasn't happy about those comments, I made that clear to Richard Thompson and also rang Rodney to tell him. After all, he was supposed to be a QPR fan with a great love for the club.'

As autumn 1994 approached, it was beginning to look like Thompson was ratcheting up the pressure to make life as uncomfortable as possible for Francis. Knowing that his manager had not been best pleased with Rodney Marsh's comments, Thompson then set about bringing Marsh in as director of football.

'On 31 October 1994 we were due to play Liverpool that night live on Sky,' says Francis. 'All morning my answer phone at home had been very busy with journalists leaving messages. They wanted to get my opinion on a story in a couple of the papers that Rodney was going to become director of football at QPR. I had been told nothing about this so I tried to reach Richard Thompson to ask him to make a statement to dismiss the rumours. I couldn't get hold of him and left various messages.

'I was now listening to Rodney on the radio talking about how he had been approached by Richard Thompson and that he was going to be sitting with him at tonight's game. I checked with my secretary, Martina Leonard, to see if Rodney was in fact scheduled to come to the game and found out that indeed he was due to sit with Richard Thompson. I was now receiving so many phone calls from friends and relatives who wanted to know what was going on. I still couldn't get hold of Richard. It's hard to explain just how I felt by now. The success I had already had at the club. All the years of hard work. The £10m they'd already made from selling players. Now they want me to sell my best player. It all seemed to count for nothing and I knew, with my character, that I had been pushed to a point where I would have to resign straight after the QPR v Liverpool game.

'I took my girlfriend Julie and our 18-month-old boy Adam to the game and picked up my parents Roy and Pauline on the way to the stadium. They all knew that I was going to resign. We beat Liverpool 2-1, but for the first time in my career I didn't turn up at the post-match press conference. With the Sky cameras having shown Richard Thompson sitting alongside Terry Venables, and Rodney Marsh draped in a QPR scarf during the match, I would have felt humiliated going to a press conference before having been told anything officially about the situation.

'Having refused to return any of my calls, it wasn't until the morning after the game that Richard finally allowed me to talk to him. I have to say I made my anger clear to Richard as I tendered my resignation. He accepted it but told me I had to go and meet his father David on 2 November. Richard told me his dad was the owner of the club, which was news to me. The following statement, which I released to the media a few days later, explains what happened next:

QUEENS PARK RANGERS FOOTBALL CLUB
Rangers Stadium, Shepherd's Bush, London, W12 7PA
Statement from Gerry Francis

It is with deep regret that I find it necessary to issue this statement with regard to my resignation from Queens Park Rangers Football Club.

Due to the events that took place on Monday 31 October, which I knew nothing whatsoever about, I felt I had no alternative but to resign as manager of Queens Park Rangers FC on Tuesday 1 November. This resignation was accepted by Mr Thompson subject to me meeting him again on Wednesday morning, 2 November, which I did.

I was then asked to meet Mr David Thompson, who I haven't met in three and a half years of being at the club, on Wednesday evening where again I was asked to work with Rodney Marsh. I left that meeting at 10.45pm having resigned from QPR FC.

Later that evening at 11.30pm I had a telephone call from Mr Thompson saying that they were not accepting my resignation and that if I left I would be in breach of contract and that they wanted further talks with myself and asked if I would carry on with the team for the Newcastle game. This I agreed to do because of the lateness of the situation.

I have had subsequent meetings with various people over many issues and although I regret the fact that for once in my life I have had to break a contract, I found I was left with little alternative.

I would again like to thank my staff and players for three excellent seasons in difficult circumstances and everybody associated with the club for their outstanding support for me over my time with QPR, particularly the supporters who, through my stay here, have been absolutely outstanding with their support.

I sincerely wish Queens Park Rangers FC, the players and supporters every success possible for the future.

Gerry Francis

Francis adds: 'One thing will always puzzle me about the whole affair. If, as both Richard Thompson and his father David told me, Rodney Marsh would be such a valuable asset to the club, why was he never appointed when I left? I will leave you to reach your own conclusions.'

Alan Sugar seized the moment. Although the Thompsons had officially rejected Francis's resignation, when Sugar phoned them for permission to speak to Francis, he was given the go-ahead. QPR would be entitled to some compensation in the event of Francis leaving.

'When Alan called me I told him after what had happened at QPR I wasn't sure I was interested in staying in football,' says Francis. 'Alan, though, can be a very persuasive man, and by the end of that phone call I had agreed to meet him at his home in Chigwell. I found him a precise man who chose his words carefully. He was very straight about the situation concerning the position of the club. He told me that although he would fight the issue, he didn't envisage the return of the six points or the FA Cup place.

'They were right in the relegation dogfight. So, there was no FA Cup, and the team were fighting for their lives in the league. They hadn't kept a clean sheet all season and had only one win in their last seven games – a run that included a humiliating 3-0 League Cup defeat against a Notts County team who were bottom of the First Division. Alan also made it clear that there was no money left to spend in the transfer market and I would have to raise any cash myself through selling players.

'So it wasn't the most attractive proposition, but I listened to what he had to say. I think there are two sides to Alan. Of course he wasn't doing *The Apprentice* at the time, but there is that side to him. I think that is the side he likes people to see, but really there is a much warmer side to him, and that's the real Alan, and the Alan that I got to know.

'On my part, I explained to Alan in detail my management career, what I had learned from my experiences at Exeter City and that at both Bristol Rovers and Queens Park Rangers – despite severe financial restraints and having to sell my best players – I had managed to bring great success.'

It's easy to see why Sugar would have been impressed by Francis's track record. Prior to what he had achieved at QPR – finishing above Tottenham every season since he had arrived in 1991, despite having to sell his players – he had also over-performed at Bristol Rovers.

His managerial career had started as player-manager at Exeter. Despite having spent so many years playing at the very highest level, he was willing to cut his teeth in the lower leagues with the Grecians. 'I made a lot of mistakes at Exeter,' says Francis. 'I was trying to play the sort of football I had been playing all my career. The players were willing, but at that level they weren't capable of doing the things I wanted. I was still playing, and I was having to deal with the directors too. I learnt a great deal about managing, but I was bitterly disappointed when we were relegated in 1983/84. It led to my first and only sacking.'

In 1987 he succeeded Bobby Gould as manager at Bristol Rovers – also in the third tier. There he built a team for £20,000 – £10,000 of which was his own money. 'I loaned them that to buy Ian Holloway from Brentford,' laughs Francis. 'It wasn't the most sensible thing to do when you consider the club was in danger of folding at any time and therefore I would have lost every penny.'

Under Francis, Rovers had four fantastic years. They finished eighth, then reached the play-off final where they were edged out by Port Vale over two legs. Then, huge success followed in 1989/90. Francis was named Division Three's Manager of the Year after leading Rovers to their first title since 1953, losing just five games along the way. He also guided them to Wembley for the first time in their history as the club took 36,000 fans to the Leyland DAF Cup Final where they were narrowly beaten 2-1 by Tranmere. His final year saw a highly-respectable mid-table finish in the second tier – the first time Rovers had played at that level since the early 1960s.

Francis had a remarkable association with Rovers fans. He had played for them in 1986/87 when the club's supporters got together to help pay his wages. In 1988/89, having just missed out on promotion, Francis was a much sought-after manager. He was interviewed by West Ham and Aston Villa with the media linking him with several high-profile jobs. He was out of contract and could have left. The Bristol Rovers fans were desperate for him to stay. Ten thousand of them sent him postcards which read: 'Don't go Gerry.'

'I've still got those postcards in my loft,' says Francis. 'They meant a lot to me. I am so pleased I stayed on, because the next year was amazing. What made me stay for that year was the fact that the fans got together to persuade me. They had paid my wages as a player, and you remember things like that. It was a chance for me to repay that loyalty.'

The loyalty was indeed repaid as Francis led them to the title and the Leyland DAF Cup Final. He did that despite losing two of his best players in the space of a week. With the team top of the table, Watford signed his top goalscorer Gary Penrice for £500,000 and a young Nigel Martyn became Britain's first £1m goalkeeper when he was sold to Crystal Palace. The two players had cost Rovers nothing.

'I'd signed Nigel after he had been recommended to me by my tea lady at Bristol Rovers,' says Francis. 'She'd seen him playing while she was on holiday and recommended him to me. It nearly didn't happen. Rovers at the time were in a precarious situation financially. Nigel was working in a warehouse on £100 a week and wanted about £130 from us. Speaking to my chairman, he felt that we had a good young keeper in Nicky Carter, which we did. He said we couldn't afford another keeper. I had to explain that Nigel was a different level, and it would be a massive mistake not to sign him. Luckily I managed to convince him. He went on to become England Under-21 goalkeeper while at Bristol Rovers.

'Gary Penrice was a midfielder who I had played alongside at Rovers. When I became manager I made him into a striker straight away. I was fiercely opposed to both of them being sold. Now if you lose two players of that calibre in the space of a week – your top scorer, and a future England goalkeeper – then that really is frustrating as a manager. On the bright side I was given my £10,000 back, although without any interest. I was also handed just £70,000 from the £1.5m worth of sales to replace Penrice and Martyn. This I did by taking goalkeeper Brian Parkin on a free transfer from Crystal Palace and eventually buying Carl Saunders from Stoke City for £70,000. At the time Carl was a reserve right-back for Stoke. I made him into my replacement striker for Gary Penrice and he became my leading goalscorer as we won the title.

'The money the club got for Penrice and Martyn saved them financially. As it turned out, I won the title and got to a cup final without those two, so the owners were certainly pleased their decisions had worked out. However, for me, I felt they had made a mistake selling both players at the same time and they were very fortunate that I was able to bring in those players and still keep the success going. In doing so, I had made a rod for my own back. People felt I could perform miracles all the time.'

It was a reputation which Francis built on at QPR, and one which clearly impressed Alan Sugar. 'At our first meeting Alan said he wanted to bring in David Pleat as director of football, with me working as head coach,' says Francis. 'I told him I didn't work like that. Alan said he was interviewing other candidates, and as I left his house I wished him good luck with his appointment, whoever that might be.

'The morning after I had been at his house Alan rang again. He wanted me to go back for another meeting that evening. I went over and, whereas in the first chat I had with him he had been very businesslike, this time he seemed much warmer. He came over as a man who had made up his mind. He wanted me to take over at Tottenham as manager. His obvious enthusiasm for Tottenham to do well came across in a very positive way. In fact, his whole family – especially one of his sons Danny, who I met for the first time that night – were very optimistic about the club's future. Alan was determined to try to make Tottenham a force to be reckoned with again. He wanted the club to try to become the Manchester United of the South. He agreed that he wouldn't be appointing a director of football.

'At this stage my head was spinning. I had now been offered the job at one of the biggest clubs in the country two days after resigning at Queens

Park Rangers and at a point when I was considering finishing in football management. I asked Alan to give me 48 hours to think it over and talk to my family as so much had happened so quickly.

'I got home in the early hours of that Thursday morning. Julie was fast asleep and I saw no point disturbing her. I went straight to bed but couldn't sleep as my mind was very active. Eventually, I must have nodded off as the next thing I remember was Julie waking me up with a much-needed cup of tea. I spent most of that day talking with Julie and a number of people that I knew and trusted, like my dad and Dave Sexton who was the England Under-21 coach and had once been my manager at Loftus Road and Highfield Road when I played for Coventry. Dave was a person for whom I had the utmost respect, both as an outstanding football coach and also a friend.'

Although Francis was initially reticent about returning to football, as he sounded out friends, family and colleagues, they urged him to take his chance at one of England's biggest clubs.

'The over-riding message from everyone I spoke to seemed to be that after what I had achieved at Bristol Rovers and Queens Park Rangers in difficult circumstances that I now had a real chance at a top job,' says Francis. 'This was also how I was beginning to think and it was Alan Sugar's ambition in particular that had left a big impression on me. Most importantly, for the first time in my career, a chairman was telling me I wouldn't have to sell any players that I wanted to keep. Believe me, that was music to my ears.'

On Friday 11 November 1994, Francis went to see Sugar at his house again and told him, that yes, he would like to accept the job as Tottenham manager. 'I said to Alan I would do it until the end of the season and see how it went – a trial if you like,' says Francis. 'I had virtually always worked with either a year's contract or no contract at all. This was certainly a different approach to nearly all managers' agreements, where security is of the utmost importance. Security is usually established with a long-term contract. I felt it was crucial to see whether myself and Alan could work together because in my experience the two most important men at any football club are the chairman and the manager. Their relationship is vital. In my position, at the end of the season if I wasn't successful then I could be out of a job – with no compensation whatsoever. Yet, at the same time, if I was successful but I wanted to leave for one reason or another, I could do so. This gave me the freedom – without breaking contracts and letting people down – to decide what I wanted to do with my life. This situation certainly doesn't stop you being loyal to any particular club as throughout my career as both player and manager I had acquired a reputation for being so.

'Alan was really surprised and couldn't understand why I didn't want a long-term contract, but he agreed to it. Thankfully, there wasn't a game the following day. It was international week. That gave me the chance to look for someone to be my assistant. First, I tried to get Frank Sibley to join me from Queens Park Rangers. When I took over at QPR I had appointed Frank as my assistant manager after he had been sacked as Chelsea reserve team manager. I had known Frank and his family for some 25 years and I was a player at Rangers when he was manager briefly back in the late 1970s.

'Initially, he agreed to come to Spurs and I had negotiated a great contract with Alan Sugar for him, but obviously only until the end of the year. At the last minute, Frank turned it down and signed a new, improved three-year contact with Rangers.

'At this stage, I had also decided to bring Des Bulpin, my youth team manager at Queens Park Rangers, with me to take charge of the Tottenham youth team. I had first met Des at Bristol Rovers where he was my youth team manager and also my reserve team manager. He had followed me to QPR and was a very good friend. We had developed some great youngsters at QPR like Kevin Gallen, Danny Dichio, Trevor Challis, Chris Plummer, Matthew Brazier, and Nigel Quashie. Des had just won the South East Counties Championship the year before with QPR but he was delighted to follow me again to Tottenham.

'I then returned to my search to find an assistant manager. I contacted my reserve team manager at Rangers, Roger Cross. He had also been offered a new three-year contract at Loftus Road. Roger turned down the contract offer from Rangers and agreed to come to White Hart Lane. I was delighted, but felt responsible for both Roger and Des after their rejection of the security that the Rangers contracts would have provided. For both of them it was something of a gamble. After all, I might not even be at Tottenham at the end of the season for whatever reason but both were very angry and upset, as I was, at the treatment I had received from QPR.

'There was another person at Queens Park Rangers who was upset and angry about the way things had gone – and this was to work to my advantage. When I joined QPR as manager in 1991/92, Martina Leonard had been working at QPR for a short while. Unfortunately for her, she drew the short straw, because she was appointed as my personal secretary! She was excellent at her job and made my life a lot easier, as did club secretary Sheila Marson and also Terry Springett and Terry Dormer. After I resigned, Martina told my girlfriend Julie that she was so upset by the treatment I had received that she couldn't work there anymore and that she was leaving to find another job. She asked Julie not to say anything to me about the matter. As you can imagine Julie was quite upset by this and eventually reluctantly mentioned it to me. While you might take your backroom staff with you when moving to another club, you don't usually take your former secretary. Fate then lent a hand. At my next meeting with Alan Sugar, Daniel Sugar and the chief executive Claude Littner, I was informed that, at that moment in time, I hadn't got a secretary. Bingo! Now Martina had drawn the short straw again.

'There is of course a less pleasant side of moving into a club and bringing your own assistant with you. It means that, invariably, someone has to go and in this case it was Steve Perryman, who had been serving as assistant to Ossie Ardiles, and who of course was in caretaker charge for the last match against Blackburn. With Roger coming in, it was obvious Steve had to go. It was unfortunate and I spoke to him myself about the situation. He understood. Steve is a great professional and had been an outstanding servant to Spurs over the years.

'Moving to a new club with a third of the season gone created problems of its own. There had been no pre-season preparation for me, no chance for me to get to know the players who were going to play for me. I had a very short time in which to gain their respect. If you take over in the summer you at least have the advantage of having six to eight weeks to get an association with the players and the pattern of play and tactics that you are going to use. At Tottenham, I didn't know them, and they didn't know me.

'There was also the drawback of taking over in international week. Many overseas players had been brought to the club that summer. So, as well as Teddy Sheringham being away with England, I had first-team players all over the continent. Jürgen Klinsmann was with Germany, Gica Popescu and Ilie Dumitrescu with Romania, Ronny Rosenthal with Israel, and Gerard McMahon with Northern Ireland. Also away with the Under-21s were Sol Campbell with England, Steve Carr and Andy Turner with the Republic of Ireland and Gareth Knott with Wales, so I had been left with just a handful of first-team players for most of the week. I couldn't have waited until Friday when they all returned for my first talk to the squad, so I assembled those that were still with me in the canteen at the training ground.

'I kept my message brief and simple. All I did was to introduce myself, Roger and Des. I told the players: "I have come here because I want to be successful and to try to win things. It is not going to be easy and we are just going to have to work hard on the training pitch and make it work together." Then I took my first press conference.

'The next day I became aware of the media attention there is at a club like Spurs. It is totally different to QPR. All the headlines in the papers were FRANCIS CLEAR-OUT, saying that I was going to be selling all the players and bringing in new ones. One of the papers had mugshots of the players all printed in a line-up. I didn't like this at all, and was worried how it would have gone down with the players. Spirit is important to me, very important. I felt it may be damaged if the players named in the story thought I was looking to sell them when it simply wasn't true.

'I saw it as the worst possible way to start because the players concerned might be thinking that was really what I had in my mind. The good thing was that I always made sure my press conferences were recorded. I called all the players together and said: "I can tell you one thing – I will always tell you the truth. Come and see me and I will let you know what the position is." I believe it is vital to be truthful and loyal to your players. The reaction from the players to the story seemed to be that this sort of thing always happened at Tottenham. I told them that they could listen to the recording of the press conference at any time and I just stressed again that if any player came to see me, I would tell them what, if anything, was going on.

'It was not until the Friday morning that I was able to sit and talk with Jürgen Klinsmann, Teddy Sheringham, Ronny Rosenthal, Gica Popescu and Ilie Dumitrescu. On the two previous days I had spoken at length with Gary Mabbutt. He had been at the club a long time, was respected by the players and could give an insight into the situation from the players' point of view. That was a big help to me. Jürgen came over as a very articulate person but, perhaps understandably, a little wary on our first meeting. It was a help having Roger Cross there when it came to Teddy Sheringham. I had never met Teddy before but Roger had worked with him when he was youth coach at Millwall.

'I had asked Roger to talk to Teddy after the England game on the Wednesday night and to let him know of my plans and that he and Jürgen were a very important part of those plans. I have always believed in wingers to supply my front men and in Jürgen and Teddy I had two outstanding strikers – particularly from a finishing point of view. It was going to be vital to supply these two front men with as many chances as possible. This is what good natural wingers can achieve – but unfortunately it was clear to me that we were very short of natural wingers at the club. Darren Anderton – a great crosser of the ball – had been out injured for over six weeks and hadn't even had a reserve game yet, but had just returned to training.

'Another situation I had to resolve quickly, was one concerning the media and the fans coming to our Chase Lodge training ground in Mill Hill. Every day seemed like a press day or an open day. It was like a circus. Hundreds of people had been turning up in coaches, and there were complaints from our landlords about damage to the pitches. I had to put a stop to that. I couldn't have all those people there every day. After all, the training ground is a place of work. Outside of matchday, it is the most important place for preparation and concentration. I'm not saying the press and public should never be allowed up there, because they are vital elements in all football clubs. But what I did was to set aside certain days when they would be given access. No one would be allowed up there the day before a game. That is when I wanted the minds of the players to be focused on the game ahead, nothing else.

'Before I knew it, it was time for my first big decision as manager of Tottenham – picking the team I would put out against Aston Villa at White Hart Lane for my first match. That is a decision I always make myself. Naturally, I talk to the people who work with me but I take the responsibility for the final choice. This was a difficult one. I knew how I wanted to play but it was a question of whether I was going to be able to do it successfully with the players that I had at the club.

'The lack of natural wingers was a real problem for me. Tottenham had been playing in different triangle systems all season without much width, basically a narrow diamond. Over the years I had used a certain formation and pattern of play in both defence and attack that could be adaptable to all kinds of systems and tactics, and width played a big part in it.

'The most important ingredients for me, however, are ability, organisation and consistency – a team working as one unit with great skill and flair, when allowed, and great tenacity when required. Unfortunately, though, this takes time, and time was something I was short of in the build-up to this first game. So, to put it mildly, it was a difficult night for me before the game. I don't think I got any sleep at all, the way I was tossing and turning. I don't like to be unprepared – and never had a team of mine been so unprepared as the one I sent out there that day.

'With Ilie Dumitrescu out suspended, I decided on my team line-up and it included what many people might regard as my first controversial decision. I decided to leave out Nicky Barmby. I had no doubt at all that he was a talented player and I reckoned that in the months to come he would have a big part to play for me, but Nicky was an out-and-out attacking player and I saw Teddy and Jürgen as my front two. I knew I would be bringing Nicky into the team but I wanted to do more work with him on the role I wanted him to play on the left-hand side. He was disappointed at my decision and I could understand that, but management is all about making decisions – and I took a major chance with another one. Darren Anderton was a player I had always rated and even though he had been out for six weeks, I decided to play him. I knew he would give me the width I needed to supply the service to the front men.

'At the back I went for David Kerslake at right-back, Colin Calderwood and Gary Mabbutt in the middle, with Sol Campbell at left-back. With Nicky Barmby left out, Darren Caskey was my wide player on the left and I kept David Howells in midfield to give us some bite alongside Gica Popescu. Now we were ready for my first match, and it turned out to be a real rollercoaster, which is exactly what the next few months had in store too.'

Indeed, so eventful were those next few months, that Francis was moved to commit many of his experiences to paper. It is a great privilege to be able to reproduce those writings in this book over the next few chapters.

8

Changing of the Guard

*'The team was still attacking, still vibrant,
because Gerry retained that Ossie freedom,
but with a balance. There were some
sensational performances after a while.'
(David Howells)*

A S Gerry Francis steps on to the White Hart Lane pitch, dozens
of flashbulbs pop around him. The fans here for today's match
against Aston Villa can barely make out the figure of their new
manager, drowning as he is in a sea of photographers. Francis takes a few
steps and waves to all four sides of the ground, turning his entire body as
he does so; the imperfect circle of cameramen surrounding him wobble
in time like a drunken hokey-cokey. With Christmas now just six weeks
away, the nights are drawing in. Even ahead of a three o'clock kick-off
the North London gloom lends intensity to the flashbulbs: sparks of
light beneath slate-grey skies. Sparking Spurs back into life in the depths
of autumn is the task Francis has been set. The mission: to reverse the
dramatic loss of form that has seen Spurs win just one of their last seven
games and slip towards the relegation zone.

Diary of Gerry Francis
Saturday 19 November, 1994
I drove mum and dad, along with Julie and Adam, to White Hart Lane.
From the outset, it was clear that this was a different situation for all of us
to what we were used to at QPR, because even a good few hours before

kick-off we were caught up in heavy traffic. I had to leave the main A10 route that I knew and go around the back way to Tottenham, straight into more traffic. I certainly didn't want to be late for my first game. I was pretty nervous and the traffic didn't help matters. Eventually we managed to get there in good time and I found my way into my office. From the window I saw masses of people arriving at the club and it was obvious this was going to be a huge crowd. I left Julie, Adam and my parents at about 1.30pm and it was a relief to get down into the dressing room area and get things going.

One thing that has made an impact on me straight away is the size of the club. Until you work here you don't realise just how big it is and how much tradition there is attached to the place. It is massive. You see people like Bill Nicholson around and you know you are somewhere special. I noticed a replica of the FA Cup standing proudly in the foyer of the main entrance. You have to be associated with a club like Tottenham to appreciate the true history of the game. At 1.45pm it was time to reveal my first Tottenham team to the players. Before I did so, I had a quiet word with Nicky Barmby who was being left on the bench. He was disappointed, but I assured him he has a future here under me.

Just before the game I was introduced to the crowd and was given a tremendous reception. It was a good moment but sometimes you fear it is like winning the Manager of the Month award – it is great to get, but sometimes it can be the kiss of death. The dressing room I had left was a pretty quiet one but that was to be expected. As the players get to know you, they become aware of the level of formality that you like. I quite like the players to relax and for it to be quite a noisy dressing room. Before the game I decided to put the television on for half an hour, just to break the silence and help people unwind a bit. It helps to settle nerves. Obviously, 30 minutes before the game, the television went off and we talked about what we had to do. We had gone over things on Friday and just before they left the dressing room we went over the same points again. If I had tried to put everything into their heads that I wanted, it would have been a nightmare. It just wasn't possible. They wouldn't have been able to take it in so I went with the real basic stuff in the hope that it would work out. It didn't.

FA Carling Premiership
Tottenham Hotspur 3-4 Aston Villa
Sheringham 40, Klinsmann (pen) 53, Bosnich (og) 74
Atkinson 8, Fenton 21, 27, Saunders 90
After ten minutes we were behind. Then there was another, and within 27 minutes we were 3-0 down. All of the nervousness and lack of

confidence that had been apparent in the videos I had been watching of the home defeat by Forest, the thrashing at Manchester City and the cup shock at Notts County, were evident. And there was an absolute stone-cold silence at White Hart Lane. Except of course, for the ecstatic Villa fans who had come along. I looked over to Roger Cross alongside me in the dugout and thought: 'What have we done? How are we going to pull this around?' The first thing that struck me as the game progressed was how unfit they were – to my level of fitness anyway.

Then just before half-time, another blow. We lost David Kerslake through injury and I put Stuart Nethercott on. Fortunately Teddy Sheringham got a goal back. That at least gave the crowd a little something to cheer about. Now I was going into my first half-time meeting with plenty to do, to say the least. On the way back to the dressing room I was thinking that if this was my QPR team then this would have been 'a tin hats job' because they would know me well and realise that this was well below the level of performance that I would expect from them. But I have always felt that the most important thing is to be constructive. So my half-time message was a mixture of the two. First a bit of a rant and a rave to liven them up and show them what I won't accept on the pitch, but then a constructive tactical chat. There was a lot to put right tactically, and quickly.

I asked them about what had happened with two of the goals. No one said anything. For me, accountability is crucial, that's something I will be instilling in them. I told them this was a time to go out and show real pride and character. I wanted them to show me what they had got and what sort of players I was working with at the club. I asked them straight: 'Can we do it or are we going to lay down and die?'

I also decided I had to make a switch at half-time. On came Nicky Barmby for Darren Caskey and Nicky did very well indeed on the left-hand side of midfield. He's had a hectic week. His partner Mandy gave birth to their first child, Jack, on Monday, then I left him out of the starting line-up, and he has responded well.

The second half showed me that there is indeed a tremendous amount of pride and character here and I ended the game knowing I had something to work on because in that second 45 minutes we were magnificent. The tactical changes that we implemented worked and we stormed back to 3-3 with two goals from Jürgen – the first from a penalty, and then a scrappy close-range finish. We really should have gone on and won it. We missed a couple of good chances to have done so but in injury time Dean Saunders went past Gary Mabbutt on the right-hand side and curled a fantastic shot into the far corner. So inside a matter of seconds, instead of coming in and giving them a lot of praise for what had been a remarkable comeback, I had to go into the dressing room upset for the players and yet convinced there was enough heart in the squad to build a decent team. They had picked themselves up off the floor and came so near to pulling off a fantastic win.

What an amazing first game, even though it didn't go our way. Everyone was really down when I came into the dressing room – as it should be after a home defeat. But I said: 'Right, I am really pleased with that. You have shown me in that second half that you have spirit. Now we will get back on the training pitch on Monday and we will get it right.'

There is a game against Chelsea on Wednesday and then a really hard match at Liverpool on Saturday. The games are indeed going to come thick and fast which means we have very little time to prepare.

Fittingly, it was a picture of David Howells that adorned the programme for the first match of the Gerry Francis era. Howells was the immediate beneficiary of the change in management. Having been recalled to the holding midfield position by Steve Perryman for his one match in charge against Blackburn, he kept his place under Francis and had a good game against Villa. Colin Calderwood, who had been used in the holding midfield position by Ardiles, was switched to his more familiar central defensive role.

Under Francis, Howells would become possibly the most important component of the team. 'I speak to people now,' says Howells, 'and they ask me what we could have done if we'd had Gerry and Ossie working together. If we could have mixed the flair of Ossie and the stability and defensive mind of Gerry? Well, actually that's probably what we had for the first five or six months of Gerry: the perfect mix. The team was still attacking, still vibrant, because Gerry retained that Ossie freedom. He wanted you to go out and play, but he worked on the back four with the midfield and on how to defend, and we were very much stronger on set pieces because we all knew our jobs. The mix of Ossie's freedom to go and play, go and express yourself, and Gerry coming in and saying, "Well, that's all well and good, but what about when we haven't got the ball and we're playing against good teams?" That mix worked really well, there were some sensational performances after a little while.'

Darren Anderton says the confidence Francis showed in him by telling him on his first day that he wanted him in the team despite the fact he'd been out injured for six weeks, was really important. 'That was exactly what I wanted to hear,' he says. 'It really surprised me, but it was great to know from the off that I was rated by him. I'd only been back training two days and it really gave me a lift. Ossie had been good for me, but the change of management took me to another level and also the

The transfer that stunned the football world. Alan Sugar signs Jürgen Klinsmann

World Cup winners. Ossie Ardiles meets Jürgen Klinsmann

Klinsmann climbs aboard his 1967 VW Beetle

Fans mob Klinsmann at the pre-season friendly against Watford

Klinsmann launches into his famous dive celebration after scoring on his competitive debut at Sheffield Wednesday

EXIT

Fire door
Keep shut

Photographers snap Ardiles as he
leaves his final press conference
following his sacking by Alan Sugar

New manager Gerry Francis at work on the Mill Hill training ground

Francis in the Anfield dugout for his third game in charge, a 1-1 draw at Liverpool on 26 November 1994

Klinsmann celebrates his sensational volley in the 3-1 win against Sheffield Wednesday on 10 December 1994

Francis assesses proceedings from the dugout in the home win over Sheffield Wednesday

A joyous Teddy Sheringham after hitting a spectacular equaliser in the FA Cup sixth round tie at Anfield. Spurs went on to win 2-1

David Howells celebrates his only goal of the season as Tottenham beat Manchester City 2-1 on 11 April 1995

team to another level because of the work we did defensively. After that Villa game we went on a great run with some terrific performances. The Newcastle game a few weeks later was just brilliant. The talent and the flair was still there. The players were still allowed to express themselves, but now we had a spine, a shape, and some stability too.'

Spurs fans felt they had already seen promise of a revival under Francis too. 'It was a wonderful atmosphere that day,' says Daniel Wynne. 'The team did everything to get back into it when it seemed like they were dead and buried at 3-0 down. When Klinsmann finally hit the equaliser, scrappy though it was, he pulled out the dive celebration for the first time since his home debut against Everton. Everyone loved seeing it again.'

Perhaps Klinsmann was making a point to the referee with the celebration on this occasion. He had been furious not to have been given a penalty for a challenge by Bosnich in the first half. He had already been engaged in a few verbals with the Villa keeper who suggested to the referee Paul Durkin that Klinsmann had dived. Durkin didn't think it was a foul or a dive, yet Klinsmann was so angry that his protestations were still going on a minute later when he was then booked for dissent. It was his third yellow card in English football, and his third in four games.

Klinsmann was the key to Tottenham's comeback. After Villa made it 3-0, most Spurs fans would have looked at the clock and feared an absolute annihilation with 63 minutes remaining. Klinsmann though stood on the halfway line, frantically waving both arms at the crowd, cajoling them to get behind the team. He alone believed there was a way back.

Sheringham gave Spurs hope just before the break, then Klinsmann got his opportunity from the spot early in the second half. It was Howells who started the move which led to the penalty. He prodded a pass forward to Sheringham. The England striker threatened to get the better of Phil King, who pulled at his shirt, leaving the linesman no option but to flag. The foul began outside the box, but continued into the area, legitimising Durkin's decision to point to the spot.

For Spurs, by now penalties were no longer the straightforward scoring opportunity they should be. Sheringham had missed his last three. Barmby and Anderton had both had penalties saved by Villa keeper Bosnich in the same match at The Lane the previous season. Penalty specialist Dumitrescu was not involved, so Klinsmann – as many felt should have happened earlier in the season – assumed spot-kick duties.

As he faced up to Bosnich from the spot, and the opportunity to bring Spurs back to 3-2, many home fans feared yet another Tottenham miss. Even the über-cool German had been losing his rag in this match, and Bosnich had a good penalty-saving record. The outcome was far from a foregone conclusion, but Klinsmann strode up and side-footed his effort low and just beyond the reach of Bosnich, who went the right way but just couldn't get a touch on the ball.

The goal which brought Tottenham level at 3-3 was probably the team's scrappiest of the season. The ball ricocheted off Paul McGrath to Barmby, who turned and teased it through a crowded area to Popescu who was standing just inside the area. He spun and fired a shot straight at Bosnich, which the keeper fumbled. As Barmby rushed in for the rebound he had so much of the goal to aim at, but seemed to slip and crash the ball straight into Bosnich – again at point-blank range. The ball bounced off Bosnich and Barmby sprang to his feet, tripping over Bosnich as he tried to get to it before two Villa defenders. The ball rolled loose to Klinsmann who struck it low and hard; it smashed into Bosnich and flew into the net.

It was originally credited to Klinsmann, but in April 1995 the Dubious Goals Panel put it down as a Bosnich own goal. It was hard to tell what had happened in real time, but in slow motion Klinsmann's shot went under Bosnich's body, hit his left arm to move away from the goal, and crashed into the keeper's back before flying into the net. These days the panel makes its rulings on a weekly basis, rather than waiting months. By today's criteria, with Klinsmann's initial shot on target, it seems highly likely he would have kept the goal and ended the season with stats of 21 league goals and 30 in all competitions.

'Goals are important as a striker,' says Klinsmann. 'But it is much more important to work for the team. We could already sense that things were going to change under Gerry. As I have mentioned, I learnt a bit from all my managers. I played for some wonderful managers, including both Ossie and Gerry. What Gerry did though – which is really important – is he concentrated on consistency. After all, that is the only way you will be successful as a team, because you need to deliver a certain level of performance every week. Consistency was one of his key words. There was a tremendous energy in the team and he wanted to keep that, but he also knew that in a way we had to calm that energy, we had to control it, and channel it in the right way. Tottenham has always been a high-energy environment, full of dreams and high expectations, but you need some realism too, and we figured out how to find that consistency under Gerry. Every coach has his own style and his own approach. As a player, it is your duty to take the best out of that approach. I will forever be thankful to Gerry for what I learnt from him.'

9

The Francis Revival

'Newcastle were flying at the time, but we were really hitting our stride now. We had great balance as a team, and so much quality going forward.' (Teddy Sheringham)

FORMER Spurs right-back Dean Austin has been riddled with pain since his mid-20s. His life today as a coach is as hectic as it was as a player. There's a crucial difference, though: what he does to earn a living nowadays doesn't physically hurt him. It's common to hear managers and retired players say that nothing beats playing. Austin, now in his mid-40s, disagrees. 'I have a different buzz now, because I enjoy coaching far more than I did playing,' he says.

In the recent past he has done well as an assistant manager at Watford whom he helped win promotion to the Premier League in 2015, and then stay up comfortably. 'I enjoy coaching more, because I don't remember many times being 100% fit as a player and on many occasions I played in pain, even if it meant taking an injection to get out there,' he says. That pain is etched in his face. It resonates in his voice. Those years have clearly taken their toll.

'I've got to be honest,' he adds. 'I am very, very thick-skinned now. I never worry about what people are saying about me as a coach, because I know I am good at my job. When you're playing and you're younger, and you kind of feel that you're getting criticised when people don't know what you're going through, don't understand what you're going through on a daily basis to get yourself on the field for the team: that's tough. I've got four sons now. One of them is a very keen footballer, he just wants to play. He's only 11, but even with him I tell him if you're not feeling well enough to play, don't play; because one thing I've learnt is that when you cross that white line you are judged. No one cares whether you are fit or not. You might think you're doing yourself a favour but you're not. You're kidding yourself really if you think you can still be at your best, but you do it because you want to play. I kidded myself for two reasons. One, I loved playing, but the other was I loved my club even more than that.

'I realised from about the age of 26 that every day it was a challenge to get out of bed. Now I've got arthritis in both my knees and in one of my feet. You don't expect to be struggling to get out of bed at that age, and hobbling to the toilet. I would think, "Oh, I'll pop a Voltarol or take a couple of Ibuprofen, and that will get me going by the time I get there for training. It might take me 20 minutes or so to wind the body up, but I'll be all right." That was how I lived my life for the last seven years of my career, really.'

Aside from the physical pain, he also admits it hurt to be left out for David Kerslake by Ossie Ardiles at the start of 1994/95. He had to wait until 1 October for a kick when he started the 2-1 win at Wimbledon. He kept his place for the 3-2 defeat at home to Watford in the League Cup second round, second leg tie at White Hart Lane three days later, but was then left out again until the end of the month, when, with the pressure really growing, Ossie Ardiles recalled him.

'So at the start of the season Ossie told me I wasn't going to play, and I was available for transfer and I could do whatever I wanted. Now, though, he was saying he was putting me back in and that I was going to get three games. The game he put me back in for was Notts County, which was a nightmare. I got injured with a nasty gash in my shin in that game, which needed stitches. We lost 3-0. I made myself available for the next game against West Ham but Ossie didn't want to risk me, and after that game he was relieved of his duties.'

Four days after the thrills and spills of that 4-3 defeat to Aston Villa – in which David Kerslake went off with a torn calf muscle – Dean Austin was back in the starting line-up for the second game of the Gerry Francis era as Tottenham ran out in front of the highest White Hart Lane crowd of the season so far. With some of the works on the South Stand now completed, 27,037 were present to see the London derby with Chelsea.

On this Wednesday night in late November, Austin was part of a Spurs team which achieved something they hadn't managed in their previous 17 games all season – they kept a clean sheet. In the few days Francis had been on the training ground, he had worked almost exclusively on the defence and fitness, and it was to have an immediate impact.

Diary of Gerry Francis
Tuesday 22 November, 1994

I had a word with Ian Walker on the training ground. He knows now that I'm not someone who is easily satisfied. I wasn't happy with one or two of the goals that he conceded against Villa and I made my feelings known. He knows he has to work hard, and that goalkeepers are not exempt. Hopefully he will respond against Chelsea.

We've not had much time to prepare for Chelsea's visit tomorrow, and we are taking on a team who have enjoyed a fairly decent start to the season. Yesterday and today were the first real days that I have had an opportunity to work with the entire squad. We started by going over the video of the Villa match. We looked at who was responsible for the goals. This wasn't a process of making players feel as though they were the scapegoat. I am the first to admit that we all make mistakes. For me, this is part of the learning process. I spend two and a half hours after each game, with the tape of the game and two VCR players, editing it down to the 20 minutes that I want to show the players next time we are in. This is so much education in terms of the learning process, accountability and showing players where they are in relation to the ball. It's a process that has served me so well as a manager and a coach.

You can learn from mistakes and as manager you can show players what they have done right as well as what they have done wrong. I was able to show how well we had done in that second half with the goals that had brought us level in the match against Villa. I also made it clear to the players that I didn't think they were fit and I was going to get them a lot fitter. They were not as fit as they could or should be. We then went out and started working defensively. I want them as a unit to be working better, because at this stage of the season they still haven't achieved a clean sheet.

Wednesday 23 November, 1994
FA Carling Premiership
Tottenham Hotspur 0-0 Chelsea

For the Chelsea game I brought Dean Austin in to replace the injured David Kerslake and Nicky Barmby started the game on the left-hand side. It was 4-4-2, but really we were playing as a 4-4-1-1 with Teddy dropping in to the hole position. I know that he can take the centre-half with him and Nicky from the left-hand side can move easily into the open space. The back four was Austin on the right, Calderwood and Mabbutt in the centre of defence and Sol Campbell at left-back. Ahead of them from left to right it was Barmby, Howells, Popescu, Anderton, then Klinsmann and Sheringham up front.

The match ended up being goalless – but it was not what you would call a boring or lifeless game. We could have won it when Teddy Sheringham hit the post but to be fair Ian Walker needed to make a great save in the last couple of minutes. All right, so we didn't win and that was now one point from the last two home games, but it was a clean sheet and it was the first time I can remember the back four players smiling since I came to the club.

The team as a whole was also pleased with the situation. I was particularly happy for the defenders who had taken so much stick from the media in the previous months. I sat down afterwards thinking that there were further signs of a real good spirit in the squad. I made a point of telling them how well they had done and how they proved that the system works when everyone plays their part. It was a performance we can build on.

The first clean sheet means a lot as well. It gives them belief in what I have been telling them. I have never had too many worries about the forward play here, what with Teddy Sheringham and Jürgen Klinsmann in the team. Put them alongside Nicky Barmby and Darren Anderton and I know we have players who can score goals. That isn't a problem for me. My priority at this moment in time is that everyone knows where they should be defensively. Tonight has been a good start on that front.

Ian Walker said in his media interviews after the match: 'We are certainly more organised. Under Ossie, the method seemed to be to go forward and see what happened. With Gerry it's, "This is what is right, this is what is wrong." As a goalkeeper it is a lot better for me now. It is no good for the team to keep losing thrilling matches 4-3. Gerry has a tremendous tactical awareness of what is going wrong, and what needs to be put right. Since he came here all he has worked on is the defence, and that is beginning to show. He says if we keep a clean sheet we can't lose. We have to build on that, and it will give the defenders confidence not to have conceded any goals. There is a lot more responsibility on the midfield now, and today the covering at the back was much better than it has been. Ossie would rarely have a go at people. In many ways, he was too nice. Gerry lets you know in no uncertain terms if you don't do what he wants.'

Looking back today, Dean Austin says of the Chelsea game: 'I remember not playing very well that night to be honest, but I wasn't match fit because I hadn't been playing. As the season went on I got more confident because I got fitter. I was training hard, but there's nothing like playing matches. I remember in that year, I think I played 31–32 games. It's the best playing year that I had; but obviously the year before I had broken my leg and had a groin operation.

'The 94/95 season became really tough, because in the Man U game in March 1995 I broke a bone in my toe – no one would know that. I played with injections every game after that, which I suffer from now because I have hallux rigidis in my foot where basically my toe is just solid. It needs an operation really, but I will leave it as long as I can.

'I kept playing because I was in the form of my life, but three games before the end of the season we were playing Newcastle away – we drew 3-3. I actually tore my cartilage the day before the game. I should never have played, but I did. I feel that was the beginning of the end of my Spurs career. I had six knee operations in probably about the next two years. It wasn't just the beginning of the end of my Spurs career, but the beginning of the end of my career. Aside from the injury though, 1994/95 was a brilliant time for me and most of my team-mates.'

Diary of Gerry Francis
Friday 25 November, 1994

The Chelsea game means I've got my first point as Spurs manager, and Spurs have their first clean sheet of the season. Now it also sounds like we might soon have something else to celebrate. Alan Sugar has won his arbitration case against the FA. An independent hearing has ruled that the club should be allowed back into the FA Cup and have the six-point deduction cancelled.

We can't yet crack open the champagne, because there needs to be another hearing between the independent panel and the FA in 14 days' time to determine whether the FA will accept the recommendations. However, the panel has ruled that the FA should pay the costs of the previous two hearings, which makes it look highly likely that the final decision will indeed go our way.

Putting that to one side, I need to prepare for the tough trip to Anfield to take on Liverpool. The draw against Chelsea has given the team hope. It was the first clean sheet in 19 matches going back to last season. The team has let in 30 league goals this season, and that is the joint highest in the top flight along with Ipswich. I find that incredible. I believe in good attacking football, but I would have been very disappointed in the past if my team didn't keep 11 or 12 clean sheets a season. We have made progress defensively. You could see that against Chelsea. Liverpool will be a really tough match though. They have had a good start and have only drawn once at Anfield and won the rest.

I still haven't had a chance to introduce my proper fitness running sessions yet. Monday and Tuesday were spent preparing for Chelsea, Thursday was a day off and today we've had to travel to Liverpool. I've been worried about this match, but there's a more confident air about the squad now after the Chelsea result.

Saturday 26 November, 1994
FA Carling Premiership
Liverpool 1-1 Tottenham Hotspur
Fowler (pen) 39
Ruddock (og) 77

Anfield has always been a difficult place to go. As usual Liverpool have been doing well in the league and are sitting fourth. With our six points not yet definitely returned, we went into this game in 19th place.

I left the team the same as it was for the Chelsea game. During the first half we played really well defensively because we had to – they put us under an awful lot of pressure. But we didn't look like we were going to concede until just before half-time when Sol Campbell was adjudged to have brought down Steve McManaman in the box and they were given a penalty. Robbie Fowler smashed home his 15th of the season, and coming off at half-time I felt sorry for the players. We had done a lot of good things, we had a couple of half-chances ourselves but we were still 1-0 down. I felt we needed to change it a bit and gamble. So I put Gica Popescu to sweeper and brought Ilie Dumitrescu on to play in the hole behind the front two. I took off Darren Anderton who was injured so we needed to change things around anyway and I decided we would have a go at them.

Because of the change to the defensive system, we were a bit disorganised at the back. To be fair they had a lot of chances but Ian did well in goal and we were beginning to get more and more into the game. From one attack Sol went past the full-back and whipped in a fabulous cross. Teddy Sheringham was coming in behind and Neil Ruddock really had to stretch to make contact and prevent Teddy from getting a touch.

He ended up putting it into his net. That stung Liverpool and we held on quite comfortably after that. So that was one more point. Two out of the first nine may not seem much of a return but the last two performances have been very encouraging. The problem is the six-point deduction. If that does stay then we are still in the relegation area. At least now though, for the first time since I got here, I have a full week to prepare for our next game at home to Newcastle.

Dean Austin says the arrival of Francis brought an immediate upturn in fortunes. 'The training regime changed drastically because the things that we were doing with Ossie we then weren't doing,' he says. 'We started working on the back four, the shape of the midfield, so we worked for hours and hours and hours on the structure of the team. Gerry's view was, "We have great players in attack, we don't need to work on stuff showing you how to attack, but what we do need to do is work on how to be a team, so we're gonna work on the structure of the team. We're gonna work on stuff that will bore you." Looking at things now from a coaching side, I think the first thing that you have to do is to get your organisation from the back sorted. That's what we did. We equalled a club record that year; six clean sheets in a row, so obviously the hard work paid off, but that wasn't just a back four thing, it was a team thing.'

Austin was about to embark on the best run of form of his career. Given how hard he pushed himself, though, leaving physical scars that last to this day, does he have any regrets? 'We do what we do. And we do it because we want to do it. What's meant to be is meant to be. I managed to fulfil a dream that probably thousands and thousands of kids have out there. I managed to fulfil it and do it for a sufficient period of time. I played over 100 games for my boyhood club, which for me is the best club in the land. It's one of the big six clubs in this country, it's a European super-power and is going to be even more so when the new stadium is there. I never have regrets. I made the choices I made. I made some good choices, I made some bad choices, but I don't cry over spilt milk. I had a great time.

'There is massive pressure on medical people within football clubs to get people on the field to play games. The game's changed. We're talking about 20 years ago. These days if players don't want to play, if they've got a broken fingernail, they won't play. I think the English mentality was in that era, if you felt that you could get through it you had to do it. With hindsight, the problems that I've got now with arthritis are to do with that, but they are choices that I made because I wanted to play. I don't regret any of those. The first year (1992/93) and the third year (1994/95) of my playing days at Tottenham have been the best two years of my life.'

Again the emotion stirs in his voice. 'When I go back now to watch games,' he says, looking around almost as if he is envisioning himself in his seat at Spurs, 'I sit there, and I kind of think, "I used to do that."' In the six years that he was with the club, he took more than his fair share of stick from a section of the Tottenham fans. He went on to make 151 appearances, almost all at right-back, after joining from Southend for £375,000 at the age of 22 in the summer of 1992. Injuries prevented him from adding more to that tally, and likely prevented him from fulfilling his early promise.

Spurs were the club he supported as a boy. Born in Hemel Hempstead, he had represented Watford's Under-18s and was playing for non-league

St Albans when he was spotted by Southend and signed for £14,000 in 1990. His manager at Roots Hall was a former QPR team-mate of Francis, Dave Webb. Webb was a useful mentor given that he had also been a defender in his playing days, and one who had experienced some difficult moments. Webb endured a torrid time at right-back for Chelsea in the 1970 FA Cup Final against Leeds before being switched to central defence, from where he scored the extra-time winner in the replay at Old Trafford.

Austin played the last seven games of the season as Southend won promotion to Division Three in 1989/90, and then was a key member of the side that went up again to Division Two in 1990/91. The following summer he was on his way to Spurs, having done enough to come to the attention of Terry Venables. He may well have replicated his solid form of 1992/93 and 1994/95 had it not been for the injury troubles that plagued his career. Those troubles kept him out for much of 1993/94, 1996/97 and 1997/98, when he left to join Crystal Palace where he was signed by the man who initially brought him to Spurs – Venables.

Slight of build, it would sometimes look as though Austin's Tottenham kit was too big for him, that it was almost as if, when he changed direction, he would do so before his jersey caught up with him, leaving him disorientated in a sea of fabric. In his early days at the club he styled his blond hair in spikes, making him an unmistakable figure on the pitch, which ensured there was no place to hide. He was a fighter, though, determined to get through the injuries and through the criticism. Even as a youngster he could be vocal on the pitch, certainly more so than some more experienced and more talented team-mates. Over the next few months following the arrival of Francis he would really start to enjoy his football again, as would many Tottenham players and fans.

For Sol Campbell, who had played left-back again against Liverpool, the learning curve was steep. 'Playing at left-back was a challenge,' he says, 'but by the end of the season I remember Jürgen saying he had taken a good look at me over four to six months and he said, "This man is the best left-back in the world." He was saying, "Wow, going forward he's incredible." And Jürgen's not stupid. He's seen it all before. He's one of the best players ever to grace this planet, so for him to say you're one of the best left-backs in the world at such a young age was obviously heart-warming, and I appreciated that kind of comment.

'I was diligent, I worked hard. Obviously I took the good and the bad from some players, but what I took from Jürgen was a desire to keep on pushing yourself to win games, to win trophies and push yourself every time you're on the pitch: to squeeze the absolute most out of every performance, and out of your entire career.'

Diary of Gerry Francis
Monday 28 November, 1994

We went through the video of the Liverpool game. Spirits were high after our result but I was very selective with the parts of the game I was showing. I emphasised how well we had done defensively in the first half. I decided not to highlight how poor defensively we were at times in the second half after I had changed the system. It was important to keep the spirit and belief intact. I showed our equaliser from the Ruddock own goal which raised a good cheer. You have to be as much of a psychologist as a manager and know when to do things and when not to. The spirit and confidence levels have to be assessed at all times.

As this is my first full week I explained to them the programme that lies ahead. Tuesday will be the real day of hard fitness work, the day of running. I tell them I feel they can get a lot fitter. Wednesday will be a day off. This will be a vital rest day, particularly after the Tuesday running session. Thursday we will be working tactically on our defensive and offensive pattern of play, with our next opponents Newcastle in mind. Friday will be short sprints, all the dead-ball situations like free kicks, corners and throw-ins and any more of the pattern of play work that we feel we need to cover. As for today, after we ran through the incidents that occurred in the Liverpool game we had a five-a-side game. The players always love this. As usual the team I was playing on won – then again, as usual, I was also refereeing.

Tuesday 29 November, 1994

Tuesday is the day that I am most interested in. The running sessions I implemented at Bristol Rovers and QPR served me so well at those clubs. Unfortunately, today the Tottenham players were only able to do half of it. They were just not capable of completing it. The times they did achieve on the whole were very poor. I had been anxious to see these times as I wanted to know that the fears I had about the fitness levels were correct. They were.

The times more than confirmed my suspicions. It was clear from early in the session that there was no way they were going to be able to finish it. A few players were physically sick. To their credit, no one moaned. I reassured them that no one likes running – I certainly didn't when I was a player. I stressed though that fitness is very, very important if you want to be successful. It makes so much sense. For example, if you have an extremely skilful forward player, but his level of fitness is low, then the first thing he will lose when he gets tired is his skill factor. With a defender, his concentration level will suffer along with his ability to cover ground when he's tired. The fitter you are, the longer all these attributes will remain at their top level.

This is no ordinary running programme. The system I have devised is based on nearly 30 years in football as player, coach and manager. In my early days as a young player, in pre-season you wouldn't touch a ball for a week. You did all types of running, up hills, down hills, long-distance running, six miles, ten miles. All sorts. You would run on sand, run through water. My programme though was a running programme that went on throughout the season, and it was all about the sort of running that players have to do during a game for those 90-plus minutes. It was designed specifically for the running that you have to do on a football pitch.

The players understand it has to be done. The only problem I've had this week has been with Ilie Dumitrescu who clearly did not like being substitute. He had been suspended for the first game against Aston Villa and I had brought him on in both the other games against Chelsea and Liverpool but there was no way I could accommodate Anderton, Sheringham, Barmby, Klinsmann *and* Dumitrescu in the same team without committing football suicide.

Ilie is an instinctive player and a talented one but has absolutely no idea or inclination towards defending, unlike Jürgen and Teddy who are very intelligent all-round footballers. So for me Ilie can play in only two positions – up front as a striker or in the hole just behind the front two strikers. As I'm not going to use a player in the hole he's going to have to take either Klinsmann's or Sheringham's place. I'm more than happy with Jürgen and Teddy so this leaves Ilie on the bench. I was quite content for Ilie to be there because you need squad back-up – but unfortunately, Ilie wasn't happy with that at all. He came to see me and asked to be put on the transfer list. This I have agreed to do.

Saturday 3 December, 1994
FA Carling Premiership
Tottenham Hotspur 4-2 Newcastle United
Sheringham 15, 39, 71, Popescu 80
Fox 30, 42
I felt so much better prepared going into this game than the previous matches because it's the first clear week we've had. Having that time made all the difference. The game attracted yet another big crowd. Although the work on the South Stand is still going on, reducing the capacity, there were more than 28,000 here today.

I felt the crowd were fully behind the team. It was an outstanding attacking game. Newcastle are having a great season, and are third.

I have great respect for Kevin Keegan, Newcastle's manager and my team-mate during my days as captain of England. I do like the way Kevin approaches the game of football, although I would probably be a little more pragmatic defensively.

It started in a lively fashion with both ourselves and Newcastle having early chances. We managed to score in the 15th minute when Darren Anderton put Teddy through the middle with a great ball. Teddy finished superbly, curling the ball with the outside of his right foot past Pavel Srnicek and into the net.

Newcastle came back to equalise in the 30th minute through Ruel Fox who, not for the first time, caught my eye today. Lee Clark delivered a cross from the left and Ruel scored a lovely header.

We took the lead for a second time with half-time approaching. It was the Anderton–Sheringham corner routine again. They pulled it off a couple of months ago, before I arrived, against Wimbledon at Selhurst Park, but we've had to tweak it because it's been shown on TV many times. As a team we have really been concentrating in training on our dead-ball situations as they account for 50% of goals. So Darren hit the corner and Teddy got there to strike it low on the volley and into the back of the net.

Unfortunately that man Fox struck again just before half-time when a deflected shot came back to him off the post and he made it 2-2. In the dressing room during the break I was quite pleased. It had been an excellent game of football and although we had twice lost the lead and conceded two goals, we had done well both offensively and defensively and were a little unfortunate with the deflection for their second goal.

I told them it was vital that we kept up the pressure and maintained the tempo of our first-half performance. I said I felt sure that we could go on to win the game. The second half started just as brightly as the first with both teams looking to score goals. Fortunately for us we were the team to do so when Teddy managed to complete his hat-trick with a volley in the 71st minute to make it 3-2. This time the players were determined that we were not going to concede another equaliser, so much so that with about ten minutes left Gica Popescu managed to make the game safe for us when he finished off a good passing move.

So we had our first win since I arrived here. The dressing room was a great place to be after the game. Everyone was congratulating each other. I had a quick chat about what we'd done well – and not so well – but basically I told them I was very pleased with the performance and that they had deserved their win. It was the happiest I've seen them. I'm delighted for them. It's also the first time since the start of the season that they've gone three games without defeat and it's vitally important to maintain that momentum and keep that consistency of performance going throughout the season.

Thanks to this result, this weekend will be the most relaxing and certainly the most pleasing one for myself, Roger Cross, and our families for quite some time. We now have another clear week until we play Sheffield Wednesday which is another important bonus.

The match featured Sheringham's second hat-trick for the club since joining in 1992. His first goal of the afternoon was his 50th for Spurs. 'That was a brilliant game,' he says. 'The first goal was something I did a few times in my career. I scored that type of goal a lot. The keeper would always be unsure in a situation like that. Often they expect you are going to hit it with your left, but then you catch them by surprise by knocking it off the outside of your right.'

Indeed, for the fans, it had been a tremendous goal to witness. With Sheringham through one-on-one he seemed to have several options as to how to beat Srnicek, and appeared to choose the most difficult one to pull off. Rather than hitting it low to the keeper's right, he whipped it up off the outside of his right boot, bending it round him and into the top corner.

'Newcastle were flying at the time,' says Sheringham. 'They were a team full of attacking intent, just like we were, and both teams gave it a real go that day. We came out on top, we were really hitting our stride now, we had great balance as a team, and so much quality going forward.'

Tuesday 6 December, 1994
Yesterday we went over the video of the Newcastle game and it was a good, positive meeting. There were even a few little jokes flying around. I'm beginning to sense a major belief on the part of the players in what we're doing. This is absolutely vital in regard to whatever system you try to play. Not only do the players have to believe in you as a manager, what makes the system work far better is that the players themselves know exactly what they should be doing at any given time.

During the meeting I laid out a defensive situation on the tactics board. I then asked the players to show me where they should be under those circumstances in relation to the position of the ball. The position of the ball is, in my opinion, the most vital element of attacking and particularly defensive play. The players came up and put themselves in the positions they felt they should be adopting to cope with that situation.

They all positioned themselves correctly. I acted pleased. But there was a sting in the tail. What they didn't realise is that the scenario I had laid out was in fact the attacking move that led to Ruel Fox's second goal.

It's interesting after showing this on the video and asking the players where they thought they should have been. They knew where they should have been, so why weren't they there on Saturday? This for me is how we learn and also how we accept we're accountable. Gary Mabbutt says he's benefiting from the work we've been doing. As a whole the squad are enthusiastic and willing to learn. They're getting more information from me and we're able to do more and more work as a unit. They're learning different things every day. The fitness work is also improving. We were able to do our Tuesday running session today thanks to the clear week ahead. It's impossible to do it during the week if you have a midweek game. They're now doing 75 per cent of the programme and times are improving.

With word getting round about the running sessions, some of the media have wanted to come along and film it or even to take part. But I'm not having that. This isn't a novelty thing, it is serious, and I'm not prepared to have my players ridiculed.

As regards to how the team has been playing, I've been impressed with David Howells. He's really important to me. You have to have that link, that holding player who is disciplined enough to protect the back four, because the back four were totally isolated before my arrival. In defence I've got Gary Mabbutt, who is a great player but who is coming to the end of his career. I have a real outstanding defender in Sol Campbell, but he still needs to learn the game. He's been playing centre-forward not long ago. He's my best defender. He's quick, strong, low centre of gravity, people can't go past him.

It's about moving and playing as a team. It's like an engine. You've got to get back and defend from the front. David Howells wins the ball and breaks it up, he gives it to Darren Anderton who will make things happen. I was lucky enough to play against Pelé, Rivellino, Neeskens, Cruyff, Beckenbauer, top, top players – but you wouldn't win anything with 11 of them. It's all different things that create a team, all different skills and abilities. Tackling is an art. Winning the ball back, turnovers. It's no good having three or four midfielders in there who can't tackle, you'll never get the ball back.

Looking back now, David Howells believes the rebuilding job under Francis began immediately after the Villa game. 'He was the first manager we had worked with who would video games. He would do the proper video analysis and brought in "culpability", whereby if you weren't doing your job, in the team meeting you would get nailed. "Where were you?" he would demand. No excuses any more. You couldn't hide from it, you were shown what you had done wrong. Gerry would always have team meetings where you would go through the game. He would have edited it himself. One of the first things I remember him doing is getting Alan Sugar to set him up this thing at home where he could do all the editing.

'Nowadays you get a team of people who do it; you see them sitting behind the dugout with their laptops. But Alan Sugar had set him up with that, some system whereby he could do it himself where he would get the video – as it still was – after the game, and be able to cut it and get it all in and then bring his version in on a Monday and we would go through it.

'He'd say, "Howellsy – the first goal, who were you marking?" And I would say, "Oh I was marking my man," and he would say, "Oh, okay, well look at this." And you'd think, "Oh shit." There's no hiding place all of a sudden, so everyone's on their toes. You'd know your roles, you wouldn't go out on the pitch wondering, "How we gonna play today? How's it all gonna come off?"'

Dean Austin felt that, as Christmas 1994 approached, Tottenham were in a great place. 'As regards physically fit, I'd say come December time, after six weeks of the new running programme, there wasn't a fitter team than us in England,' he says. He was also impressed by the way the team's talisman took to the training regime. 'The running sessions we used to do on a Tuesday were so tough, but Jürgen never batted an eyelid. Up at the front, he used to be like he was gliding across the turf, he never moaned. Never moaned about it. The only time I ever heard him moan was when he used to come short for the ball and Colin Calderwood used to hit it over his head,' he laughs.

10

Up for the Cup

'There was massive elation because you ask
any footballer in the English game, they
want to play in the FA Cup.' (Gary Mabbutt)

TOTTENHAM have always had a special affinity with the FA
Cup. For the FA to ban the club from the competition hurt the fans
perhaps more than it would those of any other club. At the time
the punishment was meted out, during that summer of 1994, no other
club had won the famous trophy more times than Spurs. Their record
of eight triumphs had just been equalled by Manchester United in May
when Alex Ferguson's men crushed Chelsea 4-0, but in the eyes of many,
Tottenham were still the ultimate cup team.

The ban hurt because there had been a magic associated with each
and every one of those eight Tottenham triumphs. It hurt because down
the years it felt as though Tottenham had found their true identity in this
competition. It hurt because it felt as though it was the competition in
which their destiny lay. Not for Spurs fans the dull drudgery, and quite
frankly hard work, of a league campaign; no, much rather the cut and
thrust, do-or-die nature of cup football. Now that had been taken away
from them for a season. While fans of every other club could dream
about a sunny day out at Wembley come May, Tottenham's only realistic
trophy chance had ended with the League Cup humiliation at the hands
of Notts County.

Through the years Spurs teams had provided the FA Cup with
some of its greatest matches: in 1962 the 3-1 win against Burnley, a

final between two of the most gifted teams in the land; the 1981 final replay against Manchester City which ended 3-2; the 1991 semi-final against Arsenal, the first ever to be staged at Wembley, which Spurs won 3-1. Spurs players had also provided the FA Cup with some of its greatest moments: Bobby Smith and Terry Dyson scoring the goals to clinch the Double in 61; Ricky Villa's incredible solo goal in 81; Gazza's stunning free kick ten years later. Spurs had arguably done as much to boost the competition's profile worldwide as the competition had done for Spurs.

Captains of the calibre of Danny Blanchflower, Steve Perryman and Gary Mabbutt had seen their reflections glinting back at them from the silver curves of English football's most recognisable prize, before hoisting it towards the sky above Wembley. They had left everything out there on the hallowed turf and then hauled their weary limbs up those 39 steps nestled below the old Twin Towers, followed by the team-mates who alongside them had shed blood, sweat, and tears for the Lilywhites' cause. As the trophy was handed back down that line of players, each of those team-mates would lift the cup again to cheers from the Spurs faithful.

The old Wembley provided the perfect backdrop for trophy celebrations – raw, unscripted, emotion-filled occasions. Cup finals 20 years ago felt different. Today everything is structured, everything is choreographed. Trophy ceremonies didn't need fireworks back then, or a platform on the pitch for the photo-opportunity. Today there is no room for fluidity, no room for a pure, authentic expression of joy. Everything is timed to perfection, to suit the needs of the broadcasters and the desires of the sponsors who want to make sure their brand is featured in every defining image. The whole thing takes forever and sucks so much joy out of the occasion. Instead of the captain lifting the trophy and handing it back down the line, there is now the rather clumsy process of getting every player, substitute and seemingly every member of coaching staff up the steps and on to the platform, before the captain finally wriggles through all the bodies to raise the cup.

Tottenham's absence from the 1994/95 FA Cup was going to hurt, because until then almost every generation of fans who had followed this great club had enjoyed the opportunity to see their team play in the showpiece event of the English football calendar. In 1901 Tottenham, then of the Southern League, became the only non-league team to win the FA Cup when they beat Sheffield United in a replay at Burnden Park. In 1921 there was a victory over Wolves at Stamford Bridge, courtesy of a goal scored by a man who remains Tottenham's youngest FA Cup finalist. At 20 years 139 days, left-winger Jimmy Dimmock – Jinkin' Jimmy Dimmock as he was known – hit the only goal.

Tottenham then endured their longest ever absence from the FA Cup Final – 40 years. They returned in style, sealing the first league and FA Cup Double of the 20th century as they beat Leicester 2-0 at Wembley in 1961. Further victories over Burnley in 1962 and Chelsea in 1967 brought Tottenham's FA Cup wins record to five. Then came another glorious decade in the competition, from 1981. Spurs beat Manchester City 3-2 in a replay that year, with Ricky Villa scoring his magnificent solo goal. They retained the trophy the following year against QPR, again in a replay. In 1987 Tottenham suffered their only FA Cup Final defeat, to Coventry. The unfortunate Gary Mabbutt scored an own goal in extra time, to give the Sky Blues a 3-2 win. He was at least able to make amends four years later, when he captained the team to victory against Nottingham Forest in what remains, at the time of publishing, Tottenham's most recent FA Cup win.

The general public's affection for this great competition once knew no bounds. It's probably true to say that the last time Tottenham won the FA Cup in 1991, the average man or woman in the street would be better able to name Spurs as the FA Cup winners than Arsenal as that season's league champions. By 1994/95 that was possibly just about still the case. However, the Premier League's profile was rising, the Champions League was soon to take off, and perhaps no one had quite foreseen just how severely both would detract from the FA Cup.

Of course the FA Cup Final always felt like a special occasion in the 70s, 80s and early 90s, because there were far fewer televised matches then. The knockout blow to the competition's prestige was delivered when Manchester United were allowed to opt out of the 1999/2000 FA Cup, in order to compete in FIFA's inaugural World Club Championship in an ultimately futile attempt to boost England's chances of winning the bid to host the 2006 World Cup. The FA Cup has never fully recovered its lustre. It never will. Still special, but the final is no longer the defining match of each season. No longer the first point of recall for anyone rifling through the memory banks, trying to remind themselves what year it was they first went abroad, bought their first car or got their first job. 'Was it 84 or 85? Definitely 84. I remember Watford were in the cup final.' The FA Cup doesn't have that about it any more, but in 1994/95 it still meant everything. And Spurs weren't allowed to play in it.

To Tottenham fans it felt like a heavy-handed sanction. Teams had of course been docked points in the past for financial misdemeanours, and Swindon had been relegated two divisions, reduced to one on appeal, as recently as 1990. Expulsion from the FA Cup, though, was unprecedented. The announcement on Friday 25 November 1994, that an independent arbitration panel had ruled that the FA had erred in the severity of the punishment, meant there was now hope for Spurs. The club would have to wait 14 days for ratification of that decision, but it looked like it was going to be an embarrassing defeat for the FA. It also meant an extra headache for football's governing body, because in the meantime the draw for the FA Cup third round had to be conducted, and no one knew for sure whether Spurs were back in the FA Cup or not.

On Sunday 4 December the draw took place live on BBC television. The FA had decreed Tottenham's name would be in the hat, but whoever Spurs were paired with would be given a bye through to the fourth round in the event of Spurs not being allowed to take part. Tottenham were drawn at home to Altrincham, a team positioned in the Vauxhall Conference, the highest non-league division. The minnows from Cheshire were delighted at the prospect of facing one of the biggest names in the game; but that joy was tempered by the knowledge that it might all be taken away from them. Even the consolation of a bye straight through to round four in that event wouldn't make amends for missing out on such an opportunity. Altrincham chairman John Maunders insisted the club would claim compensation from the FA if the match didn't go ahead – he estimated £200,000 would pass them by. The following day the FA promised they would indeed compensate Altrincham in the event of the fixture being cancelled.

Five days later though, the news was confirmed – Tottenham were officially back in the FA Cup. The independent arbitration panel had ruled that 'the penalty was unreasonable to such an extent that it was irrational to impose any penalty other than a fine'. It was an embarrassing decision for the FA, whose chief executive Graham Kelly looked shell-shocked as he read a prepared statement to the media on the steps outside the FA's Lancaster Gate headquarters: 'The Football Association, for its part, is absolutely committed to taking the strongest action against any financial irregularities in our national sport,' he said. 'We believe any punishment must have the effect of deterring others. We welcome the fact that the tribunal confirms the powers of the Football Association to deduct points and decide who should play in the FA Challenge Cup. We are surprised, therefore, that they don't consider such penalties are appropriate in a serious case like this one.'

The arbitration panel's decision was the final item on the BBC's *Nine O'Clock News*. Anchorman Michael Burke told viewers: 'Tottenham Hotspur will compete in this season's FA Cup, and they no longer face having six Premiership points deducted at the end of the season. The club appealed against the punishment imposed last June for making irregular payments to players. The Football Association accepted the decision of an independent tribunal.'

Esteemed sports correspondent Kevin Gearey began his report outside Lancaster Gate. FA chief executive Kelly was pictured reading out his statement. Gearey described it as a 'humiliating defeat for the FA, and one which may well have implications for the ruling bodies of other sports who find their authority coming under legal challenge'.

Alan Sugar was shown leaving the training ground in his chauffeur-driven Rolls-Royce with its personalised AMS1 licence plate. He had refused to comment to the media. A small group of fans had gathered outside White Hart Lane. 'I'm absolutely elated,' one told the TV cameras. 'I think it's a wonderful thing for Tottenham,' said one, before another chipped in, 'They've got a great chance now [to actually go on and win the cup]. Spurs are the best and they're gonna beat the rest.'

Jürgen Klinsmann says of Sugar's fight against the FA: 'It showed his spirit. He threw himself into that battle and he won that battle, and that showed us players that now it was down to us to take it as far as we could. That created a team spirit, in fact it was more than a team spirit – it was a club spirit, because everybody was involved in it, whether it was front office, back office, the playing squad, or the fans. All of that is what created that energy that season. The energy built, and built and built up, and made it just a really exciting place to be. That kind of feeling is what you dream about as a player. It was not down to money, or individual guys, or egos. It was all about the club, and about how we could make a statement in a season where a lot of people thought we had no chance.'

David Howells says he had every confidence that Alan Sugar would win the fight with the FA. 'I always thought we kind of knew he was gonna do it,' he says. 'He's that sort of bloke. He told us he was going to appeal, and you always thought, "Yeah, he's gonna make sure it goes for us. It's unjust, nothing to do with us, or him, or anyone running the club any more; surely it's gonna be overturned." I think most of the players thought he was gonna do it. It wasn't a surprise when we got our points back and were put back in the cup.'

Gary Mabbutt adds: 'From our point of view it was all down to politics and certain financial things. We thought it was very unfair that things off the field were compromising our on-field situation. Alan Sugar, full credit to him, got the bit between his teeth and fought it and won the case. There was massive elation because you ask any footballer who plays in the English game, they want to play in the FA Cup. They want to win games, to win competitions.' Sugar says in his autobiography that 'the newspapers had a field day and Kelly was made to look a real prat. For once, it seemed I had achieved something positive in the football world.'

Sugar's former PR man Nick Hewer remembers how much the victory over the FA meant to his boss. 'There had been a terrible feeling of injustice, because Alan had gone into buying Spurs with Venables and put a lot of money in, and Terry was a bit slow coming up with his share. After that initial frustration, to rescue this club, and then find out that the previous regime had broken the rules, and now he was getting lumbered with the fall-out; well, that just felt deeply unfair.

'One of the investigative TV programmes wanted to confront Alan and one of the players. They wanted to grill him, but we knew it would all be about how they edited it afterwards, so I said to Alan, "I tell you what we should do, we're gonna take our own television crew along." Of course we could do that, because we had our own cameras to film the matches. So when the TV crew pitched up they were surprised to find another TV crew, and they said, "Who's this? Where are these people from?" "Oh, that's our team," we said. "That's our crew."

'They were furious because of course they knew we would now also have every second of footage that was filmed, and if they messed around we would have the evidence. They were livid about it, but it was quite a neat stroke on our part which I was rather pleased about. They'd never seen anything like it and they didn't want us to go ahead with our filming, but we said that if they wanted to do the interview we would be filming everything too and we explained why.'

So did he ever find the circus surrounding Alan Sugar and Spurs stressful? 'Oh yes, it was very stressful. My fax machine would start at six in the morning because I had all the news coming in then, and I would be taking calls until midnight. It was a nightmare. In fact the management at the flat I was living in asked whether I was running a business from my apartment and I had to explain that no, I wasn't. It was very stressful for everybody, and stressful for Alan Sugar who has the heart of a lion, actually. He's a very strong advocate of carrying on the fight if he thinks he's been unjustly treated. So he'll take on the most fearsome opponent if he believes he's right and the other lot are wrong. He took on everybody. He is a very persuasive character. Everyone believed in him. He is the kind of bloke you would follow over the top, because he instils great confidence and everybody would fight for him.'

Hewer says that Alan Sugar would freely admit that he enjoyed the profile football offered him. The feud with Terry Venables and the signing of Jürgen Klinsmann had transformed him into one of football's first celebrity chairmen. Now victory over the FA brought him the adulation of the fans. It must have been the closest a football club owner could come to feeling like a player: as though he had scored a winning goal, or lifted a trophy. In the game between Tottenham and the FA,

Alan Sugar had been man of the match. Now – for a short time at least – he could revel in the glory.

It had been quite a turnaround for a man who had been public enemy number one when he forced Terry Venables out of the club two years previously. 'The Venables High Court battles were actually pretty scary,' says Hewer. 'There was quite a lot of anti-Semitic abuse, even up in the courtroom. We legged it down the judge's staircase and we could see the mob out in the Strand. I could see Alan's driver turning his Rolls-Royce into the judge's car park, and I sort of waved him away. I got a taxi and brought the taxi in, because people didn't know who I was. Then we stuck Alan in the middle and gave him a file to read to keep his head down. We sat either side of him with another two in the jump seats, and we drove through the crowd. If they'd seen him there'd have been trouble. We had our own film crew in the crowd and we gave the footage to the police, because there were some very nasty people in there.'

Diary of Gerry Francis
Saturday 10 December, 1994
Tottenham Hotspur 3-1 Sheffield Wednesday
Barmby 61 Klinsmann 72, Calderwood 80
Nolan 38

The news that we were back in the FA Cup and have our six points back gave everybody connected with the club a massive lift, we were all absolutely delighted with the outcome. The media went to town on the story and Alan was quite rightly hailed as a saviour. Today we played Sheffield Wednesday and there was a mass of euphoria about the place.

The players were laughing and joking, all around the stadium there were banners and posters commending Alan for what he had done and I shared in everyone's delight. However, I was just a bit concerned that the party atmosphere was not taken out on to the pitch by the players. This would indeed spoil the party. Unfortunately, despite several warnings from Roger Cross and myself, that is exactly what happened. From the first whistle we were second best in every department.

Wednesday dominated the game and we were very fortunate to be only one goal down at half-time. I certainly was not very happy. We had lots of things going on around the ground, but you have to focus yourself mentally for the game ahead. I don't want ten out of ten performances one week and one out of ten the next. I don't want to beat the league leaders one week and lose to the team who are bottom the next. I accept that you can't always play your best but you can give a certain level of consistency in performances. You have to keep on at the players week in, week out if you are going to achieve that. Let's just say I reminded the players of this in no uncertain terms. They must have listened to me at half-time because they went out in the second half and completely changed it around. We won 3-1. Nicky Barmby equalised in the 61st minute through a set piece training routine that we had rehearsed – always pleasing when that happens – Jürgen Klinsmann got a wonder goal with a volley from about 25 yards, a truly magnificent effort in the 72nd minute, and then Colin Calderwood scored his first goal for the club from another set piece routine from a corner to round off what has been a magnificent week for the club.

Just to make life that bit happier, we moved into the top half of the table in tenth place. And this time, they couldn't change the tables. We have now gone four games without defeat and we have won the last two. The manner of the wins has also pleased me a lot. There has been a lot of good attacking football and we have scored a good few goals. Perhaps we are conceding one or two too many for me, but these are still early days.

Today's match against Sheffield Wednesday was also significant for another reason. I was forced to change a winning team as Gica Popescu and Ilie Dumitrescu were away on international duty. I therefore made a big change concerning Darren Anderton. From the first time I had the opportunity to watch Darren play on a regular basis I knew he had everything that was needed to be an outstanding central midfield player. I knew everything about that role from my playing days. But I too, also played wide on a number of occasions. I felt that Darren was the sort of player you wanted to get on the ball all the time. When you play wide it is easier for opposing teams to stop you getting the ball and make you less effective. Also it can be very tight for space when you play up against the touchline and you can only go one way sometimes to find room. In the middle of the park you have the chance to go either side with a lot more space.

Darren also has tremendous stamina which gives him the ability to get into the penalty box and just as importantly, to get back. He can score goals with either foot, he is an excellent passer of the ball with superb vision and I really feel that long-term, centre midfield will be his best position. The great bonus for me is that Darren also wants to play in that role and really enjoyed it today. With Darren in the middle alongside David Howells and Nicky Barmby on the left, I played Ronny Rosenthal on the right, and he had a good game too.

More than 20 years on, Dean Austin says he will never forget Klinsmann's wonder goal against Sheffield Wednesday. 'I remember that goal because it kind of came out of nowhere. It gives you so much confidence when you have team-mates of that calibre. You know they can deliver, you know they will deliver, and when they pull off something like that you can only stand back in wonder and admire it all. Wednesday didn't know what had hit them because they'd played quite well till that point.

'It was a massive thing to win for us though, because of the excitement of the news about getting the points back and getting back into the FA Cup – we didn't want to let the fans down. It also meant we had finally got back-to-back home wins for the first time in a long time. Jürgen was just the ultimate professional. On the pitch he just never gave up, he was always encouraging everyone to keep going. You never accepted you were beaten with him in the team.'

David Howells, who provided the assist for the goal, agrees: 'When you've got players like that on the pitch, Teddy, Gazza, Jürgen, you just know where they are heading,' he says. 'You've got the next pass in your mind anyway before the ball even comes to you, and you know where they're gonna be and that they're gonna be able to deal with it even if you've got to smash it into them with a bit of pace, which they probably prefer anyway.

'It's just lovely playing with players like that, you know you can give them the ball in any situation. A lot of times I'd know exactly where Jürgen's runs were, and if Teddy might be dropping off into the hole. If the ball broke to me, or was played from the full-backs into me, I could play it round the corner first time or into an area where I knew Teddy would be, or into a channel where I knew Jürgen was running.'

On this occasion Howells pulled off a fancy bit of footwork himself and then lobbed a lovely long ball forward. Klinsmann headed it on and then smashed it on the bounce from just outside the box.

Lifelong fan Daniel Wynne says: 'If you were to ask me of my opinion about one of the most special, magical games that actually counted for nothing, it would probably be from that 94/95 season – Sheffield Wednesday. The day before the match we had got our points back and were back in the FA Cup. When we turned up on the Saturday, there was a buzz all around the ground. The PA announcer asked the fans to say thanks to the chairman, and everyone was on their feet clapping him. It's probably the only time the crowd sang, "There's only one Alan Sugar!".

'Klinsmann's goal in front of the Park Lane End – I don't think I've ever seen a ball hit as hard as that in my life. He ran on to it and he connected with it from about 20 yards, and it just flew in. The overhead kick goal against Everton raised the roof, but this goal … Wow. I mean obviously Alan Sugar was the chairman and he got the points and the FA Cup place back, but it was almost like it was all down to Klinsmann. It was almost like a fairy tale. I think Jürgen's bond with the fans was all the more extraordinary because of the whole England–Germany thing, which was still a big deal at the time. When he signed he wasn't particularly well-liked because he had this reputation among some of being a diver and a cheat, but he turned it all around. Performances speak louder than anything and his performances got the Spurs fans on board. 'We would sing "Walking in a Klinsmann wonderland" and "There's only one Jürgen Klinsmann". When you perform consistently well, you tend to get your own song. It happened with Ossie Ardiles, Glenn Hoddle, Gareth Bale with "He was born to play for Spurs", and Harry Kane now with "He's one of our own". The performances speak for themselves.'

On Tuesday 13 December, the FA confirmed they would not be appealing the independent arbitrators' decision. It was a mere formality, since both Spurs and the FA had previously promised to abide by the outcome. It did also bring with it confirmation that the club would still have to pay the £1.5m fine. The arbitration panel had said the club would be within its rights to ask the FA to reduce or revoke the fine. The club made that request. The FA rejected it.

Alan Sugar was typically forthright in his criticism of the FA for allowing the fight to go on so long. 'The FA are obviously resentful of what they have been recommended to do by the arbiters,' he told the media. 'At the end of the day we can celebrate getting back the six points and getting back into the FA Cup. But the FA have also made it clear they are delighted that the arbiters have endorsed their own powers to impose such penalties again in the future. And if you see what they are saying, it gives no excuses to anyone else who, like us, might want to clean the slate. It won't encourage any kind of clean-up in the game.'

The FA of course saw things differently. Spokesman David Davies said: 'The commission specifically noted that Tottenham had been engaged in a wholesale, systematic abuse of football rules. Over six years, secret payments of more than £500,000 had been agreed with 19 players. Those secret payments disadvantaged other clubs which did not have such a policy and Spurs benefited, notably in reaching two FA Cup finals during the relevant period. It wasn't satisfactory to totally blame a previous management, when several directors and officials from that period remained in office.'

Diary of Gerry Francis
Saturday 17 December, 1994
FA Carling Premiership
Everton 0-0 Tottenham Hotspur

I had to change a winning team yet again. For the first time this season we were without Jürgen Klinsmann because he is still away with his country – he scored one and set one up against Moldova this week and tomorrow Germany play Albania in another Euro 96 qualifier. This has been a major blow to us, especially after two great wins. I decided to play Nicky Barmby up front with Teddy Sheringham.

With Gica Popescu available he went into midfield alongside David Howells and I moved Darren Anderton back to his wide position. Ronny Rosenthal also started out wide. The defence, from right to left, was Dean Austin, Gary Mabbutt, Colin Calderwood and Sol Campbell. We really missed Jürgen. Everton were also without their main striker Duncan Ferguson but their other danger man – Paul Rideout – was available.

This was the first week in which my players have proved themselves fit enough to complete my full running programme, and it showed out there on the pitch against Everton. We had to work so hard against them. They have been on such a great run. We've worked really hard all week at defending corners because Everton have been really successful at these. In Andy Hinchcliffe they have probably the best corner taker in the league. Corner takers like Hinchcliffe try to put the ball over the top of the opposing centre-half so that the striker can attack the ball on the move with a running jump while the defender is underneath it. I want my players to move out with them and come in on the run thereby also attacking the ball on the move.

The game turned into a real battle. It was dull at times, but I was really pleased with how we defended. We nearly won it when Darren Anderton hit the post with a free kick near the end. It finished goalless though. I was happy with a point and delighted with another clean sheet. You really need to be strong to get anything at Everton these days and we were.

Looking back over the years my impressions of Tottenham as a team have always been of a talented but inconsistent side - capable of beating anybody on their day but just as capable of losing to anybody. Whenever I was up against them while with other clubs - as either a manager or a player - I always felt that if you gave them time and room they would beat you because they could really turn it on when they had the space. But they did not look so good if you got at them and put them under pressure. Their record in the league since they last won the title in 1961 possibly reflects this. Their cup record is outstanding and you can't deny that. All I would say is that in cup competitions you only need consistency for those six or seven rounds. The league is different, particularly our Premiership. I reckon it is the hardest league in the world to win. Forty-two games a season - as it has been for most years - with the possibility of any one of the teams in the division capable of beating you. It is played in all kinds of weathers without a break for nine months. To win the Premiership title means you need real consistency and a big squad of players.

During my managerial career I personally feel one of my strengths has been to make individuals, and thereby teams, more consistent. At Bristol Rovers for example we never lost two games on the trot for two and a half years and that was reflected in winning the Third Division title and reaching Wembley in the Leyland DAF Cup. At Queens Park Rangers, despite selling some £10m worth of talent, we went on some magnificent runs and for that you need consistency. I spent just £2m in over three years when I was in charge at Loftus Road and with that sort of outlay you shouldn't finish higher than much wealthier clubs like Tottenham, Liverpool, Arsenal and Chelsea. But we did. If you talk to someone like Bill Nicholson – someone I have known and admired over the years – he talks the same language. The team has to function in attack and defence. You have to play for each other, pass the ball when you can and battle when you have to.

He won the league and the FA Cup in 1961 and managed the first British team to win a European trophy when Tottenham won the European Cup-Winners' Cup in 1963. His record is exceptional. To this day the same qualities that won you the league 35 years ago are needed to win you the league now.

These days you can play the Newcastles, the Manchester Uniteds, the West Hams and they are magnificent open football matches. But then you come across teams that just won't let you play so you say to the players, 'Right, do we lose this game because they won't let you play football, or do we knuckle down, roll our sleeves up and get something out of the game?' That's the name of the game. You have to go to places like Everton, where they have steamrollered teams, really good teams, and make sure they don't do it to you. Adaptability is the name of the game. A system is important but that system must be adaptable. If you play one way all the time, people are going to stop you. You become too predictable if there is no variation.

Sunday 25 December, 1994
So today – Christmas Day – was spent travelling to Norwich. This is the first time that people like Jürgen and Gica have been involved playing football over Christmas. They are most unaccustomed to this tradition and I feel Jürgen in particular has found it hard to understand. Like the rest of us he wants to be with his family at Christmas. I have been involved with professional football at Christmas all my life and it is virtually non-stop. Your family tends to suffer the most. As usual we

tried to make the best of the situation. There was a bit of a laugh and a joke around the hotel as the boys went up to their rooms on Christmas night. Fortunately we have had nine days to prepare for this match. There has been time to work on pattern of play, improve the running even more and get things sorted.

Monday 26 December, 1994
FA Carling Premiership
Norwich City 0-2 Tottenham Hotspur

Barmby 12, Sheringham 90

Norwich had been in pretty good form coming into this game. At kick-off they were seventh in the table following consecutive wins over Chelsea and Palace, still unbeaten at home, and they had the second-best defensive record in the top flight behind Manchester United.

I was delighted to be able to welcome Jürgen back from international duty. I decided to bring him straight back into the team to play alongside Teddy so I moved Nicky Barmby back to his normal position on the left-hand side at the expense of Ronny Rosenthal who dropped to the bench. Nicky gave us the lead with his sixth goal of the season. Norwich were furious that Jürgen was adjudged not to be interfering with play, despite standing in an offside position as a clever reverse pass from Teddy came through to Darren Anderton.

The flag stayed down, and Darren squared it to Nicky for an easy finish in the 12th minute. TV replays showed the linesman was probably right, because Jürgen was running away from goal and not looking to gain an advantage.

At half-time I had to ask Jürgen if he was okay. He hadn't worked anywhere near as hard as he usually did. He said he was okay, but I told him he didn't look like he was. It was important for me that the players would see that I would treat them all the same. It didn't matter who you were, you had to be pulling your weight – and if you weren't I would call you out. Jürgen is one of the hardest-working players at the club, I've never had a problem with him before.

With Norwich pushing everyone forward in search of a last-gasp equaliser, we sealed the points in the second minute of injury time. Norwich goalkeeper Bryan Gunn came way out of his goal to punt a free kick upfield, but Darren Anderton headed it straight back and Teddy was on the charge. Gunn hadn't quite got back on his line, and as Teddy hit a shot from 25 yards it deflected off Rob Ullathorne and looped over the keeper's head into the net. We won 2-0. We're now eighth in the table with 29 points, and we're London's top club. It's our sixth game unbeaten, three wins, three draws and three clean sheets. Norwich's unbeaten home record has gone, leaving Newcastle and Liverpool as the only top-flight teams yet to lose on their own turf.

After the game the spirit and the mood of the players was excellent, but Jürgen seemed a bit subdued. He hadn't played well and would be the first to admit it. He seemed rather down. On the coach journey back home I called him up front and had a long chat with him. He's not just finding it hard to be playing over the Christmas period but also being away from Debbie, his fiancée. We had a good discussion and I feel we now know each other even better. We have arranged to go out for a meal to an Italian restaurant in London called La Paesana, a place I've been a regular at for more than 20 years.

I've been absolutely delighted with the response I have had from the whole squad of players to what we have tried to achieve, both defensively and offensively. I am really impressed with our consistency level which is so important in terms of trying to win something.

Tuesday 27 December, 1994
FA Carling Premiership
Tottenham Hotspur 0-0 Crystal Palace

I'm so annoyed that we had to play again today - two games in two days is ridiculous. According to the club secretary Peter Barnes, Ossie Ardiles had the chance of changing the date and I can't for the life of me understand why he didn't take advantage of that option. We had to travel all the way back from Norwich and then play again the very next day. It's hard enough when you have two games in three days, let alone two in two. Nearly all the other teams in the league took the chance to have at least a day's break. The only other teams to play twice in two days were Nottingham Forest and Norwich. Forest won that game at the City Ground today 1-0.

At The Lane, our players, and those of Palace, were all flat on their feet. I fielded the exact same team as yesterday. When you have had a good result, you don't want to change the team unless you have to. There was precious little time for anyone to recover from any knocks. David Howells picked up a minor injury at Norwich, but he's a really important player for me because he gives us bite in midfield and can pass the ball well. He was desperate to play and despite picking up that knock I sent him out there. It can be a dilemma though. You want what is best for the team but you also want to make sure the player will last the game and not make himself worse and end up missing three or four weeks. When you are on a good run like we are, everyone wants to play, no one wants to lose their place. In the middle of a bad run, you tend to get more injuries. People don't make it.

We got the players in early this morning before the game. We did some light work, obviously nothing too strenuous, just to get the lactic acid out of their systems. Before leaving the dressing room for kick-off the mood of the players was terrific, everyone wanted to go for it, even though it was a big ask to be playing again so soon. Palace boss Alan Smith made three changes. The pitch was sodden, and it was cutting up badly from the start. Windy conditions didn't help either. The South Stand redevelopment is nearing completion. Today there were 27,730 here for a 3pm kick-off. The size of the crowd proves there is a desire from the public for festive football, perhaps the main reason why the organisers remain intent on cramming the fixture list at this time of year.

It was apparent in the first 45 minutes in the mud, that this was two very tired teams going through the motions. Both sets of players were exhausted and it turned into a long, hard slog on a very heavy pitch. Alan Smith also lost John Salako who pulled up with a hamstring injury in the 26th minute. His replacement was Paul Williams who forced the only save of note from Ian Walker. We only created a couple of chances, the best was a 30-yarder from David Howells which was well saved by Nigel Martyn, my former keeper at Bristol Rovers.

Predictably it finished 0-0. Palace ended up happier than us because it was a vital point in their relegation battle. They strung five across the back and made it very difficult for us to break them down, but the point we won has kept us in eighth position.

I told the press that I think it's virtually impossible for two teams to play at their peak for two days running, particularly in such conditions. It's not that the players are not physically fit enough to play twice in 24 hours, but what happens is a loss of quality. When I walked into the dressing room afterwards I saw Jürgen sitting there, absolutely exhausted, just shaking his head and wondering what on earth was going on. The only real plus point for us is that we have kept three consecutive clean sheets, the first time Spurs have done that since 1992/93. We've got a rest day tomorrow, then we will be back in on Wednesday to prepare for Saturday's match away to Coventry.

After the match, Palace boss Alan Smith was fuming. He called the fixture planners 'bloody idiots', and added: 'The fans are the people being ripped off. The top prices were £25, and if any of our fans came here after seeing us against QPR yesterday, you are talking about £50. It's bloody greed. It's like going to watch *Phantom of the Opera* and seeing 11 stand-ins. I blame the Premier League. They don't pay to watch games so they don't understand it. [Premier League chief executive] Rick Parry says we play too many games, but we're still doing it.'

Despite all the injury problems he endured during his Tottenham career, one man who coped particularly well with the hectic festive fixture list of 94/95 was Dean Austin. 'We played on the 26th and 27th,' says Austin. 'I played as well on the 27th as I did on the 26th. I showed that I could do it. When you know that a manager believes in you it makes a massive difference. I hadn't had that feeling of confidence since the days of Terry Venables. Terry signed me and told me, "Don't worry, you've got time to work your way into the first team." But that wasn't really in my make-up. I wanted it now. If someone told me I had got a couple of months to do something, I wanted to be there in three weeks. That was how I used to think. Now Gerry believed in me too.'

Diary of Gerry Francis
Friday 30 December, 1994
Talking to Jürgen on the coach on the way to Coventry, it was clear he now really appreciates the British player. He is so impressed by the abilities here, by the pace of the game and the sort of fixture list that no other European league has to go through. I was talking to him about English football and he said the reason that there are so many misplaced passes is because of the pressure and the pace of the game in this country. He thinks it is staggering that the game has to be played at such a speed here because of the demands of the fans, and he really respects the high skill level needed to play at the pace that we do.

Ilie Dumitrescu has left us on loan for Sevilla. After asking to be put on the transfer list just after I took over, there was only one enquiry from an English club, and that was from Middlesbrough in the First Division. Ilie was not interested in going below Premiership level so he turned it down. Sevilla are in the top flight in Spain. They have agreed to pay a £350,000 loan fee with the option to make the transfer permanent for £2.6m in the summer.

Saturday 31 December, 1994
FA Carling Premiership
Coventry City 0-4 Tottenham Hotspur
Darby (og) 7, Barmby 67, Anderton 77, Sheringham 81
A trip to the West Midlands for any fans who had plans to celebrate New Year's Eve wasn't ideal, but at least the performance and the result made it all worth it. Julian Darby headed Darren Anderton's corner into his own goal to give us a seventh-minute lead. Anderton's corner was heading for Teddy Sheringham, but Darby intervened to leave his goalkeeper Steve Ogrizovic with no chance.

It took us until midway through the second half to double the lead. Three quick low passes moved us from inside our own half to the edge of Coventry's area. From the right of midfield Gica Popescu fed Teddy, who spun inside the centre circle and moved the ball on first time with a diagonal pass to Nicky Barmby. Nicky used his right foot to drag the ball inside Brian Borrows, and then with his left hit a low shot from just inside the box. It wasn't the most powerful shot, but it beat Ogrizovic and hit the inside of the post. It looked like Coventry had escaped, as the ball bounced out; but it then span backwards and crossed the goal line halfway along the goalmouth.

Ten minutes later, we made the points safe. Darren Anderton scored his first league goal since the opening day of the season and it was a rarity – an Anderton header. The move started with Dean Austin. He moved it on to Jürgen, who played a one-two with Nicky. As Jürgen received it he turned in the left-hand corner of the pitch and again rolled it back to Nicky, who measured a perfect cross to Darren who headed in from ten yards.

Teddy added another with nine minutes to play. Jürgen flicked on Dean Austin's long pass and Teddy raced on to it. He got there just before Sean Flynn who was left grounded after diving in. Teddy then kept his cool to dink it over Ogrizovic for a lovely goal.

It is now eight consecutive matches unbeaten for us; four wins, four draws, and five clean sheets and I've been awarded Manager of the Month for December, just 46 days after taking over, which I'm told equals John Bond's record at Manchester City in November 1980 as the quickest time in which to win the award after being appointed by a club. The award is a tribute to the team and all the hard work the players have put in on the training ground and in the matches. It's a great way to finish 1994.

Monday 2 January, 1995
FA Carling Premiership
Tottenham Hotspur 1-0 Arsenal
Popescu 22
Schwarz sent off 86

We saw the new year in on Saturday night when we got home from Coventry, but we were straight back to training in the morning for this live Sky Monday night game – my first North London derby and our fourth game in eight days. I was obviously feeling a bit nervy before kick-off because you know how much it means to the fans. I had experienced similar when QPR played Chelsea and when Bristol Rovers played City.

We went into the game without Nicky Barmby who was injured at Coventry. He had no time to recover from that knock. I brought Ronny Rosenthal into an otherwise unchanged team. There was something of a scare before kick-off when Gica Popescu complained of suffering from a heavy cold. He wasn't feeling too well. He was reluctant to play but the lads had a few words with him and we managed to get him out there. It turned out to be well worth it because, in an excellent move involving David Howells and Darren Anderton midway through the first half, Gica put us 1-0 up from Darren's great cross.

It proved to be the winning goal although Gica had to come off at half-time because he was feeling so unwell. We won what was a very hard-fought derby in which I felt we outbattled Arsenal.

Listening to people connected with the club afterwards, they felt that the reverse has often been the case in the past. So we not only beat our greatest rivals and outfought them on the day, we also had another clean sheet which makes it five on the trot. We are approaching a club record with this sequence and yet, before I arrived, we hadn't recorded a clean sheet all season. We've gone nine games undefeated, winning five and drawing four. Not only have we dramatically improved the goals against situation - conceding 50% fewer than when I arrived - we have also managed to score more than Spurs did before I got the job too. To achieve one of these objectives is hard enough, but to achieve both is very difficult.

The dressing room after the game was buzzing. Myself, Roger Cross, the players and Alan Sugar are all delighted at the progress being made by the players and listening to the supporters as we left the pitch at the end of the Arsenal game, they were ecstatic. The characters in the side are also becoming evident to me. Jürgen has respect for who he is and for what he has achieved. Gica is an intelligent man, quiet, but very bright. Teddy is another who has respect in the dressing room. I think Teddy is a good leader in the way he gees people up and gets people going. Gary Mabbutt leads by example. His experience is important to keep things together. He is a great ambassador for the club and for football. People like Darren Anderton and Nicky Barmby are quiet and happy to let their football do the talking. Basically, the dressing room is in good shape. I like it to be fairly noisy. There is nothing worse than a quiet dressing room an hour before kick-off. It isn't like that at Tottenham at the moment. Everyone is pleased with the way it's going. We are stopping goals at one end, scoring them at the other. We are solid and we are competitive - and we are prepared. Anyone who knows me will tell you how important preparation is to me. I don't feel comfortable unless I am prepared in every way. We are also playing some fantastic football with exactly the same players who were at the club when I took over.

After the game, I spoke with Arsenal manager George Graham. I like George. Over the years George has been at a lot of football clubs that I have been involved with and I have a lot of time for him. His club record is very impressive. You know that if you beat a George Graham team you have had to work hard to do it. He admitted afterwards that we had deserved to win. Arsenal have been the only really successful London side in the league since Spurs won it in 1961. Since then the Gunners have won the title three times. So although, as Tottenham manager you want to beat Arsenal, you have to respect their success. One of the reasons I feel that London clubs haven't done better is because of the number of local derbies that we have to play - sometimes as many as 14. As we all know with local derbies, the form book can sometimes go out of the window.

The form book certainly hadn't gone out of the window on this occasion. Tottenham had come into the North London derby on a great run and were worthy victors against their fiercest rivals. It had been a bitter night weather-wise. The cold gnawed at the bone, crept its way into any carelessly-exposed neckline or open sleeve. Fans huddled tight, stomping their double-socked feet. The breath hung heavy, as if inscribing the chant of 'Come on You Spurs' into the frozen air.

'One-Nil to the Arsenal,' sung to the tune of 'Go West', by the Pet Shop Boys, had become the favoured chant of Gunners fans at the time, because of the regularity of that winning scoreline under George Graham. On this occasion Spurs fans had been able to sing it right back at them, and the single decisive goal had been beautifully worked. Spurs seized on a Nigel Winterburn mistake with ruthless speed and precision. Winterburn's sloppy pass forward from the left-back position barely made it into the Spurs half. There it was cut out by Dean Austin. He headed it to Darren Anderton, standing just inside the Arsenal half facing Spurs territory. Anderton prodded a first-time pass backwards to David Howells, who – with his first touch – dinked a wonderful pass straight back over Anderton's head. Anderton was already in the process of turning and immediately set off to chase the ball down the right wing towards the Arsenal box.

He had a five-yard head start on Winterburn and Steve Bould, and was in complete control of the situation. Despite the fact his run started from virtually on the halfway line, he needed just two touches to set up Gica Popescu. The first, off the outside of his left boot some 30 yards from goal, sent it to the right-hand corner of the box. There, with the inside of his right, he centred a pass weighted to perfection towards the penalty spot. Popescu had been charging down the centre, and just managed to stay onside as he received Anderton's pass before sweeping a first-time shot with his right boot beyond goalkeeper David Seaman. The ball hit the net exactly ten seconds after Winterburn played his wayward pass.

Those ten seconds constituted a golden moment in a season littered with them. If you could bottle Spurs moments from throughout the ages, the 1994/95 collection would be a vintage one. In those ten seconds, four Spurs players had taken six touches between them to propel the ball from ten yards inside their own half to the back of Arsenal's goal.

As he wheeled away, Popescu almost slipped, but stayed on his feet as he peeled off to celebrate in the corner between East Stand and Park Lane. He brought both hands, with his navy and white 'SPURS' gloves, to his lips. He blew a kiss to the fans and received their acclaim in return, then stretched both arms out wide. Ronny Rosenthal, Teddy Sheringham and Jürgen Klinsmann joined the celebrations. By the time of their next match, Spurs fans had come up with the following refrain, which they would sing for the rest of the season:

> Who put the ball in the Arsenal net?
> Gica, Gica.
> Who put the ball in the Arsenal net?
> Gica Popescu.
> Gica Popescu, Gica Popescuuuuuuuuu
> Who put the ball in the Arsenal net?
> Gica Popescu.

It was to be George Graham's final North London derby as Arsenal manager. On the pitch in the Arsenal team that night was Danish midfielder John Jensen. Jensen became famous for his pile-driver of a goal in the 1992 European Championship Final for Denmark, when they shocked Klinsmann's Germany to win 2-0. Graham signed him from Danish side Brøndby that summer. He was bought on the back of a glorious goal, but his shooting in an Arsenal shirt would prove to be wayward. Coming into the North London derby he had only just ended his very long wait for his first Gunners goal. On New Year's Eve 1994, in his 98th appearance for the club, he finally got on the scoresheet to make it 1-1 against QPR. The Arsenal fans sang his name for the rest of a match which they lost 3-1, and some of them were wearing 'I was there when Jensen scored' T-shirts at White Hart Lane three days later.

Jensen's transfer to Arsenal would become infamous for another reason. In February 1995 Graham was sacked by Arsenal after admitting receiving an unsolicited gift of £400,000 from Norwegian agent Rune Hauge as part of the deal which brought Norwegian full-back Pal Lydersen and Jensen to Highbury. Graham denied it was a bung, but in July 1995 he was found guilty of misconduct by the FA and banned from football for a year.

He was the only football manager found to have committed wrongdoing by the enquiry set up in the wake of the Brian Clough allegations which had surfaced as a result of the Alan Sugar–Terry Venables feud. Somewhat ironically, less than four years from now, Sugar – who had been so forthright in condemning any wrongdoing regarding transfer dealings – would be employing Graham as Spurs manager.

11

On our way to Wembley?

'Ronny was a very unorthodox player and a very unpredictable player. That day he just came out and kept scoring wonder goals.'
(Teddy Sheringham)

WITH Tottenham having won their FA Cup place back, the media were enthralled by the idea of the club winning the famous old trophy in a season in which they had initially been banned from it. The first task was to try to avoid potential embarrassment at the hands of Altrincham from the Vauxhall Conference. The Robins had come close to pulling off a huge shock against Tottenham once before. Back in 1979, when they were a Northern Premier League team, they had also been drawn away to Spurs in the third round.

They had managed to come away from White Hart Lane with a surprise 1-1 draw. The replay took place at Manchester City's Maine Road ground with Spurs running out 3-0 winners in front of a crowd of just under 28,000 thanks to a Colin Lee hat-trick. As well as being drawn away to Spurs in the third round, there was also another similarity between Altrincham's FA Cup runs of 1978/79 and 1994/95. On both occasions they had beaten Southport at home in the first round, so was this an omen that they were on their way to another famous result at The Lane?

Altrincham were flying high in the Conference, and had earned a fearsome reputation as FA Cup giant-killers throughout the years, having knocked 16 league teams out of the competition as a non-league side. They had a plasterer, a scaffolder and a window cleaner among their number, but the team of part-timers would be determined to raise themselves against Tottenham.

Diary of Gerry Francis
Friday 6 January, 1995

Tomorrow's match provides a vivid contrast to the Arsenal game. Strangely enough, if there is one game that has really been bothering me, it is this one. From the day the draw was made, it has been on my mind. Ask any league manager whose team are playing non-league opposition and they will tell you the same thing – they do not like this type of game.

It doesn't matter how well you are doing in your division, these games are always a nightmare. You have everything to lose, they have everything to gain. Some people expect you to run up double figures against this type of opposition but that rarely happens. Those days are long gone. It comes down to 11 against 11. It is their cup final. Everyone on their side is going to give their all, in fact it is a golden rule of mine never to buy a player from a lower level purely based on a very good performance against a team in a higher division in cup matches.

Someone may take your eye, yes, but it is important to then go and watch them on a regular basis in their own league against teams of similar quality. They will always raise their game by an incredible amount when they have nothing to lose. They are expecting to get beaten, and anything else is a bonus. There is no pressure on them. The incentive is to show how good they can be against players from the Premiership. They are more relaxed than they would be normally. So that is another reason why this game worries me.

I recall while I was at Bristol Rovers we were top of the league and playing really well – and then we were drawn away in the FA Cup to Kettering. It's even harder when you get this sort of game away from home. When you are playing a team from a lower level it can sometimes be a difficult surface and in unfamiliar surroundings too. Kettering were a good side, virtually a league side who were top of the Conference. But we were the ones expected to win – and we didn't. We lost unluckily 2-1 to a last-minute goal.

That defeat had an adverse effect on our league form and for the next five or six games we were very wobbly. From being at the top of our confidence and with everything going well we were suddenly faced with a lot of publicity that went with the defeat at Kettering. All the spirit that had been built up over the season suddenly came under threat. I also tasted a similar kind of defeat when I was at QPR and we lost at Stockport County. They were top of the Third Division at the time. The pitch was a treacherous one and the match should really not have been played. Nevertheless, it was regarded as a real upset. So I am well aware of what can happen.

The media have also been bringing up Tottenham's recent troubles against lower-division teams in cup competitions. In recent years they've suffered FA Cup defeats to Port Vale and Bradford, and last year they only just squeezed past Peterborough on penalties. Then of course, a few months ago, just before I arrived, they were knocked out of the League Cup by Notts County.

The FA Cup was by far the most realistic route for Tottenham to reach Europe; it looked like it would be a tall order to do so through the league position. In the papers Jürgen Klinsmann was pictured alongside a miniature FA Cup, beaming at the prospect of making his debut in the competition. 'It would be great to score in my first game and also at Wembley, and I'm so glad we've got the chance to play in this competition because when I came here we weren't even in it. Now we are,' he said. 'Can we win the FA Cup? We've got a good team and we can beat any side in England. It's a long way to go, but we hope to be at Wembley in May.

'The defence is playing very well at the moment. The whole team is a lot more compact than we were at the beginning. In attack we have the talent to give any team in the country problems. My own dry spell doesn't concern me. The only important thing is that we have climbed the league. For sure, it's a pleasure for a striker when he scores a goal. But I'm very satisfied with my performance at the moment. I have never been knocked out of a cup by a non-league team. We have to work very hard and be very, very careful. We cannot afford to slip up. It is too important to everyone at the club.' What Klinsmann called a dry spell, was only five games, but by his high standards it felt like a long time.

Diary of Gerry Francis
Saturday 7 January, 1995
FA Cup Third Round
Tottenham Hotspur 3-0 Altrincham
Sheringham 9, Rosenthal 34, Nethercott 82
As soon as we got our FA Cup place back we were made one of the favourites to win the competition. These are the expectation levels I now have to deal with as manager of Tottenham. I can't ever remember

Bristol Rovers or QPR being among the top ten fancied clubs to win anything.

Again, the euphoria around the stadium with regard to Spurs being back in the FA Cup could have been a distraction for the players. Before kick-off, just like at the Sheffield Wednesday home game when we learnt we were back in the cup, the PA asked the crowd to extend a round of applause to Alan Sugar. He got a standing ovation before the Chas N' Dave song 'Spurs are on their way to Wembley' was played.

The biggest problem for the manager in games like this is getting through to the players. It doesn't matter how many times you tell them, or how many times you try to warn them, they still think that when you are playing a team from four or five divisions below, all you have to do is turn up, put on the shirt, and everything will be all right. I know because I did it myself as a player. It doesn't matter what the manager says before you go out to the pitch, in these sorts of games as a player you just do not get motivated in the same way as you do when it is a game like the one against Arsenal a few days ago. It is not intentional, it just happens that way. And if you are going out at 50% when the other team is going out at 120%, then you start to have problems. You also have to learn how to handle the pressure of playing against these teams in front of your home crowd who are expecting an easy, convincing win and can quickly get frustrated.

I wasn't able to select Gica Popescu, whose goal won the North London derby. He was ruled out with the heavy cold that almost stopped him playing against Arsenal. I brought Darren Anderton back into central midfield alongside David Howells. Nicky Barmby was fit again, having missed the Arsenal game, and I played him on the right-hand side. Ronny Rosenthal kept his place in the team.

Fortunately, we got off to a great start to help ease any fears of an upset. Jürgen won a free kick, which he took quickly to send Ronny down the wing. Ronny raced into the area and crossed it to Teddy who put us ahead in the ninth minute.

With just over half an hour played, Ronny doubled our lead. Altrincham were playing well, so it was important to get the second. His goal came from a Darren Anderton corner. Darren whipped it towards Jürgen, who beat keeper Paul Collings in the air and headed across goal. An Altrincham defender hacked it off the line and it fell to Ronny, who squeezed his shot between all the bodies in the box for his first goal of the season.

Stuart Nethercott, who I sent on for the injured Ronny Rosenthal just after half-time, scored his first goal for Spurs to make it 3-0 with eight minutes to go. It was a decent goal too. Teddy Sheringham and

Darren Anderton played a quick one-two just outside the box before Teddy crossed to Stuart who headed in to the top corner from virtually on the penalty spot.

It finished 3-0. Although we were fortunate not to concede today, we have managed to equal the club record of six consecutive clean sheets. We had stopped Everton, Norwich, Palace, Coventry and Arsenal scoring against us, and here were Altrincham having better chances than any of them, but we had kept another clean sheet. It was the most indifferent performance since I came here, the worst performance since the first half of the Villa game on the day I took over, but as I've said, you can never win in these situations. As we walked back down to the dressing room I told Roger Cross that I wasn't very pleased with the performance but that I wasn't going to say too much about it right now, instead we will work on a number of things during training in the week. I didn't want to jeopardise the great self-belief and spirit that we have built up in recent weeks on the basis of this performance.

Stuart Nethercott came off the bench against Altrincham to play his part in Spurs equalling the club record of six consecutive clean sheets. It was a record set in 1922/23 and also matched by Spurs sides in 1970/71, 1981/82 and 1986/87. It has again been equalled once since – by Harry Redknapp's team in 2009/10. For Nethercott though it was a memorable day for another reason – he scored what proved to be his only goal in his 62 appearances for the club, spread across seven years. He can still visualise it clearly. 'Teddy put a ball in for me,' he says. 'He put one on my head and that was one of my strengths – I sent it right into the top corner. I was so pleased to get my first goal for the club, the club I'd grown up with, and in the end it was my only goal. I should have scored more in my career. I had the chances to score, but just didn't put them away. It was a special, special day.'

Altrincham thought they had ended Tottenham's run of clean sheets when Shaun Constable hit the back of the net with a sensational long-range shot with 20 minutes to go. It would have made it 2-1, but was correctly chalked off ... eventually. Andy Reid had taken a throw-in midway inside the Spurs half, and the linesman immediately signalled for a foul throw, but the referee somehow failed to spot it. Play went on for a good ten seconds before Constable, who had only just come on, smashed in his wonder goal. Still the referee hadn't seen his linesman's flag. He was instead focused on calming down the Altrincham celebrations.

As the howls and boos from the Tottenham fans rose in volume, Gerry Francis sprinted from his dugout to make sure the linesman didn't put his flag down. Teddy Sheringham also went over to ensure the linesman got the attention of the referee. Eventually the referee spotted the flag and rightly ruled out the 'goal'. It was tough on Altrincham and Constable, but it was the correct decision.

Diary of Gerry Francis
Saturday 14 January, 1995
FA Carling Premiership
West Ham United 1-2 Tottenham Hotspur
Boere 10
Sheringham 58, Klinsmann 79
We had a clear week in the run-up to this match, and we desperately needed that after five games in 13 days. My main concern going into this one had been that things have been going too well and on a couple of occasions during the week both Roger Cross and I felt that a little bit of complacency had crept in during the training sessions with one or two of the lads. I've experienced this sort of thing a number of times as a manager, particularly during an excellent period of results. It's not the sort of attitude you need going into a major game like West Ham.

The danger is that having gone six games without conceding a goal, some of the players might start getting a bit blasé. I've been keeping on at Ian Walker all the time, because I feel he is the kind of player who needs that. He is a very talented goalkeeper. He is a young man with a fantastic future ahead of him. But I told him from the moment I arrived that I would be on at him all the time to be consistent in his performances, because if I'm not on at him, Ian can become a bit sloppy. He is learning to handle that situation now, and I haven't eased up on him.

I was soon made aware that West Ham like to beat Tottenham. Quite simply, at the start of this game, we were dreadful. We were 1-0 down after ten minutes when Jeroen Boere scored. It was the first goal we had conceded since Ian Nolan struck for Sheffield Wednesday way back on 10 December. That was 602 minutes we had gone without letting a goal in, but by then we could easily have been 3-0 down. We were being out-thought, out-battled and outplayed. I was absolutely fuming. It was the angriest I have been since arriving at the club. I didn't like what I was seeing out there at all. I felt the attitude among the players seemed to be that they could just put their shirts on, pass the ball a couple of times, and then we would win the game.

At half-time I went absolutely berserk. Normally, during the break, my priority is any tactical situations that I have to deal with. Not this time. I gave one of the fiercest half-time team-talks in all my days as manager. It was time to let them know exactly how I felt about what I was seeing out there. I told them that it was completely unacceptable.

Games can often be won or lost in those crucial 15 minutes at half-time. What I have found is that if you tell people the truth, if you tell them how you see it, then you will always get respect. Players have to handle both praise and criticism.

To their credit, the players knew how poorly they had played in the first half and it was a completely different Tottenham team in the second period. Just before the hour mark we equalised. Boere gave away a free kick for a foul on David Howells near the touchline. Darren Anderton whipped it in; Ludek Miklosko's punch went straight to Teddy Sheringham, who controlled it on his chest, let it drop and then volleyed the ball through a crowded box. With 11 minutes to go Jürgen got his first goal in seven games. Nicky Barmby headed it forward to Jürgen, who was being played onside. He ran into the area and dinked it over Miklosko.

We were now unbeaten in 11 games in all competitions. We also preserved our proud record of not having lost to a fellow London club all season. We're still sixth – one point and one place behind Newcastle.

The match proved to me the importance of the half-time interval. I was critical at half-time, but in the dressing room at full time, I gave credit where it was due. I wanted to let the players know how pleased I was with their second-half performance, and not even Alan Sugar could get into the dressing room while I was talking. The directors normally come down after I have finished speaking. They want to show their support, win, lose or draw. On this occasion they were so pleased with our comeback and the result that they were knocking on the dressing room door almost immediately.

I opened the door. 'Excuse me Alan, I haven't finished yet,' I said. He understood. He waited outside with the other directors while I spoke to the team. I spent as long giving credit as I did being critical at half-time, but I signed off by reminding them that I never want to see another first-half performance like the one I saw against West Ham today.

Saturday 21 January, 1995
FA Carling Premiership
Tottenham Hotspur P-P Manchester City
Referee Alan Wilkie took the decision to postpone today's match at 2pm, an hour before kick-off, because of a waterlogged pitch. It was far too late for the away supporters, who had made a long trip down from the North-West, and even for some of the home fans. It was the right decision though.

The rain had been falling heavily since midday. Typically it stopped at five past two; the clouds blew away and even some blue sky was visible. In truth, though, there was too much standing water on the pitch by then.

We've been suffering with the pitch for quite a while. There was a problem because the undersoil heating had not been laid low enough. It's been positioned just nine inches or so below the surface. That means the soil around the heated pipes becomes rock hard and therefore the water can only drain away a couple of inches below the surface before it starts to come back to the top. Constant torrential rain means that the water comes back up and lays on top of the pitch. The effect is like playing on sand with divots coming up all over the place.

Something will need to be done, but it's not going to be possible this summer because of a contract with an American football team who will be using the stadium so there won't be time to sort it before the start of next season. It will have to be done eventually, because it is vitally important that we have a pitch as good as any in the Premiership.

In total, 26 league fixtures, five from the top flight, were postponed because of the weather today. In the Premier League, London was badly hit with QPR v Ipswich and Wimbledon v Liverpool also called off. Leicester v Leeds and Southampton v West Ham were the other top-flight matches to be postponed.

Wednesday 25 January, 1995
FA Carling Premiership
Aston Villa 1-0 Tottenham Hotspur
Saunders 17

I had been looking forward to this game against Aston Villa, hoping to get some revenge for that last-minute 4-3 defeat in my first game in charge – the only defeat I had experienced so far at Tottenham. Coming into this game we had gone 11 games unbeaten, with seven wins and four draws, including seven clean sheets.

Villa were now managed by Brian Little who had taken over from Ron Atkinson. Jim Barron had been in temporary charge when they came to White Hart Lane for my first game. On our way to Villa Park, we were feeling buoyant thanks to our recent run.

There was a major blow before the game when it was clear that David Howells wasn't going to make it because of injury. He is such an important player for me. He has been a major factor in the changes that I have made since taking charge. I countered his absence today by bringing Sol Campbell into midfield from left-back and putting Justin Edinburgh into the full-back position. It's the first time I've changed my back four since my second game in charge when Dean Austin replaced David Kerslake who had been injured in my first game against Villa.

Tonight's match turned out to be one of those games where we played very well for 90 minutes but ended up with nothing. Dean Saunders scored the only goal of the game in the 17th minute. We also lost Jürgen Klinsmann in the first half after an horrific clash with Villa goalkeeper Mark Bosnich. Jürgen had to be stretchered off the pitch after being hit in the head by Bosnich's knee after the keeper charged out of his box and jumped up.

I brought Darren Caskey on with Nicky Barmby moving up front. It made us a little bit lopsided, but the important thing was Jürgen's welfare and thankfully, as the game progressed, we started receiving reports that he was recovering well and there were to be no long-term ill effects.

We had lost, but on this occasion there was no ranting and raving with regard to this performance. We had played well and certainly deserved something out of the game, possibly all three points. I told the players to get their heads up. I told them we have had a great run and now we have to get out there and show everybody that we have character, that we have to bounce back and show everyone we can do it again.

After the match, the major talking point concerned the challenge by Mark Bosnich on Jürgen. I accept the fact that Bosnich certainly didn't mean to hurt Jürgen, but I thought it was a terrible challenge which could easily have broken Jürgen's neck. I was also absolutely amazed that the challenge was not punished in any way. It left us without a highly influential player.

The Spurs fans never forgave Bosnich for his challenge on Klinsmann. The mini feud between the two players actually started in that 4-3 match in November 1994, the first game of the Gerry Francis era. There had been verbals between the two that day, with Klinsmann denied what looked a certain penalty after a challenge by Bosnich who suggested he had dived.

Tottenham fans continued to wind Bosnich up even after Klinsmann left. They chanted their hero's name every time the two clubs met. In 1996/97 this led to an unsavoury incident at White Hart Lane, when Bosnich responded to those chants with what he insisted was a 'joke' Nazi salute. He was warned by the FA and fined £1,000.

Bosnich's head-high challenge on Klinsmann would probably have been bigger news but for the fact that on the very same night, Eric Cantona was also airborne at Selhurst Park, launching an assault on a Crystal Palace fan. Three minutes into the second half of the match between Crystal Palace and Manchester United, Cantona was sent off for the fifth time in his United career, this time for kicking Palace's Richard Shaw. As he was leaving the pitch he was abused by a Palace fan, and responded by jumping into the stands with a kung-fu kick on the supporter.

Two days after the match he was banned by his club for the rest of the season. They also fined him £20,000. The FA went on to extend the suspension to nine months and fined him an additional £10,000. Further punishment was to come on 23 March when Cantona was found guilty of assault at East Croydon Magistrates' Court and sentenced to two weeks in prison. At an appeal hearing at the Crown Court the following week the custodial sentence was overturned, with Cantona instead sentenced to 120 hours of community service.

United then held a press conference at which Cantona uttered the unforgettable line: 'When the seagulls follow the trawler, it's because they think sardines will be thrown into the sea.' He then promptly got up and walked out. With Cantona absent from the team for the rest of the season, United missed out on the title to Blackburn by one point and lost the FA Cup Final to Everton.

Jonathan Pearce was at Selhurst Park for London radio station Capital Gold. His commentary of the Cantona kung-fu kick won a prestigious Sony award. 'It's the most bizarre moment I have ever seen in football,' he says. 'There have been strange moments, you know, the president of South Africa and the president of FIFA wrestling over the World Cup trophy for the right to give it to Spain in 2010. I can still see that to this day, but I can still live the Cantona moment. I was so close to it at the back of that stand – 30 rows away from it. It was bang in front of me. I'm still bewildered; for all the talk of provocation from the Palace fan and verbal provocation from Richard Shaw who had man-marked Cantona, you don't react like that.

'It was the reaction of a flawed genius. Someone who lived his life very much on the edge. He was someone who was beset by inner demons, certainly. There were depths to Cantona that no one quite plumbed and worked out. I was horrified, and the horror came out in the words and I think that expressed the revulsion that people felt around the country.'

Coming up next for Spurs was a long trip to the North-East to play Division One outfit Sunderland in the FA Cup fourth round. Gerry Francis had to prepare his team for the 'Roker Roar'. The locals had seen their team pull off many shocks at the famous old ground, shocks which took them, as a second tier team, all the way to the trophy in 1973 and to the final in 1992.

Diary of Gerry Francis
Sunday 29 January, 1995
FA Cup Fourth Round
Sunderland 1-4 Tottenham Hotspur

P. Gray 74

Klinsmann (pen) 51, 87, Sheringham 57, Mabbutt 64

Bennett sent off 50

We went to Roker Park looking to respond to our first defeat in 12 games. Could we bounce back immediately and start another run of consistent results? Just like the Altrincham game, this was another one I hadn't been looking forward to. Sunderland are a First Division side, and were desperate to cause an upset. We were the BBC televised game, and there was only one reason for that. People are always looking for shocks in the FA Cup, and many people felt like Sunderland might be able to provide one. We had everything to lose, and the whole country was watching to see how we coped after the midweek setback.

It was a bitterly cold and windy day. Before kick-off there was snow, hail, the lot. The good news for me was that Jürgen was given the all-clear to play despite the injury at Villa Park and that David Howells was back too. Dean Austin was suspended so I moved Sol Campbell to right-back with David coming into midfield.

The Sunderland fans were in great voice. Their team is a sleeping giant, and the players were certainly up for their biggest game of the season. Every time they got anywhere near our goal, a huge roar went up. It was a difficult first half but overall we handled most defensive situations okay. Sunderland worked very hard and gave it everything. At half-time, with the score 0-0, I felt we had done all right and that Sunderland hadn't caused us too many problems. I also felt that as a side we could increase the tempo and put them under pressure. We needed to raise our game. To be fair to the players, they did just that.

As the rain lashed down, five minutes into the second half, the match burst into life. Teddy Sheringham charged into the area from the right-hand side and looped a delicate cross-shot towards the far post which struck the woodwork and rebounded all the way to Nicky Barmby on the edge of the area. He rolled a short pass to Gica Popescu, who smashed a first-time shot goalwards. Sunderland keeper Alec Chamberlain was beaten, but his captain, defender Gary Bennett, flew across goal to save it with his hand.

Referee Mike Reed saw the handball, and had no option but to point to the spot and send Bennett off. Jürgen scored it and it was clear what his first FA Cup goal meant as he celebrated in front of our fans. We were now a goal to the good against a Division One side who would have to play almost the entire second half with just ten men. Six minutes later Teddy Sheringham took advantage of our extra man. With Sunderland's defence not yet fully reorganised, Sol Campbell took a long throw-in just inside the Sunderland half on the right. Lee Howey failed to get his head to it and it dropped to Teddy in the right-hand corner of the pitch. Completely unchallenged he continued his run, cutting in to the side of the area and towards the corner of the six-yard box and then chipped it over Chamberlain.

We then quickly made it 3-0 from a Darren Anderton corner. His inswinger was only half-cleared to the edge of the box, where Gary Mabbutt thumped in a volley which found its way into the back of the net via a deflection off Sunderland's Andy Melville.

We were in total control of the game. So it was disappointing to concede a consolation goal from a former Tottenham player, when Phil Gray scored in the 74th minute. Jürgen got our fourth with a lovely header right near the end and we were all delighted that we had not only won a difficult away tie in some style in front of the whole country, but we had also bounced back in excellent fashion from the defeat at Villa.

The draw for the fifth round was made immediately after the game and we were given a home tie against either Southampton or Luton Town who need to replay after a 1-1 draw at Kenilworth Road. You have to be pleased with a home draw, but people are already making us favourites. It won't be easy, especially if it is Southampton who have Matt Le Tissier. He can do something special in any game. We'll worry about that if it comes to it. We've had a terrific win and it's time to savour it a little bit. Before the fifth round we have two league fixtures to concentrate on and an international break to contend with, as England continue their preparations for Euro 96 with a trip to Dublin to play the Republic of Ireland in a friendly.

Against Sunderland, captain Gary Mabbutt celebrated his first goal since one he scored against Everton in February 1993. He threw both arms to the heavens and beamed with delight as his volley crashed into the back of the net after deflecting off Andy Melville. The BBC at the time put it down as a Melville own goal, as does the *Rothman's Football Yearbook* for that season. Tottenham's official records credit the goal to Mabbutt, and the FA take their records from the clubs. So as far as Tottenham are concerned, it was this goal against Sunderland that ended up being the final one of Mabbutt's illustrious career, seeing him end with figures of 38 goals in 611 appearances in all competitions.

'As a player you will take any goal that is given to you,' says Mabbutt. 'Absolutely it was my goal. It was a deflection, but it was flying into the back of the net anyway. It was a similar situation to the 1987 FA Cup Final against Coventry, when there was discussion over whether I got the one that put us 2-1 up, or whether it was a Brian Kilcline own goal. In the end it got given to me. The cross came in from Chris Waddle and we both collided. If you watch it on TV it was a mass scrum. It hit us both and went into the net, but I got the biggest touch.'

Mabbutt seemed to have a habit of finding himself in these sorts of situations in the FA Cup. Of course, sadly it was an own goal from him, a deflection off his knee, which led to a 3-2 defeat after extra time in that 1987 FA Cup Final against Coventry. Then, four years later, he was the nearest Spurs player to Nottingham Forest's Des Walker, who headed into his own net in extra time to give Tottenham a 2-1 victory in the 1991 FA Cup Final.

Diary of Gerry Francis
Sunday 5 February, 1995
FA Carling Premiership
Tottenham Hotspur 3-1 Blackburn Rovers
Klinsmann 18, Sherwood 48, Anderton 30, Barmby 80

In the run-up to this game the lads had been telling me and my assistant Roger Cross how impressive Blackburn were when they beat us 2-0 at Ewood Park in the final match before I became manager. This game was live on Sky and Blackburn are top of the league and having a great season, so there was no doubt this was going to be a big test for us.

I knew this match was going to give me a good indication of how far we have come. The spirit is good in the squad and I was very pleased with how we bounced back from the defeat at Villa by winning so well at Sunderland.

We had a full week to prepare for Blackburn which was really important because David Howells had aggravated his knee injury against Sunderland but had managed to receive a week of treatment so he was fit to face Rovers. A week's break also meant we had time to look at the video and see what we didn't do too well at Sunderland and also enabled us to work on our fitness running programme and to look at the reports on Blackburn. They mainly play a straightforward 4-4-2 formation going into a 4-2-4 when they are in possession of the ball. They have two excellent front players in Alan Shearer and Chris Sutton who are both having an excellent year and as a team they like to get at the opposition whenever they can.

One part of our game that has improved immensely is our ability to counter-attack. For me, this is an absolutely vital element of a team's ability to be successful. I have watched European teams do it very successfully for years. It is equally valuable both home and away. It is a very important weapon to have in your armoury. It is also my belief that if you want to be successful in Europe it is an absolute must. We have worked on it a lot because I believe we have the players to make it work perfectly. When we lose possession we defend as a team and Teddy Sheringham and Jürgen Klinsmann become my first defenders. But when we win the ball back we strike forward immediately with the pace of Jürgen, Nicky Barmby and Darren Anderton. More often than not it is Teddy who is playing them through with a pass. Against Blackburn today we worked it superbly.

In the 18th minute we won the ball back just inside our half; with a few quick passes Darren then put Jürgen clear to shoot through the legs of Bobby Mimms and into the net. Former Tottenham keeper Mimms was standing in for the injured England keeper Tim Flowers, and Rovers were also missing England left-back Graeme Le Saux.

We repeated the move on the half-hour mark and this time Darren's long-range shot deflected into the net for 2-0. At this stage we were playing so well that I didn't want half-time to arrive. There are times when you can't wait to get the players in the dressing room at half-time, and there are also times when you don't want the game to stop. This was one of those times. You realise their manager has the chance to put a few things right and to try and liven up his players. So I had to be careful. I didn't want to give the lads too much praise even though I was very pleased with the way they had played. I reminded them that Blackburn hadn't got to the top of the table by packing it in when they are two goals down. I warned them to expect a real game in the second half and told them we would have to be ready for Blackburn.

Unfortunately, after defending so well in the first half, we conceded a very poor goal when Tim Sherwood scored two minutes into the second half to get them right back into the game. Management can certainly be frustrating. We managed to survive a Blackburn surge and held very strong defensively before getting ourselves back into the game. Eventually we made sure of the three points with an outstanding goal ten minutes from time. A great cross from Darren Anderton was superbly headed home by Nicky Barmby. It was a brilliant goal in a cracking game that had been live on television. We have received tremendous praise for how we played today and having beaten the league leaders people are really starting to take notice of what we are achieving at the club.

In the last 15 games we have won nine, drawn four and lost just two. We have also scored 30 goals and conceded just 12, keeping seven clean sheets along the way. I am really pleased with how things are going.

The result against the eventual 1994/95 champions had again stirred hopes of UEFA Cup qualification via the league. The win put Tottenham back in sixth place ahead of Leeds and four points behind fifth-placed Nottingham Forest. Blackburn's defeat at The Lane also gave renewed belief to Manchester United. They had beaten Aston Villa 1-0 the previous day with Andy Cole getting his first goal for the club since he arrived from Newcastle in a British record £7m deal on 10 January. United were now just a point behind Rovers, but of course crucially, that is also where they eventually finished.

From Tottenham's perspective, Darren Anderton remembers the performance against Blackburn as one of the team's best of the season. 'You go back over in your mind the games, how entertaining we were and how well we played,' he says. 'I mean beating Blackburn, who went on to be champions, 3-1 at The Lane was brilliant. We absolutely battered them. Three great goals, it just felt fantastic. Another magnificent atmosphere at White Hart Lane and live on the telly as well.'

Now Spurs headed to Stamford Bridge, hoping to keep the good run going. It had been a difficult week for the Blues. Three days prior to Tottenham's visit, trouble flared at the ground in an FA Cup replay which Chelsea lost on penalties to First Division Millwall. Away fans ran on to the pitch at full time, sparking scuffles between rival supporters. Seats were ripped up, and 38 arrests were made.

A few days before Tottenham's visit, Chelsea's captain, Dennis Wise, had also been found guilty of an assault on a London taxi driver. The following month he would be sentenced to three months in prison, before being acquitted on appeal. Chelsea player-manager Glenn Hoddle kept faith with his skipper and sent him out against Spurs still wearing the armband. Hoddle's side weren't in great form. They were without a league win in two months since beating Southampton 1-0 at The Dell on 3 December. For Tottenham though it was almost exactly five years to the day since they had last beaten Chelsea home or away. Gary Lineker's goal had given them a 2-1 win on 10 February 1990. This is a stat which would continue to be trotted out for many years yet!

Diary of Gerry Francis
Saturday 11 February, 1995
FA Carling Premiership
Chelsea 1-1 Tottenham Hotspur
Wise 79
Sheringham 8
I kept being reminded by a number of people that Tottenham haven't beaten Chelsea for some time. They were my second opponents when I

took over in November and that game ended in a goalless draw, getting the team their first clean sheet of the season.

Today Dean Austin was available after suspension and he has done well for me since I came to the club. While he's been out, Sol Campbell and Justin Edinburgh have also done a good job in the full-back positions. When someone returns from injury or suspension it isn't always a straightforward decision to put them straight back in the team. Yes, Dean hasn't let me down, but neither Sol nor Justin deserved to be left out. These are the difficult decisions managers have to deal with every week. On this occasion I decided to stick with the team that beat Blackburn last week but I included Dean on the bench at the expense of midfielder Darren Caskey.

We played well today and created more than enough chances to win. I was disappointed we didn't take all three points. In the eighth minute the Darren Anderton-Teddy Sheringham corner routine worked for the third time this season as Teddy volleyed home a low shot at the near post. We created and missed a lot of chances in the first half and really should have been leading by more. When we went in for the break I told the players that we should have put the game beyond Chelsea by now and that we had been in so much control that we really should have made our opponents pay. I told them that Glenn Hoddle wouldn't be happy with his team's performance and that we should expect a different Chelsea side in the second half. Chelsea did indeed do better in the second half, but did not really cause us too many problems.

Again we created and missed several chances to increase our lead. However, with the game nearing its end, Glenn Hoddle brought himself on for David Rocastle which woke the Chelsea crowd up a bit and at the same time, as a team, we had started to back off and get deeper and deeper. This often seems to happen in the later stages to teams who have been controlling a game. When you have been the better side but are only leading by a goal, for no apparent reason, you seem to back off into the last third and park yourselves in the penalty box thereby giving the opposition the initiative to come forward and knock balls into the box. This is exactly what happened to us today.

With just over ten minutes to go, Glenn Hoddle was given plenty of room to deliver a fine cross for Dennis Wise, of all people, to head the equaliser against the run of play. All the good work we had done for nearly 80 minutes counted for nothing as we finished the game with one point when I certainly felt we should have had all three.

The transformation under Francis had been spectacular. The Chelsea match was his 16th game in charge, the same number Spurs had played this season prior to his arrival. So how did his record compare with that of his predecessors?

	P	W	D	L	F	A	Clean Sheets
Ardiles	16	6	2	8	29	35	0
Francis	16	9	5	2	31	13	7

While the defensive improvement had been dramatic, Francis had also coaxed even more goals out of the team. How had he effected such a transformation with the same players? Well, he had got the team fit. The running sessions were now reaping full dividends. The video analysis seemed to have played a part too, with the players now learning from their mistakes. His technical coaching knowledge and awareness, and the emphasis on defensive drills and set pieces in training, meant the team was now far better organised.

Diary of Gerry Francis
Wednesday 15 February, 1995
International Friendly
Republic of Ireland A-A England
Kelly 22

Match abandoned after 27 minutes due to crowd violence with Rep. Ireland leading 1-0

I was in the Sky studio as a panellist. The game was in progress, Ireland were 1-0 up and deservedly so. I am sure at that stage that the England coach Terry Venables was desperate to get to half-time so that he could sort out a number of problems that England were having. Then, unfortunately, there were dreadful scenes of hooliganism that spilled on to the playing area and forced the game to be abandoned. As an Englishman born and bred and proud of it, I am ashamed to say that it seemed without doubt that a section of the English supporters were totally responsible for this outrage. A few mindless idiots totally ruined a great evening for thousands of people. There were many women and children in the crowd, possibly enjoying their first international match against England. What really annoys and saddens me is that many of the people responsible were adults, not kids. It makes you wonder what type of mentality these people have to endanger others in this way. All I know is that this was a very sad night for English football.

From a selfish perspective it also means as club managers that we have suffered the disruption of an international week and that the England and Republic of Ireland lads have got nothing out of it. International week is always a worrying time for a club manager. In our case, as many as 17 players can be away with the international teams, including the Under-21s. It can be a very frustrating time. You cannot work on any preparation for the game ahead as you have so few players with you. You just have to keep your fingers crossed that your players will come back injury-free, which often isn't the case.

With your English internationals, due to the cancellation of Premiership games, at least they don't miss matches. However, other internationals from Germany, Romania, Israel, Norway, Scotland and Ireland can end up playing for their countries and missing club games. We have had times where we have missed the likes of Jürgen, Gica Popescu, Ilie Dumitrescu, Erik Thorstvedt, Ronny Rosenthal and others. Without doubt it affects the standard of the squad you can name on a matchday.

It also causes a knock-on effect. If you are missing an international player and the person you replace them with has a great game, then you are left with a selection dilemma the following week. Travelling back from international games on a Thursday or Friday morning will often leave the player jaded for the weekend club fixture. I have been advocating for some time that international matches should be played on a Saturday with the players coming back to their clubs on the Monday which would give them time to recover before the next weekend fixture. This would also give the national manager the chance to go over the game with the players on the Sunday.

There is so much you can learn from a game whether you win, lose or draw, but the national manager doesn't get a chance to properly assess things with the team because they all have to rush straight off back to their clubs. They don't see them again for weeks or even months. By playing internationals on a Saturday you would be fairer to both the clubs and the national team. After all, it is both the club managers' and international managers' futures at stake if they don't produce the right result. From a players' point of view I know what it means to play for and captain England. I would never, ever stand in the way of a player representing their country. It is a great honour.

With the Republic of Ireland v England match being televised live on Sky, hundreds of thousands of viewers witnessed the destructive scenes. Twenty people were taken to hospital and 43 arrests were made. Coming just a week after the trouble between Chelsea and Millwall at Stamford Bridge, there were real fears that UEFA might strip England of the right to host Euro 96. Terry Venables missed out on a valuable chance to experiment with his team, while players from both sides were left mentally scarred by the experience, as were the innocent supporters caught up in the mindless violence.

Darren Anderton remembers: 'There were five of us Tottenham boys involved: myself, Teddy Sheringham, Sol Campbell, Ian Walker and Nicky Barmby; but I was the only one to start. The game was going along just fine, and then we went behind as David Kelly scored for the Republic.

'Then there was complete uproar behind us and all sorts of big wooden objects coming on to the pitch. We had no idea what was going on. The referee told us to get off the pitch quickly. There were sticks coming down and chairs being ripped up as we made our way to the dressing room. We were all hoping it wouldn't escalate. None of us wanted to be part of a major disaster.

'I had seen terrible incidents on telly as a kid, but thankfully I had never experienced it. The work of the security and the stewards meant that we all felt safe as we went to the dressing room. I thought that we would get back out soon, that the game would resume, but obviously it was even worse than we realised because the referee had to call it off. It was the only professional match I was ever involved in where that happened. It all felt a bit odd as we left the stadium for our flight home in the early hours.'

Diary of Gerry Francis
Saturday 18 February, 1995
FA Cup Fifth Round
Tottenham Hotspur 1-1 Southampton
Klinsmann 21
Le Tissier (pen) 22

All the media wanted to talk about in the run-up to this one was this idea that we're fated to win the FA Cup because we were initially banned from it. I find it really annoying. When the TV cameras came down to the training ground on Thursday, this was the theme of all their questions. I've been worried that this talk would start to get through to the players, who can't afford to believe that winning any game is a formality.

The media were also looking at it as a good home draw for us, and with Southampton close to the relegation zone they were assuming we would go through easily. It was up to me to make sure that all those thoughts were put out of the players' heads. Today we prepared for the game as usual. I knew Southampton would play their normal pattern and that they were a hard-working side. In the dressing room before kick-off we went through who was marking who, what positions we were going to take up, which players were going to pick up the others in the Southampton team and again we went over what we were going to do with our free kicks, corners and throw-ins.

Southampton also have Matthew Le Tissier, who on his day can cause you problems by his sheer brilliance. On other days he can be totally anonymous. That makes him so dangerous because you don't know what he is going to produce. He is one of those players who often rises to the occasion. As far as I am concerned, he is a 'big game' player and this was a big game for Southampton.

Southampton were clearly really up for it. They started very well. For the first 20 minutes or so they were much the better side. Despite their good start, we took the lead against the run of play. Ian Walker's clearance was flicked on by Teddy Sheringham and Jürgen chipped it over Bruce Grobbelaar. It was a lovely finish.

I felt this might help us relax and settle down a bit, but within a minute Southampton were level. Jeff Kenna was tripped by Justin Edinburgh. TV replays showed that the foul actually happened outside the box. Just as he did in the league meeting back in September before I took over, Le Tissier made the score 1-1 with a penalty. He smashed this one towards Ian Walker's top left-hand corner. Somehow, just as he had done against Le Tissier and Shearer (before I took over) in the league, Ian got a hand to it. But now, as on those previous two occasions, he couldn't keep it out. Le Tissier has only ever missed one penalty – saved by Mark Crossley of Nottingham Forest.

At half-time I made it clear to the players that I wasn't at all pleased with the way we started. I reminded them of what I said before kick-off, that this was going to be a tough game. This is Southampton's last chance of achieving anything this season other than avoiding relegation and they're going to fight us all the way for a place in the FA Cup quarter-finals.

We dominated the second half in terms of possession, but apart from a couple of half-chances, we didn't create a great deal. Grobbelaar made a couple of decent saves, but it ended 1-1 and I'm sure Southampton will be confident they can finish the job back at their place.

Wednesday 22 February, 1995
FA Carling Premiership
Newcastle P-P Tottenham Hotspur
Match postponed due to waterlogged pitch
Our evening match against Newcastle was called off at 1pm due to a waterlogged pitch. Unfortunately many of our travelling fans would have already started their long journey towards the North-East when the decision was taken.

The postponement was not necessarily a bad thing for us, because we would have been without Jürgen who is away with Germany for a friendly against Spain. Without playing, our hopes of European qualification have been boosted today. UEFA announced England will have five places in the UEFA Cup for 1995/96. Liverpool are currently fourth in the league and also huge favourites to win the Coca-Cola League Cup, meaning that fifth place in the league will probably be enough for any team to qualify. The Reds are favourites for the League Cup because they lead Crystal Palace 1-0 after the first leg of their semi-final, and already know they will play Division One opponents in the final. Bolton are trailing Swindon 2-1 after the first leg of the other semi-final. Both second legs were due to take place tonight, but were also rained off.

Saturday 25 February, 1995
FA Carling Premiership
Tottenham Hotspur 1-2 Wimbledon
Klinsmann 49
Ekoku 39, 64

Wimbledon are always difficult opponents. I know that because I was a coach there with Dave Bassett back in the 1985/86 season when they won promotion to the old First Division, which is now the Premiership. I also spent the 1986/87 season with them when they finished sixth – their highest position in the top division so far. The spirit at the club during my time there was magnificent. Wimbledon were always regarded as the underdogs with a small ground, limited support and very little money to spend. No one gave them much chance of staying in the top division for very long, but nearly ten years on they are still there which is huge credit to their resolve and their competitiveness.

They arrived at White Hart Lane today on the back of a disappointing run, having not won in four in the league and having recently been thumped 7-1 at Aston Villa. Before this game they were 11th in the league with 36 points. We were seven points above them in sixth place and aiming to protect our unbeaten record against London opponents this season. It was important for us to try to continue to pick up points.

They decided to play with just one up front – Efan Ekoku. They went with five at the back and packed the midfield in the hope of catching us on the break. I knew it was going to be difficult to break them down and told the players we would need to be patient. We started well enough and had a lot of the ball and the play. Clear-cut chances, however, were not so plentiful despite the amount of possession we had. As we approached half-time, Wimbledon had hardly been in our half of the field although they had defended well in numbers.

Sol Campbell was attacking down the right wing with the ball at his feet. As he crossed the ball he tore his hamstring and collapsed on the floor. Play continued although we were at this stage shouting to our players to knock the ball out so Sol could have some treatment. Within seconds Gica Popescu had gone into a tackle and strained his ankle ligaments. He was now hobbling around along with Sol. Play still continued, and the next thing we knew Efan Ekoku had put Wimbledon ahead. The ball hitting the back of the net was the first opportunity we had to get treatment to two of our players. Unfortunately they were both badly injured and had to come off. I sent on Ronny Rosenthal for Gica and Dean Austin for Sol.

It was the only shot Wimbledon had in the first half and they were in front. I was absolutely fuming when we got into the dressing room. I felt we had been very unprofessional by not knocking the ball out of play when we had the injured players. Although this all happened in just over a minute we had won the ball on a couple of occasions during that period and could easily have put it out of play.

Now we had an uphill task being 1-0 down against a team that was prepared to defend for the whole game. I told my players they were really going to have to make it happen now. We were going to have to put our heads and bodies in there and force the situation. The message seemed to get through and we started the second half brilliantly. Within four minutes we were level. Justin Edinburgh hit in a high cross, Teddy Sheringham beat Wimbledon keeper Hans Segers to it and Jürgen sent a diving header into the net. At that moment I was convinced that the only outcome would be that we would go on to win the game. I certainly couldn't see us losing.

For the next ten or 15 minutes we just bombarded the Wimbledon goal. But we just couldn't get the second. Then from nowhere, Wimbledon took the lead again. In the 64th minute a long clearance from their defence came through the middle and Ekoku picked the ball up and forced his way through despite being surrounded by four of our players. First he went past Dean Austin and Gary Mabbutt. As Ekoku knocked the ball into the box, Colin Calderwood seemed like a strong favourite to get there first, but Ekoku shoulder-charged him. It looked like a foul to me, but the referee saw nothing wrong and at the same time as charging Colin, Ekoku hammered a left-footed shot across Ian Walker and into the far corner.

I've spoken to Colin on a number of occasions about using his upper body strength. He's done very well for me, but he must learn to be ready for people who are going to use their body weight to shoulder-charge him.

For the last 20 minutes we dominated the game, but we just couldn't get the equaliser despite hitting the bar and the post. Jürgen also came close with a spectacular overhead kick which was brilliantly saved by Segers. It finished 2-1, and it was a very disappointed dressing room. It's not for a lack of passion or effort that we have lost, but because of a lack of thought, certainly in the scenario when we were down to nine men and didn't kick the ball out. We have thrown away three points. The injuries look like bad news too with Gica and Sol likely to be out for a long time now.

Wednesday 1 March, 1995
FA Cup Fifth Round Replay
Southampton 2-6 Tottenham Hotspur (aet)
Shipperley 6, Le Tissier (pen) 40.
Rosenthal 57, 59, 102, Sheringham 113, Barmby 115, Anderton 120

This was one of the most incredible matches I have ever been involved in. Going into this game, I was very aware of the problems posed to us by Matthew Le Tissier and in particular by his role in the Southampton team. He plays in the hole, just behind the front two strikers. He caused us a number of difficulties in the first game. My system normally handles that situation well with my back four looking after the front two and the man in the hole behind them. Le Tissier though is a special talent.

That concerned me, especially as Sol Campbell and Gica Popescu were injured. Dean Austin came back in for Sol and we brought Stuart Nethercott into midfield in place of Gica alongside David Howells to look after Le Tissier. I don't often use man-marking tactics for the man in the hole position. It is easy to man-mark a midfield player. It is not so easy when you have someone in Le Tissier's role. They have no defensive duties at all and they can go anywhere and do anything. It is a lazy sort of role. Le Tissier only needs a tiny area to hurt you. It was something I agonised over but my decision was made after I watched the video of the first game again. With two players out already, I thought it was worth trying. I thought that if you could stop Le Tissier, you were left with an average hard-working Southampton side. He was the talent in their team, he could make them play. After doing some work in training we decided to go with the man-marking tactic. Unfortunately, as so often happens in football, we were 1-0 down before Le Tissier had even had a meaningful touch of the ball.

Jason Dodd set up their new £1.2m signing from Chelsea, Neil Shipperley, who finished from just inside the six-yard box. 1-0 Southampton. All my planning was out the window. I left the system alone for a little while to see if we would come back into the game and we didn't do too badly. Then Dean Austin was adjudged to have fouled Neal Heaney and Le Tissier scored from the penalty. Again Ian Walker got his hand to it – in fact this time both hands – but he couldn't keep it out. So we were 2-0 down after 39 minutes and I had to change my thinking.

It was no good worrying about Le Tissier any more. We had to go back to our normal formation and try to get forward in an attempt to get back into the game. Moments later, just before half-time, I brought Stuart Nethercott off and sent Ronny Rosenthal on. Ronny had only recently recovered from damaged knee ligaments, but he was fit enough to play.

As Ronny entered the fray, no one could possibly have had any inkling about what effect he would have on this tie. At half-time I told the players that we had been good at forcing our way back into games this season and that we could do it again now. Most people must have been thinking our FA Cup run was over, but we had to prove them wrong. I urged the players to get at Southampton and to take a few gambles, to push on, because 45 minutes was more than enough time for us to turn this around. So the players went out to battle for our place in the sixth round.

What happened next was the most extraordinary comeback in my entire career, as Ronny Rosenthal completely transformed the game. Teddy Sheringham appeared to be trapped in the left-hand corner of the pitch with two Southampton players on his back. He back-heeled it into the path of Nicky Barmby, who swept a lovely first-time left-footed cross into the area. Ronny got ahead of his man and, as the ball bounced, he hit a first-time shot with his left foot over goalkeeper Bruce Grobbelaar from the corner of the six-yard box. An absolutely brilliant goal to bring us back into the game at 2-1.

The Spurs fans were urging us on now, and a chant of, 'Come on you Spurs' was echoing around the ground at full volume when Ronny struck again. Dean Austin picked up the ball just inside our half, and knocked a high ball out to the right flank towards Ronny who let it bounce, brought it under control, and then with some lovely trickery bamboozled Kenna and Dodd as he cut inside and smashed a brilliant long-range shot beyond Grobbelaar at his near post.

He had struck twice in two minutes to bring us level. There was only a minute or so between Ronny's two goals, but in that time Ian Walker pulled off a stupendous save. In its own way it was as important as Ronny's goals because had we gone 3-1 down just after getting back into it, it might have been a killer.

After our second goal, Southampton quickly regained their composure and both sides came close to winning it before the final whistle. Strangely, as manager, I felt more pressure at 2-2 than I did at 2-0 down. When we were losing 2-0, any Southampton attack didn't really matter. We had to win the ball back and score two goals. But now we'd achieved that, any Southampton attack took on a completely different complexion. Myself and Saints boss Alan Ball were both kicking every ball with our teams. We were really feeling it.

Although neither goalkeeper was beaten again in the 90 minutes, both made some great saves and it finished 2-2. Alan Ball and I both went on to the pitch to speak to our teams before extra time. I stressed to my players that we had to keep going, we had to keep playing to try and win the game in extra time rather than allowing it to go to penalties.

When you've got someone as lethal from 12 yards as Le Tissier in your ranks, you've got an advantage in a shoot-out. Sometimes extra time is dull because teams play for penalties. This half-hour was anything but. The Spurs contingent at The Dell, and the thousands watching live on Sky, were in for a treat. Three minutes before the end of the first period of extra time, David Howells picked up the ball near halfway. He hit a lovely ball out to Ronny on the left-hand side. Ronny collected it just five yards into Southampton's half, and immediately set off on a charge towards goal. He took it on, and on, and on, and then he just hammered it from 35 yards with the outside of his left foot and the ball flew into the top corner.

Down on the touchline we were all falling out of the dugout amid the amazing scenes. It was just the most incredible hat-trick. A half-volley and then two long-range strikes. It had been a tight game until this point, but then we went on to dominate the second period of extra time. With just seven minutes remaining, David Howells hit a lofted clearance from the edge of our box which left Ken Monkou in difficulty on halfway. Jürgen beat him to it, ran through and set up Teddy to take it round Grobbelaar and make it 4-2.

Two minutes later David Howells and Jürgen were the providers again. David's pass found Jürgen just inside the Southampton half. He chose the perfect moment to knock it through to Nicky Barmby, who broke the offside trap. Grobbelaar's defence left him stranded and he was already on the edge of his area so Nicky simply nudged it past him and then knocked it into an open goal for 5-2.

In the final minute of extra time, Darren Anderton completed the rout against the team he grew up supporting. David Howells started the move again, playing Nicky Barmby into the area. Grobbelaar again found himself in a difficult position, as Nicky lured him to the bottom corner of the area well outside his right-hand post.

With Grobbelaar out of goal, Nicky changed direction and charged out of the area. Grobbelaar pursued him for a split second and tried to get a tackle in from behind, leaving himself grounded. Nicky then turned a complete 180 degrees, and hit a pass back to Anderton just outside the area.

Darren did well to bring it down with his right foot and then smash it on the half-volley with his left. Just as Grobbelaar was getting back towards his goal the shot flew beyond him. 6-2 and a welcome goal for Darren, who had been barracked by the Saints fans throughout.

I will never forget this game. I feel for Alan Ball to have been 2-0 up at half-time and thinking he was through. I think the 6-2 scoreline was unfair on Southampton. In the FA Cup though, when you are behind you have to take your chances. You have to push people forward. There is no other option. You may get beat 4-0 or 5-0, or you might turn it all around like we did.

The dressing room afterwards was buzzing. Now though we had to endure the really dangerous talk of Tottenham being destined to win the FA Cup. That talk was really irritating me. Although this sort of media talk is part and parcel of the game, you can't allow yourself to believe it as players.

As the final whistle blew on an incredible 6-2 scoreline, the Sky cameras cut to Ronny Rosenthal, who didn't seem to know what to do as he was handed the match ball. The hat-trick scorer told the press: 'You don't expect to come on and score three goals like this. They were the best I have ever scored; I will always remember them as beautiful goals. The one regret I had was that I had to score these goals tonight against Bruce, because he was a good friend at Liverpool. He is a good lad and a good goalie.'

Some wondered whether Grobbelaar had been affected by the scrutiny he was under following recent accusations of match-fixing. He had also made a mistake against Ipswich in the weekend's Premiership game and in the interim he had flown home to Zimbabwe for a few days, only arriving back in England on the morning of the Southampton v Tottenham replay. There is no suggestion he wasn't trying his best against Ipswich or Spurs, but was he feeling the pressure of the media storm?

In November 1994 *The Sun* had accused Grobbelaar of helping to throw games to aid an illegal betting syndicate. Despite the allegations, the former Liverpool keeper was allowed to continue playing. Three years later he was cleared, after two successive trials both saw juries fail to reach a verdict. He then sued *The Sun* for defamation and was awarded £85,000 in damages, but when the newspaper appealed to the House of Lords they won. Grobbelaar's damages were reduced to £1, because the House of Lords believed there was sufficient proof of dishonesty. Grobbelaar was also ordered to pay *The Sun*'s costs.

Whether or not Grobbelaar was feeling under pressure because of the accusations, none of that takes away from Rosenthal's achievement. Nethercott says, 'Few people will score a better hat-trick than that. Sensational stuff. Even though I didn't complete the game, I was in celebratory mood. It was clearly the right decision to take me off and put Ronny on. Games like that you just don't forget.

'Ronny was hit and miss, wasn't he?' he continues. 'To be honest, in shooting practice he was bloody awful, so to rifle the goals he did that night was just amazing. He was a great character though, another great lad who was just coming to the twilight of his career.'

'You never knew what Ronny was going to do,' says David Howells. 'That night everything went for him. What a night, what a cup tie.'

Jonathan Pearce was commentating on the match for Capital Gold: 'Rocket Ronny,' he laughs. 'Oh dear, oh dear. Rocket Ronny. What a character. We were in the old wooden press box at The Dell and it was all compressed up there, with not much room. When Le Tissier scored the penalty, the whole stadium seemed to move, I thought that was it for Spurs, it would be another frustrating season for them. Then it was one of the most remarkable comebacks I've ever seen. Coming back from 2-0 down was impressive, but to then absolutely destroy the opposition as they did was hard to comprehend.

'I remember saying to Ronny after one game, "You know what your nickname is, don't you?" And he said, in his thick Israeli accent, rolling his Rs, "Yes, of course, R-r-r-ocket R-r-r-onny R-r-r-osenthal." It really made me laugh.'

Rosenthal's hat-trick provided the main plot line, but the fact that Spurs ran out such comfortable winners in a match which went to extra time, also made it notable. 'It was a great game to play in,' says Anderton. 'When Gica was fit he had to play, he was so good. But when he wasn't, like on this occasion, I played in the centre which I absolutely loved.'

With his 23rd birthday just two days away, the win over Southampton was the perfect way to celebrate. 'Even though I was a Southampton fan growing up, I always got a lot of stick there because of having played for Portsmouth, so it was one I always wanted to win. I had a bit of a birthday night out that night, which was nice. I made sure we didn't go to any proper Southampton pubs, though, because I might not have been welcomed. We went out of town. That night with Ronny summed us up that season; even if we weren't playing well, there were moments when someone would come up with a piece of magic to make us click.'

Teddy Sheringham says: 'Ronny was a very unorthodox player and a very unpredictable player. That day he just came out and kept scoring wonder goals. I remember celebrating one of them with Justin Edinburgh and saying to him to just keep giving the ball to Ronny.'

Kit man Roy Reyland had his own nickname for Rocket Ronny. 'I used to call him "Lino Ron",' he says, 'because he was always on the floor. He was always falling over on the pitch.

'I remember in a team meeting after he had skied one from six yards, Gerry said to him, "Ronny, Ronny, what happened?" And Ronny said, "It hit the booble, Gerry, it hit the booble." Everyone fell about laughing.

'"It hit what?" said Gerry.

'"The booble," said Ron.

'"He means a bobble, boss," said someone. He made us all laugh.'

While there were many occasions when Ronny Rosenthal left Spurs fans bewildered and frustrated with some of his erratic performances, it was all worth it for the memory of this one incredible night on the south coast.

12

Ovation

'I can still see it in my mind. The Liverpool players had already left the field and their fans were clapping us. It shows the English spirit.' (Jürgen Klinsmann)

THE victory against Southampton meant Tottenham would now head to Anfield for an FA Cup sixth round tie with Liverpool. Before that they had two league matches to attend to.

Diary of Gerry Francis
Saturday 4 March, 1995
FA Carling Premiership
Nottingham Forest 2-2 Tottenham Hotspur
Bohinen 84, Lee 85
Sheringham 79, Calderwood 87

After the extraordinary night at Southampton, the players had Thursday off and then were back in on Friday feeling elated, but pretty tired. Extra time in midweek wasn't the best preparation for today's game. Forest have been enjoying a really good season and we knew they would be difficult to beat. They were fifth at kick-off, two places and four points ahead of us. Stan Collymore and Bryan Roy had been in excellent form up front. This turned into another topsy-turvy game with all the drama coming late on.

At half-time it was still goalless, but we had been the only team threatening to score and we should have been in front. I was pleased with the way we had been playing and told them that in the dressing room at half-time. I was pretty sure that Forest manager Frank Clark would be having a real go at his players because they had given a very disappointing first-half performance. He probably did his best to fire them up, but the game followed the same pattern in the second half.

With ten minutes to go, Teddy Sheringham gave us the lead against his former club. Nicky Barmby picked up the ball about halfway inside the Forest half and passed it between two defenders for Jürgen who pulled it back from the byline for Teddy to hit home from five yards.

That for me was three points because I certainly couldn't see them scoring on the basis of their performance so far. Then they struck twice in a minute. Just as he did in the first meeting of the season between the two teams in September before I took charge, Lars Bohinen beat Ian Walker from distance. He picked up the ball on the halfway line, ran ten yards with the ball at his feet and then David Howells came at him. Before David could get there, Bohinen hit a shot that went like a rocket into the top corner. At the time I thought Ian Walker should have saved it, but having seen it on video afterwards, the ball flew in. It was unstoppable.

Worse was to come. We lost the ball from the kick-off and it ended up being knocked high into the air down the middle of the pitch. Ian Walker just sort of strolled out to catch the ball with the Forest player Jason Lee, who is 6ft 4in, closing in. Ian seemed to hesitate rather than just coming out and catching it. Lee thought he had a chance and he got his head in to knock it out of Ian's hands and then tap it into the empty net. It was a poor mistake from Ian and he was very disappointed with himself.

With five minutes to go we were now losing a game that we had been in complete control of. Thankfully there was still time for Colin Calderwood to ensure we went home with a point. Darren Anderton's outswinging corner fell to Jürgen, who flicked it on to Ronny Rosenthal at the side of the six-yard box. He volleyed it across goal and Colin tapped it in from a couple of yards. It finished 2-2 and we know we should have won. Frank Clark really criticised Collymore and Roy after the match for being lazy and not working hard enough. We had kept them quiet and totally dominated. This was two points dropped.

Wednesday 8 March, 1995
FA Carling Premiership
Tottenham Hotspur 3-0 Ipswich Town

Klinsmann 2, Barmby 15, Youds (og) 83

We could have done without this midweek game three days before having to travel to Liverpool for a huge FA Cup quarter-final. I was a bit uneasy going into this one, because at the weekend Ipswich were annihilated 9-0 away to Manchester United – a Premiership record defeat. Everyone was expecting us to hammer George Burley's side today. They are second from bottom and fighting for their Premiership lives.

A lot of people have been making jokes at Ipswich's expense and that was worrying me before kick-off. I knew those players would be hurting from the result at Old Trafford. They are professionals and I knew they would be desperate to make amends. Because we have been enjoying such a good run, teams have been coming to White Hart Lane and playing five across the back, which is exactly what Ipswich did. It would have been nice to have a free week to prepare for Liverpool in the cup, but this was also a really important game to try and maintain our push for a European place through the league, so it was crucial that we won.

This was something like our 14th game in two months. We were still without Gica Popescu and Sol Campbell, and David Howells had been having problems with his knee. Since we had pretty much been playing two games a week since Christmas, he really hadn't had much time to recover, but he was fit to start tonight.

I made sure my players knew that they couldn't afford to be complacent. It was also a concern that some of the players might have one eye on the cup tie at Liverpool. It is difficult to maintain great cup runs and good league form at the same time, particularly when you get to the later stages of the cup. You need consistency which is really hard to achieve.

I felt that if we could get a good start, and an early goal, then it would knock the stuffing out of our visitors. The message must have got through because we took a very early lead. In the second minute, Darren Anderton's outswinging corner picked out Jürgen. He arced a header towards goal but it was cleared off the line. It came straight back to him, and he simply smashed it into the net from ten yards. I turned to Roger Cross and said, 'Perfect, just perfect.' Their whole plan of getting people behind the ball to frustrate us had been to no avail.

By the quarter-hour mark we were 2-0 up. Again the goal came from one of Darren's corners. This time Jürgen flicked it on to Nicky Barmby, who hooked a well-controlled volley into the back of the net. The game was over in terms of a spectacle. Ipswich stayed basically the same shape which surprised me. Maybe they didn't want to be more adventurous and were more concerned with avoiding another hammering. We scored our third about eight minutes from time when Eddie Youds deflected Darren Anderton's cross into his own net off his arm, before Teddy Sheringham could get to it. It appeared as though the game was won so I took off David Howells to protect his knee and sent Darren Caskey on.

It was three really important points for us. We have stayed in sixth place and are still four points behind fifth-placed Forest, who won 2-1 at home to Everton tonight.

Saturday 11 March, 1995
FA Cup Sixth Round
Liverpool 1-2 Tottenham Hotspur
Fowler 39
Sheringham 45, Klinsmann 89

This was another incredible game. We were really hoping that Sol Campbell would have been fit for this match but it wasn't to be. The midweek game against Ipswich meant we only had one day - Friday - to prepare for our biggest game of the season. At least we were able to keep the same personnel, although I did make one adjustment to our tactics - I switched Nicky Barmby and Ronny Rosenthal around. I wanted Ronny on the left to handle the runs of Rob Jones and I felt with Nicky on the right-hand side, we could make use of what I saw as a gap on their left flank. They were playing Mark Walters out there and I felt that Nicky could use his strength to get into their box. I saw Walters as a mainly forward player and because of that he wouldn't be able to track Nicky back into their box, but I knew Nicky would track him. As it turned out, it worked superbly well.

Every player and manager cherishes the chance to play or manage a team in the FA Cup Final. Jürgen Klinsmann went into the game making no secret of the fact that it was his dream to play at Wembley. These cup games were always going to be special for him. I would say it is an ambition shared by all foreign players who come to this country because it is such a prestigious event and is shown worldwide. It certainly annoys me at times how in this country we belittle the attributes and abilities of British players. People forget that our record in Europe at club level is second to none in terms of winning trophies and that's despite a five-year ban. And in the majority of cases, those trophies have been won with mainly English, Irish, Scottish and Welsh players in the teams.

There weren't too many foreign players around in our league during the 60s, 70s, and 80s. The majority of foreign players that have come here have a great regard for our football, our players and our set-up. AC Milan, when managed by Arrigo Sacchi, dominated Italian and European football for a number of years in the late 80s and early 90s, and yet they played with a back four, not the sweeper everyone associates with Italian football and with Europe in general. In fact Sacchi used to show his players videos of Liverpool's performances, in particular their back four, because he admired their football so much. Now Ajax are the talk of Europe. These things go in cycles and it is important that you look at the abilities and the strengths of your home players, while keeping an eye on what is happening in Europe. You can always learn and get better whether you are a player or a manager. Jürgen has certainly been excited by what English football has to offer.

He was a crucial figure today and this game, like the replay at Southampton, will stay in my memory forever. It was outstanding. Both teams played very well but I felt we were tremendous. We unfortunately went a goal down in the 38th minute against the run of play when Mark Walters crossed for Robbie Fowler to head Liverpool in front. That was a major blow as we had started the game well. We were positive, going at Liverpool and denying them space. That for me is very important against them. The only one giving us problems when Liverpool had the ball was Mark Walters who was a handful when he was on the ball. He has the ability to take people on and get his cross in.

To find ourselves a goal behind just before half-time was hard to take. I felt very disappointed for our players who had done so well. But again we showed great character. We were at Anfield, a daunting place, a goal down when we didn't deserve to be and it might have been easy to think that it wasn't going to be our day. But, no, we were having none of that. We kept at it, kept doing the things we had been working on and we got our reward when Teddy Sheringham scored a magnificent goal. The ball was laid across to him by Jürgen after a great little move. He curled it home from outside the box.

It came right on half-time and it was no more than we deserved. The timing was crucial. It gave us a huge lift going into the break. In the dressing room I told the players that I was delighted at the way we had played, I stressed that it was important that we kept doing what we had done in that first 45 minutes when we were quicker, sharper and first to the ball. Nicky Barmby was causing them a lot of problems when we broke with the ball down the right-hand side and I told them we had to maintain that.

Liverpool had a lot of the ball in the second half but didn't cause us too many problems while we looked dangerous when we broke out of defence quickly on the counter-attack. I felt Liverpool began to run out of ideas as the second half progressed. They were also looking a bit tired because of the amount of work they had put in trying to wear us down. This is where our fitness programme can really benefit us. Walters was again by far their most dangerous player but defensively he was losing Nicky Barmby – and Nicky was getting into danger areas a lot.

Come the last ten minutes, I was certain we would get a replay back at White Hart Lane. But with two minutes remaining Liverpool had a throw-in deep in their half in the right-back position. We squeezed our players in tight on the Liverpool defenders and the ball from the throw-in broke loose to Darren Anderton. He knocked the ball first time through to Teddy. Jürgen was making a run in behind Teddy and shouted for the ball. Teddy's deft touch was magnificent. It was just the slightest of touches, just a little flick. It ran straight through to Jürgen, he took it on his thigh and slotted it past David James. It was sheer elation. Most of the players were piling on top of Jürgen. We were all off the bench. Dean Austin came running off the pitch into our arms by the side of the dugout and the magnificent Tottenham supporters were ecstatic. It was a superb feeling and it was no more than we deserved. All the players came over to the touchline but we had to keep our nerve because there was one minute and injury time to go. That was the longest 120 seconds I have had to wait in football.

When the final whistle went the relief and overwhelming satisfaction were evident. We all went out on to the pitch to celebrate what had been an outstanding performance. It has certainly been one of the greatest highlights for me this season. We have beaten Newcastle, Arsenal, and Blackburn and played very well. But to go to Liverpool in the quarter-final of the FA Cup and win, is special. It was also pleasing to have produced a tactic that had such a big influence for us – switching Ronny Rosenthal and Nicky Barmby. That is why you look at the video tapes in preparation. The coach journey back was electric. It took three hours but it wouldn't have mattered if it had taken three days. You have got to appreciate the times when things have gone as you would like. There are enough bad times in football. The coach was full of drinks, full of jokes, full of laughter. It was great to see everybody in such great spirit and buzzing.

At the final whistle, despite seeing their team lose right at the death, the Liverpool fans afforded the Tottenham team, and Klinsmann in particular, a standing ovation. 'I can still see it in my mind,' says Klinsmann. 'When the referee blew the whistle and we were walking towards the Spurs fans to say thank you to them, the Liverpool players had already left the field and their fans were clapping us. It shows the English spirit. They were prepared to honour that we had been the best of two very good teams, and that we deserved to win. I will never forget that moment.'

It certainly was a game that will never be forgotten. Liverpool v Tottenham is always one of the standout fixtures, but when it is an FA

Cup quarter-final, it's huge. Some Spurs fans had even risked missing the kick-off against Ipswich on Wednesday night because they were still outside in the Paxton Road queuing for a ticket for Anfield which went on sale at 5pm. With 5,000 available, lengthy queues formed as supporters prepared to part with £15.

For Spurs there was more riding on it than for Liverpool. Eleven days into March, Tottenham's season would have been reduced to an unlikely quest for enough points to secure the final European qualification place via the league if they were knocked out. Liverpool had already reached one cup final. Earlier in the week they had beaten Crystal Palace 1-0 at Selhurst Park in the League Cup semi-final second leg. Robbie Fowler, just as he had in the first leg, scored the only goal of the game, to complete a 2-0 aggregate victory and send Liverpool to Wembley, where they would eventually go on to beat First Division Bolton. Fowler, 19, was one reason so many had taken such a shine to Liverpool in 1994/95. He epitomised the youthful enthusiasm with which the team managed by Roy Evans played.

The match wasn't on TV. If you were a Spurs fan who couldn't get a ticket to Anfield, there was another way to watch the game. If you had £12 to spare, it was being beamed back to White Hart Lane and shown live on the screens inside the premises formerly known as Whites on the Paxton Road and in the Bill Nicholson Suite inside the stadium. The match itself was an all-ticket affair, meaning no tickets were available at Anfield on the day. The official attendance was a 39,592 sell-out. Referee Martin Bodenham had to delay kick-off by ten minutes because of crowd congestion.

These days all four FA Cup sixth-round ties are televised live. Even in the highly unlikely event that a match of this magnitude wasn't on telly today, the first port of call for many would be to seek out an internet stream, be it legal or not. That wasn't an option, of course, in 1995. Watching on the big screens at White Hart Lane was one alternative; another was to listen to the match on the radio.

Jonathan Pearce was at Anfield to commentate for Capital Gold. 'When you commentate on Spurs in the cup you are always mindful of the tradition. Especially back then, you were always mindful that they were likely to be a better cup team than they were a league team,' he says. 'You knew how important the FA Cup was for them and the fans, and the affinity that they had with the competition. And that meant every cup tie that you commentated on with Spurs was a massive occasion – it still is. To go to Liverpool and to win at Liverpool was really phenomenal. The result meant the whole season came alive. You were thinking Spurs were going to get to Wembley again.'

Among the fans who did manage to get a ticket to Anfield was Daniel Wynne. 'This was an absolutely unbelievable atmosphere. I think most of us went there not expecting to win; if anything we would have been happy to get them back to our place for a replay. It was a proper FA Cup atmosphere. Away teams get more tickets in the cup so there were thousands of Spurs fans, balloons and songs, and of course the Liverpool fans always create an incredible noise themselves.'

The ticketless fans back inside Whites Club and the Bill Nicholson Suite had converted those venues into a kind of mini White Hart Lane within White Hart Lane. To them it must have seemed like The Paxton, The Park Lane, The Shelf and the West Stand combined in one room. A joyously communal experience with eager viewers happy to grab any vantage point they could find: standing on chairs, peering over heads and through armpits. Those rooms were bedecked with scarves, flags and balloons.

Liverpool were favourites to win – they had only been beaten at Anfield once all season, bizarrely by the much-maligned and soon to be relegated Ipswich. It was a venue at which Tottenham had managed just three wins since 1912, and Spurs had never got the better of Liverpool either home or away in an FA Cup match.

To those assessing the desired destiny of the 1994/95 FA Cup from a Spurs perspective, it seemed only right that Jürgen Klinsmann should get his day out at Wembley. 'Ossie's Dream' of 1980/81 had been replaced by 'Jürgen's Dream'. Klinsmann had spoken so enthusiastically and so often since joining Spurs about what it would mean for him to play at the Home of Football, that those who idolised him so dearly hoped he would get the chance to do just that.

Tottenham would have to get to the final itself to make that Wembley dream a reality. These days every FA Cup semi-final is played at the new Wembley. In the mid-90s, the FA had started to use the old Wembley for the semis, but the day before Tottenham's trip to Anfield they announced that wouldn't be happening this year.

Wembley had been used for both semi-finals in each of the last two seasons. The trend had first started in 1991, when Tottenham met Arsenal. With no neutral venue in London big enough to stage such a huge fixture, the clubs argued it would be ridiculous to send two sets of rival fans trekking up the motorways and clogging the rail networks to a ground like Villa Park or Old Trafford. Even those stadiums wouldn't be big enough to satisfy demand for tickets for a game which in truth could probably sell out Wembley twice over. The FA agreed that Wembley should stage the tie, and they were rewarded with an absolute classic. Gazza's howitzer of a free kick and two goals from Gary Lineker saw

Spurs beat their arch-rivals 3-1 and end Arsenal's hopes of a league and FA Cup Double.

When Spurs and Arsenal were again drawn to meet each other at the semi-final stage in 1993, the FA couldn't really do anything else but select Wembley as the venue. The other semi-final was also a huge local derby between Sheffield United and Sheffield Wednesday. The South Yorkshire clubs had been told they would play at Elland Road, but understandably protested that they would also like the opportunity to play at Wembley, thank you very much. They too could sell out the game, and why should the London clubs benefit from the healthy gate receipts that they would be denied? In the end the FA bowed to the pressure, and both 1993 semi-final games went ahead at Wembley.

The FA stuck with Wembley in 1994, even though neither semi-final had quite the lustre of the previous year. This time round it was Chelsea v Luton Town and Oldham Athletic v Manchester United. So it seemed the status quo was now Wembley as the official home of the FA Cup semi-finals; but in 1995, the day before sixth round weekend, the FA changed tack. The old Wembley was only used once more for the semi-finals, when in 2000 Aston Villa beat Bolton on penalties and Chelsea won 2-1 against Newcastle. The new Wembley has been used for every FA Cup semi-final since 2008, the year after the venue opened.

For the players, thoughts of where they might play in the semi-finals didn't really concern either Spurs or Liverpool; getting there was all that mattered. Liverpool had needed a replay in all three previous rounds to get to the sixth round. They finally saw off Second Division Birmingham on penalties in the third round, beat First Division Burnley 1-0 at Anfield after a goalless draw at Turf Moor in the fourth round, and then dispatched Premiership rivals Wimbledon 2-0 at Selhurst Park following a 1-1 draw at home in the fifth round.

Darren Anderton remembers travelling to Merseyside in a state of nervous excitement. 'Liverpool were a good team with so many good players. Robbie Fowler, Ian Rush, and John Barnes who was still able to be a match-winner. People like Jamie Redknapp and Steve McManaman too, who everyone was really starting to talk about. Most people felt that Liverpool were going to win. But yes, we did have the feeling now that perhaps it was going to be our year. And we knew with Teddy and Jürgen in the team we were always capable of scoring against anyone.'

Dean Austin agrees. 'I think we felt we'd been written off a bit already,' he says. 'Most people were talking as though Liverpool were already through. People were talking about a potential Liverpool v Manchester United final. I think because their record had been so good at Anfield that year, and that they had home advantage with the Kop and the great atmosphere there, most neutrals felt they would probably make it through to the semis.'

Stuart Nethercott, who was on the bench for this game, says he couldn't contemplate the cup adventure ending at this point. 'What had happened with Ronny in the previous round just made it feel like anything was possible,' he says. 'By now I really had the feeling that this season was special, that it was taking us somewhere. We knew how strong Liverpool were, we knew it wasn't going to be easy. I guess I fancied we could at least get them back to our place.'

The game lived up to its billing from kick-off right until the final whistle. The teams took to the pitch to a crescendo of noise and colour, a sea of red in the Kop and of white in the packed away end. A soul-stirring rendition of 'You'll Never Walk Alone', sung before every home game, was belted out with extra gusto. The Spurs fans made an impressive but futile attempt to drown out the Liverpool anthem with songs of their own.

They kept up their support throughout, and were rewarded with Sheringham's sensational equaliser. 'Sheringham celebrated right in front of us,' says lifelong fan Daniel Wynne. 'It was a wonderful goal. And you could see the glory of it all over his face. The fact that we had got level so quickly after Liverpool went ahead was really important. It had been a really good first half, both teams had been playing well, but when Liverpool scored you did fear the worst because they were such a good team and they were at home. I think Sheringham scoring just before half-time really gave us hope, and you could see the players believed again.'

Of course there was even better to come. When Klinsmann's shot hit the back of the net, there was a split second of stunned silence inside Anfield as the away fans right down the other end took a while to realise the ball had gone in. Darren Anderton remembers: 'That was the moment of the whole season for me, really. The last minute. The way people spoke about the game as being a real classic. We were fairly young but also with good experienced players; Liverpool were the same.

'It was a magnificent FA Cup tie. It caught fire. We knew a lot of the Liverpool boys from the England squad; they were gutted but they acknowledged we were a good team who deserved to win on the day. Teddy's goal was a wonder goal right on half-time, and Jürgen's was a classy finish. That's the sort of thing he did, though. That was the sort of occasion he was made for. Quarter-final of the FA Cup, last minute, one-on-one, Klinsmann? Never any doubt. To be a part of that and to really be feeling like I was on the top of my game too was incredible. Afterwards I was absolutely buzzing.'

Of the standing ovation, Anderton adds: 'Liverpool fans are wonderful football fans. That game could have gone either way. Those fans could just as easily have been celebrating a win as having to get over a defeat. The way they reacted to Jürgen was first class. That game will always be one of my favourite games that I have ever played in. The way the game panned out, and at Anfield too, one of the great stadiums of English football. Me and Howellsy in the middle had a great battle against Digger [Barnes] and Jamie Redknapp. It was a battle of real quality.'

Klinsmann chooses his Anfield goal as his favourite of all those he struck for Spurs. 'The partnership with Teddy was one of the most enjoyable experiences I had in my career,' he says. 'We were always there for each other. This was a goal we scored as a partnership. It was a lovely flick from him and then I just had to put it away.'

Stuart Nethercott watched the drama unfold from the bench. 'It was just unbelievable,' he says. 'It was really special, a really special game. To score with virtually the last kick was the perfect finish for us. I hold the Liverpool fans in such high esteem, the fact that they stayed to clap us off. It was a great performance, a great result, and it really felt like we were heading places.'

For David Howells, whose performance was described as 'outstanding' by *The Guardian*'s David Lacey, it was also an occasion he will never forget. 'Aside from the 1991 semi-final, the Liverpool quarter-final remains one of the great highlights for me. It was a Saturday afternoon, three o'clock kick-off. A proper old-fashioned cup tie at Anfield.

'Fantastic crowd, great Spurs support all behind one end. And Liverpool support, as always, brilliant. It was just a heck of a game to play in. You feel amazing when you're involved in something like that. It's hammer and tongs at each other. We gave as good as we got. People a few months previously would have written us off at 1-0 down away to a very good Liverpool team.

'Teddy scored a worldy just before half-time, and we looked the better side in the second half. It was just a great occasion. Jürgen scored that great winner. Even the Liverpool fans were staying behind and clapping us off. At the end you think, "Ah, this is what it's all about – this is proper."'

Back in North London the fans had enjoyed a Hollywood ending to the cinematic experience of cheering on their team on the big screen. Hugs were shared between complete strangers. One supporter emptied a near-full pint glass over his head in disbelief. Another did likewise, then they jumped and cheered in beer-sodden unison. As they blinked their way out of White Hart Lane into the late afternoon sunlight along the Tottenham High Road, flags and scarves were waved in jubilation. Passing cars blared their horns in celebratory response. One had the window wound down with Chas N' Dave's 'Ossie's Dream' on full volume. 'Spurs are on their way to Wembley, Tottenham's gonna do it again.'

Anyone and everyone with a Spurs connection was celebrating a famous, never-to-be-forgotten FA Cup win. Tottenham had beaten Liverpool in the FA Cup for the first time ever and they'd done it in dramatic style. The media were again asking if Tottenham's name was really on the cup? The incredible win over Southampton coupled with the late heroics at Anfield had them tipping Spurs to win the trophy they were initially banned from.

Saturday's other quarter-final had ended in a 1-1 draw between First Division Wolves and Premiership strugglers Crystal Palace at Selhurst Park. The following day, there were two all-Premiership affairs. Everton beat Newcastle 1-0 at Goodison Park and Manchester United saw off QPR 2-0 at Old Trafford. The draw for the semi-finals was as follows: Tottenham Hotspur v Everton and Manchester United v Crystal Palace or Wolves.

Having struck off Wembley as a semi-final venue, the FA went on to choose Villa Park for Manchester United v Palace/Wolves and Elland Road for Spurs v Everton.

Kit man Roy Reyland says the Liverpool FA Cup game stands out as much as any of those he experienced in his near three decades working for the club. 'Anfield was always a special place for me because I had a good relationship with former Spurs coaches Doug Livermore and Ray Clemence, who were at Liverpool at that time. I got on very, very well with Roy Evans,' he says.

'I used to go in the famous Boot Room. When you walked into Anfield, this place was like a mecca of football. So to go there and win any game is a massive, massive achievement. But to go and win a game of that calibre, in that environment and win it at that stage in the game, that late on, was just majestic. I don't know how many games I worked on – probably something like 1,800 at Spurs – but that would certainly have to rank right up there as one of the best, even though it only took us to a semi-final, not to a final or a trophy or anything.'

Teddy Sheringham says his abiding memory of the game is of Klinsmann only just managing to stop himself from throwing up after scoring because of the emotion of the occasion and the effort he had put into it. 'The match exhausted all of us mentally and physically,' he says. 'For me, that was the standout game of the season. That was the only time in my career that I experienced a standing ovation from the

THE TEAM THAT DARED TO DO

opposition fans. The euphoria of the cup was carrying us through the second half of the season.'

Before they could start to seriously plan for the FA Cup semi-final against Everton, Gerry Francis and his players had four Premiership fixtures to navigate their way through.

Diary of Gerry Francis
Wednesday 15 March, 1995
FA Carling Premiership
Manchester United 0-0 Tottenham Hotspur

You couldn't ask for a harder match just four days after the exertions of Liverpool away than to have to travel to Manchester United. Their previous game at Old Trafford was their Premiership record 9-0 thumping of Ipswich. No one was expecting a similar scoreline tonight, but United were firm favourites to pick up maximum points against us. They had won five of their last six in the league, and are fighting leaders Blackburn all the way for the title.

We went into the match seven points behind fifth-placed Nottingham Forest, but with three games in hand on them. Such is the mood in the squad right now that we feel we can go anywhere and get a result. We needed that self-belief tonight because United had scored in every home game in every competition this season.

I knew it would be a big test. Having to play Manchester United away in the league straight after Liverpool away in the cup highlights just how much you have to put up with in English football. We play a lot more games than other teams in Europe, we have game after game with little time for preparation. It seems the more successful you are, the more you get punished, playing two or three games a week. That means you can lose the ability to perform at the very highest levels of fitness all of the time. So, then you have to consider resting players, but that can cause ill-feeling because you are changing a winning team.

I named the same team that took to the pitch against Liverpool and I opted to stick with the tactic that worked so well at Anfield by keeping Nicky Barmby on the right and Ronny Rosenthal on the left where he could help Justin Edinburgh cope with Andrei Kanchelskis. For me, Kanchelskis is a very dangerous player. Ryan Giggs on the other flank was also a threat, but I stuck to the format that had worked so well at Anfield.

To be honest, we could have been three- or four-nil down at half-time. My players seemed pretty pleased with themselves coming off at half-time with the score 0-0, but I certainly wasn't. In no uncertain terms I told them that we were extremely lucky to be level and that if we didn't liven up, defend better, and sharpen up all round, then we were going to get beaten.

It may seem strange to criticise your team when they are holding Manchester United to a draw at Old Trafford, but I felt it was necessary. We needed to get hold of the ball and to start to cause them some problems. In the second half there was a complete transformation. We were first class, and how we didn't win the game, I don't know.

Just minutes after the break Nicky Barmby had a great chance to become the first player to score against Schmeichel in the league at Old Trafford for 11 months. Jürgen played him in and Nicky lofted it over Schmeichel, but saw it drop wide of the post.

With six minutes to go, we were grateful to Ronny Rosenthal for a goal line clearance. A shot from Giggs was heading towards the top corner, and Ronny sprung into action to make an acrobatic clearance from under our crossbar. We had been by far the better team in the second half. I had been happy to hear the half-time whistle go, but it was Alex Ferguson who was happiest when the referee blew to end the match. It finished goalless. We have become the first team to prevent United scoring at home in any game in the whole of 1994/95. I'm very proud that we've lost just three times in the 23 games since I took over.

Francis had again helped deal a blow to Alex Ferguson's title chances just as he had done back on New Year's Day 1992. In a match shown live on ITV in the final season before the Premier League was launched, QPR went to Old Trafford and stunned a huge TV audience by beating United 4-1. The defeat played a part in Man U missing out on the title to Leeds.

This time around, in 1994/95, a goalless draw at Old Trafford between Spurs and United left the home team three points behind leaders Blackburn with nine games to play. The two dropped points would prove crucial, as United eventually lost out on the title to Blackburn by one point.

Tottenham were beginning to look like a really strong team under Francis. 'We had many more spectacular games, of course, but from a defensive point of view, Manchester United away was a really good performance,' says Dean Austin. 'No one was going there and keeping clean sheets, but we did it. This is the match where I broke a bone in my foot, though. So that's why for the rest of the season I had to play with injections in every game, and it's why I have so many problems now. My toe is just solid, and I will have to have an operation one day.'

United manager Alex Ferguson said to the press after the game: 'Spurs are definitely a different team since Gerry took over. There is a sense of discipline about them now. They're tougher and more resilient. They all work so hard for each other. We had all the play in the first half, but when Spurs started asserting themselves they looked impressive.'

The point meant Tottenham were now seventh, with Leeds overtaking them on the night by beating Leicester 3-1. It was still the case that fifth place would probably be needed to qualify for the UEFA Cup, with a slim chance that sixth could be enough if other variables all fell in to place.

Diary of Gerry Francis
Saturday 18 March, 1995
FA Carling Premiership
Tottenham Hotspur 1-0 Leicester City
Klinsmann 83

Mark McGhee is Leicester boss now. He took over from Brian Little who left for Aston Villa in November. Mark's side arrived at White Hart Lane in a relegation battle and without a win in eight games. I was again without both Sol Campbell and Gica Popescu who were hurt in the Wimbledon game three weeks ago. Unfortunately neither of them were ready to be considered today.

We got back from Manchester in the early hours of Thursday and only had one day to prepare for this game. On the training ground on Friday the players were obviously tired. This was our sixth game in 18 days, one every three days. We walked through our positions and did some pattern of play work in attack and defence. I had to take into account the emotional drain on the players from the two games against Liverpool and Manchester United, so I didn't want to do too much.

I know what it's like as a player. I can recall what it was like coming home from England matches all over Europe. The adrenaline is still there, it's the same as a manager. Sometimes you get home in the early hours, and even though it's 3am or 4am you just can't get to sleep after a long coach journey.

We knew that Leicester would be difficult opponents, playing five at the back and making it hard for us. The pitch was wet and heavy, and the fans were growing frustrated. Sometimes one of the hardest things to do is to help the supporters understand certain situations. They had seen us beat Liverpool away and draw at Old Trafford and now were expecting us to beat the bottom-of-the-table team easily. That kind of thinking can affect the players. The fans grow restless if you are not two or three up by half-time, and that filters through to the players on the pitch. From my decades in football though, I know that teams at the bottom can be more dangerous than teams at the top. They are playing for their livelihoods. No one can afford to be relegated.

It was goalless at half-time. We had enjoyed all of the play without creating too many clear-cut chances, but you had to give credit to Leicester for their defensive rearguard. Clearly, they weren't going to give up without a fight. We had been probing at them but we couldn't get through and suddenly the players were realising this was going to be a lot harder than they thought. At half-time I told them we had done okay in many ways, but that we were going to have to work even harder if we were going to get anything out of this game. I told them that Leicester were quite happy to stay in their own half in numbers and defend their goal and that it was up to us to make something happen in their box even if it meant getting hurt to do so. I stressed that we were just going to have to keep plugging away and plugging away even if we had to wait until the last minute to get our goal.

It looked like Leicester were going to hang on for a precious point in their relegation battle, but Jürgen struck with just seven minutes to go. Left-back Justin Edinburgh laid it back to Darren Anderton, central and 30 yards from goal. He lofted a cross towards Teddy Sheringham at the far post, but Neil Lewis was there for Leicester and intervened. He could only half-clear it and it dropped to Jürgen, who pulled off a fine volley. It was not quite an overhead kick but it was the same sort of technique, as he lifted his entire body off the ground and pivoted to hit it at waist height and hook it beyond goalkeeper Kevin Poole from eight yards.

Our biggest crowd of the season so far celebrated what could be a crucial win. There were 30,851 at White Hart Lane; the attendance was boosted by the opening of the upper tier in the new South Stand this afternoon.

It has been a great week, beating Liverpool away to reach the FA Cup semi-final, getting a point at Manchester United, and now winning against Leicester. There's only one disappointment, and that is that Justin Edinburgh has been booked today and will be suspended for the semi-final against Everton. With Sol Campbell and Gica Popescu still not fit, we're starting to get pretty depleted.

I've also got some concerns about the FA's decision to play our FA Cup semi-final at Elland Road and Manchester United's against Palace or Wolves at Villa Park. In my programme notes today, I wrote: 'If the ultimate criteria for having first played these games at Wembley were: one, the safety of supporters; two, allowing as many supporters as possible to see the game, and three, segregation, parking facilities etc., then there can only be one venue – Wembley. Tottenham and

Everton can easily sell 30,000 tickets each; Manchester United and either Wolves or Palace could do likewise. I agree that Manchester United and Everton, plus possibly Wolves supporters, would have to travel to Wembley, but most supporters I know would gladly walk there and virtually everybody that wanted to see the game would see it in safety and comfort.

'The reality is, unfortunately, that more than half of Spurs, Everton, Manchester United and either Palace or Wolves fans will not get a ticket to see the games. Tottenham supporters will have to travel to Leeds for a 1.30pm kick-off. Have any games at Wembley been delayed due to crowd congestion or anything else? Both the quarter-final ties on Saturday at Liverpool and Palace were delayed due to problems. I just cannot see the logic in the decision.'

Wednesday 22 March, 1995
FA Carling Premiership
Tottenham Hotspur 0-0 Liverpool
Klinsmann pen (72) saved by James
My selection problems have continued this week with Colin Calderwood going down with flu on Monday. He wasn't feeling at all well. It's a real shame because his Scotland manager Craig Brown was going to come and watch him play tonight against Liverpool.

When Craig called me to say he was planning to head to The Lane I had to let him know that Colin was a major doubt. Colin was also just one booking away from suspension that would rule him out of the FA Cup semi-final. With Justin Edinburgh banned for that game and Sol Campbell and Gica Popescu still recovering from injury, I can't risk anything else going wrong.

This morning, Colin said he was feeling better and that he might be able to play but that he still wasn't 100% fit. In the end, weighing everything up, I decided not to risk him and to play Stuart Nethercott instead. Stuart did well and we kept another clean sheet, but we really should have won.

Our best chance came from the penalty spot after Jürgen was brought down. The Liverpool players gave him a lot of stick about diving but we were all sure it was a definite penalty. Jürgen took it, but I feel all the fuss that the Liverpool players made had a bit of an effect on him. It ruffled him and he ended up missing it. I work with Jürgen week in and week out and as far as I'm concerned he's never been given anywhere near the number of penalties he should have been given. I feel that's because of the reputation he had when he came to this country. I think your reputation can precede you sometimes. I feel like he has certainly been hard done by a few times this season when it comes to giving penalties.

We have played seven games in 22 days without being beaten. We have won away at Southampton and Liverpool, beaten Ipswich and Leicester at home, drawn with Nottingham Forest and Manchester United away, and now got a point at home to Liverpool. It's been an outstanding run by anybody's standards and I'm very proud of the players.

The players won't get a rest though because now there is an international break. England scout Ted Buxton has been in the crowd tonight ahead of the squad announcement for the upcoming friendly with Uruguay. He's been watching Ian Walker, Teddy Sheringham, Nicky Barmby and Darren Anderton, who played despite going down with flu, and also all the Liverpool England boys. Jürgen will also be away for a few days with Germany who are playing against Georgia in a qualifier for Euro 96.

Sunday 2 April, 1995
FA Carling Premiership
Southampton 4-3 Tottenham Hotspur
Heaney 13, Le Tissier 44, 56, Magilton 61
Sheringham 17, 58. Klinsmann 35

Teddy, Darren and Nicky all played a part in midweek for England against Uruguay which ended 0-0. Jürgen scored twice as he captained Germany to a 2-0 win against Georgia. There were a few tired bodies on the training ground and we didn't have long to prepare for today's match against Southampton, especially as it was ridiculously scheduled for an 11.30am kick-off.

It turned into Tottenham's third 4-3 scoreline of the season, a win over Sheffield Wednesday on the opening day, a defeat to Villa in my first game, and now another defeat today. Southampton are fighting against the drop so it was really disappointing to lose this one.

Neil Heaney started the goal rush in the 13th minute. Matt Le Tissier whipped in a high corner and Neil Maddison outjumped Colin Calderwood to head goalwards. It was going straight towards Ian Walker, but Heaney positioned himself right in front of Ian and got the slightest touch to the ball with his head to beat him.

We hit back almost instantly. David Howells played a long curling pass to the centre of the pitch for Teddy Sheringham to run on to. Goalkeeper Bruce Grobbelaar started to come, so defender Ken Monkou stopped. Grobbelaar waited on the edge of his area so he could pick the ball up as soon as it entered the box, but Teddy got there before it reached him, nicked it away from him and turned it into the net from a tight angle.

Ten minutes before the break Jürgen put us ahead. Southampton failed to properly clear Darren Anderton's corner, and it dropped to Ronny Rosenthal 25 yards out. He knocked a lovely pass straight forward to Jürgen, who beat the offside trap and flicked it past Grobbelaar with the outside of his right boot.

A minute before half-time Matt Le Tissier equalised. Southampton took a throw-in to Neil Shipperley who put it through Colin Calderwood's legs. The pass found Le Tissier who hammered in a brilliant shot for 2-2.

Early in the second half came a crazy spell of three goals in five minutes. First Le Tissier put Southampton 3-2 up. Heaney's low cross deflected off Shipperley and over our two central defenders to the far post, where Le Tissier charged in, took it down with his right foot and then stroked it past Ian with his left. It was his sixth goal against us in four games this season.

Two minutes later Teddy pulled us level at 3-3. Monkou mistakenly let a David Howells pass under his foot and Teddy raced on to it. As he reached the edge of the area he squared it to Jürgen, who knocked it short to Nicky Barmby. A tackle came in on Nicky, but the loose ball fell for Darren Anderton who rolled it to Ronny Rosenthal. He took it to the byline and dug out a cross. Jürgen jumped with Grobbelaar, who dropped the ball, and Teddy reacted quickest to smash it home for his second goal of the game. Quite a way for him to celebrate turning 29 today.

Three minutes later Jim Magilton scored what proved to be the winner for Southampton. Once more a Heaney cross wasn't properly dealt with by us and Magilton took it on his chest, let it bounce and then fired a left-footed volley beyond Ian Walker from the edge of the box. Southampton's second consecutive win saw them climb out of the relegation zone. They beat Newcastle – who are flying high – before playing us. Our hopes of reaching Europe through the league are fading. We remain seventh and will probably need to finish fifth. The FA Cup is the best route to glory, the best route to Europe. A week from today we will meet Everton in the semi-final at Elland Road.

13

Deflation

'When you walked on to the pitch you thought, "Blimey – Everton, Everton, Everton. Their fans are on three sides. That's not right."' (David Howells)

IN stark contrast to Tottenham's action-packed run to the last four, Everton's progress had been straightforward. Late winners had been enough to see off Division One opponents in the third and fourth rounds, with Derby County and Bristol City both beaten 1-0. Cup fever took hold of Goodison Park with home ties against Premiership opponents in the fifth and sixth rounds. First Norwich were blitzed 5-0, then Newcastle beaten 1-0. Everton were through to what in 1995 was a record 23rd FA Cup semi-final.

With Everton struggling in the league, manager Joe Royle found himself in a near-identical situation to the one he had faced as Oldham manager just 12 months previously. In 1994, with the Latics fighting against relegation, they met Alex Ferguson's Manchester United in the FA Cup semi-final at Wembley. They took the lead in extra time only for Mark Hughes to equalise in the last minute with a sensational volley. Oldham lost the replay 4-0 at Maine Road.

Three weeks later Oldham lost their relegation battle too, with Tottenham putting virtually the final nail in their coffin. Spurs won 2-0 at Boundary Park to secure their own Premiership status, and as good as send Royle's team down in the process. So, a year on, Royle now had a chance to get a modicum of personal revenge against Spurs. Indeed, he had endured rum luck against Manchester United as Oldham boss in the FA Cup. He was also in charge when they were beaten by Ferguson's United in a semi-final replay in 1990; so, as Everton prepared to meet Spurs, Royle was hoping it would prove third time lucky for him in his quest to reach the FA Cup Final as a manager.

For Tottenham fans, just getting to the game was a mission. Schlepping up the M1 for a 1.30pm kick-off was far from ideal. No one connected with Spurs was happy with the choice of Elland Road as venue. The kick-off time also rankled. Given that the second semi-final venue – Villa Park – was far closer to being equidistant from Manchester United and Crystal Palace, it seemed perverse that that game should have the later kick-off. Fans of both those clubs had a shorter trip than Spurs, and yet they had more time to get there. While the broadcasters would have had as much say as the FA, if not more, in the scheduling of the kick-off times, it again added to the whiff of conspiracy. The more cynical Spurs fans were convinced that the FA was out to make life as uncomfortable as possible for the club, in revenge for having the FA Cup ban overturned.

Many Spurs fans only just made it to their seats in time for kick-off, others missed the first few minutes. Huge traffic delays around the stadium caused real problems at the exit from the M1. Official supporters' coaches were given a police escort down the hard shoulder, but those in their own cars and minibuses were not so lucky. Missing the pre-match sing-along for the biggest match of the season was a source of real disappointment for them.

Spurs were favourites to win though. Kit man Roy Reyland remembers spotting a lucky omen before kick-off: 'On the team coach on the way to the game Colin Calderwood sees two magpies. Colin says, "One for sorrow, two for joy, we might be all right today."'

Meanwhile, as they approached the ground, the coach carrying the families of the players was running the gauntlet of abuse. 'My ex-wife and my daughter went up to the game and they were on the players' families coach,' says Reyland. 'It was on its way to the stadium, and because of the blacked-out windows this Evertonian guy on the street thinks the family coach is the team coach. So he's running along and he's doing all the hand gestures and signs, and calling them all kinds of names. My daughter was then eight or nine, so she's looking out of the window and this guy's doing all these rude gestures, and as the coach gets faster and faster he's sprinting after the coach and giving it all this. My daughter says, "Mummy, look at that funny man, what's he doing?" and my ex-wife's going, "Well, don't look at that, Vicky." And with that, this fella just runs into a lamppost and just absolutely knocks himself spark out. Like a proper rugby tackle. They said it was hilarious. To this day, my

Vicky – she's grown up and married now – she still dislikes Everton because of that bloke.'

Chairman Alan Sugar's trip to Leeds was rather more comfortable. He flew to Yorkshire in a private plane with his son Simon and some of the Spurs directors. The minibus, which picked them up from the airport to take them to Elland Road, was emblazoned with the slogan 'Kelly's Minibus Hire'. It struck him as ironic, given that the man who had given the club so much aggravation was FA chief executive Graham Kelly, and he asked a member of the party to take a photo of the group next to the minibus to give to the press in the event of a Spurs win.

Royle's Everton had become known as the 'Dogs of War'. The nickname originated from Royle himself, as he praised his side for their work ethic and never-say-die attitude. He would come to regret coining that phrase, though, as it became so widely used by the press and broadcasters that it effectively denigrated his achievements at Goodison Park. The 'Dogs of War' depended hugely on their combative midfield. John Ebbrell hounded opponents as soon as they had the ball at their feet, but would be suspended for the semi-final. Wales captain Barry Horne – just over a month shy of his 33rd birthday at the time of the FA Cup semi-final – was enjoying something of a renaissance as he approached the end of his career. Tough in the tackle, Horne would go on to be voted the club's Player of the Year for 1994/95. He had already gone down in Everton folklore by scoring a wonder goal that helped save them from relegation the previous season.

Mike Walker's Everton had gone into that final game of the 1993/94 campaign at home to Wimbledon, knowing even a win might not keep them up. When they trailed 2-0 they appeared doomed; but Graham Stuart struck either side of a breathtaking 30-yard volley from Horne and the Toffees stayed up with a 3-2 win. Horne's central midfield partner in the 'Dogs of War' midfield was Joe Parkinson who, on his best days, helped form a near impenetrable force-field in front of the back four. With this formidable trio taking care of things in the middle of the park, at left full-back Andy Hinchcliffe was able to both supplement the defensive screen and, going forward, provide pinpoint accuracy from his crosses and set piece deliveries.

Royle's priority on succeeding Mike Walker in November 1994 was to keep the club in the top flight. Walker endured a tricky 11 months in charge of Everton. Having impressed by leading Norwich to third place in the inaugural Premier League season of 1992/93, he was appointed by Everton in January 1994. That fraught relegation battle of 1993/94, and a dreadful start to 1994/95, hardly endeared him to the Merseyside faithful. After just six wins in 35 games he was gone.

Royle quickly set about restoring order on the pitch. Already a favourite with the fans, having plundered over 100 goals in a 12-year playing career at the club, his managerial debut ran to perfection with a 2-0 win against Liverpool in the Merseyside derby. One of the scorers on that occasion, Duncan Ferguson, was the very embodiment of the 'Dogs of War' philosophy. The towering striker had been signed on loan from Rangers in April 1994 by Walker, in a switch then made permanent by Royle for £4m in December.

Everton had taken quite a gamble, because Ferguson had the threat of a jail term hanging over him. In the very month that they initially signed Ferguson on loan, he had head-butted John McStay in a Scottish Premier League match between Rangers and Raith Rovers. The referee neither booked nor sent off Ferguson, but on viewing video evidence the SFA took action and it then became a police matter. In October 1995 Ferguson would become the first British player to be jailed for an on-field assault, when he was sent to prison for three months. Confrontational in style, Ferguson was fearsome, 6ft 4in tall, all elbows and knees. He played with a permanent snarl. Fortunately for Tottenham he was suspended for the FA Cup semi-final.

Tottenham against Everton took the season back to where it had all started: that first home game. A match which kicked off in a burst of adrenaline, as though turbo-charged by the 4-3 win at Hillsborough four days previously. It had been an evening when the 'Famous Five' had been the talk of not just the town but the entire country: an evening when Jürgen Klinsmann hung in the White Hart Lane air before dispatching his sublime overhead kick, and then sent himself and all ten team-mates diving to the turf in joyous celebration.

So much had changed since then. Both teams were playing with added defensive discipline since Gerry Francis had taken over from Ossie Ardiles and Royle had succeeded Walker. Both were within touching distance of a Wembley final. Late spring sunshine filtered through a cloud-specked West Yorkshire sky at an Elland Road stadium that had recently been rebuilt ahead of Euro 96.

At kick-off there was a cacophony of noise from all four sides of the ground. Controversially, three of those sides were inhabited by Everton fans. Tottenham fans had been upset by the allocation that placed all of them in the huge new East Stand, which housed as many as the other three sides combined. Everton fans filled the stands behind both goals as well as the entire West Stand. It was a most unusual arrangement for a semi-final. Rather than half the stadium being dressed in Spurs colours and half in Everton's, this match had the appearance of a home game for the Merseysiders – and with the added advantage for them of shooting towards their own fans in both halves. For the aforementioned cynics, that whiff of controversy was now becoming ever more pungent: a semi-final venue far closer to Everton than Spurs; an unfavourable kick-off time; and now an unfavourable stadium layout for the fans.

As the players came out of the tunnel, it clearly struck them too. David Howells remembers: 'When you walked on to the pitch you thought, "Blimey – Everton, Everton, Everton. That's not right." I think the FA stitched us up a little bit by having it at Elland Road and giving three sides of the ground to Everton. It felt like an away game. Elland Road was hardly ever used for semi-finals. God knows how that one came about. Probably because they didn't think we should be in it anyway, and they didn't want us in their showpiece final. That's the way I see it.'

Elland Road's use as a semi-final venue had indeed been rare. This was the first time it had been chosen since 1961, although it was used for a replay in 1980. With the new Wembley nowadays staging all semi-finals at least for the foreseeable future, 1995 is likely to remain Elland Road's last.

Darren Anderton agrees that the players were affected by where the supporters had been positioned. 'I'd played in previous semi-finals and both teams get half the ground. That's the way it's supposed to be. Elland Road was a poor venue as far as I'm concerned, because the way the stands were, it made it very lopsided. I think they put 18,000 Spurs fans in one stand and Everton everywhere else. The Tottenham stand was further away from the pitch. Everton were behind both goals, which is weird because usually you know you will get a chance to kick into your own fans. It felt like an away game, which is not how a semi-final is supposed to be.'

Along with everything else that seemed to be against Tottenham, there were also injuries and suspensions to contend with. Justin Edinburgh was banned, David Kerslake and Sol Campbell were ruled out and Darren Anderton, Gica Popescu and David Howells were facing late fitness tests. A 1.30pm kick-off meant Tottenham had to arrive at Elland Road at about 11am for a final spot of training. It wasn't a great way to prepare for the biggest match of the season.

Diary of Gerry Francis
Sunday 9 April, 1995
FA Cup Semi-final
Tottenham Hotspur 1-4 Everton
Klinsmann (pen) 63
Jackson 35, Stuart 55, Amokachi 82, 90
It was a terrible build-up to the game. The media had been convinced that we were fated to win the FA Cup, and I was sick of that plot line. You earn your place, fate won't get you anywhere. We had injuries galore,

and a row going on all week about why the semi-final wasn't taking place at Wembley, and why we had to kick off at 1.30pm.

Away from the training ground, we've also had a really tough week as a family. Adam, my little boy, has been in hospital all week on a drip. That's been scary as he was seriously ill. He had toxoplasmosis. I didn't mention it to the press because I feel it's a private thing, but I know they were annoyed that I kept cutting short my media commitments to get to the hospital.

Then I was left with hardly enough available players for this game. Justin Edinburgh was suspended, Sol Campbell still wasn't fit, neither was David Kerslake. That meant a crisis in the full-back positions. I decided to go with Stuart Nethercott at left-back and leave Dean Austin continuing on the right. Stuart is a great lad, who is primarily a centre-back and has filled in for me a number of times in different positions, but we knew this was going to be a very tough experience for him in an unfamiliar position against a very good player in Anders Limpar. I knew with Stuart's character he would give it a go. In midfield David Howells, Darren Anderton and Gica Popescu all had to have late fitness tests, but the medical staff gave them the green light to start. Darren had to play with strapping around his knee, and Gica, of course, wasn't match fit having been out since February.

Joe Royle switched Limpar from left to right to take advantage of Stuart Nethercott being in an unnatural position at left-back. With Ferguson suspended there was less temptation for them to send the ball long. Instead Swedish international Limpar was the obvious outlet for them.

Ian Walker had already made two decent saves from Limpar and seen a Dave Watson header fly over the bar before Everton took the lead, ten minutes before half-time. David Howells lost possession, and Gary Mabbutt got back to clear it out for a corner. Andy Hinchcliffe whipped it in and and Matt Jackson got a flick at the near post. 1-0 to Everton.

At half-time I said to the lads that we didn't seem like we wanted it as much as them. We had played Everton just before Christmas when they were flying and beating everyone in sight, with their 'Dogs of War' label. We got a great 0-0 up there and really had to match them, because they were a team who put so much effort in.

I could see they wanted it more than us in the first half. I said to my players, 'Look, we have played 26 games since I got here, we've won 13, drawn nine and only lost four. I can't fault you in the time I've been here, but today I'm asking you, do you want it enough?' I said, 'Forget about all the problems we had getting here, forget about the injuries, forget about being 1-0 down, just concentrate. We've got to get back in the game.' In no uncertain terms I told them we had been second best in that first half and we had 45 minutes to put it right. 'It's the FA Cup semi-final and a one-off chance to get to Wembley', I said. As we headed out for the second half, in my mind, from the players' response in the dressing room, I felt that we could turn the game around.

We started well and missed a good opportunity to draw level when Gary Mabbutt's header was well saved by Southall. But then came a mistake from Ian Walker. He hurried a free kick from inside his box given for an offside decision and scuffed it. It didn't even reach the halfway line, catching Gary Mabbutt by surprise. Paul Rideout nipped in, got the ball, charged down the pitch and was clear on goal. Ian saved his shot, but it fell to Graham Stuart who tapped it into an empty net. All the hard work at half-time, and our good response, had been undone.

With 35 minutes to go we were now 2-0 down. It was going to take the sort of miracle Ronny Rosenthal inspired at The Dell to keep us in the cup. Eight minutes after Everton's second goal, it looked like a glorious comeback could be on the cards again. Nicky Barmby picked up the ball on our right and dinked a left-footed pass into the area. Jürgen headed it on and Dave Watson pushed Teddy Sheringham over. The referee pointed to the spot.

Teddy kissed the ball before handing it to Jürgen. He had been on spot-kick duty ever since I took charge. Jürgen had taken three before this one, scoring against Villa and Sunderland and missing against Liverpool. Jürgen had made no secret of his Wembley dream; now it was down to him to keep it alive.

Southall went the right way, but Jürgen's shot was hard and true, and hit the back of the net. Our fans were brilliant after that, keeping the singing going from their section of the ground and doing well to try and drown out the surround-sound from Everton's three sides. Then, with just under ten minutes left, we almost pulled level.

Darren Anderton, on the right wing, sent in a lovely left-footed cross from about 35 yards out. Nicky Barmby did brilliantly to get in front of his man on the penalty spot and flick the ball on to Nethercott who hit a decent half-volley which hit the post and bounced all the way out of the area. The ball went straight to Limpar who ran the length of the pitch, then laid it off to Horne who crossed it in for Daniel Amokachi. Amokachi headed it past Walker, and seconds after it had so nearly been 2-2, we were 3-1 down. Game over. Amokachi got another one right in the dying seconds with us all pushing forward in desperation. 4-1. A terrible, terrible day.

'I think Everton simply overpowered us,' says Klinsmann, looking back on the result that ended his Wembley dream. 'They were hungry. Maybe we thought after the Liverpool win that we could play our way through that game, but they were just very physical and tough. It was their momentum that carried them through.'

Stuart Nethercott says playing at left-back made it the toughest assignment of his career. 'It was difficult,' he says. 'We turned up at the stadium and Leeds had a little training pitch there. Justin's not available. Sol's gone down. David Kerslake's injured. We're thinking, "Bloody hell, who's gonna play left-back today?" It was just one of those days. It's hard enough to play right-back on your stronger foot, but to play left-back on your weaker one is a little bit more difficult and it was a tough, tough afternoon. You've got a raging Anders Limpar running at you …

'You know I've got no hard feelings about it, at the end of the day I had to do a job. It was a torrid afternoon. I'd like to give anyone a go at left-back that hasn't played there before in their life. It was a tricky gig.'

Speak to anyone who was at Elland Road about the 1995 semi-final and most will remember Stuart Nethercott having a chance to make it 2-2 but hitting the post and Everton breaking straight up the other end to go 3-1 up. If you watch a replay though, what actually happened is that Southall made a tremendous save. He got such a strong palm behind it that the ball rebounded all the way out of the area to Limpar who then charged the length of the pitch to set up the goal which killed off any hopes of a comeback. There must have been something about the ferocity with which the ball crashed off Southall and back into play that convinced many that it hit the frame of the goal. Since few people of a Spurs persuasion would have ever wanted to watch a replay, they wouldn't know any different. Even Nethercott remembers hitting the post. For him, it must be the case that the story has been repeated so often, that an incorrect version of events has been ingrained in his memory.

'I can still see that chance,' says Nethercott. 'Neville Southall in goal, I've hit a left-foot shot that would have made it 2-2 and it comes off the woodwork. You look back over the course of your career, and you think, "Bloody hell, if that had gone in…" We'd have probably gone on and won it. I think they would have been deflated. It wasn't a great day for me. To have a chance to level the scores and maybe go on to a cup final. It wasn't meant to be. Yeah, it still hangs around me. They turned up and we didn't. We just couldn't get Jürgen into the game. They out-battled us that day. There's not many teams that did that to us under Gerry, but they did.'

Kit man Roy Reyland remembers the feeling of utter desolation, compared to the optimism in the build-up to the match. 'If I'd have seen them two magpies Colin Calderwood spotted I'd have wrung their bloody necks,' he says. 'I just thought we weren't at the races. They had Limpar – he just had one of them days. He couldn't have another game like that. He was just frightening.

'I felt sorry for Stuart Nethercott. He played left-back, he's a centre-half so he's playing out of position. We had no option. Limpar tormented him. It was difficult. Sometimes you say we didn't deserve to get beat 4-1. But, yeah, we did. It wasn't gonna happen that day. Losing any game is difficult, but I think losing a semi-final is worse than losing a final.'

Alan Sugar was able to get out faster than most. His private plane flew him and his son Simon back to Heathrow, where they caught Concorde to New York to connect down to Florida and join his wife Ann. Sugar says in his autobiography that he and his son never exchanged a word throughout the flight, and that they were both gutted with the result. He says that they had worked so hard to get back in the cup, and then been 'scuppered by a series of disasters' in the build-up to, and on the day of, the game.

Darren Anderton describes the 1995 semi-final as the lowest point of his entire club career. 'I've been involved in five semi-finals and lost them all,' he says. 'The Euro 96 one hurt the most, but after that, this was the one that was hardest to take, because we were a good team. I think the country wanted us to get through, wanted us to play against Man United. It would have been the dream FA Cup Final, because of the way we played that year and the players we had – entertainers. To lose and lose in that manner was tough.

'Joe Royle had come in for them and devised a system that was very direct. Route One. Free kicks, corners, whip it in the box. Very effective football – not for the purists, but they got the job done. They won the FA Cup that year. Fair play to them.

'After the semi-final we felt rotten, really rotten. That was the longest journey home. The chairman, Alan Sugar, came in after the game. There was just a silence. No one really knew what to say. It just hit home really; from after the Liverpool game and feeling what an opportunity we had here, to lose in that manner was a tough one. You want to play well in big games, but we didn't. They stopped us playing. Kicking and grabbing and getting free kicks and putting the ball in the box. Stuart Nethercott hit the post, and they went up the other end and it was 3-1. That's football, little moments in games that define them.'

Sol Campbell says he wishes he could have recovered in time to play. He says it was incredibly hard to be injured and to have to watch from the sidelines. 'I was young then. These moments don't come round often. Being injured is a huge disappointment, and watching your team when you can't do anything about it is really hard. You can't be there to add another dimension and give Everton more problems. I couldn't recover in time, I was helpless and it was a big score against us.'

Everything that could go wrong for Tottenham on the day, did go wrong. 'Sorry about your "Dream Final", lads?' joked Joe Royle to the

BBC in his post-match interview, mocking the tag the media had attached to the prospect of a Wembley showdown between Manchester United and Tottenham Hotspur. That dream had turned into a nightmare for everyone connected with Spurs. There was to be no reward of a trophy, but throughout their run to the last four Tottenham had certainly played their part in making 1994/95 a vintage year for the FA Cup.

After beating Southampton and Liverpool in such dramatic circumstances in the fifth and sixth rounds, to Tottenham fans it had felt like it was destiny that their team would win the competition they had started the season banned from. Looking back now, though, it almost appears the club has been cursed for the financial misdemeanours which were alleged to have helped them sign some of the players who lifted the cup in 1991 before Sugar arrived.

Since 1991, Spurs have reached seven FA Cup semi-finals and lost them all. In the long and illustrious history of the competition, which dates back to 1872, no other club has been defeated in seven consecutive FA Cup semi-final appearances. Controversial refereeing decisions against them have contributed to defeats in five of those games. In 1993, at Wembley, Darren Anderton was brought down just inside the box by Arsenal's Andy Linighan, who was the last man. The referee – who could have sent off Linighan and given a penalty – did neither. Spurs lost 1-0.

In 1999 Nikos Dabizas of Newcastle committed a handball in the area, with the semi-final at Old Trafford still goalless in extra time. No penalty was given. Spurs lost 2-0. In 2010 Tottenham were 1-0 down to Portsmouth in extra time at Wembley. Peter Crouch thought he had equalised, but the 'goal' was chalked off with Niko Kranjcar adjudged to have fouled Pompey keeper David James. Spurs lost 2-0. In 2012, referee Martin Atkinson adjudged a shot by Chelsea's Juan Mata to have crossed the line to put the Blues 2-0 up. Replays showed Spurs defender Benoît Assou-Ekotto hadn't just stopped it on the line, but in front of the line. Spurs went on to lose 5-1. When Spurs and Chelsea met again in 2017 Son Heung-Min, playing in an unfamiliar left wing-back role, made a last-ditch tackle on Victor Moses in the box. The referee awarded a penalty and Willian put the Blues 2-1 up. Replays showed Moses had anticipated contact from Son but had gone down before he was actually touched.

Another of the seven FA Cup semi-final defeats contained an element of misfortune. Sol Campbell injured himself while conceding a free kick near the halfway line in the 2001 semi-final against Arsenal. Spurs were leading 1-0 at Old Trafford through Gary Doherty's early goal. As Campbell limped off to receive treatment on his ankle, leaving Spurs momentarily down to ten men, Arsenal equalised from the free kick and went on to win 2-1. Campbell was not fit to carry on, and had to be replaced by Ledley King. Conceding that free kick turned out to be Campbell's final act in a Spurs shirt. He was injured for the rest of the season, and then joined Arsenal in the summer.

When assessing the 1995 semi-final against Everton there were no controversial refereeing decisions, but there was controversy over the choice of venue, kick-off time and stadium layout, and bad luck concerning the amount of injuries and suspensions.

Spurs fans in the cars and coaches, heading up the M1 before the game in a mass of navy blue and white, had undertaken the journey in optimistic spirit. It truly felt like the football gods had determined to overrule the FA, that they had decided it was to be Tottenham's year. It felt like this journey would be one that would ultimately carry their team to Wembley. Scarves were flown from windows, flags draped over seats, ribbons tied to aerials as a sea of Tottenham colour moved slowly northwards. In those cars cassette tapes and CD players blasted Tottenham songs at full volume. The complete repertoire: Chas N' Dave's 'Ossie's Dream' from 1981; 'Hot Shot Tottenham' from 1987; 'It's Lucky For Spurs When the Year Ends in One' from 1991; and many more. To get them in the mood, fans on the official supporter coaches had been treated to videos of the wins over Southampton and Liverpool.

The FA Cup had displayed its full magical lure in both those games. As supporters relived Ronny Rosenthal's sensational hat-trick at The Dell, the beauty of Teddy Sheringham's equaliser at Anfield and the glory of Jürgen Klinsmann's late, late winner in front of the Kop, it didn't seem possible that all of that could be in vain. Could the FA Cup really be so cruel as to work Spurs fans into a frenzy of excitement, of near-expectancy that the famous trophy would again be theirs, just to rip it all away again? Of course it could.

And so, out of the FA Cup, and with little chance of qualifying for Europe through the league, a season that had promised so much felt like it was all over. Another Tottenham false dawn. Another White Hart Lane mirage. The nature of the semi-final defeat to Everton eventually sucked the life out of Spurs, though the initial response was promising. They had just over 48 hours to recover from the FA Cup semi-final defeat before having to face a Manchester City side fighting for their Premiership lives.

The City game had originally been set for 21 January, but was postponed an hour before kick-off because of a waterlogged pitch, so was rescheduled for Tuesday 11 April. Once it was known that Spurs were due to play their semi-final on Sunday 9 April, it could theoretically have been put back 24 hours. That though would not have helped much, since Spurs were also due to meet Crystal Palace on Good Friday, 15 April. So it would just have meant playing Wednesday-Friday instead of Sunday-Tuesday.

Dean Austin says he actually relished the swift return to action after the events of Elland Road. 'I know English football still has problems with fixture congestion, but it probably wouldn't happen nowadays – a Premier League match two days after an FA Cup semi-final,' he says. 'I think it actually helped, though. It helped me get over what happened against Everton. We had to get straight back into it. No time to think. "Time to go again, lads." For me that's partly why it was a bit easier to get over than the semi-final defeat to Arsenal in 1993, when we had to wait a week.'

Diary of Gerry Francis
Tuesday 11 April, 1995
FA Carling Premiership
Tottenham Hotspur 2-1 Manchester City
Howells 53, Klinsmann 86
Rösler 49

This was a massive game for myself personally and the players. Although there had been many problems prior to the semi-final at Elland Road, not least with the players we had lost through suspension and injury, the arguments about Wembley, the early kick-off and the way the fans were seated, we all felt we owed the great support we had received throughout the last few months at White Hart Lane an apology for our overall performance in the semi-final.

It was a great way to respond to the setback of just two days earlier. I'm really proud of the lads, and really pleased for the fans too, who were brilliant. To see more than 27,000 turn up on a Tuesday night after losing in the semi-final was fantastic and for me showed once and for all what a big club this was in that respect.

I was able to field ten of the team who started against Everton on Sunday. Justin Edinburgh returned from his suspension to replace Stuart Nethercott who dropped to the bench, but other than that we were unchanged. We played so well tonight, and our fans were sensational. I just wish we'd been able to put in this kind of performance for them on Sunday. I'm sure if we had played at this level it would have been good enough to beat Everton.

Dean Austin almost gave us the lead with his first goal for the club when he cut in from the right but shot a little too close to Tony Coton.

But football being football, we were to go behind against the run of play when four minutes into the second half Uwe Rösler flicked it beyond Ian Walker with the outside of his right boot for his 20th goal of the season. Despite the setback, the atmosphere at The Lane was brilliant. The response of the fans to the City goal was a crescendo of noise that swept the stadium to try and immediately lift the team. It was an acknowledgement that we had been playing well and were unlucky to be losing.

Four minutes after City had taken the lead, we deservedly equalised. Teddy Sheringham kept possession on the edge of the box and laid it back to Darren Anderton, who swept a diagonal pass to his left to Jürgen five yards outside the area. Jürgen let it run through his legs to David Howells. His first touch took him square of his defender along the top of the box, and opened up enough space for him to drill a low right-footed shot between Coton's outstretched arm and the keeper's right post. It was David's first goal of the season.

It looked like we might have to share the points though until, with about five minutes to go, Jürgen got us the winner. Darren Anderton whipped in a free kick and Jürgen stood his ground, got huge leverage from a standing jump and thumped his header inside the near post from six yards.

The most incredible thing about tonight was the reaction of the fans. I had worried about how they might react to the weekend when we had let them down, but it was a full house and they were fantastic. I was amazed by their support. I just thought, that's what this club is all about. We have a big waiting list for season tickets here. You could probably have 50,000 or 60,000 people who would want to be here even after what happened at the weekend.

'I remember that game, I remember my goal,' says David Howells. 'We played really well. We owed it to the crowd that night. They were terrific. It was a really good win, one of those really good displays which we proved we were capable of putting in throughout that season. It's just a shame we didn't do it two days earlier.'

Imagine if your place of work, your office, was the pitch at White Hart Lane, or any Premier League football stadium for that matter. Imagine the splendour of that. Working within the confines of a structure that exudes history and tradition, one that resonates meaning for all who enter it.

Well, Howells had that, and now, following his retirement as a professional footballer in 2000, he has it again in the place that has become his new office. As director of football at Charterhouse School, he is coaching the game he loves in the grandest of surroundings. Driving up to the entrance of this majestic public school building in Godalming, Surrey, is like approaching Harry Potter's Hogwarts. Set back from manicured lush green lawns are imposing geometric spires and minarets which have stood here since the 1870s, and which seemingly have the power to bestow excellence on all who move beneath them.

For all its grandeur there is warmth here too, lasting friendships formed, respect between teachers and pupils. On this particular day, the low sun is streaming through the trees on an early autumn morning. Overnight rain has left the grass and hedgerows glistening with a silver hue. As the bell goes, the young boys (and girls when it comes to the sixth form) busily zig-zag the corridors, hallways and pavements outside the building. Emerging from the sea of blazers and ties is Howells, who looks almost out of place as he saunters among them in his tracksuit. He walks with a limp, the effect of recent reconstructive surgery on his anterior cruciate ligament, he explains. Even long after the boots have been hung up, the rigours of the Premier League continue to take their toll on the bodies of those who have had to dance to the beat of its congested fixture list, its crowded festive programme and its seemingly ever-expanding pre-season.

With boarding fees of £35,500 a year, the parents who can afford to send their children to Charterhouse School expect the very best: the very best in the classroom and the very best on the sports fields. 'It's a magnificent place to work. There's pressure too, as there should be. We're expected to create winning teams, but teams that play the right way,' says Howells. After almost 15 successful years playing at the top level of English football, working under some of the highest-profile managers in the game, Howells is in a position now where he is the one who imparts his wisdom. It is now his responsibility to decide the important messages to pass on to the young boys and girls in his charge.

It seems fitting that his post-playing career finds him based in one of the spiritual homes of football. The first Football Association rulebook of 1867 relied heavily on the rules favoured by the Charterhouse and Westminster Schools.

Those schools (as Howells himself did in his playing days) put the emphasis on a passing game, rather than the dribbling game favoured by Harrow and Eton. If there weren't already enough signs that he was fated to work here, then what about its FA Cup connections? In 1876, ex-pupils of Charterhouse School founded the Old Carthusians football club, which went on to win one of the early FA Cup finals, beating Old Etonians 3-0 at Kennington Oval in 1881. The achievements of those players would be matched by Howells 110 years later, as a member of the

Tottenham side of 1991. It's perhaps easy to see why he feels very much at home at Charterhouse.

Seated in a small room set back from the pitches, which are laid out as pristinely as the hallowed turf of Wembley, he doesn't speak in clichés. He is of an era, the last remnants of an era, when footballers were still allowed to think and speak for themselves: from a time before the media and the football clubs got themselves into such a state that few meaningful questions are asked nor meaningful answers given. He is a thinker. He considers his answers carefully. His career clearly meant something to him; it's important to him to give as accurate a reflection as possible of his memories and feelings. Some sportsmen and women can be blasé. Some actually do not care much for their sport; they have an extraordinary gift and through it a route to fame and fortune, but it is not actually all that important to them. He isn't like that, though. The style in which he played the game is mirrored by the way he talks about it. Pausing, stopping the ball dead. Thinking of the perfect phrase to move the conversation on, in the way he used to see the perfect pass to move the game on.

He still loves football, he still loves Tottenham too. They have always been his club. Born in Guildford, he says he supported Spurs because his dad was a huge fan: 'We had no choice,' he laughs. Unlike most youngsters he was able to go on to achieve his dream of playing for the club he supported; not just that, but of lifting the FA Cup in their colours beneath the Twin Towers of the old Wembley. That was the obvious highlight of a career which provided him with more happy memories than unhappy ones.

As with many of the Spurs generation of the 90s, though, the whirlwind months of 1994/95 have left their mark on him – for good and for bad. 'By the time of the Newcastle home game in December we were playing really well,' he says. 'Personally, winning the FA Cup in 1991, and that whole season with Gazza, is more highly regarded by me. That all came on the back of the World Cup, and to see the way football was re-invigorated means that was my favourite season. But 1994/95 is close. It's just a shame the way it ended, losing to Everton in the semi-final and then seeing it all fizzle out when it had promised so much. So much happened with the points deduction and the highs and lows of being back in the cup, and the change of manager. My own situation was up and down. I was in the team, out of the team, then back in the team,' he laughs.

For Howells the 1995 semi-final would prove to be the last big day out. He had experienced the joy of a semi-final win over Arsenal in 1991, the frustration of being injured for the defeat to the Gunners in 1993, and now the agony of being knocked out by Everton at the last hurdle.

He left White Hart Lane for Southampton in 1998, and when it came to hanging up his boots in 2000 there would always be the pride of an FA Cup winners' medal from 1991, but the missed opportunity of 1995 still haunts him. 'It was hard to take. It was such a sad way for the season to peter out. The momentum had started to build, it really felt like we were going somewhere with this team. We let ourselves down on the day.'

Howells says he himself was partly culpable for the first Everton goal. 'One of my positions was near post for corners,' he says. 'So I'd be on the post, and anything in front of me I'd come off the post and try and head it. So I came off and I didn't make it. It was a bad decision from me. They scored.

'After the penalty we had got right back in there and were dominating. Stuart Nethercott hit the post and literally – I'm sure it went like this, but you'd have to watch the videos to be sure because I've tried to never look at the match again – the rebound goes straight up the other end and they score.'

Of Nethercott's torrid afternoon, Howells adds: 'He was a lovely kid. Wherever you played him he would give his best. I felt a little bit sorry for him at the semi-final, he's not a left-back; Justin Edinburgh was suspended, Sol's not available, David Kerslake's not available. That's not an easy thing to be asked to do, and he tried his best.'

Howells also remembers the ugly scenes at the end of the game when dozens of Everton fans ran on to the pitch. Most were intent on celebrating with their own heroes, but some wanted to give the Tottenham players grief. The layout of the stadium, with Everton fans streaming on from three sides, probably didn't help the stewards.

'It was horrible at the end of the game. The Everton fans ran on to the pitch and were pushing, spitting at you, taking the piss out of you,' says Howells. 'Jürgen got some horrific stuff and it was just really, really poor from an FA point of view to allow that sort of thing to happen. We were having our shirts ripped. It was humiliating. One of the worst days of my career, no doubt.

'Other than that day though, it was a fantastic season. We were the big-news club at the time. We generated more headlines than anyone else. Some seasons I can barely remember, but that season there were lots of great games. It was a good group of lads too. We would play golf together and socialise. Jürgen would be part of that; it would be great, especially if we had won. Socialising does bring you all together, it makes you a closer-knit team. You share more than you would usually. You don't just share things from a football perspective, but you share more of what you do in your lives, and it does definitely make you a stronger unit. They were lovely times.'

PART THREE

April 1995–June 1995

FOOTBALLER OF THE YEAR

14

Footballer of the Year

A T HIS family home in Bagshot, Surrey, a house he bought in 1976
when he was in his pomp as a QPR player and captain of England,
Gerry Francis shows me a collection of the 1994/95 memorabilia
he has in his possession. As well as his writings, writings that it has been a
privilege for me to reproduce in this book, he flicks through thumbnails
of the many photos that were taken for the Tottenham matchday
programme and the official club magazine.

In one he stands alongside Jürgen Klinsmann at the training ground.
Both have huge smiles on their faces. Another is an action shot as Francis
directs proceedings from the dugout. It's not clear what match it is, but
so many times in those first few months after his arrival the tactical
decisions he made from the touchline proved to be correct. Then he
chuckles at a series of photos of him dressed in a blue and white Father
Christmas outfit. It's hard to imagine a modern-day Premier League
manager being persuaded to do likewise.

Next out of the file comes a four-page paper pamphlet. It is simple
in design. A thin blue border on a white background. At first glance the
colours make it appear as though it is connected to Tottenham, but the
text reads:

FOOTBALL WRITERS' ASSOCIATION
The Footballer of the Year
DINNER & PRESENTATION
Royal Lancaster Hotel
Thursday 18 May 1995

Down the left-hand margin, in blue biro, is a handwritten thank you message: 'To Gerry. Only because of you I get to sit here. Thank you very much for everything you have done for me!! Your friend, Jürgen Klinsmann'. Klinsmann was thanking his manager for his seat at the top table. He had been named Footballer of the Year by the journalists who make a living from covering the game. Blackpool's Stanley Matthews had been the first recipient of the prestigious award back in 1948. The Spurs greats who had made it on to the esteemed list of winners since then were Danny Blanchflower (1958 and 1961), Pat Jennings (1973), Steve Perryman (1982), Clive Allen (1987) and Gary Lineker (1992). Klinsmann had now joined them in his first season in English football.

'It was a measure of the man that he had changed opinions so quickly,' says Francis. 'You have to remember, the narrative that the press, and the TV and everyone was interested in when he came to England just a few months previously was that he was a diver and a cheat, that Germany were the enemy. Not only had he disproved all that, he won everyone over with his brilliant performances, and his magnificent goals, and he had also shown he was a lovely person, a true sportsman, someone who was willing to teach the younger players, and someone who – even at the age of 30 – knew he could still learn from the English game.

'That message he wrote to me means a lot. I like to think I helped most of the players I worked with improve their game. That's what I took pride in. Someone who had won the World Cup was saying thank you to me for helping him become England's Footballer of the Year, and that was great.'

One statistic which demonstrates the effect Klinsmann's arrival had on the English game is that at the time he was only the third player from outside Britain and Ireland to have won the award. Manchester City's German goalkeeper Bert Trautmann was honoured in 1956 as was Dutchman Frans Thijssen of Ipswich in 1981. At the time of this book's publication, just eight of the 22 winners since Klinsmann picked up the trophy have been British or Irish (incidentally, that number includes one Tottenham winner – Gareth Bale in 2013), while the other 14 have been from overseas (likewise, one Spurs man is on that list; David Ginola – a man signed by Francis – won it in 1999).

Klinsmann finished ahead of Blackburn duo Alan Shearer in second, and Colin Hendry in third. Incidentally, it was Shearer who won the Players' Player of the Year award in 1995. By the time of the Football Writers' Award ceremony, Klinsmann had already made it public that he was leaving Tottenham. Of course, the votes had been cast weeks in advance, and it's possible he wouldn't have garnered quite so many had his decision been out in the open before then.

Following the 2-1 win against Manchester City – the perfect response to the debilitating FA Cup semi-final exit at the hands of Everton – Spurs had just seven games to try and pick up enough points to qualify for Europe via the league. The press had made great play of the fact that UEFA Cup qualification was essential if Klinsmann was to stay. The player himself placed an importance on that throughout the season. Francis though doubts it would have made much difference. 'Bayern Munich were set to offer him a brilliant deal,' says Francis. 'Image rights were built into it, which is routine these days, but was a big deal then. Add to that the fact he was going home, to one of the biggest clubs in the world. I'm pretty sure that even if we had qualified for the Champions League, let alone the UEFA Cup, Jürgen wouldn't have been persuaded to stay.'

As it was, Spurs won just one of their final seven games. This is how the results panned out:

14 April	D 1-1 C.Palace (a)	Klinsmann
17 April	W 1-0 Norwich (h)	Sheringham
29 April	D 1-1 Arsenal (a)	Klinsmann
3 May	D 3-3 Newcastle (a)	Barmby, Klinsmann, Anderton
6 May	L 1-2 QPR (a)	Sheringham
9 May	L 1-3 Coventry (h)	Anderton
14 May	D 1-1 Leeds (h)	Sheringham

The Palace game was a sort of depressing FA Cup third-place play-off. Live on Sky on Good Friday, the Eagles had hardly had any time to recover from Wednesday night's semi-final replay defeat to Manchester United. They went down 2-0 to United at Villa Park in a match where Roy Keane was sent off for stamping on Gareth Southgate and Palace also had Darren Patterson red-carded for getting involved in the aftermath.

Palace had endured a tough few weeks. Leading scorer Chris Armstrong was about to return for the Tottenham game. He had just served a four-week FA ban and been ordered to undergo counselling after traces of cannabis were found in a random drugs test back in January.

There had also been a tragic incident at the weekend when a Palace fan attempting to flee trouble between rival fans at a service station prior to Sunday's original semi-final tie with Manchester United had been run over by a coach and killed. It put football in perspective.

Armstrong gave Palace the lead with a neat 20-yard shot beyond Ian Walker four minutes before the break, but with just three minutes of the game remaining Klinsmann equalised with a terrific free kick which went in off the bar.

Of the two scorers that day, it would actually be Armstrong who would line up in a Spurs shirt the following season. Palace's fight against the drop was in vain. They eventually finished 19th, but with the top flight being reduced from 22 teams to 20, they became the only team in the Premier League era to be relegated having finished fourth from bottom.

After the Palace game, Klinsmann was asked about his future by the media. He told the press: 'I have to analyse the situation and compare certain things – there are a few of them to consider. I will discuss the situation with Gerry Francis when the season is over and see what happens.'

Francis says: 'When I joined Tottenham I knew nothing about the clause in Jürgen's contract. I was out for dinner with Jürgen when he told me about that. I didn't know anything about it. It was a real blow to me. I was looking forward to the new season and how I could build. How could you replace Jürgen Klinsmann? He wasn't gonna go for much money, either. Who do you get in?

'I was just starting to build a good team there. I had just got us playing really well. We were expansive. We never got the credit for some of our performances. That win over Liverpool in the quarter-final was tremendous. We tore Blackburn apart, and they went on to be champions.'

David Howells agrees Spurs were rocked by the departure of their talisman. 'Chris [Armstrong] was a good player,' says Howells. 'In the first season with us he actually scored more goals than Dennis Bergkamp who joined Arsenal at the same time [Armstrong hit 15 in the league and 22 in all competitions while Bergkamp's figures were 11 and 16] – but obviously he wasn't the same level as Jürgen, few players are. I just felt that there were many times throughout my 12 years at Tottenham when we were so close to having a really strong team, and it never quite materialised.

'I made my debut in 1986. David Pleat's 1987 team was built off the back of what Peter Shreeves had done plus the signing of Richard Gough. With the talent that we had we should have won the league. Steve Hodge was a really good signing for that team too.

'That team didn't win anything and then fell apart quite quickly. Pleat sold quite a few players, and then had to leave because of the stories concerning his private life. Then Terry Venables came in – he built a team which won the FA Cup in 91, but Lineker was retiring soon and Gazza had to be sold, injured or not, because of the financial situation. So that team changed quickly as well. Paul Stewart left in 92 because of the Venables thing. Neil Ruddock left around the same sort of time, and

Vinny Samways too. Ruddock and Samways were in their prime. We were constantly having to rebuild the team. Now it was happening again at the end of the Klinsmann season.

'So instead of doing what Arsenal and Man United were doing, building teams, keeping players and adding to them, we didn't ever manage to do that. Three or four times in my career I had the sense that this could be something quite special, but it never materialised. Klinsmann left and we didn't really replace him.'

On Easter Bank Holiday Monday, three days after the Palace game, with Spurs fans still believing European qualification was both possible and also necessary if Klinsmann was to stay, Tottenham beat Norwich 1-0 at White Hart Lane. Darren Anderton set up Teddy Sheringham for a lovely goal nine minutes before the break. Sheringham just managed to stay onside, pulled the ball out of the air with his right foot, let it roll in front of him and then dinked it over City's 20-year-old goalkeeper Andy Marshall. It was a victory watched in double vision. The new South Stand was fully opened for the first time, so a crowd of 32,304 – the highest of the season at that point – was in attendance. On the top of the stand was a huge screen, christened 'the Jumbotron'. It was a slightly strange, and some would say pointless, experience to be able to watch the match on the pitch, and on the big screen at the same time. The players could occasionally be seen glancing up at it during the game.

Before kick-off an interview with Klinsmann was shown on it in which he joked that the referees would now be able to see properly the many penalties which he should have been awarded during the season. The FA had ruled though that no replays of any controversial incidents could be shown.

Norwich were desperate for a win. Manager John Deehan had resigned eight days ago and Gary Megson was in caretaker charge. Ultimately he was unable to turn things around and Norwich were eventually relegated along with Palace, Leicester and Ipswich. It had been an incredible fall from grace for the Canaries. When Tottenham visited Carrow Road on Boxing Day they had inflicted the first home defeat of the season on a team who were placed seventh. After that result they would go on to win just two of their remaining 22 league games as they crashed through the relegation trapdoor.

From this point, there wasn't much more for Spurs to celebrate in 94/95 either. The three points against Norwich proved to be their final win of the season. 'I think at the time of the Norwich game we still felt we could qualify for Europe,' says Darren Anderton. 'I don't think it was the case that the season caught up with us. Yes there were a lot of games to play, but we had initially responded well to the Everton defeat and I don't think it was the case that we switched off after the FA Cup exit. I think it's just the way football goes. No one gives you anything in the Premier League. Every game is tough. So many teams are playing for something at the end of the season, and even if they're not, no one rolls over and does you any favours. That's what makes it a great league.'

The Norwich match was Tottenham's fifth in 15 days, but now they had a 12-day gap until the next match. It was an international break, but the FA had messed up and failed to find opponents. They had announced months ago that they would instead hold a training session at Bisham Abbey. Terry Venables called up a squad of mainly uncapped players including goalkeeper Ian Walker. Of the three capped players, two were from Spurs – Nicky Barmby and Darren Anderton. In the end, Barmby had an ankle injury and Anderton went down with tonsillitis so they both missed the training session anyway.

Tottenham's league programme resumed with a sell-out crowd of 38,377 present at Highbury for a fiercely-contested North London derby against Arsenal. Stewart Houston was now in charge of the Gunners with George Graham having been sacked in February following allegations that he had accepted a bung.

Before the game the screen at Highbury showed endless replays of Arsenal's European Cup-Winners' Cup semi-final penalty shoot-out win over Sampdoria in midweek. David Seaman's three saves had put them through to the final where they would be taking on a Real Zaragoza team containing former Tottenham midfielder Nayim.

The North London derby turned into a really ugly affair. Highbury was a swirling mess of vitriol and abuse. When Justin Edinburgh was adjudged to have brought down Ian Wright in the box midway through the second half, some Spurs fans tried to get on to the pitch as a penalty was awarded. Many were angered at how easily Wright seemed to go down, and the fact that he appeared to throw an arm at Gary Mabbutt. Wright scored from the spot to give Arsenal the lead, then picked up an empty whisky bottle which had been thrown at him. It didn't hit him, but landed close by. Referee Robbie Hart momentarily halted the game to pass it on to police. A dozen people were ejected from the stadium as police continued to battle with Spurs fans trying to make it on to the Highbury turf.

Back at The Lane, there was news of a bit of trouble too. The Jumbotron had been used to broadcast the game for those who hadn't been able to get a ticket. Some Arsenal fans sneaked in too, and when Wright gave them the lead they were either brave enough or stupid enough to celebrate. A minor scuffle ensued leading to the worrying, if admittedly rather comical, sight of stewards chasing Arsenal fans around the largely empty East Stand before throwing them out.

Arsenal led for just 13 minutes, before that 'blur of blond', as one newspaper put it, was there again to save the day for Spurs. Howells found Rosenthal, who sprayed it wide to Edinburgh. He took it beyond Lee Dixon, who dived in and left himself grounded. Edinburgh stretched to get his cross in just before it went behind for a goal kick. Klinsmann surged between Nigel Winterburn and Tony Adams, then leapt and sent a bullet header crashing down and beyond Seaman from six yards.

It finished in a 1-1 draw, but with Leeds having won 1-0 at home to Villa, Tottenham now trailed the Yorkshire side by six points. Spurs still had a game in hand, and still had to play Leeds on the final day, but Europe was now looking unlikely.

At least Spurs were now almost certain to finish above Arsenal – a feat which it would take them until 2016/17 – a full 22 years – to repeat. Francis says: 'I'm proud of my record against Arsenal. In my whole time at Spurs I only ever lost one game to Arsenal, and those games are huge, massive, they mean everything to the fans. You would never have thought Spurs would take nearly a quarter of a century to finish above them again.'

Next up came a long midweek trip to St James' Park. For some fans it was the second time they had undertaken the journey, or at least a portion of the journey, this season. The original evening kick-off back in February had been called off at 1pm because of a waterlogged pitch. Some of the fans were already on their way to the North-East at that point. Anyone who did make the effort to return to Tyneside was rewarded with what the *Daily Mail* hailed as 'a contender for game of the season'. Spurs had had a few of those. To the list of goal-crazy games that contained Sheffield Wednesday 3-4 Tottenham, Watford 3-6 Tottenham, Manchester City 5-2 Tottenham, Aston Villa 4-3 Tottenham, Tottenham 4-2 Newcastle, Southampton 2-6 Tottenham, Southampton 4-3 Tottenham, you could now add Newcastle 3-3 Tottenham.

Newcastle were among Tottenham's main rivals for the final UEFA Cup place. At kick-off they sat fifth, and had only just suffered their first home league defeat of the season. The fact that they had gone down 1-0 to Leeds a fortnight previously hadn't really helped Spurs, because Leeds were also chasing the European place.

For those who couldn't make the trip, the game was again shown live on the Jumbotron at White Hart Lane. Within ten minutes Tottenham were 2-0 down after goals from Keith Gillespie and defender Darren Peacock, a man who had played under Gerry Francis at QPR before being sold to Newcastle for £2.4m. Spurs though hit back with three goals in four minutes to lead 3-2 before even half an hour had been played. Nicky Barmby played a one-two with Jürgen Klinsmann before dispatching the goal which gave Spurs hope in the 22nd minute. Two minutes later Klinsmann himself smashed in a right-footed volley – which proved to be his final goal of 1994/95 – and then in the 26th minute Darren Anderton hit a 25-yard screamer into the top corner. It was a stunning goal which Francis went on to choose as his favourite of the season when asked by the club to select one.

Ten minutes into the second half, Spurs had a great chance to make it 4-2 and boost their European qualification hopes. Barmby broke the offside trap ten yards into the Newcastle half. He charged forward into the box, and as he attempted to round Srnicek on the penalty spot, the keeper brought him down. Referee Dermot Gallagher pointed to the spot and sent Srnicek off. Sheringham sportingly tried to plead that the Czech keeper should stay on. He put a hand across Gallagher's red card. By the letter of the law Gallagher was right, and of course he wasn't going to change his mind. Newcastle were down to ten men and Klinsmann, the man who had been desperate for the team to qualify for Europe, had the perfect opportunity to keep the embers of that fading dream alive.

Substitute keeper Mike Hooper came on with midfielder Ruel Fox sacrificed by manager Kevin Keegan. There was a lengthy delay, which gave Klinsmann too much time to ponder his many alternatives, and the St James' Park crowd plenty of time to get on his back. He drilled his penalty straight down the middle. Low and hard but against Hooper's legs. It was the fifth penalty Spurs had missed in the league all season: three by Sheringham (against Everton, Manchester United and Nottingham Forest), and two by Klinsmann (against Liverpool and now Newcastle). Successful penalties could conceivably have led to a draw with United and wins over Forest, Liverpool and Newcastle. Ten points from those games instead of two. Those points could perhaps have meant a place in Europe.

Ten minutes after Klinsmann's penalty miss, Tottenham lost their numerical advantage. Calderwood was sent off for a second bookable offence, a fairly innocuous challenge on Steve Watson inside the centre circle. Spurs had surrendered the initiative, blown a chance to go 4-2 up, and now lost a man. Five minutes later they lost the lead. Calderwood's dismissal led to Francis taking off Barmby and sending on Sol Campbell, his first action since injury against Wimbledon on 25 February. Campbell obviously wasn't match fit. He was lacking pace as a long pass cleared his head and bounced behind him on the edge of the box. A 34-year-old Peter Beardsley beat him to it, and quickly got a shot away which eluded

Walker at his near post for 3-3. It was Beardsley's 100th goal in his two spells with Newcastle.

Both teams came close to grabbing a winner. Robert Lee's shot was cleared off the line; then Klinsmann's effort from way out on the right, with Hooper stranded out of goal, drifted just wide. 3-3 is how it finished and Tottenham's European hopes were hanging by a thread.

Three days later Francis made an emotional return to Loftus Road where he had enjoyed such success as a player and a manager. The Rangers fans welcomed him back before kick-off, grateful for everything that he had achieved. There was only one name on the lips of the Tottenham fans though. They were desperate to convince Jürgen Klinsmann to stay. 'There's only one Jürgen Klinsmann', 'Don't go Jürgen', and 'Jürgen stay another year', were sung for the entire 90 minutes in an attempt to persuade their hero to snub the much-reported potential move to Bayern Munich.

QPR's goalless draw with West Ham in midweek had guaranteed that Tottenham had finished the season as London's top club, which meant Francis had repeated the feat he had also pulled off with QPR back in 1992/93. He remains the only manager to do that with two London clubs in the Premier League era. Spurs started the game knowing that if they lost, they would no longer be able to reach Europe.

Teddy Sheringham put Spurs ahead in the final minute of the first half, smashing in his 22nd of the season from close range after good work from Nicky Barmby. As news filtered through at half-time that relegation-threatened Norwich were beating Leeds – Tottenham's rivals for the last European spot – cheers went up from the School End where the away fans were gathered.

It fell apart for Tottenham in the second half though. Les Ferdinand struck in the 64th and 75th minutes. QPR were 2-1 winners, and Tottenham's European hopes were mathematically over. In fact even if they had won, Leeds came from behind to beat Norwich which would have meant they missed out anyway. Klinsmann waved to the travelling fans as they continued to chant his name at the final whistle.

Don't go Jürgen,
Don't go Jürgen,
Don't go Jürgen, don't go.
Don't go Jürgen,
Don't go Jürgen,
Don't go Jürgen, don't go.

With European qualification now beyond their team, the focus of Tottenham fans was on trying to keep Klinsmann at the club. Three days after the QPR defeat, Spurs were at home to relegation-threatened

Coventry on Tuesday 9 May, in a match which had originally been due to take place on FA Cup semi-final weekend until Spurs reached the last four. There were banners and songs pleading with Klinsmann to stay.

The Sky Blues were now managed by Ron Atkinson, who had taken over from Phil Neal in February to try and pull off a great escape. Tonight, they picked up three crucial points with two goals from Peter Ndlovu (one from the penalty spot) and one from Dion Dublin and went on to secure safety on the final day of the season. Darren Anderton restored a fragment of respectability to the scoreline for Spurs when he struck a consolation goal with seven minutes remaining. Throughout the game and, as the final whistle blew on a 3-1 defeat, the crowd sang:

Jürgen stay another year,
Jürgen stay another year,
Jürgen stay another year.
Jürgen sta-a-a-ay another year.

The home team trudged off, with Klinsmann waving to all four corners of the ground again. This time, though, he was waving goodbye.

Diary of Gerry Francis
Friday 12 May, 1995

Klinsmann has called a press conference at The Comedy Café in Hackney, East London. It's the announcement every Spurs fan has been dreading. Their hero is heading back to Germany to join Bayern Munich.

'Since I've been over here I've learned to appreciate the English humour because, as you know, we Germans are not renowned for our sense of humour. That is the reason I invited you to the Comedy Café,' said Klinsmann.

PR-wise Klinsmann has barely put a foot wrong since he arrived in England, but this seems a misjudgement. He got it spot on at his very first press conference, with his jokes about diving. His intentions this time were also good; he chose this setting to allow him to make some self-deprecating comments about the German nation's supposed lack of humour, but while Tottenham fans can respect his decision to leave, no one is in the mood to laugh.

He thanks the fans for being 'Wunderbar' and explains his reasons for quitting White Hart Lane. He says he wants to end his career by winning trophies. 'Because of the wonderful support [of the fans], especially in the last months, this has been the most difficult decision of my career,' he says. 'At the age of nearly 31 I had to give serious consideration to my final career move. I had to consider where I want to build up my life and I've never won a national title. Only the next years will show me if this was the right decision.' He adds: 'When Colin Calderwood was picked for Scotland he said to me, "This is because of you", and that was the biggest compliment I could have got from a team-mate.'

Alan Sugar calls a separate press conference later in the day, to confirm that Gerry Francis has agreed to stay on as manager for another season: 'As good a player as Klinsmann is, the most important person at a club is the manager,' he says. 'He is the one who decides the strategy that wins titles and in Gerry we have one of the best in the Premiership.'

Sugar also makes clear his displeasure at Klinsmann's decision. 'I have a different interpretation to his contract than him. Disappointment is the word. I shouldn't be. I've been in business 30 years and when I looked into the whites of his eyes in Monaco last July I genuinely felt we had an agreement for two years.

'If there's anyone to blame it's me. I brought one of the world's greatest players here to fix a problem but it created another one. It relaunched his career and attracted all these offers for him. It's been a lesson to me. I'll be looking for a far clearer documentation in the future.'

Two days later, on Sunday 14 May, White Hart Lane was sold out again with 33,040 in attendance for the final match of the season. The home fans had come to say goodbye. There was no anger, only gratitude and respect. In one season Klinsmann had won his place in the hearts of the Spurs fans. No other Spurs player has achieved legendary status despite having such a short Spurs career.

Whoever was choosing the music for the stadium PA system selected, 'You don't know what you've got till it's gone'. But Spurs fans knew what they had all right. Huge banners were unfurled. 'Goodbye and good luck, Jürgen', read one in English. Another in German, 'Sehr Glück, Jürgen'.

In recognition of his wonderful performances throughout the season, Gerry Francis made Klinsmann captain for the day. As the player led the team out of the tunnel, his song was chanted from all four stands. He turned and waved to every part of the ground.

> There's only one Jürgen Klinsmann,
> One Jürgen Klinsmann,
> Walking along,
> Singing a song,
> Walking in a Klinsmann wonderland.

Klinsmann was presented with a huge bouquet of flowers. The entire stadium was on its feet. The Leeds fans too. The match meant nothing to Tottenham in terms of points; they knew that whatever the result they couldn't make it to Europe. Leeds needed a point to be sure of fifth place and the final definite UEFA Cup place.

Sheringham put Spurs ahead on the half-hour mark from Edinburgh's cross. Klinsmann celebrated by jumping up, grabbing the crossbar and swinging from it. As the game restarted the crowd was willing him to score, to get a goodbye goal. But it didn't come.

Brian Deane equalised midway through the second half. Again Colin Calderwood wasn't strong enough as Deane barged him out the way, just like Efan Ekoku had done in the defeat to Wimbledon at The Lane back in February. As well as saying goodbye to Klinsmann, there have been a few songs at Arsenal's expense. 'Nayim from the halfway line' rings around the ground on more than one occasion in celebration of the Spurs old boy netting an extraordinary long-distance winner for Real Zaragoza against Arsenal in the last minute of extra time in Wednesday's European Cup-Winners' Cup Final in Paris.

The real drama of the final day of the Premiership season unfolds at Anfield and Upton Park. As they still do today, the final Premiership games of the season all kicked off at the same time. Leaders Blackburn went into their last match two points ahead of second-placed Manchester United. Rovers knew if they slipped up at Liverpool, then United would win the title by beating West Ham. As those matches reached the final minute, Blackburn and Liverpool were drawing 1-1 while it was still goalless in East London.

In injury time Liverpool got a free kick, and Jamie Redknapp scored to put his side 2-1 up. Just as the ball hit the net, the full-time whistle blew on a goalless draw at Upton Park. Man United's failure to beat West Ham meant Blackburn were champions, despite having lost to Liverpool. The timing almost made it seem like Blackburn's fans were celebrating Liverpool's goal, when in fact they were revelling in being English champions for the first time since 1914. Liverpool fans were equally delighted that their fierce rivals Manchester United had missed out, so Anfield was in raptures.

Back at The Lane, Leeds manager Howard Wilkinson gave his post-match press conference. 'Klinsmann's contribution to overall entertainment in the British game this season has been considerable. It is a pity he is going. The only plan we had today was to spoil the party for Jürgen Klinsmann. In the end he had a party and so did we. Everyone came away smiling.'

At full time, Klinsmann led the traditional end-of-season lap of honour around White Hart Lane. He was leaving the fans with memories of 29 goals, so many of them spectacular, and of performances which had seen him voted as the Football Writers' Player of the Year. Looking back now, does Klinsmann have any regrets about leaving after just one season?

'I was already 30,' says Klinsmann. 'Joining Bayern Munich meant winning trophies straight away. We all knew that Spurs wouldn't be going for the Premier League title or for European titles. I had to make up my mind. I had to say to myself, "Look, I'm in my thirties now, do I want to win something or carry on being happy with where I am?" It just drove me inside to know that I wanted to win things, and that is how it turned out because we won the UEFA Cup and then the German championship. I always missed Spurs. I always missed the people, and that special energy there, but as a player you have to go to the highest level possible, and if you get the opportunity to play for Bayern Munich, you have to go for it.'

No one begrudged Klinsmann the captain's armband for his final game except, perhaps, a certain Alan Sugar. Francis says: 'I think Alan had just got off the plane from somewhere, and I was telling him my team for the final game of the season. I never allow anyone to interfere with my team, never in a million years, never at any club – I would be out of there like a shot. I told him, "I'm making Jürgen captain for the last game." There was silence. I said: "Are you still there?" He mumbled back at me, "I'm not too happy about that."

'"What do you mean, you're not too happy about that? What's it got to do with you?"

'"I'm the eff-ing chairman."

'"Well, I'm the eff-ing manager, and if you want to run the team, I'm off."

'I even met him the next morning, and told him again never ever to do that. He never did. We had a few rows, but never again over team selection. That was the only one. And to be fair he was one of the best chairmen I worked for.'

Sugar was furious about Klinsmann's decision to leave. He felt duped by the contract. Somehow a man of his esteemed business acumen had failed to grasp that the break clause meant Klinsmann could leave at the end of the season, regardless of whether Spurs were relegated or not.

His anger had still not subsided five months later, when he appeared on the BBC's *Sportsnight* programme and tossed the signed Spurs shirt Klinsmann had given him towards reporter Ray Stubbs. Sugar said he wouldn't wash his car with it now. He said he wouldn't be signing any more 'Carlos Kickaballs', the type of foreign players, he said, whose agents would send him a few DVDs insisting they were good, when in fact they were nothing special. It all felt quite disrespectful. Sugar seemed to have misjudged the public mood. Most people felt Klinsmann had done far more good than harm for Spurs and the English game. But Sugar had clearly had his fingers burnt. Spurs fans would pay the price for his new-found reticence in the transfer market when it came to signing top overseas players.

Of course, there was a major U-turn from Sugar over Klinsmann two and a half years later. Francis resigned as Spurs boss on 19 November 1997, three years to the day since his first game. The team was struggling. Sugar's choice of successor proved to be a disaster. He appointed the unknown Swiss boss Christian Gross, who became a figure of fun with the English media from the moment he arrived late at his first press conference clutching a tube ticket and saying, 'I want this to be the ticket to my dreams.' Results worsened. By Christmas relegation was a distinct possibility. Having once said he wouldn't wash his car with Klinsmann's shirt, Sugar went out and re-signed him, this time on loan from Italian side Sampdoria.

By now Klinsmann needed Spurs as much as they needed him. He wasn't getting much game-time in Serie A, and was desperate to make it into Germany's World Cup squad for France 98. Now 33, which was also the number he wore on his shirt with Norwegian striker Steffen Iversen occupying the No.18, he was unable to make quite the impact he did first time round. Nevertheless, he still scored nine times in 15 Premier League appearances, and played a crucial role in keeping Tottenham up. His most vital intervention was his four-goal haul (his first Premier League hat-trick) away to Wimbledon, in the penultimate game of the season. Tottenham's 6-2 win at Selhurst Park secured their top-flight status.

His initial departure in May 1995 clearly affected Sugar. Never again did the chairman show the same level of ambition to transform the club into a top outfit. When Sugar sold Tottenham to current owners ENIC in 2001, he said there had been 'no highlights' of his time in charge. It seems like a depressing assessment, but his former PR man Nick Hewer agrees with the sentiment. 'I never enjoyed it at Spurs. The only high was when we beat Leicester to win the League Cup in 1999. I remember the look of relief and happiness on Alan's face when I met him immediately afterwards and he said, "Ah, thank God for that." We had a dinner for all the players and people at the club, and actually it was as flat as a pancake because nobody said "thank you" to him.

'I don't think there were any highlights, really. He might have had a bit of fun with Klinsmann and Dumitrescu and Popescu, but even when they were winning it was the manager who got the credit. That's the law of football, and it's not what he understood when he went into it. I think eventually his family were distressed that he was being given so much abuse. I think he just thought he couldn't do this any more.'

On Tuesday 16 May 1995, Klinsmann's transfer to Bayern Munich was confirmed. It was announced that he would travel with Tottenham on their end-of-season tour of the Far East and then sign for the German club at the end of June. The fee was undisclosed, but the press reported it as £1.3m, down on the £2m they had spent on him. There was a further blow for Tottenham fans on the same day with the announcement that Gica Popescu was leaving for Barcelona. The press reported the fee as £2.8m, again just under the £2.9m Tottenham paid to bring him to The Lane.

Sugar has since said that Popescu 'arrogantly walked out' on the club, and that he literally walked out too, telling the players at the last game with Leeds that he was off and then simply leaving White Hart Lane. Sugar also claims he got £4m out of Barcelona, a much higher fee than widely reported at the time.

Darren Anderton remembers the players saying goodbye to Klinsmann on the end-of-season tour of the Far East. 'We had to play one match in Singapore, one match in China, and one in Hong Kong. We didn't really want to watch the FA Cup Final when we were out there, we wanted a night out, but [assistant manager] Roger Cross came and got us and told us we had to come back to the hotel. It kicked off at about 11pm their time, and we watched Everton beat Manchester United 1-0. It was really tough of course because we knew it could have been us. As soon as the game was over Roger went to bed and we snuck straight back out again. It was really late.

'There had been quite a few rumblings about Jürgen leaving towards the end of the season before it was confirmed. The boys all understood it. He wanted to go home. He'd been a top player all his career, he'd been all round Europe. It's understandable. I went home to Bournemouth at the end of my career. We were on that tour to the Far East, and after the last game Jürgen put his credit card behind the bar to say thank you to all the players. He just said, "Thanks boys, and stay in touch." He loved playing with us. During the season we would sometimes go to the stadium the day before games to train, and then we would go to the café on the High Road to have a fry-up. Jürgen would be with us. He was one of the boys. It was a pleasure to play with him.

'It was gutting to lose him, and of course Gica and Nicky [Barmby] too. Ilie was gone too, then I picked up injuries. So from that one year there was a massive, massive change.'

Stuart Nethercott also remembers the big send-off to Klinsmann in Hong Kong. 'We were a good group of lads. We socialised together. Christmas parties were eventful. At the end-of-season tour Jürgen put his gold card behind one of the bars and said, "Here you are boys, drinks are on me for the night," and we took full advantage of that,' he laughs. 'The dentist's chair it was! We managed not to get photographed like the England team did the following year, so we were lucky. I think Teddy probably took the England team back to the same place the next year. He probably thought, "This is good, we'll come again." For us, it was a nice end-of-season trip, getting drunk for three days!'

The dentist's chair in a Hong Kong bar became infamous in the run-up to Euro 96. Pictures emerged of England stars including Teddy Sheringham and Paul Gascoigne looking the worse for wear. The occupant of the reclining chair would have neat shots poured down their throat. The press and public pilloried England's players for their rowdy night out just days before the biggest sporting event in England since the 1966 World Cup. All was forgiven by many when Gazza scored his brilliant solo goal in the group match against Scotland and mocked the criticism in his celebration, lying on the Wembley turf on his back, mouth wide open, while Sheringham squirted the contents of a water bottle into his mouth.

In the summer of 1995, the preparations for that tournament were continuing with a friendly competition called the Umbro Cup. England's final game of three was against World Cup holders Brazil at Wembley on 11 June. Blackburn left-back Graeme Le Saux gave his team the lead with a stunning volley just before half-time, but Juninho, Ronaldo and Edmundo all struck in the second half to give Brazil a 3-1 win. The game was overshadowed by huge transfer news that day. Both Tottenham and Arsenal had splashed out club record fees. Arsenal had spent £7m on Inter Milan star Dennis Bergkamp, while Tottenham had paid £4.5m for 24-year-old striker Chris Armstrong who had just scored 18 goals in all competitions for relegated Crystal Palace.

With Klinsmann and Popescu having left, Francis was then hit by another blow as Nicky Barmby – who had just signed a new contract – announced that he wanted out too. Teddy Sheringham has since claimed that it was the arrival of Armstrong that led to Barmby's departure, saying the England youngster 'kicked up something of a fuss'. Francis says that wasn't the case, and that Barmby said he wanted to leave before the Armstrong move happened, but he admits he and Barmby had different ideas about his strongest position. 'The way we were playing was really working,' says Francis. 'I used to have Teddy coming off Jürgen. Then Nicky, for me, he wasn't strong enough to play up front. Nicky had a good football brain – he was best to come in late, so I played him wide on the left. He didn't like it, but years later he admitted to me I was right: wide on the left was his best position. He said thanks. That was nice. Teddy would come out and bring the centre-half out and Nicky would be in that slot, and he got 11 goals that season and played for England. Jürgen was going, Gica was going, but the plus point was that Ian Walker and Nicky Barmby had just signed three-year deals. Then, though, Nicky comes to see me with his girlfriend and says she can't settle here and they've got to leave.'

Barmby and his partner turned up together to see Francis. It was an emotional meeting. Francis, it's clear, is a family man. Family comes before football. Family comes first. 'They turned up to see me here at this house,' he says. 'The contract had already been signed, about a month earlier. So you can either force him to stay, or let him go. She was in tears, she really couldn't settle in London. People have got to be happy. If they're not happy then they won't play at their best.

'You want people to want to be at the club. Footballers are not robots, neither are managers. They have a life as well, they have a family as well. I've always respected that. If you have a wife or baby and there is a problem, then you go home and sort it. The most important thing is your family and when you think long-term, if players know that's how you see things, they respect you for that and give their best.

'I treated everyone how I wanted to be treated myself. You can't please everybody, because with 30-odd players at the club you can only pick 11 and the other lot will be unhappy with you. You have to make your decisions as you see it. But if the only thing they're unhappy about when they leave the club is that you didn't pick them enough, then that's all you can do.'

Is it typical for a player and his partner to both come and see the manager? 'It's usually just the player,' says Francis. 'But Nicky wanted to do it together. He felt they were both in it together, and they wanted to come and see me together.'

Barmby, who was born in Hull, left North London that summer for a place nearer home as Middlesbrough spent a then club record £5.25m to take him to Teesside.

Kit man Roy Reyland worked under a succession of Tottenham managers. He says Francis had the human touch. 'Gerry was the most family-orientated person I worked with,' he says. 'Because of the nature of the game you're doing six or seven intense days a week. You do a lot of travelling. If things aren't going right the training sessions seem to drag on. But with Gerry, he was quite tactically minded but he also had this big passion for his family, because he had children later in life and I think he appreciated home life a bit more than some of the other managers did; so he would make you have a day off.

'He came in one day and said, "Shut this place down. Everyone's off on Wednesday." And in a professional environment that is physically impossible. In my job I've still got to prepare the next training kit; Wednesday was my morning for starting to prepare the match kit for the weekend. So he comes in and drags everyone off, and I obviously went in anyway. He came into my kit room and says, "What you doing here?" I said, "Gaffer …" He says, "Get out now or I'll sack you." So I went home, which was great. But I come in Thursday and I've got so much to do it's ridiculous.

'But I could really appreciate it, and I have a lot of time for Gerry. He was very compassionate and considerate with family and children. If you went to him and said: "Gaffer, I've got a problem with my little one," he would say, "I don't want to know the problem. You go. Make sure you're covered here, but you go and do what you've got to do." That wasn't just with me, he was like that with anyone in the club. And that bonds you, because you think, the gaffer's gonna look after us here with family. You don't mind doing that extra bit. When Gerry came in and brought this culture into the club it was quite refreshing, because I'd never really experienced that before. My daughter was born in 87.'

For Darren Anderton, it was a blow to hear that Barmby was leaving, and he also had a big decision to make. He put in three fine performances for England in the Umbro Cup. In the opening game he scored England's first as they beat Japan 2-1. Then came a thrilling match at Elland Road against Sweden. The visitors led 2-0 before Teddy Sheringham pulled one back just before half-time. Sweden went 3-1 up in the second half and looked certain to win as the final whistle approached. In the last minute David Platt made it 3-2, and then as the clock ticked over into injury time, Anderton unleashed a stupendous volley which crashed off both posts and into the back of the net to secure a 3-3 draw.

He then played really well in the 3-1 defeat to Brazil and as he was about to leave the stadium his agent Leon Angel, who had been watching the game at Wembley, pulled him to one side. He told him Alan Sugar wanted to meet him tonight. Just eight months previously Anderton had signed a new four-year contract with Spurs worth £7,000 a week, plus a signing-on fee and a clause that said that if another club came in with a £4m offer he would be allowed to leave. Sugar also told Angel that if the clause was kept quiet then Anderton would be allowed to keep half of any amount above £4m.

By the summer of 1995 though, Anderton was a wanted man. Rumours were persisting that Manchester United manager Alex Ferguson wanted to take him to Old Trafford. When Anderton arrived at Sugar's Chigwell mansion that night, Gerry Francis was already there.

As Anderton remembers it: 'I had a lot of communication with the chairman at the end of the 1994/95 season. We'd lost Jürgen, we'd lost

Gica, we were about to lose Nicky.' So was it nerve-wracking meeting the chairman at his mansion? 'To a point, yeah. He's got the butlers there. It's all quite grand. But I was in such a good position and I'd grown up a lot.

'Coming to Spurs at 20, and the fact that I struggled in the first three or four months and came out the other side, meant I had learnt so much. The chairman said, "I can't let you go, Gerry's desperate for you to stay." Who knows what Gerry would have done if I'd gone? He'd lost half his team.'

Anderton didn't put pen to paper that night. At the airport the following day, as he prepared to check in for a flight to the US for a holiday, it was clear that his recent performances for England had heightened his fame. He was offered an upgrade to first class and was told the captain would like him to join him in the cockpit for landing.

While he toured New York, Washington and Philadelphia and watched the NBA final in Houston, he was aware of the newspaper stories back home linking him with Manchester United, Blackburn and Newcastle. Man United boss Alex Ferguson came out and said Anderton was the only player he wanted to sign. On the final night of his holiday, Anderton's friends toasted his likely move to Old Trafford.

The day that Anderton returned home, England team-mate Gary Pallister of Man United called and asked Anderton if it was all right for him to give his number to his manager. Anderton agreed. Later in the day, when Anderton got back from playing golf, his brother Scott told him Fergie had phoned and that he would be calling back in an hour.

'I was a bit nervous talking to Fergie,' says Anderton. 'You don't really know what to say. I was kind of, "Oh, okay, yeah, sounds cool." He said, "Just come up and have a look around, have a chat with us." I said, "Yeah, okay."'

Anderton admits that his head was spinning as he put the phone down. The following day he and his agent met with Gerry Francis and Alan Sugar again. Spurs were aware of United's interest. Andrei Kanchelskis was about to leave, and Ferguson wanted Anderton as his replacement on the right side of midfield. The wider football world hadn't heard much about United youngster David Beckham yet, and clearly Ferguson didn't feel he was quite ready to be the main man in that position in his first team.

Anderton stepped outside with Francis and they left Alan Sugar and Leon Angel to negotiate. Angel told Sugar that Manchester United and Blackburn were both offering £6m, and that would mean a £1m bonus for Anderton. Sugar hit back that he could simply do a £4m swap deal for Kanchelskis, meaning Anderton wouldn't get anything. Angel retorted that if Sugar really wanted to keep Anderton, he should pay him the £1m bonus on top of what he was offering. Sugar agreed and got out a bottle of champagne.

'The chairman wouldn't let me leave his house until I signed,' says Anderton. 'So that was that. The truth was I didn't want to go. United were in transition. They'd lost Hughes and Ince. I honestly felt we had as much chance as them at that time,' he laughs. 'We didn't know about the youngsters they had coming through.'

The next season started with United losing 3-1 to Aston Villa, and *Match of the Day* pundit Alan Hansen famously asserting, 'You can't win anything with kids.' United's kids were special though – Paul Scholes, Nicky Butt, Gary Neville, Phil Neville and a young man who might not have played much had Anderton moved to Old Trafford – David Beckham. Those players helped carry United to the Double in 1995/96. Does Anderton have any regrets? 'I'd like to have won more. Yeah, you look at it now and how big Man U are around the world, and I'd like to have been part of that,' he says.

'But more importantly, the following years I started getting the injuries and at Spurs I didn't feel we had the best medical facilities. That's why I struggled ... you know, at that point my career should have been on an upward trajectory rather than a downward one. So that is a regret. I wanted to be the best that I could be. A lot of people now will talk about the injuries as opposed to ...' His voice nearly tails off. He recovers: 'Well, anyway, a lot of people would still say I was a good footballer.

'If it happened again, I'd probably still make the same decision because I'd be left with the same reasons. I wouldn't say I let Fergie down. I was more than happy to go and meet, but I didn't want to leave. Spurs had done nothing wrong to me and I was happy there. Euro 96 was coming and I wanted to play centre midfield; Gerry was going to play me there and build the team around me.

'I still speak to Teddy about it now. He heard there was going to be a press conference about me, and phoned me in a panic. He said, "Oh shit, you're not going too, are you?"

'"No, I'm staying. They want to do a press conference because I'm staying."

'"Oh, thank God for that."'

Sheringham, of course, later went on to have his own successful career at Old Trafford. He left Tottenham in the summer of 1997. His first season was frustrating, as United finished trophyless. But then came the Treble in 1999, with Sheringham scoring in the FA Cup Final win over Newcastle, and the Champions League Final victory against Bayern Munich at Barcelona's Camp Nou.

'Nowadays Teddy feels bad for wanting me to stay, because he went on to see how good it was at United after that,' says Anderton. 'I would love to have been involved in Champions League finals and winning the league – who wouldn't? But before I started playing football, if someone had said to me I was going to spend 12 years at Tottenham, be part of teams like that and be thought of in a great way as a footballer and at a top, top club, of course I would have taken it.

'The chairman was great. He gave me a ridiculous contract, and made it clear that I was the top man. I had lots and lots of conversations with him. He was asking my opinion on stuff and he really wanted to do well. Unfortunately, the next season I had a bad injury and everything started to peter out at Spurs. Chris Armstrong came in and other players not quite at Jürgen's level – but you weren't going to get players at his level.'

Klinsmann, Popescu and Barmby had gone. Sevilla had lost faith with Dumitrescu; he wasn't getting in their team. They refused to meet Tottenham's reported £2.6m asking price and he returned to North London after his loan, but it was clear he wasn't in Francis's plans. As it was Dumitrescu actually started the first three games of 1995/96 but didn't play again until the end of the year. He was then named in the team against Blackburn on 30 December and against Man United as Spurs won 4-1 to go fourth in the Premier League in a Sky match on New Year's Day. Bizarrely this was the second time Francis had chalked up a 4-1 win over Alex Ferguson's United in a televised match on New Year's Day having done likewise with QPR in 1992.

That match proved to be the final match of Dumitrescu's Tottenham career. A few weeks later he left, having scored five goals in 20 matches for Spurs in all competitions, and signed for Harry Redknapp at West Ham where he went on to make just ten appearances before moving to Mexican side Club America.

In the summer of 1995, Francis had lost key players, but he still had Anderton and Sheringham, two England internationals in the prime of their careers. Goalkeeper Ian Walker was in the England squad, and had enjoyed a fine first season as Tottenham No.1; Sol Campbell was still raw but had in the main played well in whatever position he'd been asked to fill. In the holding midfield role David Howells had helped transform the season since Francis arrived, but it was going to be hard to recover from the loss of three key players.

'I'd lost a team. I had to start again,' says Francis. 'I wanted Les Ferdinand from QPR, really. I wanted him in his prime. He was my player, but we couldn't afford him. He went to Newcastle for £6m. The most I had, and that was at a push, was the £4.5m for Armstrong.'

The only other arrival at Tottenham in the summer of 1995 was 33-year-old left-back Clive Wilson who had played under Francis at QPR. He left Loftus Road on a free transfer to team up with his former manager again. In October 1995, Francis also spent £4.25m on Newcastle midfielder Ruel Fox.

Francis says: 'In 1995/96 we got almost exactly the same points tally as 1994/95, one less I think, from four fewer games because it was a smaller league. We had a really good team. Not as much flair as the 1994/95 team, but a really consistent side. In fact we were in the top three, three times, we spent at least eight weeks in the top four and we were still fifth as late as March. Again we were really unlucky not to get into Europe. We went to Newcastle on the final day needing a win. We drew 1-1. Sol had to come off injured, and Colin Calderwood got caught with Les Ferdinand for their equalising goal. Otherwise we would have been in Europe.

'For me at Tottenham there was always just something missing. We were always nearly there, but not quite. Just before Christmas 1995 we were 2-0 up at home to Bolton. A win would put us second in the table. We drew 2-2. If that game had finished as a win we'd have finished with the same points as Villa who were fourth. It comes down to silly things like that.'

Indeed that match with Bolton was a missed opportunity, and one in which whoever was operating the Jumbotron at White Hart Lane may regret the choice of pictures they decided to cut to during the game. At 2-0 up with 15 minutes to go they showed former player Nayim, who was sitting in the crowd. The fans went wild. The PA then asked supporters to welcome him back to The Lane. Thanks to his match-winning heroics against Arsenal for Real Zaragoza in the 1995 Cup-Winners' Cup Final when he struck the winner from the halfway line in the final minute of extra time, Nayim received an ovation as great as any he ever had during his Spurs playing days. The entire stadium sang 'Nayim from the halfway line' at top volume for a solid ten minutes. The players on the pitch must have wondered what on earth was going on, and promptly went and conceded their first goal for 602 minutes before throwing away the 2-0 lead entirely to draw 2-2. The chance to go second was missed.

After losing Klinsmann, Barmby and Popescu, the 1995/96 squad lacked a bit of star quality. Did it lack team spirit too? There were newspaper reports of a bust-up between Sheringham and Armstrong. 'That was a complete fabrication in the press,' says Francis. 'They said that Teddy Sheringham and Chris Armstrong had a fight at a petrol station. That never happened, but it became "The Truth". I think it was even mentioned in another team's match programme. It never even happened. It was ridiculous. What was good about Alan Sugar, though, was that he used to sue everyone who got things wrong and put it into his charity fund.'

In the three seasons before Francis arrived, Tottenham finished 15th, eighth and 15th again with Francis's QPR above them every year. His record of finishing seventh, eighth and tenth with Spurs measures up well compared to his successors. After his departure Christian Gross, George Graham, Glenn Hoddle, David Pleat and Jacques Santini all came and went before Spurs finished higher than Francis's seventh with Martin Jol eventually guiding them to fifth in 2006.

What did Francis take from his first season as Spurs boss? 'The biggest thing I learnt is that there is a massive difference between managing QPR and what you would call a really big club like Spurs. I learnt the difference between the expectation levels. For example, pre-season with QPR, no one outside the club would give a toss about the results; no one would care if you won, lost or drew, no one would even know where you were playing. With Tottenham, you lose a pre-season game and it's the end of the world. When I arrived, all the pre-season games for the next summer had been planned before I got there. We were playing all the top teams in Europe, and we'd only just come back from the break; we were getting beaten and it was "Crisis" everywhere.

'So, we'd lost Jürgen and Gica and Nicky and the "Crisis" carries on. It's "Crisis" already. It was hard to take. The season hadn't even started, and it's "Crisis".'

Does he have any regrets that, with the team on a poor run of form, he decided to resign in November 1997? 'I made the decision to leave for many reasons, primarily because of a section of the media, and also Spurs being a very political club,' he says. 'The Venables–Sugar row had rumbled on for years. Half of Fleet Street was in favour of Alan, half in favour of Terry, which meant win, lose or draw, there were people who didn't want to write good things about Tottenham. Also, I had played with and under Terry and knew him for many years, which made it difficult. At the time he was England manager and a number of our players were playing for England and he needed to come to White Hart Lane on a regular basis.

'Added to that, it was also one of the few clubs to be a plc, which brought its own pressures. I didn't think I was really appreciated for what I had done there. After all it would be 12 years before anybody beat my best league position there at the club. To be fair to Alan Sugar, he pleaded with me not to go. At the time people said he had sacked me but that couldn't have been further from the truth. He had been a very good chairman for me. We have seen over the years that managing Tottenham certainly isn't easy. Winning isn't enough. You have to win with style. This isn't always possible, whether you are Manchester United, or whoever, but I managed to do that in the first two seasons.

'I had been a manager for eight and a half years already when I went to Spurs. I knew all about the pressures of the job, but at the really big clubs the media attention, good or bad, can be intense and often totally unfair and factually wrong. Given the political situation there was between the two sections of the press, it can gradually wear you down.

'Exeter was the only club that sacked me. Tottenham, during 1997/98, is the only time I felt under real pressure from the media. I wasn't particularly under pressure from the fans, especially the away fans who were fantastic. I really enjoyed the club and I love that over the years supporters come up to me and tell me how much they enjoyed some of the performances, particularly at the beginning of my spell there. As I explained to Alan Sugar just before I left, I felt I had done a really decent job in difficult circumstances, and I just felt it was time to leave.'

In the first half of Francis's tenure, Spurs were a real force to be reckoned with. Indeed, Francis experienced fewer defeats in his first 50 league games (ten) than any other Spurs manager. He beat the record of 11, set by the great Arthur Rowe (orchestrator of the back-to-back Division Two and Division One title triumphs in 1949/50 and 1950/51). The record has not yet been bettered.

'I was interviewed twice for the England job during my career,' says Francis. 'The first time, at QPR, I felt I was too inexperienced as I had only had a couple of seasons in the Premier League. The second time, after that first good season with Tottenham, I could have taken the job then but was really enjoying my time at the club and looking forward to building a good side. I loved the day-to-day coaching with the players as opposed to international managing. If we had won the FA Cup that year, I really think we could have gone on to bigger and better things. But that's football, all ifs, buts and maybes.'

* * * * *

A schoolboy today flicking through *The Complete History of Spurs* is unlikely to have his attention drawn to the stats for 1994/95. The league table shows the team sitting there in seventh. The cup competition columns show depressing exits: 3-0 to lower division Notts County, 4-1 to Everton. Despite all that, somehow, it was incredibly special.

'It was my favourite season,' says 1999 League Cup winner Anderton. 'We had loads of attention on us. At the start of the season we were either so good or so bad that there was always something for people to talk about. On *Match of the Day* they'd be trying to figure out how we could be inconsistent to that degree, that good and that bad. We'd get thrashed and people would say, "They can't play in that system," and then we'd go out and beat someone. We were something different.

'Other than Cantona there weren't any overseas players of that calibre playing in our league. Jürgen, Dumitrescu and Popescu were first. Then it was Bergkamp at Arsenal. Then Zola at Chelsea. Look at it now. We started a trend. Well done. Well done, Mr Sugar. The players that we have in this league now all began from that day at Watford in pre-season.'

If Alan Sugar had gone into football to boost his profile, then in 1994/95 it certainly worked. Eighteen months earlier he had been abused in the stadium and the street for his sacking of Venables. In 1994/95, White Hart Lane gave him a standing ovation before the matches against Sheffield Wednesday and Altrincham. He had brought great players to the club, then taken on and beaten the FA. He would never be so popular again. It seems strange that this man, who made his fortune in computers, didn't stick with the programme.

Sugar has spoken about how he believes a key factor in his success with Amstrad was building excitement for a new product and powerful marketing to get the media and the public going. In his 2010 autobiography he says that in the summer of 1985 he did this by launching the PCW8256 with QWERTY keyboard for £399, and telling the assembled hacks that this wouldn't just change the lives of journalists, but the lives of every person in every office who used a traditional typewriter. He then led the journalists into a separate room where they could try out 20 of the machines. Sugar says they clambered over them and then started to call their offices, leading to even more journalists and lots of photographers turning up.

Nine years later, he did the same with Tottenham. Klinsmann, Dumitrescu and Popescu were the football equivalent of the computer with QWERTY keyboard. But he only did it once – in the summer of 1994. As Teddy Sheringham remarked in 1998, a year after joining Manchester United: 'Arsenal bought Dennis Bergkamp and David Platt. Chelsea bought Gullit. Tottenham, apparently, were the only club who hadn't learned from what they themselves had started.'

His Spurs career ended in acrimony, but Sol Campbell looks back on 1994/95 with joy. 'For me the football we played was special,' he says. 'You know, you had Jürgen, Teddy, Dumitrescu, Popescu, Barmby, Anderton. I think the whole team's style of play was in the real kind of Tottenham way; in the history of Tottenham that is how they played football.'

So, was the highlight of Campbell's Spurs career winning the League Cup in 1999? 'That was great,' he says, 'as was being the first black captain to lift a cup, any cup, at Wembley; but the highlight really was the learning, and going a couple of seasons when I was playing nearly full seasons as a youngster. I wanted to learn and wanted to bust my gut to get better. Ardiles and Perryman then Gerry Francis spent time with me and gave me the opportunity. Gerry made me captain. I always trained all the time as a youngster, going in before training and sometimes afterwards going back to work on my technique and things like that. There were really good people there at the club, from the tea lady to the press people, nice people. Yes, winning the League Cup was great, but it was the football, trying our best and going for it in that 1994/95 season that was incredible.

'For me it was just an exciting time to be around the club and be around these top players. I learnt a lot from winning and I learnt a lot from losing; that's the key to your development as a young player. I just absorbed everything. From being on the coach and listening to some of the lads, being on the pitch and things working out, things not working out. It was just the whole experience, seeing all that's going on. That's the beautiful thing about football, the memories and the history. I really enjoyed my time there. It's a really good football club and one of the biggest clubs in the world.'

What must it be like to be a professional footballer when the team is winning, playing with flair, and everyone in England wants to come and watch you play? 'You do have lows in football,' says David Howells. 'But they are far outweighed by the highs. Even though the genuine highs of winning a trophy are few and far between, just the games where you come off and you've all played well and you can sit in the dressing room afterwards and all look at each other and know it's a job well done, and you've pleased thousands and thousands of people out there. Emotions take over. We certainly experienced that feeling plenty of times in 1994/95.'

Gerry Francis says: 'I think football gives so many people throughout the world a sense of belonging. It makes people happy, it makes people sad. I can remember fantastic games that I watched as a kid, and then to be involved in them as a player and manager, was incredible. Life is memories and football is a great sport because of that.'

The late great former England manager, Sir Bobby Robson, probably put it better than anyone when he said: 'What is a club in any case? Not the buildings, or the directors, or the people who are paid to represent it. It's not the television contracts, get-out clauses, marketing departments or executive boxes. It's the noise, the passion, the feeling of belonging, the pride in your city. It's a small boy clambering up stadium steps for the very first time, gripping his father's hand, gawping at that hallowed stretch of turf beneath him and, without being able to do a thing about it, falling in love.'

The memories handed down are the glue that binds generation to generation – in essence those memories are all a football club is. The owners, managers, and players change. The kits change. The stadiums change. In some cases even the club's name changes. The memories are the one true constant. In 1994/95 at Tottenham, thanks to Alan Sugar, to Ossie Ardiles, to Jürgen Klinsmann, to Gerry Francis, and above all to 'The Team That Dared To Do', there were enough of those to last a lifetime.

What Happened Next to the Boys of 94/95

The following players – listed in alphabetical order alongside their 1994/95 squad number – all made at least one first-team appearance during the campaign.

9. Anderton, Darren (1992–2004)
Spurs Starts (Sub Apps): League 273 (26), FAC 26 (2), LC 30 (1)
Spurs Goals: League 34, FAC 6, LC 8
Spurs Trophies: 1999 League Cup
After 12 years with Spurs, midfielder Anderton left in 2004 to join Birmingham who were starting their second consecutive season in the top flight. Made 20 league appearances as he helped the Blues to a 12th-place finish before moving on to second tier Wolves where he teamed up with his former Spurs and England boss Glenn Hoddle. In his one season at Molineux the club narrowly missed out on the play-offs before he left for third tier Bournemouth in the summer of 2006. He was part of a Cherries side that was relegated at the end of 2007/08. Midway through the following season, Anderton announced that the weekend's match against Chester City on 6 December 2008 would be his final game before retirement. He signed off in style by coming off the bench to score a spectacular winner in the 88th minute. Made a club record 299 Premier League appearances for Spurs and won the 1999 League Cup, a competition in which he also finished as a runner-up in 2002. Played for England at Euro 96 and the France 98 World Cup, winning 30 caps and scoring seven goals.

2. Austin, Dean (1992–98)
Spurs Starts (Sub Apps): League 117 (7), FAC 16 (1), LC 7 (2)
Spurs Goals: 0

Terry Venables – the man who signed Austin for Spurs – came calling again in 1998 when he took him to Crystal Palace. The right-back went on to become a popular figure with Eagles fans after agreeing – along with several of his team-mates – to take a huge pay cut when the club entered administration. In 1999 he was named Palace club captain and he stayed at Selhurst until his retirement in 2002. His most notable success in coaching so far came at Watford where he helped manager Slavisa Jokanovic win promotion to the Premier League in 2015. Jokanovic was sacked that summer, but Austin stayed on under Quique Sanchez Flores as the club comfortably stayed up in 2015/16 and also reached the FA Cup semi-finals.

7. Barmby, Nicky (1992–95)
Spurs Starts (Sub Apps): League 81 (6), FAC 12 (1), LC 7 (1)
Spurs Goals: League 20, FAC 5, LC 2
After leaving Spurs in a £5.25m move to Middlesbrough in the summer of 1995, Barmby stayed on Teesside for just 17 months before heading to Everton for £5.75m. Four years later he made the switch across Stanley Park to Liverpool for £6m. Was part of the Reds' Treble cup-winning side of 2000/01 though he didn't play in the FA Cup Final or the UEFA Cup Final. Joined Leeds for £2.75m in August 2002 but injuries restricted his appearances. In 2003/04 he played just six times for the Elland Road club as they were relegated from the Premier League. After a loan spell with second tier Nottingham Forest he joined hometown club Hull in 2004. Helped the Tigers win promotion to the Premier League in 2008 and made 41 top-flight appearances, mainly from the bench, over the next two seasons before they were relegated back to the Championship at the end of 2009/10. In November 2011, a month after making what turned out to be his final professional appearance against Cardiff in the Championship, he was appointed manager – initially on a caretaker basis – following the departure of Nigel Pearson to Leicester. Sacked in May 2012 following a disagreement with the club's owners.

5. Calderwood, Colin (1993–99)
Spurs Starts (Sub Apps): League 152 (11), FAC 15 (1), LC 19 (1)
Spurs Goals: League 6, FAC 1, LC 0
After his breakthrough on to the international scene during the 1994/95 season, Calderwood remained a part of Scotland manager Craig Brown's plans. The central defender played in all three group games at Euro 96 where he came up against club-mates Teddy Sheringham, Darren Anderton and Sol Campbell (who came on as a late sub) in a game that England won 2-0. Also played in two of Scotland's three matches at the

1998 World Cup. Left Spurs for Premiership rivals Aston Villa in 1999. The following year he moved on to second tier Nottingham Forest where he suffered a broken leg. That injury eventually forced his retirement in 2001 after a short spell at Notts County who were then in the third tier. Went on to manage Northampton, Forest and Hibernian. In recent years he has worked alongside manager Chris Hughton – who was once one of his coaches during his time as a Spurs player – at Newcastle, Birmingham, Norwich, and most recently Brighton. Left the Seagulls in November 2016 to join the coaching staff at Aston Villa.

23. Campbell, Sol (1992–2001)
Spurs Starts (Sub Apps): League 246 (9), FAC 28 (2), LC 28, Europe 2
Spurs Goals: League 10, FAC 1, LC 4, Europe 0
Spurs Trophies: 1999 League Cup
Skippered Tottenham to their first silverware for eight years when he lifted the 1999 League Cup and in doing so became the first black captain to win a Wembley trophy. Angered Spurs fans by leaving on a Bosman free transfer for arch-rivals Arsenal in the summer of 2001. Won the Double in 2002 and a further title as part of the Gunners' side which went through the entire league season unbeaten in 2003/04. He also won a further two FA Cups with the club, though he was suspended for the 2003 final and did not make it off the bench in 2005. In 2006 he left Arsenal for Portsmouth whom he captained to FA Cup glory in 2008. His career ended with brief spells at Notts County, a return to Arsenal, and then a move to Newcastle before retirement in 2012. Won 73 caps for England and was named in the squad for six major tournaments (the World Cups of 1998, 2002 and 2006, and the European Championships of 1996, 2000 and 2004).

20. Caskey, Darren (1993–96)
Spurs Starts (Sub Apps): League 20 (12), FAC 6 (1), LC 3 (1)
Spurs Goals: League 4, FAC 0, LC 1
Midfielder loaned out by Gerry Francis to First Division Watford for the start of the 1995/96 season. Returned for the busy festive fixture list and started the 4-1 win over Manchester United on New Year's Day 1996. Kept his place for the next five games until the 1-1 FA Cup fourth round tie at home to Wolves on 27 January which proved to be his last game for the club. Joined second-tier Reading in the summer of 1996 and made more than 200 league appearances in five years with the Royals. Left the Berkshire club for Notts County in 2001 and racked up more than a century of league appearances for the Magpies before moving on loan to Bristol City in March 2004. After being released by Notts County

that summer he also had spells with Football League clubs Peterborough and Rushden before dropping into non-league. Has worked as a coach at York City and Wrexham.

12. Dozzell, Jason (1993–97)
Spurs Starts (Sub Apps): League 68 (16), FAC 4 (1), LC 8 (2)
Spurs Goals: League 13, FAC 1, LC 0
A regular starter under Francis in 1995/96 and frequently part of the matchday squad in 1996/97, Dozzell then returned for a month on loan at the club where he made his name – Ipswich – at the start of 1997/98. After eight appearances with the Portman Road club the midfielder was released by Spurs and joined third tier outfit Northampton just before Christmas 1997. Helped the Cobblers reach the play-off final that season but wasn't in the team for the Wembley final where they were beaten by Grimsby. In October 1998 he left Sixfields for Colchester who had just been promoted to the third tier. Went on to make more than 100 appearances for the U's. Following his retirement in 2001 he had spells with non-league sides Canvey Island and Grays Athletic. On 16 April 2016, Dozzell's son Andre made his professional debut for Ipswich at the age of 16 and scored, which is exactly what Jason himself had done at the same age in 1984.

8. Dumitrescu, Ilie (1994–96)
Spurs Starts (Sub Apps): League 16 (2), FAC 0, LC 2
Spurs Goals: League 4, FAC 0, LC 1
Spanish side Sevilla refused to meet Tottenham's £2.6m asking price for Dumitrescu at the end of his loan spell in the summer of 1995, so the midfielder returned to White Hart Lane. Started the first three games of 1995/96 but did not play again until 30 December when he was named in the team which lost 2-1 at Blackburn. Kept his place for the 4-1 win over Manchester United on New Year's Day 1996, which turned out to be his final appearance for the club. A few weeks later he signed for Harry Redknapp at West Ham, but after just ten appearances he was off to Mexico. Spent two seasons there with, first, Club America, and then Atlante before returning to Romania with Steaua Bucharest in 1998. He retired later that year aged just 29. Has had numerous managerial spells in countries including Greece, Cyprus and Romania, most recently at Steaua where he was sacked in 2010.

3. Edinburgh, Justin (1990–2000)

Spurs Starts (Sub Apps): League 190 (23), FAC 27 (1), LC 25 (4), Europe 4 (2)

Spurs Goals: League 1, FAC 0, LC 0, Europe 0

Spurs Trophies: 1991 FA Cup, 1999 League Cup

Left-back who finished the 90s the way he started it, with a Wembley medal for Spurs against a team from the East Midlands. In 1991 it was the FA Cup against Nottingham Forest, in 1999 it was the League Cup against Leicester. Edinburgh wasn't on the pitch when Allan Nielsen headed home the last-minute winner. He had been sent off for a 'headbutt' on Robbie Savage who has since admitted his play-acting was 'disgraceful' given that Edinburgh didn't touch him. He is Tottenham's most decorated player since 1990, being, as he is, the only man to have played in two winning cup finals for the club in that time. Left Spurs for second tier Portsmouth in 2000 and, after retiring in 2003, then had several spells as a manager at non-league level before taking Newport up to the Football League via the play-offs at the end of 2012/13. He was manager of third tier Gillingham (where he appointed former Spurs team-mate David Kerslake as his assistant) from February 2015 until he was sacked in January 2017. Within a fortnight he landed the job at fellow League One club Northampton Town and again brought Kerslake on board.

16. Hazard, Micky (1980–85 & 1993–95)

Spurs Starts (Sub Apps): League 88 (31), FAC 9 (3), LC 12 (4), Europe 22 (1)

Spurs Goals: League 15, FAC 2, LC 5, Europe 3

Spurs Trophies: 1982 FA Cup, 1984 UEFA Cup

Midfielder whose final game for the club proved to be his appearance as a substitute in the 2-0 defeat to Blackburn at Ewood Park on 5 November, 1994 in what was Steve Perryman's sole game as caretaker manager following the sacking of Ossie Ardiles. Retired in April 1995 and was recently working as a black cab driver in London. Displayed flashes of brilliance after rejoining the club from Swindon under Ardiles at the age of 33 in November 1993, but his first period at Spurs had been by far the more successful. Won the FA Cup in 1982, starting both the final and the replay against QPR. In 1984 he scored a brilliant free kick to give Spurs a 1-0 win at The Lane in the UEFA Cup semi-final second leg against Hajduk Split. It proved enough for Spurs to advance to the final on away goals, having lost the first leg 2-1. In the final he set up both Tottenham's goals as the first and second legs against Anderlecht finished 1-1. Spurs won the trophy on penalties. Hazard frequently hosts Tottenham Legends events.

21. Hill, Danny (1992–96)
Spurs Starts (Sub Apps): League 4 (6), FAC 0, LC 0 (2)
Spurs Goals: 0
Never played again for Spurs after his substitute appearance against West Ham on 29 October 1994 in what was the final game under Ossie Ardiles. Midfielder who went on to have loan spells with Birmingham, Watford and Cardiff. Joined Oxford in 1998 then returned to Wales with Cardiff later that year. Dropped into non-league with Dagenham & Redbridge in 2005.

15. Howells, David (1986–98)
Spurs Starts (Sub Apps): League 238 (39), FAC 17 (4), LC 26 (5), Europe 6
Spurs Goals: League 22, FAC 1, LC 4, Europe 0
Spurs Trophies: 1991 FA Cup
After 13 seasons with Spurs, Howells left for fellow Premier League club Southampton in the summer of 1998. Fittingly, the midfielder's only goal in 11 appearances for Saints was the equaliser in a 1-1 draw against Arsenal at Highbury in October 1998. Ended the 1998/99 season on loan from Saints at second tier Bristol City where he scored once in eight appearances. A persistent knee injury then kept him out for the entirety of the following campaign and led to his professional retirement in 2000. Had spells in non-league with Hartley Wintney, Havant & Waterlooville and Guildford City. Is now director of football at Charterhouse School. Won the FA Cup with Spurs in 1991 and scored the winner on his professional debut – a 2-1 victory at Sheffield Wednesday – in February 1986. At 18 years 69 days of age, he remains the youngest Spurs player to score on their competitive debut.

22. Kerslake, David (1993–95)
Spurs Starts (Sub Apps): League 34 (3), FAC 1 (1), LC 5
Spurs Goals: 0
Right-back who had loan spells with Swindon and Charlton before being released by Spurs in 1997. Joined second tier Ipswich where he made just seven appearances. Was loaned out to Wycombe and then signed for Swindon in 1998. Started his coaching career in 2006 working under former Spurs team-mate Colin Calderwood who was manager of Nottingham Forest. Joined Watford as assistant under manager Malky Mackay in 2011 and worked with the same manager at Cardiff. Was appointed Gillingham assistant manager by Justin Edinburgh in February 2015, and followed his former Spurs team-mate to fellow League One side Northampton Town after they were sacked by the Gills in January 2017.

18. Klinsmann, Jürgen (1994–95 & 1997–98)
Spurs Starts (Sub Apps): League 56, FAC 9, LC 3
Spurs Goals: League 29, FAC 5, LC 4
Won the UEFA Cup with Bayern Munich in 1995/96 and the Bundesliga – his first league title – in 1996/97. Re-signed for Spurs in December 1997 with the team desperately fighting against relegation under manager Christian Gross. Scored nine goals in 15 league appearances, including four (his first and only Premiership hat-trick) in the penultimate game of that season away to Wimbledon when a 6-2 win ensured that Spurs stayed up. The following week he scored on his final appearance for Spurs – a magnificent long-range volley – in a 1-1 draw at home to Southampton. Retired after the 1998 World Cup having hit 40 goals in 82 games for his country, and having won the 1990 World Cup and Euro 96. Began his managerial career as head coach of Germany in 2004. Led the hosts to third place at the 2006 World Cup before resigning. Appointed manager of Bayern Munich in the summer of 2008 but was sacked the following April when his team were knocked out of the Champions League by Barcelona at the quarter-final stage. Served as USA national team manager from the summer of 2011 until November 2016 when he was sacked. During his time with the States he led them to one continental title – the 2013 CONCACAF Gold Cup.

6. Mabbutt, Gary (1982–98)
Spurs Starts (Sub Apps): League 458 (19), FAC 45 (2), LC 60 (2), Europe 22 (3)
Spurs Goals: League 27, FAC 5, LC 2, Europe 4
Spurs Trophies: 1984 UEFA Cup, 1991 FA Cup
Was a near ever-present in the heart of defence during Gerry Francis's second season in charge (1995/96), but broke his leg on the opening day of 1996/97 in a 2-0 defeat away to Blackburn. That injury kept him out until the start of the following season. His final appearance for the club came as a substitute on the final day of the 1997/98 campaign during a 1-1 draw at home to Southampton, in what was also Jürgen Klinsmann's last game for the club. Retired after 16 seasons playing for Spurs. Won the 1984 UEFA Cup and the 1991 FA Cup and was an FA Cup runner-up in 1987. Now works as a club ambassador.

28. McMahon, Gerard (1995–96)
Spurs Starts (Sub Apps): League 9 (7), FAC 0 (1), LC 3
Spurs Goals: 0
Attacking midfielder who made his Spurs debut as a 21-year-old in the penultimate game of 1994/95 when he started against Coventry, and

kept his place for the final match of the season against Leeds. He was used regularly as a substitute by Francis in the first half of 1995/96. In September 1996 he moved on loan to second tier Stoke before joining them permanently for £450,000. Never scored for Spurs in a major competition, but did get one in the 2-1 defeat to Swedish side Öster in the much-maligned InterToto Cup in the summer of 1995. Went on to play for St Johnstone and Glenavon. Won 17 caps for Northern Ireland.

14. Nethercott, Stuart (1993–97)
Spurs Starts (Sub Apps): League 31 (23), FAC 5 (3), LC 0
Spurs Goals: League 0, FAC 1, LC 0
Joined third tier Millwall in 1998 after an initial loan spell with the Lions. In 2001 he helped them win the title and promotion to the second tier. Loaned out to third tier Wycombe for the second half of 2003/04, meaning he missed out on the South London club's run to the FA Cup Final where they lost to Manchester United. In the summer of 2004 he moved to Adams Park on a permanent basis and in total he made more than 50 appearances for the Chairboys. At the end of 2005/06 he dropped down to non-league and had spells with Woking, Heybridge Swifts, Wivenhoe Town and Welling United. Is now a PE teacher in Braintree where he also runs coaching schools.

4. Popescu, Gica (1994–95)
Spurs Starts (Sub Apps): League 23, FAC 3, LC 2
Spurs Goals: League 3, FAC 0, LC 0
Left Spurs after one season to join Barcelona in the summer of 1995. Won the Copa del Rey and Cup-Winners' Cup in 1997 before heading to Turkey with Galatasaray. In Istanbul he won three league titles (1998, 1999, 2000), and two Turkish Cups (1999, 2000). After Popescu struck the winner in the North London derby on 2 January 1995, the song 'Who put the ball in the Arsenal net? Gica, Gica!' was doing the rounds for months. It was given a new lease of life after the 2000 UEFA Cup Final when Popescu struck the decisive penalty for Galatasaray in a shoot-out against... yes, Arsenal. Scored 16 goals in 115 games for Romania, playing in the 1990, 1994 and 1998 World Cups as well as Euro 96 and Euro 2000. Was voted Romania's Player of the Year on no fewer than six occasions. On 4 November 2014 he was released from a Romanian prison having served one year of a three-year sentence for money laundering and tax evasion relating to player transfers.

11. Rosenthal, Ronny (1994–97)
Spurs Starts (Sub Apps): League 55 (33), FAC 7 (2), LC 3
Spurs Goals: League 4, FAC 6, LC 1
After three and a half seasons at White Hart Lane, Rosenthal left on a free transfer for third tier Watford in the summer of 1997. That season he was a regular in the Hornets team which won the Second Division title, and his goal against Blackpool was voted the club's goal of the season. Injuries restricted him to just five league appearances the following campaign and he retired at the end of 1998/99. During his career he won 61 caps for Israel and scored 11 goals for his country. On the domestic scene he won league titles in Israel (Maccabi Haifa 1983/84, 1984/85), Belgium (Club Brugge 1987/88) and England (Liverpool 1989/90). He also played a part in the Reds' 1992 FA Cup-winning run although he was not in the squad for the final. He now works as a football consultant in England.

19. Scott, Kevin (1993–95)
Spurs Starts (Sub Apps): League 16 (2), FAC 0, LC 0 (1)
Spurs Goals: League 1
Scott spent the second half of 1994/95 on loan at second tier Port Vale. The centre-back returned to The Lane to make a couple of substitute appearances under Francis at the start of 1995/96, but was then sent back out on loan to Division One side Charlton. In February 1997 he left Spurs for good when Norwich – who were now midway through their second season back in Division One having been relegated from the Premiership – paid £250,000 for his services. Made 33 league appearances for the Canaries before moving to fourth tier Darlington on a month's loan in January 1999. It was while with the Quakers that he played his final professional game – a 1-0 home defeat to Hull on 16 February 1999. Scott then dropped into non-league with Guisborough Town and Crook Town. Since retirement he has worked as a coach at Middlesbrough and also as a driving instructor.

10. Sheringham, Teddy (1992–97 & 2001–03)
Spurs Starts (Sub Apps): League 230 (6), FAC 20, LC 20 (1)
Spurs Goals: League 97, FAC 14, LC 13
Left Spurs for Manchester United in a £3.5m deal in June 1997. Won the Treble of Champions League, Premier League and FA Cup in 1999, scoring in both cup finals. Won the league again in 2000 and 2001 before returning to Spurs on a free transfer as one of Glenn Hoddle's first signings. Was part of the Spurs team that finished runners-up in the 2002 League Cup. He left The Lane for a second time in 2003 for Portsmouth, and also went on to play for West Ham and Colchester

before retiring in 2008. Came on as a substitute in the 2006 FA Cup Final and was the only West Ham player to score from the spot as they lost 3-1 on penalties to Liverpool after a thrilling 3-3 draw at the Millennium Stadium. Remains the oldest goalscorer in Premier League history having struck for the Hammers against Portsmouth on Boxing Day 2006, aged 40 years 266 days. Four days later he made his final Premier League appearance in a 1-0 defeat against Manchester City and remains, at the age of 40 years 270 days, the oldest outfield Premier League player. After a spell on the coaching staff at Premier League West Ham in 2014, he went into management with Stevenage in May 2015. He was sacked by the League Two club in February 2016. In July 2017 he made a surprise move to the Indian Super League when he was appointed as manager of reigning champions Atleticó de Kolkata.

1. Thorstvedt, Erik (1989–94)
Spurs Starts (Sub Apps): League 171 (2), FAC 14, LC 25, Europe 6
Spurs Clean Sheets: League 40, FAC 3, LC 10, Europe 4
Spurs Trophies: 1991 FA Cup
Goalkeeper whose final Tottenham appearance proved to be the 3-1 win against West Ham on 29 October 1994 in what was Ossie Ardiles' final game in charge. For the next season and a half the Norwegian was occasionally on the bench and more often left out of the squad altogether, (with Chris Day providing back-up to Ian Walker), before retiring at the end of 1995/96. He went on to work as a goalkeeping coach with the Norway national team and their Under-21s, and as a television pundit in his homeland. The highlight of his eight seasons at Tottenham was winning the FA Cup in 1991. He won 97 caps for Norway and played in all three of his country's matches at the 1994 World Cup where they exited at the group stage.

17. Turner, Andy (1992–95)
Spurs Starts (Sub Apps): League 8 (12), FAC 0 (1), LC 0 (2)
Spurs Goals: League 3, FAC 0, LC 1
Winger whose only appearance of 1994/95 came on the final day of the season when Francis handed him a start against Leeds – it turned out to be his final game for the club. After loan spells with Huddersfield and Southend he joined Portsmouth in 1996 and then moved on to Crystal Palace, Wolves and Rotherham. Won nine caps at Under-21 level for the Republic of Ireland. His winning goal for Spurs against Everton on 5 September 1992 saw him become the youngest Premier League goalscorer, though admittedly the competition was itself only one month old. He was aged 17 years 166 days at the time and, while the record has

since been broken numerous times, he remains Tottenham's youngest Premier League scorer.

13. Walker, Ian (1991–2001)
Spurs Starts (Sub Apps): League 257 (2), FAC 25, LC 22 (1), Europe 6
Spurs Clean Sheets: League 67, FAC 6, LC 7, Europe 4
Spurs Trophies: 1999 League Cup

Goalkeeper who won the 1999 League Cup with Spurs, keeping clean sheets in both legs of the semi-final against Wimbledon, and in the final itself against Leicester. After six years as Tottenham's first choice between the sticks, he lost his place to Neil Sullivan in 2000/01. He left for Leicester in the summer of 2001 with the Foxes paying £2.5m. His first season in the East Midlands ended in relegation from the Premier League. Won immediate promotion before relegation again followed two years later. In January 2004 he was confronted by a Leicester fan who ran on to the pitch and shouted at him after he conceded five goals in 18 minutes in a 5-0 home defeat against Aston Villa. Left Leicester in 2005 for Bolton where he remained until retiring in 2008. His four England caps were strung out over eight years, from his debut against Hungary in 1996 to his last match against Iceland in June 2004. He was in the England squad for Euros 1996 and 2004 but only played one competitive fixture when he kept goal for England against Italy in a World Cup qualifier in 1997. Gianfranco Zola struck the only goal at Wembley and Walker was harshly criticised for having been beaten at his near post. Became goalkeeping coach at Chinese Super League club Shanghai Shenhua in April 2012. Moved across the city to Shanghai East Asia before leaving them at the end of 2016. Kept a joint club record six consecutive clean sheets in all competitions in 1994/95. Also kept a joint club record five consecutive league clean sheets as part of that 1994/95 run, and did so again in 1995/96.

Final Premiership Table 1994/95

	P	W	D	L	F	A	GD	Pts
1.BLACKBURN	42	27	8	7	80	39	+41	89 Champs Lg
2.MAN. U.	42	26	10	6	77	28	+49	88 UEFA Cup
3.N. FOREST	42	22	11	9	72	43	+29	77 UEFA Cup
4.LIVERPOOL	42	21	11	10	65	37	+28	74 UEFA Cup*
5.LEEDS U.	42	20	13	9	59	38	+21	73 UEFA Cup
6.NEWCASTLE U.	42	20	12	10	67	47	+20	72
7.TOTTENHAM H.	**42**	**16**	**14**	**12**	**66**	**58**	**+8**	**62**
8.QPR	42	17	9	16	61	59	+2	60
9.WIMBLEDON	42	15	11	16	48	65	-17	56
10.SOTON	42	12	18	12	61	63	-2	54
11.CHELSEA	42	13	15	14	50	55	-5	54
12.ARSENAL	42	13	12	17	52	49	+3	51
13.SHEFF. W.	42	13	12	17	49	57	-8	51
14.WEST HAM U.	42	13	11	18	44	48	-4	50
15.EVERTON	42	11	17	14	44	51	-7	50
16.COVENTRY C.	42	12	14	16	44	62	-18	50
17.MAN. C.	42	12	13	17	53	64	-11	49
18.ASTON V.	42	11	15	16	51	56	-5	48
19.C. PALACE	42	11	12	19	34	49	-15	45 R
20.NORWICH C.	42	10	13	19	37	54	-17	43 R
21.LEICESTER C.	42	6	11	25	45	80	-35	29 R
22.IPSWICH	42	7	6	29	36	93	-57	27 R

Promoted from Division One: Middlesbrough (Champions)
Bolton Wanderers (via play-offs)

FA CUP FINAL
20 May 1995 (Wembley)
Everton 1-0 Manchester United
Rideout 30
Everton qualify for Cup-Winners' Cup

LEAGUE CUP FINAL
2 April 1995 (Wembley)
Liverpool 2-1 Bolton Wanderers
McManaman 37, 68, Thompson 70
*Liverpool qualify for UEFA Cup

CHAMPIONS LEAGUE FINAL
24 May 1995 (Vienna)
Ajax 1-0 AC Milan
Kluivert 85

UEFA CUP FINAL
3 May 1995 (1st leg), 17 May 1995 (2nd leg)
Parma 1-0 Juventus
D.Baggio 5
Juventus 1-1 Parma
Vialli 33, D.Baggio 54
Parma win 2-1 on aggregate

CUP-WINNERS' CUP FINAL
10 May 1995 (Paris)
Arsenal 1-2 Real Zaragoza (Aet)
Hartson 77, Esnáider 68, Nayim 120

Tottenham Results 1994/95

Date	Result	Scorers	Att.
20 Aug	W 4-3 Sheff. W. (a)	Sheringham, Anderton, Barmby, Klinsmann	34,051
24	W 2-1 Everton (h)	Klinsmann (2)	24,553
27	L 0-1 Man. U. (h)		24,502
30	W 3-1 Ipswich T. (a)	Klinsmann (2), Dumitrescu	22,559
12 Sep	L 1-2 Soton (h)	Klinsmann	22,387
17	L 1-3 Leicester C. (a)	Klinsmann	21,300
21	W 6-3 Watford (a) LC2.1	Anderton, Klinsmann (3), Sheringham, Dumitrescu	13,659
24	L 1-4 N. Forest (h)	Dumitrescu	24,558
1 Oct	W 2-1 Wimbledon (a)	Sheringham, Popescu	16,802
4	L 2-3 Watford (h) LC2.2	Barmby, Klinsmann	17,798
8	D 1-1 QPR (h)	Barmby	25,799
15	D 1-1 Leeds U. (a)	Sheringham	39,224
22	L 2-5 Man. C. (a)	Dumitrescu (2, 1p)	25,473
25	L 0-3 Notts Co. (a) LC3		16,952
29	W 3-1 West Ham U. (h)	Klinsmann, Sheringham, Barmby	26,271
5 Nov	L 0-2 Blackburn R. (a)		26,933
19	L 3-4 A. Villa (h)	Sheringham, Klinsmann (p), Bosnich (og)	26,899
23	D 0-0 Chelsea (h)		27,037
26	D 1-1 Liverpool (a)	Ruddock (og)	35,007

3 Dec	W 4-2 Newcastle U. (h)	Sheringham (3), Popescu	28,002
10	W 3-1 Sheff. W. (h)	Barmby, Klinsmann, Calderwood	25,912
17	D 0-0 Everton (a)		32,809
26	W 2-0 Norwich C. (a)	Barmby, Sheringham	21,814
27	D 0-0 C. Palace (h)		27,730
31	W 4-0 Coventry C. (a)	Darby (og), Barmby, Anderton, Sheringham	19,951
2 Jan	W 1-0 Arsenal (h)	Popescu	28,747
7	W 3-0 Altrincham (h) FC3	Sheringham, Rosenthal, Nethercott	25,057
14	W 2-1 West Ham U. (a)	Sheringham, Klinsmann	24,573
25	L 0-1 A. Villa (a)		40,017
29	W 4-1 Sunderland (a) FC4	Klinsmann (2, 1p), Sheringham, Mabbutt	21,135
5 Feb	W 3-1 Blackburn R. (h)	Klinsmann, Anderton, Barmby	28,124
11	D 1-1 Chelsea (a)	Sheringham	30,812
18	D 1-1 Soton (h) FC5	Klinsmann	28,091
25	L 1-2 Wimbledon (h)	Klinsmann	27,258
1 Mar	W 6-2 Soton (a) (aet) FC5	Rosenthal (3), Sheringham, Barmby, Anderton	15,172
4	D 2-2 N. Forest (a)	Sheringham, Calderwood	28,711
8	W 3-0 Ipswich T. (h)	Klinsmann, Barmby, Youds (og)	24,930
11	W 2-1 Liverpool (a) FC6	Sheringham, Klinsmann	39,592
15	D 0-0 Man. U. (a)		43,802
18	W 1-0 Leicester C. (h)	Klinsmann	30,851
22	D 0-0 Liverpool (h)		31,988
2 Apr	L 3-4 Soton (a)	Sheringham (2), Klinsmann	15,105
9	L 1-4 Everton (n) FCSF	Klinsmann (p)	38,226
11	W 2-1 Man. C. (h)	Howells, Klinsmann	27,410
14	D 1-1 C. Palace (a)	Klinsmann	18,149
17	W 1-0 Norwich C. (h)	Sheringham	32,304
29	D 1-1 Arsenal (a)	Klinsmann	38,377
3 May	D 3-3 Newcastle U. (a)	Barmby, Klinsmann, Anderton	35,603
6	L 1-2 QPR (a)	Sheringham	18,637
9	L 1-3 Coventry C. (h)	Anderton	24,134
14	D 1-1 Leeds U. (h)	Sheringham	33,040

THE TEAM THAT DARED TO DO

	ANDERTON	AUSTIN	BARMBY	CALDERWOOD	CAMPBELL	CASKEY	DOZZELL	DUMITRESCU	EDINBURGH	HAZARD	HILL	HOWELLS	KERSLAKE	KLINSMANN	MABBUTT	McMAHON	NETHERCOTT	POPESCU	ROSENTHAL	SCOTT	SHERINGHAM	THORSTVEDT	TURNER	WALKER
SHE	9		7	5	6			8	3	13			2	11	12		4				10			1
EVE	9		7	5	6			8	3	12			2	11	13		4				10			1
MNU	9		7	5	6			8	3	12			2	11			4				10			1
IPS	9		7	5	6			8	3				2	11	12		4				10			1
SOT	9		7	5	6			8	3	12			2	11			4				10			1
LEI	9		7	5	6			8	3	12			2	11			4				10			1
NFO	9				5			8	3	7	12		2	11	6			4			10			1
WIM	9	2					7	8		12		3		11	6			4		5	10			1
QPR			7	5	6			8	3	12	9		2	11					13	4	10			1
LEE			7	12	6		9	8	3				2	11				4		5	10			1
MNC			7		6		9	8	3	12			2	11				4		5	10			1
WHA			7		5		9	8	3	10	13		2	11	6			4			12	1		
BLA			7		5		9		3	12		8	2	11	6			4	13		10			1
AVI	9		12	5	3	7						8	2	11	6		13	4			10			1
CHE	9	2	7	5	3			12				8		11	6			4			10			1
LIV	9	2	7	5	3			12				8		11	6			4			10			1
NEW	9	2	7	5	3				12			8		11	6			4			10			1
SHE	9	2	7	5	3							4		8	6				11		10			1
EVE	9	2	7	5	3							8			6			4	11		10			1
NOR	9	2	7	5	3							8		11	6		12	4			10			1
CPA	9	2	7	5	3							8		11	6		13	4	12		10			1
COV	9	2	7	5	3							8		11	6		13	4	12		10			1
ARS	9	2		5	3							8		7	6		12	4	11		10			1
WHA	9	2	7	5	3				12			8		11	6			4			10			1
AVI	9	2	7	5	8	12			3					11	6			4			10			1
BLA	9		7	5	2				3			8		11	6		12	4			10			1
CHE	9		7	5	2				3			8		11	6			4			10			1
WIM	9	12	7	5	2				3			8		11	6			4	13		10			1
NFO	9	2	7	5					3			4		8	6				11		10			1
IPS	9	2	7	5		12			3			4		8	6				11		10			1
MNU	9	2	7	5					3			4		8	6				11		10			1
LEI	9	2	7	5					3			4		8	6				11		10			1
LIV	9	2	7						3			4	12	8	6		5		11		10			1
SOT	9	2	7	5								4	3	8	6				11		10			1
MNC	9	2	7	5					3			8		11	6		13	4	12		10			1
CPA	9	2	7	5					3					8	6			4	11		10			1
NOR	9	2	7	5		12			3					8	6			4	11		10			1
ARS	9	2	7	5					3			4		8	6				11		10			1
NEW	9	2	7	5	12				3			4		8	6				11		10			1
QPR	9		7	5	2				3			4	12	8	6			13	11		10			1
COV	9		7	5	2				3			4		8	6	11	12				10			1
LEE	9			5			12		3				2	8	6	11	4				10		7	1

	ANDERTON	AUSTIN	BARMBY	CALDERWOOD	CAMPBELL	CASKEY	DOZZELL	DUMITRESCU	EDINBURGH	HAZARD	HILL	HOWELLS	KERSLAKE	KLINSMANN	MABBUTT	McMAHON	NETHERCOTT	POPESCU	ROSENTHAL	SCOTT	SHERINGHAM	THORSTVEDT	TURNER	WALKER
APPS	37	23	37	35	29	1	6	11	29	2	1	26	16	41	33	2	8	23	14	4	41	1	1	41
SUBS	0	1	1	1	1	3	1	2	2	9	2	0	2	0	3	0	9	0	6	0	1	0	0	0
GLS	5		9	2				4				1		20				3			18			
FAC																								
ALT	9	2	7	5	3							4		8	6		12		_11_		10			1
SUN	9		7	5	2			3				_8_		11	6		12	4			10			1
SOT	9	12	7	5	2			3				8		**11**	6			4			10			1
SOT	9	2	7	5		13		3				**8**		11	6		_4_	12			10			1
LIV	9	2	7	5				3				4		8	6				11		10			1
EVE*	9	2	7	5								8		11	6		_3_	4	12		10			1
APPS	6	4	6	6	3	0	0	0	4	0	0	6	0	6	6	0	2	3	2	0	6	0	0	6
SUBS	0	1	0	0	0	1	0	0	0	0	0	0	0	0	0	0	2	0	2	0	0	0	0	0
GLS	1		1											5	1		1		4		4			
LC																								
WAT	9			5		8	**3**	_7_	12	13	2			11	6		4				10			1
WAT	_9_	2	7		5		8				12	4	3	10	6				11					1
NCO		2	7	_5_	6		9	8	3	12				11			4				10	1		
APPS	2	2	2	1	3	0	2	2	2	1	0	1	2	3	2	0	0	2	1	0	2	1	0	2
SUBS	0	0	0	0	0	0	0	0	0	1	2	1	0	0	0	0	0	0	0	0	0	0	0	0
GLS	1		1					1						4							1			

Team name in bold = home   **Bold number** = first sub off   Numbers are positional number not squad number

EVE* = neutral   Underlined number = second sub off   12 = first sub on   13 = second sub on

Points of Interest

The following trivia – all correct at time of publication – pertain to the 1994/95 season:

1) The 'Famous Five' only played six games together. Darren Anderton, Nicky Barmby, Ilie Dumitrescu, Jürgen Klinsmann and Teddy Sheringham started the first six games of the season. They were never again all on the pitch at the same time.

2) Tottenham started 1994/95 with a World Cup winner as their manager and also one in their team – Ossie Ardiles (Argentina, 1978) and Jürgen Klinsmann (West Germany, 1990).

3) Tottenham took 11 seasons to better their seventh-place finish of 1994/95 under Gerry Francis before coming fifth under Martin Jol in 2005/06. In that time they appointed six managers: Christian Gross, George Graham, Glenn Hoddle, David Pleat, Jacques Santini, and then Jol.

4) Season 1994/95 is the last time Tottenham finished as London's top club. It also took 22 years for them to finish above Arsenal again, which they next achieved in 2016/17. It was their 2-0 home win over the Gunners on 30 April 2017 which ensured they could no longer be caught by the Gunners.

5) Gerry Francis is the only manager to lead two different clubs to the position of London's top club (QPR in 1992/93 and Tottenham in 1994/95) during the Premier League era.

6) Gerry Francis experienced fewer defeats (ten) during his first 50 league matches than any other Spurs manager.

7) On 20 August 1994 Jürgen Klinsmann scored the winner on his Tottenham debut away to Sheffield Wednesday, a feat also achieved by Spurs team-mate David Howells on 22 February 1986. Martin Chivers also scored on his Tottenham debut away to Sheffield Wednesday on 17 January 1968, hitting the opener in a 2-1 win. Len Duquemin struck on his Tottenham debut in a 5-1 win over Sheffield Wednesday at White Hart Lane on 30 August 1947. Tottenham's two league titles of 1951 and 1961 were both secured with wins over Sheffield Wednesday at White Hart Lane.

8) Two players with Tottenham connections played for 1994/95 champions Blackburn. Tim Sherwood was Rovers captain and scored in their 3-1 defeat at White Hart Lane on 5 February 1995. He would go on to make 118 appearances for Tottenham between 1999 and 2002, scoring 16 goals and finishing as a League Cup runner-up in his final season. He was also manager of Tottenham from December 2013 until May 2014. Blackburn goalkeeper Bobby Mimms, who deputised for the injured Tim Flowers in that match on 5 February 1995, had made 44 appearances for Tottenham between 1988 and 1990.

9) In 1994/95 four players who would go on to play for Spurs scored against them: Ruel Fox (two for Newcastle), Les Ferdinand (two for QPR), Tim Sherwood (Blackburn Rovers) and Chris Armstrong (Crystal Palace). Two players who had previously represented Spurs also scored against them: Paul Walsh (two for Manchester City) and Phil Gray (Sunderland).

10) In 1995 three Premiership footballers were handed prison sentences after being found guilty of assault. One served time, one had their sentence reduced, and one was acquitted on appeal. Everton striker Duncan Ferguson served three months after being found guilty of assault for head-butting an opponent while playing for Rangers before he moved to Goodison Park. Manchester United's Eric Cantona was sentenced to two weeks in prison for his kung-fu kick on a Crystal Palace fan, but had his sentence reduced to community service on appeal. Chelsea's Dennis Wise was sentenced to three months in prison for assaulting a taxi driver, but was acquitted on appeal.

11) Tottenham missed five penalties in 1994/95. Teddy Sheringham missed against Everton, Manchester United (saved, Peter Schmeichel) and Nottingham Forest (saved, Mark Crossley) and

Jürgen Klinsmann missed against Liverpool (saved, David James) and Newcastle (saved, Mike Hooper).

12) Matthew Le Tissier scored six goals in four games for Southampton against Tottenham in 1994/95.

13) Matthew Le Tissier scored a penalty in three of the four games for Southampton against Tottenham in 1994/95. Spurs keeper Ian Walker got a hand to all of them – indeed he got both hands to the one in the FA Cup replay – but he couldn't keep any of them out.

14) Ian Walker also got a hand to Alan Shearer's penalty in a 2-0 defeat at Ewood Park on 5 November 1994 – but failed to keep it out.

15) In 1994/95 Gerry Francis's Tottenham team equalled the club record of five consecutive clean sheets in the league. It had already been achieved twice previously, and has also been matched three further times since. One of those more recent occasions was by Francis's team again in 1995/96. The full six occasions when Spurs have kept five consecutive clean sheets in the league are as follows:

22 April–13 May 1967 (Manager: Nicholson – Goalkeeper: Jennings)
W 1-0 Soton (a), W 1-0 Sunderland (h), D 0-0 Liverpool (a), W 2-0 W. Ham (a), W 2-0 Sheff U (h)

24 January–22 March 1987 (Manager: Pleat – Goalkeeper: Clemence)
W 3-0 Villa (h), W 2-0 Soton (h), W 5-0 Leicester (h), W 1-0 QPR (h), W 1-0 Liverpool (h)

17 December 1994–2 January 1995 (Manager: Francis – Goalkeeper: Walker)
D 0-0 Everton (a), W 2-0 Norwich (a), D 0-0 Palace (h), W 4-0 Coventry (a), W 1-0 Arsenal (h)

21 November–16 December 1995 (Manager: Francis – Goalkeeper: Walker)
W 1-0 M'Boro (a), D 0-0 Chelsea (a), D 0-0 Everton (h), W 1-0 QPR (h), W 1-0 Wimbledon (a)

13 January–10 February 2001 (Manager: Graham – Goalkeepers: Sullivan / Walker

D 0-0 Everton (a), D 0-0 Soton (h), D 0-0 W. Ham (a), D 0-0 Charlton (h), W 1-0 Man C (a)

16 December 2009–16 January 2010 (Manager: Redknapp – Goalkeeper: Gomes)
W 3-0 Man C (h), W 2-0 Blackburn (a), D 0-0 Fulham (a), W 2-0 W. Ham (h), D 0-0 Hull (h)

16) In 1994/95 Francis's Tottenham also equalled a club record of six consecutive clean sheets in all competitions. It had been achieved four times previously and has also been equalled once again since. The six sequences of six games are:

6 January–3 February 1923 (Manager: McWilliam – Goalkeeper: Blake)
W 2-0 M'Boro (h), D 0-0 Worksop Town FAC (h)#, W 9-0 Worksop Town FAC (h), W 3-0 Oldham (a), W 3-0 Oldham (h), W 4-0 Man U (h) FAC
#played at home by mutual consent

9 September–29 September 1970 (Manager: Nicholson – Goalkeepers: Hancock / Jennings)
W 3-0 Swansea (h) LC, W 3-0 Blackpool (h), W 4-0 Dunfermline (h) TC, W 3-0 Palace (a), W 2-0 Man C (h), W 3-0 Dunfermline (h) TC

26 September–17 October 1981 (Manager: Burkinshaw – Goalkeeper: Clemence)
W 1-0 Man C (a), W 3-0 Ajax (a) CWC, W 3-0 Forest (h), W 1-0 Man U (h) LC, W 2-0 Stoke (h), W 2-0 Sunderland (a)

31 January–25 February 1987 (Manager: Pleat – Goalkeeper: Clemence)
W 4-0 Palace (h) FAC, W 5-0 W. Ham (h) LC, W 1-0 Arsenal (a) LC, W 2-0 Soton (h), W 1-0 Newcastle (h) FAC, W 5-0 Leicester (h)

17 December 1994–7 January 1995 (Manager: Francis – Goalkeeper: Walker)
D 0-0 Everton (a), W 2-0 Norwich (a), D 0-0 Palace (h), W 4-0 Coventry (a), W 1-0 Arsenal (h), W 3-0 Altrincham (h) FAC

16 December 2009–16 January 2010 (Manager: Redknapp – Goalkeeper: Gomes)

W 3-0 Man C (h), W 2-0 Blackburn (a), D 0-0 Fulham (a), W 2-0 W.Ham (h), W 4-0 Peterborough FAC (h), D 0-0 Hull (h)

FAC = FA Cup, LC = League Cup, TC = Texaco Cup, CWC = European Cup-Winners' Cup

17) Astonishingly, the two different consecutive clean sheet runs under Gerry Francis's Spurs side both saw the team – with Ian Walker in goal throughout – go exactly 602 minutes without conceding. In 1994/95 they went 602 minutes after conceding Ian Nolan's 38th-minute goal for Sheffield Wednesday on 10 December 1994 until Jeroen Boere's tenth-minute opener for West Ham on 14 January 1995. 602 minutes also passed without concession between Dennis Bergkamp's 15th-minute goal for Arsenal on 18 November 1995 and Scott Green's opener for Bolton on 22 December 1995. The runs are displayed below:

1994/95 JOINT CLUB RECORD SIX CONSECUTIVE CLEAN SHEETS ALL COMPS

	10 Dec 1994	W 3-1 Sheff Wed (Nolan 38)		I
1.	17 Dec 1994	D 0-0 Everton		I
2.	26 Dec 1994	W 2-0 Norwich		I
3.	27 Dec 1994	D 0-0 C. Palace		I
4.	30 Dec 1994	W 4-0 Coventry	602 mins between these goals	
5.	2 Jan 1995	W 1-0 Arsenal		I
6.	7 Jan 1995	W 3-0 Altrincham (FAC)		I
	14 Jan 1995	W 2-1 West Ham (Boere 10)		I

1995/96 JOINT CLUB RECORD FIVE CONSECUTIVE LEAGUE CLEAN SHEETS

	18 Nov 1995	W 2-1 Arsenal (Bergkamp 15)		I
1.	21 Nov 1995	W 1-0 Middlesbrough		I
2.	25 Nov 1995	D 0-0 Chelsea		I
3.	2 Dec 1995	D 0-0 Everton	602 mins between these goals	
4.	9 Dec 1995	W 1-0 QPR		I
5.	16 Dec 1995	W 1-0 Wimbledon		I
	23 Dec 1995	D 2-2 Bolton (Green 77)		I

18) The 602 minutes in 1995/96 constitutes the longest run duration-wise that Tottenham have gone without conceding a Premier League goal. Gerry Francis was manager, and Ian Walker played in goal throughout.

19) The longest time duration-wise that Tottenham have gone without conceding a goal in all competitions (but in the Premier League era, because tracking down goal times for all the runs before then has not been possible) is 633 minutes between 16 December 2009–16 January 2010. Harry Redknapp was the manager, and Heurelho Gomes played in goal throughout. After conceding a third-minute goal to Wolves in a 1-0 home defeat on 12 December 2009, Spurs then kept six consecutive clean sheets in all competitions and did not concede again until Liverpool's Dirk Kuyt struck in the sixth minute of a 2-0 win for Liverpool at Anfield on 20 January 2010.

20) When Tottenham met Norwich on Boxing Day 1994 their opponents were seventh in the table, unbeaten at home in the league and had the second-best defensive record in the top flight behind Manchester United. Spurs won 2-0. After that match, Norwich won just two of their remaining 22 league games and were relegated in 20th place.

21) Tottenham had two matches postponed because of waterlogged pitches in 1994/95. The home match against Manchester City, scheduled for Saturday 21 January, was called off an hour before kick-off at 2pm. It was rescheduled for Tuesday 11 April and Spurs won 2-1. The away match at Newcastle, scheduled for Wednesday 22 February, was called off at 1pm. It eventually took place on Wednesday 3 May and ended in a 3-3 draw.

22) In 1994/95, Tottenham played matches against five of their future managers; Gerry Francis (manager of QPR, the month before he became Spurs boss), Glenn Hoddle (player-manager of Chelsea), George Graham (manager of Arsenal), Harry Redknapp (manager of West Ham), and Tim Sherwood (captain of Blackburn).

23) In 1994/95 Crystal Palace were relegated having finished in 19th position, or fourth from bottom. This was because the Premiership was being condensed from 22 teams to 20, with four going down and two coming up. They are the only team ever to be relegated from the Premier League having finished fourth from bottom. The only other team to be relegated from the top flight having finished fourth from bottom are Chelsea. They finished 18th in a 21-team Division One in 1987/88. The division was being shrunk to 20 teams, with four going down and three coming up. Chelsea had to play Blackburn – who had finished fifth in Division Two – in a two-legged play-off semi-final. They won and then had to contest a two-legged final

against Middlesbrough, who had finished third in Division Two. Middlesbrough won to take Chelsea's top-flight place.

24) Ipswich Town's 9-0 defeat to Manchester United at Old Trafford on 4 March 1995 is a Premier League record. The other meeting between the teams that season ended Ipswich 3-2 Manchester United at Portman Road on 24 September 1994.

25) Manchester United's Andy Cole became the first player to score five goals in one Premier League match during that 9-0 defeat of Ipswich. That record has since been equalled by Alan Shearer (Newcastle 8-0 Sheffield Wednesday on 19 September 1999), Jermaine Defoe (Tottenham 9-1 Wigan, 22 November 2009), Dimitar Berbatov (Manchester United 7-1 Blackburn, 27 November 2011), and Sergio Agüero (Manchester City 6-1 Newcastle, 3 October 2015). Defoe is the only one among them to have struck all five in one half.

26) Ronny Rosenthal is the only player to come on as a substitute and score a hat-trick for Tottenham in a competitive match.

27) From the 1992/93 season Premier League and Football League teams could name three substitutes on the bench. One had to be specified as a player who could only replace the goalkeeper, and only two substitutions were actually permitted during the match. In 1994/95 this changed. All three substitutes could now be used – however, one could only be used to replace the goalkeeper. In 1995/96 it became the case that all three could be used with no restrictions on positions.

28) Having finished seventh in 1994/95, Tottenham were invited to take part in that summer's InterToto Cup – a backdoor way to qualify for the UEFA Cup. With several first-team players having spent much of the summer with England in the Umbro Cup, and with White Hart Lane unavailable while the pitch was relaid, they reluctantly agreed thinking they had received permission from UEFA to field a team of young players and loanees. While Gerry Francis took the first team on their pre-season tour, Roger Cross and Des Bulpin oversaw the InterToto Cup campaign, which resulted in one win and three defeats in the group stage. An 8-0 drubbing away to Köln angered UEFA who banned Tottenham, and fellow Premier League entrants Wimbledon, from Europe for a year. The Premier League fought the ban and it was overturned in January 1996.

29) Tragically, it appears two opposition players from the 1994/95 generation went on to take their own lives. Leeds and Wales international midfielder Gary Speed died, aged 42, in 2011. West Ham United's Dutch striker Jeroen Boere died, aged 39, in 2007, although there are conflicting reports as to whether he took his own life.

30) On Sunday 14 May, 2017 Tottenham beat Manchester United 2-1 in the last ever match to be played at White Hart Lane. The club invited numerous former players on to the pitch for a farewell ceremony. Of the 48 players who accepted the invitation, seven were part of the 1994/95 squad: Darren Anderton; Justin Edinburgh; Micky Hazard; David Howells; Gary Mabbutt; Teddy Sheringham and Erik Thorstvedt. Jürgen Klinsmann was unable to attend.

With no particular link to 1994/95, I also learnt, or was reminded of, the following trivia, while researching this book:

1) Darren Anderton's final five caps for England were each awarded by five different managers: Glenn Hoddle, Howard Wilkinson, Kevin Keegan, Peter Taylor, and Sven-Göran Eriksson.

2) Anderton writes in his 2010 autobiography *Take Note*, that had England scored in extra time against Germany in the Euro 96 semi-final they planned to celebrate what would have been a 'golden goal' by running straight down the Wembley tunnel. The 'golden goal' rule was used at the European Championships of 1996 and 2000, and the 1998 World Cup, with the first goal scored in extra time instantly winning the game.

3) Despite receiving plenty of criticism for his injury record, Darren Anderton made a club record 299 Premier League appearances for Tottenham.

4) Ian Walker's four England caps were won across the space of eight years. He made his debut against Hungary in 1996 and his final game was against Iceland in 2004.

5) In February 2000, referee Mike Reed was 'severely reprimanded' by the Premier League after appearing to celebrate what proved to be the winning goal by Patrik Berger as Liverpool beat Leeds 2-1. He said his 'pumped fist' motion was because of his satisfaction at his

own decision to play advantage. He was removed from officiating the match between Liverpool's rivals Everton and Newcastle the following month.

6) Gary Mabbutt went on to become one of Tottenham's finest defenders but in his debut season for the club (1982/83) he actually hit double figures from midfield, scoring ten goals, all in the league.

7) Teddy Sheringham was the top Premier League goalscorer in the competition's first season of 1992/93. He scored 22 goals, one for Nottingham Forest and 21 for Tottenham. The single goal for Forest was the first ever goal scored in a live Sky TV Premier League match as his team beat Liverpool 1-0 at the City Ground on Sunday 16 August 1992.

8) Manchester United's Neil Webb was the first top-flight player to miss a penalty in an FA Cup shoot-out, and team-mate Ryan Giggs the first to miss a decisive penalty. On 5 February 1992, Webb blazed United's first penalty over in a fourth-round replay against Southampton at Old Trafford which had ended 2-2 after extra time. When United's fourth kick, a tame effort from Giggs, was saved, Southampton went through 4-2 on penalties. By stopping Giggs's shot, Saints keeper Tim Flowers became the first top-flight goalkeeper to save a penalty in an FA Cup shoot-out.

9) Matthew Le Tissier, who scored three penalties against Spurs in the course of 1994/95, only ever missed one penalty in his career. He scored 47 of his 48 spot-kicks before retiring in 2002.

10) Mark Crossley of Nottingham Forest was the only goalkeeper ever to save a Le Tissier penalty. He also saved five penalties from Tottenham players during his time at Forest – Gary Lineker's in the 1991 FA Cup Final, Teddy Sheringham's in a Premiership match in September 1994, and three in a shoot-out from Ronny Rosenthal, Clive Wilson and Sheringham in an FA Cup fifth-round replay in March 1995.

11) Since the start of the 1990s, Justin Edinburgh is the only player to have won two trophies with Tottenham – the FA Cup in 1991 and the League Cup in 1999.

12) Gerry Francis is the only QPR player ever to captain England.

13) At 18 years 69 days old, David Howells is the youngest player to score on his competitive debut for Spurs. He netted the winner in a 2-1 victory away to Sheffield Wednesday on 22 February 1986.

Bibliography

Books

Anderton, Darren with Donovan, Mike, *Take Note! The Autobiography* (DB, 2010)

Ardiles, Ossie, *Ossie's Dream* (Corgi, 2009)

Astaire, Simon, *Sol Campbell: The Authorised Biography* (Spellbinding Media, 2014)

Blickensdörfer, Hans, *Jürgen Klinsmann* (Klinsmedia, 1995)

Duggan, Jim, *The Glory of Spurs* (Crimson Publishing, 2012)

Fynn, Alex & Blair, Olivia, *The Great Divide* (Andre Deutsch, 2001)

Goodwin, Bob, *The Spurs Alphabet* (ACL & Polar Publishing, 1992)

Goodwin, Bob, *Tottenham Hotspur: The Complete Record* (Breedon Books, 2007)

Harris, Harry, *Klinsmann* (Headline, 1995)

Reyland, Roy, *Shirts, Shorts & Spurs* (John Blake, 2010)

Sheringham, Teddy with Webb, Mel, *My Autobiography* (Warner Books, 1998)

Smailes, Gordon, *Football Records: 1871–2000* (Breedon Books, 2000)

Soar, Phil, *Tottenham: The Official Illustrated History* (Hamlyn, 1996)

Sugar, Alan, *What You See is What You Get* (Pan, 2010)

Venables, Terry, *The Autobiography* (Penguin, 1994)

Wright, Oliver, *From The Lane* (Lulu, 2007)

DVDs

Tottenham Hotspur: Season Review 1994/95

Football Club Programmes

Arsenal (v Tottenham Hotspur, 29 April 1995)

Blackburn Rovers (v Tottenham Hotspur, 5 November 1994)

Chelsea (v Tottenham Hotspur, 11 February 1995)

Coventry City (v Tottenham Hotspur, 31 December 1994)

FA Cup semi-final (Everton v Tottenham Hotspur, 9 April 1995)

Ipswich Town (v Tottenham Hotspur, 30 August 1994)
QPR (v Tottenham Hotspur, 6 May 1995)
Tottenham Hotspur (various editions, 1994/95)
Wimbledon (v Tottenham Hotspur, 1 October 1994)

Magazines
Four Four Two
World Soccer
90 Minutes

Newspapers
Daily Express
Daily Mail
Daily Mirror
Daily Telegraph
Evening Standard (London)
Guardian
Independent
Independent on Sunday
Mail on Sunday
News of the World
Observer
People
The Sun
Sunday Express
Sunday Mirror
Sunday People
Sunday Telegraph
Sunday Times
The Times

Television
BBC Sport archive (*Football Focus* and *Match of the Day*)
BBC News archive (*One O'Clock News, Six O'Clock News*)

Websites
British Pathé
Englandfootballonline.com
Rsssf (Rec.Sport.Soccer Statistics Foundation)
Soccerbase
Tottenham Hotspur Football Club
YouTube

Yearbooks and Almanacks

Rothmans Football Yearbook (various editions)
Sky Sports Football Yearbook (various editions)
Tottenham Hotspur Official Yearbook (various editions)